I0834654

Other Books by Mark Carlson:

Promises to Keep – A Civil War Mystery Novel
Paragon Press, 2010

Confessions of a Guide Dog – The Blonde Leading the Blind
iUniverse, 2011

FLYING on film

A CENTURY OF AVIATION IN THE MOVIES 1912 • 2012

MARK CARLSON

Albany, Georgia

Flying on Film: A Century of Aviation in the Movies, 1912 – 2012

Published in the USA by:
BearManor Media
PO Box 1129
Duncan, OK 73534-1129
www.BearManorMedia.com

ISBN 1-59393-219-7

Printed in the United States of America

Design and Layout by Allan T. Duffin.

TABLE OF CONTENTS

Acknowledgements		vii
Dedication		xi
Foreword by William A. Wellman, Jr.		xv
Introduction by Mark Carlson		xix
Chapter 1	The Silent Sky	1
Chapter 2	The Great War on Film	15
Chapter 3	The Golden Age 1927-1939	53
Chapter 4	This is Your Life, Hollywood Style: Biographies	65
Chapter 5	The Approaching Storm	89
Chapter 6	The War in the Air: Europe	105
Chapter 7	The War in the Air: The Pacific	145
Chapter 8	Drama and Disaster: The Airliner Films	189
Chapter 9	Blowtorches on Film: The Jets Take Over	209
Chapter 10	Faster, Louder, More Money: Action Films	245
Chapter 11	Gasbags and Whirlybirds	267
Chapter 12	Just For Fun: The Adventure Films	283
Chapter 13	A Funny Things Happened to Me in the Air: Comedies	315
Chapter 14	On the Edge of Flight: Non-Aviation Films	337
Bibliography		353
Index		361

ACKNOWLEDGEMENTS

The author wishes to thank all those who have generously provided their time and resources to making this book possible. Collectively they gave hundreds of hours of their time relating stories, anecdotes, memories and background material that could not be found from any other resource. Some of the persons listed below are no longer with us.

Lt. John W. Finn, USN MOH, gave the author the first insights into what veterans thought about the movies depicting their own experiences.

John was a good friend and a special man. He will be missed.

To these people and all those whose names are not listed below the author is eternally grateful.

And a special thanks to Linda Stull, who gave so much time, support, and most of all encouragement at a time when it was needed most. Without her this book would never have been written.

Actors, Stunts and Film Crew

Louis Gossett, Jr., David McCallum, Efrem Zimbalist, Jr., Jack Larson, Dewey Martin, William Wellman, Jr., Cliff Robertson, Sean Astin, A.C. Lyles, Paramount Pictures, Marilyn Knowlden, Sound Effects Editor Peter Berkos, Shawn Caldwell, Zona Appleby, John Kazian

NAVY/MARINE CORPS

Rear Admiral Paul Gillchrist USN, Rear Admiral James D. "Jig Dog" Ramage, Col. John Telles, USMC, Col. Dean Caswell, USMC, Capt. Rex Warden, USN, Capt. Rick "Wigs" Ludwig, USN, Capt. Wallace "Griff" Griffin, USN, Capt. C. J. "Heater" Heatley, USN, Capt. Dick Evert, USN, Cdr. Dean "Diz" Laird, USN, Cdr. Charles Beauchesne, USN, Cdr. John Stubbs, USN, Cdr. Chuck Sweeney, USN, Distinguished Flying Cross Society, Lt. John W. Finn, USN, Medal of Honor

AIR FORCE

Maj. Gen. Chris Adams, USAF (Strategic Air Command), Brig. Gen. Bob Cardenas, USAF, Brig. Gen. Stan Brown USAF (Strategic Air Command), Col. Ralph Parr, USAF, Maj. Walter Douglas, USAF, Sgt. Al Buckles, USAF (Strategic Air Command)

ARMY AIR FORCES

Col. Steve Pisanos, No. 71 Eagle Squadron/4th Fighter Group, Maj. Joe Armanini, 100th Bomb Group, Maj. Bob Sternfels, 98th Bomb Group., Capt. John Gibbons, 100th Bomb Group, Lt. Edwin Davidson, 96th Bomb Group, Lt. Roger Drinkwalter, 390th Bomb Group, Lt. Harvey Greenfield, 96th Bomb Group, Lt. Frank Bushmeier, 100th Bomb Group, Sgt. Ed Silverstone, 100th Bomb Group, Sgt. Bruce Richardson, 100th Bomb Group, Sgt. Rich Tangradi, 100th Bomb Group, Dr. Roscoe Brown, 100th Fighter Group/Tuskegee Airman, Sgt. David Thatcher, 17th Bomb Group/Doolittle Raiders, Sgt. Ed Pepping, 506th PIR, 101st ABN

GERMAN AIR FORCE

Harald Bauer, Luftwaffe

Museums and Associations

Bomber Legends, EAA AirVenture, Flying Leathernecks Marine Air Museum, Air Group One, CAF, Arizona Wing, CAF, Inland Empire Wing, CAF, Dixie Wing, CAF, Rocky Mountain Wing, CAF, Ron Twellman, EAA AirVenture, Oshkosh, George Welsh, Curator, Edwards Air Force Base Museum, Bob Adams, B-36 Peacemaker Association, Larry McKinley, National Air & Space Museum, Washington, D.C., Harold Rubin, Museum of Flight, Dan Hagedorn, Museum of Flight, Herb Phelan, Museum of Flight, Ted Huetter, Museum of Flight, Ross "Rossco" Davis, SDASM, Linda Stull, Archivist, SDASM, Pam Gay, Librarian, SDASM, Robert S. Johnson, SDASM, Dennis Stewart, SDASM, Alan Renga, SDASM, Scott Buckingham, Oakland Aviation Museum, Christen Wright, Yanks Air Museum, Penelope Hacker, Yanks Air Museum, Leon Frewin, Yanks Air Museum, Bill

Allen, Allen Aviation, Kristen Moloney, Planes of Fame, Steve Hinton, Planes of Fame, Steve "Smitty" Smith, Flying Leathernecks Marine Air Museum, Stephanie Smith, Edwards AFB Museum, Karen Jacobsen, *USS Oriskany* Museum, Elizabeth Demaine, North Bay Public Library, Virginia Bader, Bader Fine Arts, Herb Leopold, DFCS, Geoff Simpson, Trustee, Battle of Britain Memorial Trust, Ray Cheney, Battalion Chief, CAL FIRE, Marcus Brooks Mike Dralle, Air Group One CAF, Vicki Moen, Air Group One CAF, Craig Covner, Air Group One CAF, Howard Merritt, Air Group One CAF, Col. Bob Simon, Air Group One CAF, Jim McGarvie, Air Group One CAF, Rich Kenney, SkyICam, Bud Ukes, Inland Empire CAF, Michael Faley, 100th Bomb Group Foundation, Charles Marfin, Flying Tigers Living History Group, Constance Clark, John Underwood, Douglas Corrigan, Jr.

Authors and Media

Col. Walter Boyne, author and historian, Jim Busha, EAA Warbirds, Budd Davison, *Flight Journal Magazine*

Carl von Wodtke, *Aviation History Magazine*, Bruce Orriss, author, *When Hollywood Ruled the Skies*, Eric Presten, Stephen Chapis, Jay Stout, author, *The Men Who Killed the Luftwaffe*, David W. Jourdan Nauticos, author of *Finding Amelia Earhart*, Frank Thompson, author, *Lost Films*, William A. Wellman, Jr., author

Corporate Officers

Joe Bock, Aero Telemetry, Inc., Bill Hempel, Aero Telemetry, Inc., Kevin Goads, Northrop Grumman

Aircraft Owners

Alan Armstrong, Jack Van Ness, Ken Laird, Joe Shepherd, Greg Herrick, Grace McGuire, Dave Derby

Air Crew

EAA B-17G *Aluminum Overcast* crew, CAF C-53D *D-Day Doll* crew, CAF B-25 *Maid in the Shade* crew, CAF SNJ-5 *Sassy* crew, CAF B-17G *Sentimental Journey* crew, Collings B-17G *Nine-O-Nine* crew, Collings B-24H *Witchcraft* crew

DEDICATION

To my beloved wife Jane, who saw the eagle in me long before the feathers sprouted
and made me believe I could do it,

and

To my lifelong friend Monty Montgomery, who started me loving old movies
and special effects and wanting to know all the useless trivia,

and

Director William A. "Wild Bill" Wellman (1896-1975), who started us all
on a cinema graphic aerial joy ride way back in 1927,

and most of all

To the gallant men and women who long ago left our shores to risk their lives
to do battle in the skies over distant lands, to the ones who came home
and the ones who remain forever on the wind,

This book is gratefully dedicated.

IN MEMORIAM

Cliff Robertson

1921 – 2011

During the research for this book the author was fortunate to have talked and corresponded with Cliff Robertson.

An actor, veteran, pilot and aviation enthusiast, Robertson generously gave of his time, photos and memories.
The author was proud to call him a friend.

He will be missed on Earth and in the skies but lives forever on the silver screen.

FOREWORD

by William A. Wellman, Jr.

Mark Carlson has produced a remarkable and insightful chronicle of a 100-year history of aviation in the movies. He sketches an incredible portrait of the films, the diversity of aircraft, and the highly skilled and courageous flyers who helped make these films the spectacles that they became.

How spine-tingling to read the accounts of these pictures and their pilots who fly their planes into our hearts and imaginations. From early flight, through the world conflicts, into the peacetime wars of Hollywood, the filmmakers and heroic aviators navigate kite-like biplanes, ponderous blimps and transports, thunderous bombers, lightning-fast fighters, sleek and sturdy jets.

From the beginning of our country's air service and all the branches of it, the aircraft climbed into the silent era of films, the talkies, the Golden Age and the mighty studio empires ruled by the great moguls. Even when the kingpins of Hollywood began to disappear and their glamour factories faded and crumbled away, the skymen flew a steady course into the future without crashing.

The first Academy Award winner for Best Picture was the movie milestone *Wings* (1927), directed by my father, William A. Wellman. He was a decorated fighter pilot in the First World War, and his Oscar-winning film was dedicated to those young warriors of the sky whose wings are folded about them forever.

The same dedication might be said of the stunt pilots in this book, who took to the air in all manner of aircraft—many sacrificing their lives—to bring the thrilling stories to the screen.

My father made every kind of film: tough gangster pictures like *Public Enemy* (1931) with James Cagney and Jean Harlow, fast-moving action films like *Call of the Wild* (1935) with Clark Gable and Loretta Young, and *Beau Geste* (1939) with Gary Cooper and Ray Milland.

In his pursuit of making all kinds of films, he always returned to the sky for his love of aviation adventure. Throughout his 35 years as a director, there were 11 such pictures: *The Legion of the Condemned* (1928) starring Gary Cooper and Fay Wray, *Young Eagles* (1930) with Buddy Rogers and Jean Arthur, *Central Airport* (1933) starring Richard Barthelmess, *Men With Wings* (1938) top-lining Fred MacMurray and Ray Milland, *Thunder Birds* (1942) with Gene Tierney and Preston Foster, *This Man's Navy* (1945) starring Wallace Beery, *Gallant Journey* (1946) with Glenn Ford, and *Island in the Sky* (1953) and *The High and the Mighty* (1954), both starring John Wayne.

The High and the Mighty was my father's most commercially successful aviation film. Although the CinemaScope format limited the number of theaters where the film was screened, *The High and the Mighty* ranked number one at the box office and set a record for the "fastest return of negative cost," recouping its production cost of $1.47 million within two months. The film grossed $8.5 million.

The picture received six Academy Award nominations. My father was nominated for Best Director. He received a nomination from the Directors Guild as well. Other Academy Award nominations went to Jan Sterling and Claire Trevor for Best Actress, Ralph Dawson for Film Editing, and Dimitri Tiomkin and Ned Washington for Best Music/Original Song. Tiomkin received an Oscar for his musical score.

Among its achievements, the film's greatest triumph was in its legacy. For it would start a new genre of all-star "disaster" themed epics, the creation of fright films in the sky, in airport terminals, on cruise ships and other confining venues—a seemingly never ending cycle of pictures.

In addition to Dad's first flying film, the colossal hit *Wings*, his eleventh and last was the failed *The Lafayette Escadrille* (1958). Produced as *C'est la Guerre* (*It's the War*), the picture was his tribute to the young flyers of that long ago war.

It had taken almost three decades to get the "green light" and, in the end, the film was so butchered by Warner Bros. Prexy Jack Warner that dad, heartbroken, retired from the industry he helped to create—an industry that had provided 76 directed pictures and 32 Academy Award nominations with 7 Oscars.

William A. Wellman Jr. with the author at the Wings Over Gillespie Air Show in San Diego, 2012. *Courtesy Ernie Viskupic, Wingman Photography*

Of my father's aviation films, it was *Wings* of which he was most proud. With his celebrated cameraman, Harry Perry, and their staff, they created the technology that set the standard for aviation movies that followed. All flying movies owe a debt of gratitude to the first Best Picture winner.

Paramount's masterful *Wings*, a story filled with action, romance, camaraderie, patriotism, tragedy, hope and love, was the first film to depict the Great War fought in the air. The studio mogul, Jesse L. Lasky, called it "the last great silent picture." It was the *Star Wars* of its generation.

As a member of the Lafayette Flying Corps, "Wild Bill"—the nickname bestowed on him by his commandant—felt the thrill of battle and saw the horrors of war. He never forgot those adventurous young Americans who fought so bravely in a foreign land, flying French planes, sacrificing their lives in the pursuit of life and liberty.

My Dad often said that the flyers he had known in France, the pilots of his movies, and other aviators he met during his lifetime, were far more important than any celebrities or movie stars who graced the silver screen in his pictures.

In this book, Mark Carlson has flown a resolute route, through brilliant blue skies surrounded by billowy white clouds, into 100 years of aviation in the movies. It is a book my father would love.

— *William Wellman, Jr.*

INTRODUCTION

by Mark Carlson

"Most motion picture directors are a little screwy. I know that fliers are, and I have been both, so draw your own conclusions."

— William A. Wellman

A Short Time for Insanity

For a full century, film audiences have enjoyed watching projected images of airplanes winging their way across the silver screen.

The airplane and the motion picture were born within a few years of each other. It has been well over a century since the Wright Brothers took their first daring flights into the sky at Kitty Hawk and a year longer since Georges Méliès began his daring forays into early science fiction with *Le Voyage Dans la Lune* in 1902.

The newly-hatched wonder of flying captured the imaginations of people all over the world. Barnstormers and stunt flyers thrilled audiences in big cities and farming towns in the 1920s. By coincidence, the technology of motion pictures was growing in popularity in theaters and movie houses.

Of course some filmmaking pioneers recognized the allure of flying machines to further attract and captivate the public.

The early "two-reelers" were long on thrills and short on plot development or believability, but that only served to bring more wide-eyed viewers into the dark environs of the movie house to shriek in horror or laugh at the antics on the screen.

Charles Lindbergh's historic flight from New York to Paris in May 1927 had set the nation — indeed the world — on an aerial journey which continues to this day.

In that same year of 1927 Paramount released the first full-length feature about the air war over France. *Wings* took the public out of the fantasy of Saturday morning serials and into a world few had ever imagined.

Wings showed in powerful reality air combat between heroic and handsome American flyboys battling to the death against evil sneering Germans. *Wings* was the first of many films to realistically portray the air war. It also won the first Academy Award for Best Picture.

Since then it has become the standard by which nearly all air movies are measured. The allure of those first shaky black-and-white images of spinning propellers and burning planes has never been truly equaled.

Wings was quickly followed by other aviation pictures, many forgotten by all but a few dedicated film buffs.

Universal's *Flying Cadets* (1933) and Twentieth Century Fox's *Hell in the Heavens* (1934) have all but vanished on television, even in an age of 24-hour classic movie channels. Yet they are only two of the hundreds of films that emerged from RKO, Universal, Paramount, Warner, First National, Republic, Monogram and a dozen small studios in the decades before the advent of television.

The art of filmmaking has gone through many stages, using every conceivable means of creating illusion on film. Models, aerial photography, rotating backdrops, double-exposure, back-projection process, bluescreen and finally the digital universe of Computer-Generated Imagery have brought the skies into the theaters.

Some early aviation films focused on the daring war aces, the pioneering Air Mail jockeys, the courageous test pilots who tested dangerous planes or the stalwart airline pilots who carried passengers to exotic places around the globe.

By the mid-1930s women had proven that they were as capable of flying an airplane as any man. However, female characters in the movies well into the 1940s played the love interest of the handsome pilot and, in most cases, of two pilots. The "two aviators pursuing the same woman until one of them is tragically killed in either a crash or during combat" theme was born in *Wings* and lives on in the CGI-laden *Pearl Harbor* (2001). Some things never change.

In a way the real hero was the airplane. Unlike the automobile during the Depression years, airplanes were a novelty, a dream to most Americans. Today we in the 21st Century have never known what it was like not to have flown in an airplane. Our grandparents grew up in a time when having flown to another city was something to brag about to small crowds of wide-eyed listeners.

The aviation industry advanced at a rapid rate that put filmmakers "behind the curve," hard-pressed to keep up with new planes and technology. From wood-and-fabric biplanes to aluminum monoplanes, from huge four-engine bombers to sleek jets, the movie studios did their best to stay current with the aircraft.

Audiences were able to see the newest fighters, transports, bombers and jets on the screen even as those same planes soared effortlessly in the skies over the country.

Cooperation between the studios and aeronautical firms like Boeing, Curtiss, Douglas and Lockheed — eager to showcase their latest designs — was possible as long as the film made the airplane look good. The same can be said of the Army and Navy in the periods before and during World War II. *I Wanted Wings* (1940) and *Dive Bomber* (1941), among others, were often blatant recruiting films extolling the thrill of military flying. Many young men, spurred on by dreams of flying and glory, envisioned themselves as the heroes depicted in these films.

By late 1942 the exploits of the Flying Tigers and the Naval aviators who defended Midway against the Japanese Navy spawned more movies about their deeds in the skies. *Flying Tigers* (1942) and *Wing and a Prayer* (1943) were two films quickly turned out to feed the public's appetite for the world of the military pilot.

As the war progressed and the speed, agility and power of the airplane increased almost exponentially, wartime audiences thrilled to the sound of roaring 2,000-horsepower Pratt & Whitney Wasp and Wright Cyclone engines, a far cry from the sputtering rattle of the 60-horsepower OX-5 that powered the Jennies of the 1920s. The sight of hundreds of B-17 Flying Fortresses and Curtiss P-40 Warhawks in the skies doing battle with the Germans and Japanese only made filmgoers want for more. John Wayne did his part for the war effort along with Spencer Tracy, Van Johnson, Pat O'Brien, Dennis Morgan, Errol Flynn, James Cagney and dozens of others. However, they performed their military duties on film rather than in the cockpit. By contrast, Jimmy Stewart served in combat as did Clark Gable, Wayne Morris, Edmund O'Brien, Tyrone Power and many others.

The end of the war heralded the birth of fighter jets, which gave the film studios an exciting new lease on aviation. The men who tested hot new rocket planes over the Fighter Test Center at Edwards Air Force Base in California and those who dueled with Chinese jets over Korea found their way onto the movie screen.

Understandably, the companies who built and sold aircraft for commercial airlines preferred their products not be depicted as unsafe. Douglas Aircraft requested Warner Brothers make their DC-7 unrecognizable in 1964's *Fate is the Hunter*. Warner used parts from two DC-7Bs and one Boeing 707 to build a totally fictional airliner. Thus the motion picture industry found ways to make harrowing stories about doomed airliners to draw the public while appeasing the aircraft industry.

The 1970s are remembered for disaster films, but it's often forgotten that *Airport 1975* had its roots in films as far back as 1954 in *The High and the Mighty*, starring John Wayne.

Some of the most epic films of the 1960s and 1970s had strong aviation themes. Twentieth Century Fox's *The Longest Day* (1962) and *Tora! Tora! Tora!* (1970) cost far more to produce than they made for the studios.

This brings us to the subject of this book. Growing up in the 1950s I loved to watch and re-watch classic films on weekend and late-night television.

The advent of cable and video provided a stunning variety of movies totally unknown in my youth. I collected hundreds of movies on videotape, cataloging them by subject, year and title.

I volunteered as a docent at the San Diego Air & Space Museum, where I worked around real airplanes. I attended air shows to be around vintage aircraft and talk to the men and women who flew them. Occasionally I was treated to a ride in one. I began submitting stories to aviation magazines.

After several of my military and aviation articles appeared in national magazines, I thought: *Why don't I write a book about aviation in the movies?*

Early in my research I realized that I had bitten off more than I could chew. Instead of the 100-plus aviation-themed movies I thought would be enough for the book, my list quickly grew past 200 — and beyond. Every film I researched led me to others. In time the theme of the book took shape: not just about the movies, but more than that. Something for everybody.

This book is intended to be of interest to, and a reference for, anyone who enjoys watching aircraft on film.

Interviews with actors, film crew, stuntmen and pilots revealed fascinating background information about many of my favorite movies. In the case of participants no longer with us, extensive study of biographies and autobiographies, articles, documentaries, film clips, DVD commentaries and other sources filled in many missing pieces.

Since a great number of films are based on history, aviation technology, war or biographies, this gives the book much more scope.

In the case of war films, for instance, veterans who participated in or remember the actual events depicted in the film have generously provided their own thoughts and anecdotes.

I chose this theme after a conversation with my friend John W. Finn, the oldest living Medal of Honor recipient. He had received the nation's highest military award for his action at Kaneohe Bay, Oahu, on December 7, 1941, during the Japanese attack on Pearl Harbor. Navy Chief Finn used a .50 caliber machine gun to shoot down two attacking enemy planes and damage two others.

The legendary John Finn died at age 100, shortly before this book was written, but I had asked him what he thought of *Tora! Tora! Tora!* as a historical drama.

Finn replied with a smile, "That was a good movie," he said. "They got it pretty much on target. They filmed it on the base right where I was standing. You can see the kid playing me, right there shooting at the Japanese planes."

But the witty old veteran had more to say: "*Tora* was a lot better done than some others I won't name."

Pearl Harbor Medal of Honor recipient John Finn with the author. *Courtesy Linda Stull*

This is what makes this book unique: veterans, pilots and historians graciously offering their opinions, criticisms and praise. The screenplays, flying scenes, dialogue, technical aspects and combat are examined by those who have really "been there and done that."

The reader will gain a greater insight into the story and trivia behind these films.

The techniques of aircraft carrier operations and combat during the Korean War in 1954's *The Bridges at Toko-Ri* are examined by Naval aviators who flew strikes against North Korean targets.

However, overly talkative Japanese pilots chatting up Dennis Morgan in *God Is My Co-pilot* (1944) are apocryphal at best, as one P-51 Mustang ace commented.

The chapters are arranged in chronological and genre order, starting with the Silent Era. The vast number of films depicting aviation before and during World War II necessitated three chapters.

An explanation regarding films within each chapter is needed here:

The chapters titled "The Silent Sky," "Golden Age," "The Great War," "Approaching Storm," "Action Movies," "Comedies" and "Non-Aviation Films" are arranged according to their release dates.

However, the chapters covering biographies, World War II, airliners, airships, helicopters, and the Jet Age are presented in historical order.

For instance, *Memphis Belle* (1990) is covered prior to 1948's *Command Decision* because the latter film's subject takes place more than a year after the *Belle* finished her last mission.

I did this because this book is also about the films in the context of the history that inspired them.

Some chapters are specific to a genre, such as adventure and comedy.

The immensely popular *Top Gun* (1983) and its many copycat followers like the *Iron Eagle* films and *Air Force One* appear in the chapter about action films.

Comedies have always been one of the most popular movie genres. Steven Spielberg's madcap *1941* and the zany disaster film spoof *Airplane!* are covered along with the flying films of the Bowery Boys, Abbott & Costello, and Laurel & Hardy.

Some popular adventure films with aviation sequences have their own chapter. Here the reader will find the *Indiana Jones* trilogy, 1975's *The Great Waldo Pepper* and 1991's *The Rocketeer.*

A few oldies, like 1931's *King Kong,* are spotlighted in the chapter about non-aviation films.

It is not possible to discuss every movie that features airplanes. That would require a book as thick as the large print edition of *The Complete Works of Mark Twain.*

This book isn't about all of the aviation films ever made — or even the best — but in my opinion, the most interesting.

I hope this book will be enjoyed by the classic film fan, aviation buff, military historian and anybody who wants to know more about the real story behind their favorite airplane movie.

See you at the movies.

Mark Carlson
San Diego, California
2011

CHAPTER ONE

The Silent Sky

In the first decade of the twentieth century a new form of entertainment was being enjoyed in small theaters in America and Europe. The motion picture had first gained widespread exposure through the work of D.W. Griffith and Mack Sennett in America and Georges Méliès in France. They were the first of the pioneers who would make the motion picture into an industry and force of cultural change. Most of the early movies were made in New York and Chicago, but the crowded streets, high property costs and limited good weather forced a migration to the balmy lands of California.

Los Angeles had been blessed with a combination of excellent weather and diverse geography. Sand dune deserts and snow-capped mountains, picturesque beaches and towering cliffs were within an easy drive, even in the autos of the day. With very little effort the filmmakers found locations for cliffhanging stunts or romantic encounters.

The budding studios sought subjects for their films and as early as 1905 the first footage of an airplane was shot. The aircraft was hardly more than a box kite with a propeller. Little is known of the film, and nothing is recorded of the pilot.

In 1910 an air meet was held at Dominguez Field south of the city. It lasted for over a week and local spectators watched airplanes perform stunts and set records in speed, distance and altitude.

Among the spectators was a 13-year old boy who quickly fell under the spell of the airplane. In years to come that boy, whose name was Jimmy Doolittle, became one of the most famous men in aviation.

A great deal of film footage was taken of the event, and the local papers proclaimed that the air age had arrived.

A Dash Through the Clouds (1912) was one of the first true aviation films, produced by the Biograph Company and directed by Mack Sennett. It starred the pretty and plucky Mabel Normand as Josephine, an aviation enthusiast who contrary to the pervasive male heroes of the day saves her own beau from the villain.

Mack Sennett's own Keystone Films soon cranked out several shorts, including *Sky Pirate* (1914) with Normand and a young Roscoe "Fatty" Arbuckle, who also directed the film. *Dizzy Heights and Daring Hearts* (1915) was another Sennett airplane comedy, starring the walrus-mustached former Keystone Kop Chester Conklin. According to Sennett biographer Simon Louvish, this film may contain the first aerial chase scene in motion pictures. The plane used in most of Biograph's and Sennett's films was probably a Wright Model B sport flyer, favored by pilots for ease of handling and its reliable 35-hp engine.

Most of the stunts were little more than takeoffs and landings with a few low-level passes. They were interspersed with clips of actors in close-up in front of moving backgrounds. Often a cockpit mockup was given the illusion of motion by means of an off-camera crewman shaking and rocking the simulated airplane. So far the pilots had little difficulty doing what was needed for a film.

Silent film actress Mabel Normand, the plucky heroine of *A Dash Through the Clouds* in 1912.

The limited space at Dominguez spawned the need for another field near Griffith Park. More airfields and planes were soon to come.

The early planes were little more than wood and canvas, held together by piano wire and glue. Their top speed was barely above 100 miles per hour, they could only climb up to 5,000 feet, and small fuel capacity limited them to an hour in the air.

Exhibition flying began in the years before the First World War with, among others, Glenn Curtiss and Lincoln Beachey taking center stage to showcase their feats. At that time very few people saw much potential in the rickety and fragile planes.

Curtiss was a motorcycle and automobile racer who had set several speed records. He was one of the most prolific inventors of aircraft and the Wright Brothers' biggest competitor. Curtiss toured the country and established aviation schools from coast to coast. In 1910 he opened a school in Coronado, California, where he instructed Lt. Theodore Ellyson to fly a Curtiss seaplane, shepherding in the birth of Naval Aviation.

The San Francisco-born Lincoln Beachey was a true showman. He always wore a neat suit with a broad tie and diamond stickpin while flying his Curtiss biplane in expositions across the country. Beachey's most famous stunt involved a vertical "death dive" beginning at 5,000 feet and spiraling straight down to level off just above the ground. A similar stunt cost the intrepid Beachey his life in 1915.

Even the least skilled pilots were held in some awe by the non-flying public. The image of leather flying helmets and goggles served only to heighten the allure of the daring air ace who braved the skies.

Aviation had, to put it mildly, fired the public imagination.

Exhibition flyers were the most visible members of the flying fraternity.

After the war ended the sudden and vast influx of former Air Service pilots eager to use their flying skills to earn a flashy and profitable living added hundreds more to their ranks. By the 1920s they were commonly known by the sobriquet "barnstormer."

Most often the barnstormers were lone pilots travelling from state to state, looking for a small town to awe with moderately dangerous feats of airborne daring. The people who attended these "one-man airshows" were not sophisticated city dwellers but farmers and townspeople who hardly ever saw a plane. Simple loops and barrel rolls, hammerhead stalls and low passes were all it took to elicit gasps and respect for the pilots' skill and bravery.

The meager living afforded by the pilots helped them to pay for fuel and kept their rapidly-deteriorating Curtiss JN-4 Jenny and Lincoln-Standard war-surplus planes in the air a little longer. Many pilots went broke or died, and the survivors sought safer and more lucrative ways to earn a living. Those who could pass the increasingly rigorous standards set by the Air Commerce Act of 1920 went into commercial aviation. The early airlines began business taking a mere dozen passengers on cross-country flights aboard noisy vibrating Ford Trimotors.

But those who still felt the need to be daredevils-for-hire found their way to the new Mecca of entertainment: Hollywood, California.

As more studios moved to Los Angeles competition to produce the funniest, most romantic and dramatic or hair-raising films became fierce. Nestor, Biograph, Keystone, Lasky, Roach and a dozen others vied for the attention and loyalty of the rapidly growing audiences. The era of the movie star had begun with the films and celebrity of Rudolph Valentino and Douglas Fairbanks, Mary Pickford and Norma Talmadge.

The most common films were not epic or deep drama. They were more often than not of the "hero vs. villain to save the heroine" genre.

Comedies were cheap and easy to produce. Hal Roach cranked out scores of zany shorts each year. Other studios preferred cliffhanger thrillers to frighten audiences with the exploits of - Normand and Pearl White.

Two of southern California's attractions were the nearly year-round sunshine and calm climate. The weather was perfect for flying. Vast open fields offered lots of places to land a plane with a balky engine. It's no wonder so many future aviation giants were born in the region. North American, Lockheed, Martin, and Douglas established their headquarters in the sprawling expanse of valleys and farmland.

The pieces were in place: aircraft manufacturers, pilots who loved to fly, and a fast-growing motion picture industry.

Those were the years when men like Al Wilson, Ormer Locklear, Frank Clarke, Dick Grace, Garland Lincoln, Frank Tomick and others who had once fought in the skies over France found their true calling as motion picture stunt pilots.

In the context of motion picture stunts, "safe" was a relative term. Falls or jumps from a galloping horse or moving auto were dangerous enough to break limbs or cripple a man for life. At least they were performed on the ground. Adding the third dimension of height compounded the risk.

Audiences wanted to see feats of daring and hair-raising thrills for their theater admission. When the studios demanded more exciting airplane movies the pilots found they had to perform ever more challenging maneuvers in front of the camera. While some stunts were simple, others were downright dangerous.

The stunt pilots eventually formed an organization. Associated Motion Picture Pilots (AMPP) was known for skilled and experienced pilots for hire in the movies. Kentucky-born Al Wilson was the first to be hired as a professional stunt pilot. He trained other men to fly, including Cecil B. DeMille, soon to be famous for *The Ten Commandments* (1923) and other epic movies. DeMille hired Wilson to fly an American-made Bleriot monoplane in a short film entitled *We Can't Have Everything* (1918), produced by the aptly-named Aircraft Pictures Corporation. It is one of Hollywood's lost films, according to the Cecil B. DeMille Society.

DeMille formed Mercury Aviation Company in 1919 near Melrose and Fairfax Avenues. The airfield was named for DeMille and soon more were established to fit the growing need for space and planes. Mercury offered advertising flights, sightseeing tours and charter work in addition to training pilots. When the Jesse Lasky Company (soon to become Paramount) and other studios needed stunt pilots and planes for an aviation sequence, Mercury was one of the best places to go.

Syd Chaplin, brother of Charlie soon opened Chaplin Field at the corner of Wilshire Boulevard and Crescent Avenue, just across from De Mille Field. In a short time Chaplin was also in the business of providing experienced pilots and planes for the rapidly growing movie industry's needs.

Chaplin Field at the intersection of Crescent and Wilshire, directly across the street from De Mille Field.

The beloved Curtiss Jenny, built during the war, was often used in the 1920s for aerial stunts. Affordable and available in huge numbers, the two-cockpit Jenny was easy to fly and very forgiving. The narrow fuselage and network of struts and wires made it perfect for stunt work. The modest 60-hp OX-5 engine limited the Jenny to about 60 knots' airspeed, allowing stuntmen to climb out of the cockpit and walk on the wings. Movie villains were aggressively chased by policemen all over a flying Jenny.

Erstwhile Army pilot Ormer Locklear was probably the best known of the Jenny stunt pilots. His barnstorming act involved mid-air transfers from one plane to another. Many of the wing-walking stunts performed in the movies during the 1920s were devised and perfected by Locklear. He appeared as a wing-walking and mid-air transfer stunt performer in *The Great Air Robbery* (1919). The Universal Film Manufacturing Company, forerunner of Universal Pictures, willingly paid Locklear's high fees. His skill was put to the test as he climbed from one plane to another, from the plane to a speeding car and from the car to the plane. The film was so successful more studios began producing aviation-themed films.

Unfortunately Locklear's film career was short. He was killed along with his fellow stunt pilot Milton Elliott during a night filming of *The Skywayman* in 1920. The plot was written around Locklear's special stunts. It was directed by James P. Hogan, later to direct many of the *Bulldog Drummond* and *Ellery Queen* mysteries.

The fatal crash happened on the night of August 2, 1920, when Locklear and Elliot were over DeMille Field. Several bright arc lights would follow the Jenny as it fell into a spin from 2,000 feet. Locklear had told the crew manning the arc lights to turn them off before he reached the altitude where he would pull out. All went well until the point the biplane should have leveled off. The lights were not extinguished and the Jenny simply plowed into the ground close to the intersection of Crescent Avenue and Third Street.

The tragic irony is that Hogan had intended to use a miniature for the scene. But Locklear didn't think audiences would accept models as being real. He chose to do the stunt and it cost him and Elliott their lives.

There is a quote attributed to Ormer Locklear: "Safety second, that's my motto."

Other pilots were also killed due to the ever growing dangers of stunts. Earl Burgess died in a fall when he tried to work his way back to the left wing skid of a Jenny after three takes of fighting a dummy villain on a landing gear spreader bar. Although another pilot saw Burgess' dilemma and tried to help, the exhausted stuntman lost his grip and fell to his death. His body was found where the Beverly Hills Hotel is today.

Another member of AMPP, B.H. De Lay, was killed while test-stunting a plane over Clover Field, now Santa Monica Municipal Airport.

But some pilots survived the early years to become legends.

Frank Clarke, an athletic horseback rider, was captivated by flying after seeing an exhibition near Fresno, California, in 1915. He made a name for himself with wing-walking stunts in California and Arizona, attempting daring midair transfers without the use of a rope or ladder. Clarke often preferred flying sturdier Canadian-built JN-4s with the more powerful Hall-Scott engine.

Early stunt pilots Ormer Locklear and B. H. DeLay. Both pilots died during aerial stunts.

Clarke did his first major film stunt for *Stranger Than Fiction* (1921), starring the heroine Katherine MacDonald. Although *Stranger* is not an aviation film the stunt Clarke and fellow pilot Wally Timm performed is more than worthy of attention, if for no other reason than to illustrate what lengths directors and screenwriters would go to in order to include a daring airplane scene.

A nearly completed ten-story building in downtown Los Angeles at Broadway and Eleventh Street provided the venue for the stunt. A long wooden platform with a slight rise at the far end was built along the long axis of the roof. Clarke and Timm practiced with the Jenny until they could depend on a takeoff in less than a hundred feet, which is the most they could count on for the stunt. One night in December of 1920 the Jenny was partially dismantled, hoisted to the roof and rebuilt. One wing projected over the roofline, prompting early-morning city dwellers to wonder how an airplane had landed up there.

There is some dispute among Hollywood historians as to whether the City of Los Angeles ever intended to allow the plane to be flown off the platform a hundred feet over a street crowded with cars and pedestrians.

When the film crew was ready, Clarke was in the cockpit while Timm stood with a knife next to a sturdy rope tied to the tail skid and the building. Clarke revved the engine to full power and gave Timm the signal. The rope was cut and the Jenny shot off down the wooden ramp. The "ski-jump" provided some lift at the end, but the plane fell almost five stories before Clarke was able to gain control and fly down the length of Broadway.

Today it is hard to imagine that anyone would attempt something so dangerous. If Clarke hadn't managed to stay in the air the crash of the Jenny in the street below would have caused many deaths. Modern litigation attorneys would drool at the liability claims such a catastrophe could spawn. But for Frank Clarke, already one of the more daring stunt pilots, it was all in a day's work—although he never tried it again.

Clarke survived several crashes, including deliberate ones, during his nearly thirty years as a stunt pilot and barnstormer. His work in motion pictures included *The Flying Deuces* (1939) with Laurel & Hardy and continued until 1950 with *Walk Softly, Stranger,* released after his death in 1948.

Wally Timm also worked as an instructor at Mercury Aviation. One of his students was Art Goebel, the winner of the ill-fated Dole Derby from Oakland to Hawaii in 1927.

Frank Tomick was an Air Service pilot flying out of March Field in Riverside County, California, when he met Clarke. The two Franks became good friends and soon Tomick began doing movie work. Though as good a pilot as Clarke, Tomick was better suited for the careful, steady precision flying required for safe stunt work. He could be depended upon for keeping a Jenny stable while a fight or transfer was being done on the wings. His career flying for motion pictures spanned more than a decade in flying and acting, from *Wings* (1927) to *Test Pilot* and *Men With Wings* (1938).

Pioneer movie stunt pilots Al Wilson and Dick Grace. Grace would soon become the "King of aircraft crash stunts."

Dick Grace was a Minnesota-born Naval Air Service pilot who'd barnstormed his native state in a Jenny until a crash put the plane permanently out of commission. He moved to Los Angeles and began doing stunt work such as jumping from buildings and moving cars. Grace was nearly killed during an aerial stunt for a Tom Mix feature. After two full takes of climbing up and down a long knotted rope in a JN-4's 60-knot slipstream Grace was almost too exhausted to climb back into the rear cockpit. Only assistance from the pilot, who reached back over the sill to grab Grace's jacket, avoided a fatal fall.

Grace's stunt pilot career would eventually include work on *Wings* and many other aviation films. His specialty was crashes.

Mercury hired a skilled and innovative mechanic and pilot named Garland Lincoln, who was distantly related to the sixteenth president. He eventually went into business for himself, flying and ferrying actors like Gary Cooper from Los Angeles to location shoots. He was able to purchase three French Nieuport 28s as surplus and put them into flying condition for film work. These planes were used in *Dawn Patrol* (1938) with Errol Flynn. One of these is on display at the San Diego Air & Space Museum

Lincoln didn't do stunt work for some years but later flew for Howard Hughes in *Hell's Angels* (1931) and *Forced Landing* (1941) with Richard Arlen.

Dozens of aviation-themed serials, comedies, dramas and cliffhangers were filmed in the first five years of the 1920s.

Despite the seemingly terrifying risks shown on film the majority of stunt pilots were careful and well-prepared to perform what the directors and writers wanted. But things went wrong often enough to make even the most cautious pilots wary.

While not a true aviation film *The Grim Game* (1919) contains one of the most stunning aerial sequences ever filmed. The *Grim Game* starred the famous magician and escape artist Harry Houdini. The Lasky Company searched for a stuntman who could double as Houdini but several men backed off, knowing the stunt involved a mid-air transfer. Many pilots had been killed trying to duplicate Locklear's feats.

What appears in the movie wasn't scripted. It was a near-fatal accident.

Three planes were rented from Mercury. Al Wilson flew the camera plane with camera operator Irvin Willat. Chris Pickup and David Thompson flew the stunt planes, both Curtiss JN-4s. The stuntman was a former Air Service pilot named Robert Kennedy, who was to lower himself from the high plane by knotted rope to the lower plane with Thompson at the controls.

The afternoon air was turbulent and as the stunt was begun, the two planes were tossed up and down by as much as twenty feet.

Kennedy lowered himself by rope until he was almost to the lower Jenny's wing. The rough air made him have to lift his legs when the Jenny's propeller suddenly appeared under him. Just as he was ready to let go and climb into the rear cockpit a sudden updraft smashed Thompson's Jenny into the plane flown by Pickup. The upper wing and landing gear of the two planes were virtually locked together and Kennedy was sure he would be killed. For several moments the two pilots tried desperately to free the planes and finally succeeded before managing shaky crashes in Santa Monica. Kennedy had held on to the rope and yet received only scrapes and bruises.

Willat got the entire event on film, so the studio re-wrote the sequence to include the collision.

Movie audiences were amazed at the stunt and the film drew packed crowds. The studio publicity releases gave the impression—one they made no attempt to correct—that Houdini himself had done the stunt. Kennedy tried to pursue legal action against the studio; unable to pay the costs of a civil suit, he had no choice but to let it go.

The collision in *The Grim Game* was not the last near-fatal incident to appear on film.

It happened again in Fox's serial *The Eleventh Hour* (1923), which had an early credited role for Alan Hale, later to become one of Hollywood's most recognized character actors. The script required a sequence in which pilot Dick Kerwood would fly a J-1 Standard biplane over a surfaced submarine, whereupon the sub would fire upon the plane, causing the latter to explode in mid-air.

The U.S. Navy provided a submarine in San Diego Bay. The Standard was set with a charge of dynamite that was supposed to explode ten seconds after Kerwood set the timer and bailed out. When he reached the altitude of 2,800 feet over the anchored sub, Kerwood set the timer and began to climb out, but the plane suddenly exploded. He was stunned almost to the point of unconsciousness but managed to pull the ripcord and drop into the bay.

Frank Clarke crashed in a Jenny during a stunt for Paramount's *The Woman with Four Faces* (1923). The film was directed by former Vaudevillian Herbert Brenson, who would also direct *Beau Geste* with Ronald Coleman in 1926. Clarke was apparently too focused on the acting while he took off in a Jenny. Doubling for the male lead, he was supposed to wave at actress Betty Compson but failed to see he was approaching a tree near the runway. The Jenny crashed and was totally wrecked but Clarke, ever lucky, was unhurt.

The accidents continued to happen. Some were the result of bad luck, but most could be attributed to poor planning or sloppy preparation by non-skilled technicians, as in the case of the Kerwood dynamite stunt.

Around 1925 several stunt pilots, cameramen and stunt race car drivers organized themselves into the "Thirteen Black Cats." The group set rates for various stunts and exhibition feats to airports and motion picture studios.

Aircraft take off from Venice Field on Memorial Day, 1919 for an aerial show at De Mille Field. *SDASM Collection*

Specific fees were charged for stunts, the most expensive being changes with an airplane and a moving car, another plane, speedboat or train. The changes from a train to a plane cost $500, since it was one of the most dangerous. Others were crashes into trees or buildings. To spin down in a burning plane but not crash earned a steep $1,500. (Bear in mind it was a similar stunt that killed Ormer Locklear five years earlier.)

Al Wilson continued to do stunt work in several films in the mid-1920s. Wilson wrote the scripts for *The Sky Hawk* (1924) and *The Cloud Rider* in the following year in which he played a Secret Service agent. Several "standard" stunts such as plane-to-plane or plane-to-car transfers, fights on the upper wing and others were done by Wilson and other AMPP pilots. Through it all, Wilson maintained control of the entire process, overriding even the director's authority when necessary.

One of the more imaginative stunts in *The Cloud Rider* involved a woman flyer, who as usual was in need of rescue. She took off in a Jenny and lost one wheel. The "girl" was doubled by Clarke, who presumably wore a wig to appear female. Wilson's hero character saw the girl's dilemma and took off in another Jenny piloted by Frank Tomick, with a spare wheel strapped to his back. When he reached the doomed girl's plane he stood on the top wing and fitted the spare wheel onto the landing gear. Then, in the expected style of the era, Wilson climbed into the other cockpit of the Jenny and brought the terrified girl down for a safe landing.

But it must be remembered that if the "repair" was not achieved, Clarke would have to land the one-wheeled plane with all the risk that entailed.

Al Wilson was one of the first aerial stunt coordinators. He worked with the directors, cameramen, mechanics and technicians to assure safety for himself and the other pilots.

By 1926 the era of impulsive, ill-prepared stunts, ridiculous plots and needless risk-taking was almost at an end. Pilots were determined to have more control of the flying and stunts. It was a far cry from the highly regulated stunt unions that would spring up in the years after World War II, but the first steps had already been taken by the AMPP and Black Cats.

But the pilots were only part of the team that made films come to life. The names of Elmer Dyer and Harry Perry would soon become as famous in Hollywood as the men whom they filmed. Dyer, who began as an amateur filmmaker from Kansas, started working in Hollywood on *The White Squaw* in 1920. He proved to be a skilled cameraman and attracted the notice of several directors. Dyer's camera and aerial cinematography work would eventually span four decades.

Perry was another one of Hollywood's best and soon-to-be-famous aerial cinematographers. A Kansan like Dyer, Perry's film career began with Famous Players-Lasky in 1918. His skill was innovation. When director Tom Forman wanted a specific shot for *The Broken Wing* (1923) it was Perry who came up with a solution. Forman wanted the actor playing the pilot to be visible while flying the plane. But there was no room for the actor, the pilot and the cameraman in the small Jenny. So Perry adapted a remotely-controlled camera to be powered by the motor from a sewing machine. It was mounted on the rear of the fuselage to shoot over the head of the pilot in the rear cockpit. The actor's face could be seen as he turned his head against the moving sky and spinning propeller.

Cameraman Harry Perry's innovative camera mounts made possible the authentic aerial sequences in *Wings* and many other films.

The ability to show an actor in the cockpit of a flying aircraft would catapult aviation movies well beyond the crude studio mockups of less than a decade earlier.

Just seven years after the guns had fallen silent on November 11, 1918, Hollywood was ready to showcase the Great War in the air.

CHAPTER TWO

The Great War on Film

In the narrow slices of blue sky visible above the trenches of the Western Front was heard the sound of spinning propellers and wind whistling through wire.

The first aircraft appeared over the Western front soon after the stalemate began. Far short of the swift fighters soon to come, the first observation planes were used to help spot artillery emplacements and troop movements. But it wasn't long before some observers carried rifles and even pistols to shoot at the planes of the other side.

And there were born what would soon be the first fighter planes.

Soon it was possible to fire machine guns through the propellers, turning the plane into a deadly air weapon.

By the spring of 1915 Anthony Fokker's agile E.III Eindecker had begun to sweep the skies of French and British planes. The "Fokker Scourge" brought names like Max Immelmann and Oswald Boelcke to the lips of worshipful Germans and fearful Britons. The black Maltese crosses of the German Air Service were as hated as the Nazi Swastika of a later generation.

Albert Ball and Billy Bishop, Georges Guynemer and Rene Fonck were in the air to challenge the Germans. They and their foes were known as aces, the modern equivalent of the mounted knight.

The daring exploits of volunteer American pilots of the French Lafayette Flying Corps showed that Yankee pilots could hold their own against the experienced German aces. Army Air Service pilots soon bore aloft the colors of the United States, but they flew in British and

French-built planes. Eddie Rickenbacker, a former race car driver, added his own name to the legend of the flying ace.

During the last year of the war Baron Manfred von Richthofen, "The Bloody Red Baron," was a living legend. His red Albatros D.III and later Fokker Dr.I Triplane eventually brought down eighty enemy planes until he was killed by sheer chance in April of 1918. But the legend had taken root and hasn't faded to this day.

Between 1918 and 1927 only a few minor films centered on the war in France. But the subject of war in the air and on the ground was too enticing to leave for long.

In the early 1920s Cecil B. DeMille, who was producing and directing several films a year, began making movies about military pilots and planes. At least one of these films was shot at the Army's Rockwell Field on San Diego's Coronado Island in California. Several Army biplanes were flown by Air Service pilots for various sequences. While viewing the rushes, DeMille and the field commander, Col. Harvey Burwell, noticed that one plane had a man sitting on the landing gear spreader bar in flight and during landing. Burwell roared, "Ground Doolittle for a month!"

When DeMille questioned how he knew who it was, Burwell said, "Who else but Doolittle would do it?"

Jimmy Doolittle, having missed out on combat in the war, was serving as an instructor at Rockwell during the filming. The world would hear more of Doolittle in the years to come.

The year 1927 marked the height of the Jazz Age, the era of flappers and Al Capone. A major aviation event took place that year—an aerial feat that inspired thousands of young men and women to find a way to fly.

Charles Lindbergh was a handsome 25-year old Air Mail pilot from Minnesota who had dared to challenge the vast Atlantic Ocean and fly nonstop between New York and Paris. His silver-painted Ryan monoplane, the *Spirit of St. Louis*, left Roosevelt Field on the morning of May 20. He arrived in Le Bourget late on the night of May 21 after 33 hours in the air.

Bearing in mind that Lindbergh had accomplished this feat after many more famous pilots with more money and larger planes had failed and died, it is not hard to understand why he quickly became the most famous man in America.

Among the men who'd fallen in the attempt to fly the Atlantic was Charles Nungesser. He and fellow ace Francois Coli as navigator had flown a Levasseur PL.8 biplane named *L'Oiseeu Blanc* (The White Bird) into the morning sky over Le Bourget Field near Paris on May 8, headed for New York and glory. They and their white plane vanished somewhere between Ireland and Newfoundland and were never seen again. To this day the disappearance of Nungesser and Coli ranks with Amelia Earhart as one of aviation's most enduring mysteries.

Two years earlier, Nungesser had attempted to recapture his fading fame by starring in a movie, *The Sky Raider* (1925). This is the only film that shows Charles Nungesser after the war.

By 1927 the time was ripe to begin what may be the greatest action drama of the silent age, *Wings*.

Wings opens in the months as the U.S. is gearing up for war in France. The main characters are Jack Powell, played by the boyish Charles "Buddy" Rogers, and David Armstrong, whose brooding and quiet character is well portrayed by the handsome Richard Arlen. Jack is a brash and socially unconscious young man with a zest for fast cars and the love of Sylvia Lewis, the town beauty. But Jack is mulishly unaware that Sylvia and the wealthy David are in love. The girl next door, Mary Preston, played by the dewy-eyed "It" girl, Clara Bow, is in love with Jack. This love triangle plus one is placed against the backdrop of Jack and David's eagerness to join the Air Service and fight Germans.

When Jack learns David is also interested in Sylvia his pugnacious personality comes out and he mercilessly taunts David, who wants only to do his job. Eventually the two rivals find friendship. Jack still caries the unlit torch for Sylvia.

During flight training they briefly meet a lanky young man with piercing eyes. Cadet White is idolized by Jack and David as an experienced flyer. White chews thoughtfully on a Hershey's candy bar, and says with a grin, "I've got to go and do a flock of figure eights before chow." After seeing a small teddy bear in David's hand he explains he never carries a lucky charm. "Luck or no luck, when your time comes you're gonna get it!" With that he is gone. A few moments later, White dies in a collision with another plane.

Jack and David fly their first "Dawn Patrol" after arriving in France. The squadron commander tells them to patrol the region around Mervale, but to watch out for "Captain Kellerman's Flying Circus." Jack's natural vigor earns him several victories, including a Gotha bomber.

Then Jack believes David is trying to take Sylvia from him, which drives a wedge between the two friends. David tries to explain but Jack is too angry to listen. During a patrol David, who has left his lucky charm behind, is shot down behind enemy lines. Believing his friend dead, a remorseful Jack goes on a rampage of revenge on the Germans.

But David is not dead. He reaches an airfield and steals a German plane. He shoots down a pursuing Fokker and races to his own lines. But in the sky nearby is the vengeful Jack. David ends up in his sights. Jack sees only the black crosses and the hated Hun and attacks. David screams, "Jack, don't you know me?" David crashes into a farmhouse and soldiers carry him inside. Jack lands to claim the kill. A woman comes out and asks him to come inside to see the dying pilot. Jack's face turns white with shock as he realizes what he has done.

David dies in Jack's arms. As he falls limp, the shot cuts to the propeller of Jack's plane slowing to a stop.

Jack, looking older and far wiser visits David's parents to apologize for killing their son. They accept his heartfelt pain with stolid faces. He finds Mary and realizes that she had loved him all along.

Wings holds a particular place in film history. Not only was it the first major Hollywood production to realistically portray the air war, but it also took on the subject of the tragedy and waste of war.

Wings was written by former Air Service pilot John Monk Saunders. His vision of the film was of near-epic proportions. After learning that Paramount would be willing to cover the cost of the film if the Army provided the needed men and equipment, Saunders contacted the War Department. He made his pitch for a film depicting America's valiant struggle against the Germans. The U.S. military was at the mercy of a parsimonious Congress and needed all the public support it could generate. (The cooperation between the military and motion picture industry was born with *Wings* and continues, more or less, to this day.) The War Department informed Paramount that the Army would cooperate.

William A. Wellman had joined N87 *las Chats Noir* (Black Cats) of the Lafayette Flying Corps prior to U.S. entry into the war. He was awarded the French Croix du Guerre for victories over the Germans. This convinced Jesse Lasky to use Wellman. It was one of the best decisions the venerable producer ever made.

William A. Wellman (right) with French instructor and mechanic, in France, 1917. Note Bleriot training aircraft. Wellman served in N87 *las Chats Noir* (Black Cats) of the Lafayette Flying Corps. *Collection of William A. Wellman, Jr.*

The boyishly handsome Rogers was establishing himself in film by the time he was cast in *Wings*. "We hit it off well," said Rogers, "although Wellman was the toughest director I ever had. Most directors would say, 'Fine, Buddy, that's great!' But Wellman would make me do it until it really was fine."

Richard Arlen was an unknown at the time. Wellman wasn't sure Paramount's choice of Neil Hamilton was right for the role of David. When Wellman saw Arlen's screen test he said, "Jesus Christ! Who's that good-looking son-of-a-bitch?" He wasn't called "Wild Bill" Wellman for nothing.

Arlen was able to pull a great deal of film presence from a simple deep gaze into the camera. Several authentic planes, including a SPAD VII and two Fokker D.VIIs were acquired. Iron Crosses were painted on Army Curtiss Hawk P-1s used as German Albatros D.5As. A Martin MB-2 bomber was modified to be the fabled German Gotha. Tremulous music overshadows the scene where the huge plane is wheeled out of its hangar for a raid on Mervale.

The U.S. Army's nimble Curtiss P-1 Hawk played the role of German Albatros fighters in *Wings*.

Soldiers of the 2nd Infantry Division on location at Camp Stanley near San Antonio, Texas for the battle scene in *Wings. Collection of William A. Wellman, Jr.*

Five square miles of land near Camp Stanley were landscaped and built to resemble an actual battlefield near St. Mihiel, France. Trenches, dugouts, barbed wire and artillery emplacements were built along with a French village and crossroads. The ground battle used 3,500 troops of the Second Infantry Division.

During the complex battle a plane was to swoop low into the shot. It was an Army pilot and his wheels actually knocked helmets off the ground troops. Wellman was angered at the pilot. "When I saw him crash I was almost glad," he stated in his biography.

Wellman went to the crashed plane. He saw the pilot sitting against an ambulance with a bandage on his head. "He was dazed, and I suddenly realized that in all my planning, I had forgotten one terribly important factor, the human element. This pilot had flown at the front. It was not 1926 to him; it was 1918."

The aerial sequences are stunning testimony to what Hollywood had learned since 1912. The Texas sky was often cloudless, but Wellman wanted clouds. "The clouds give a sense of speed," he said. "But against a blue sky, it's like a lot of goddamn flies!"

Rogers and Arlen were photographed in scores of flights, in some cases actually flying the planes. Rogers recalled, "My flying instructor was Hoyt Vandenberg, later head of the Air Force." Arlen was already a pilot from service in the Army but never saw combat.

Perry's cameras caught close-up shots of the actors in helmet and goggles. The dizzying dogfights are very realistic. Machine guns fire through the propellers while the background spins. Burning planes cartwheel down in pyres of black smoke while victorious aces swoop low over the infantry trenches.

David's terrified face as he feels Jack's bullets striking him are unforgettable. His head droops limply as the plane spins to its destruction.

For modern audiences it's hardly even noticed the film is silent, accompanied only by a dramatic Wurlitzer Pipe Organ.

When the Gotha attacks Mervale, the bombs are seen falling away from the plane as the ground rolls by far below.

While most of the aerial scenes were done in the air, a few had to be done by the special-effects available at the time.

Gary Cooper plays the role of the doomed aviator Cadet White. The crash is only shown as shadows on the ground, then a quick cut to the planes smashing into each other. The collision was achieved with two Thomas-Morse Scouts. The planes were set on two 175-foot "V" shaped tracks with engines running. The tracks kept the unmanned planes straight until they were almost airborne and met in the center for the final collision.

The manned crashes were done by Dick Grace, who would soon become the king of aircraft crash stunts. For the scene where Jack is shot down the SPAD was modified with a steel sheath around the cockpit to protect Grace. He was to bring it down just at the edge of the barbed wire in No Man's Land at a shallow angle to provide the most dramatic crash possible. The ground had been dug up by the Army to give Grace some soft soil. The metal posts and barbed wire were replaced by thin pine and twine to prevent him being sliced. Grace's aim was off. He hit the real barbed wire, but received no injuries.

In the scene where David steals a German plane and shoots down another, the second plane was a Fokker D.VII, with Grace at the controls. Since the crash was to take place at takeoff the landing gear and lower wing was cut to let it collapse upon impact. Grace nosed it over about twenty feet from the ground, but the sturdy German plane refused to collapse. Grace suffered a neck fracture which put him in a brace for several months.

Wellman himself appears in a cameo during the final battle scene. A mortally wounded Doughboy sees Jack cut down a line of advancing German infantry. "Attaboy," he says in the title card. "Them buzzards is some use after all."

The final film was an excellent, almost unsurpassable example of the filmmakers' art. Wellman brought out powerful emotions in the actors. Even male viewers, the author among them, shed tears as David died in Jack's arms. *Wings* was the first film to win Best Picture at the Academy Awards. It is also the only picture ever to win for Engineering Effects, a precursor of Visual Effects.

Dick Grace after the crash that broke his neck during the filming of *Wings*.
Collection of William A. Wellman, Jr.

For Wellman it might have seemed as if he had peaked just after leaving the starting gate in his first Kentucky Derby. But it was only the first of many successful films for "Wild Bill" Wellman.

Wings was followed by another Paramount air war film, *The Legion of the Condemned* (1928), with Gary Cooper in a flying role. There was a great deal of unused aerial footage left over from *Wings*. Jesse Lasky decided to make another air war film in order to garner more profits without the expense of further major aerial photography.

French-born writer Jean de Lumur's script was based on a story by John Monk Saunders. Cooper was cast as an RFC pilot named Gale Price. The female lead was Fay Wray, still five years from her blind date with King Kong.

Wellman (left), Dick Grace (in plane) and Buddy Rogers on the set of *Wings*.
Collection of William A. Wellman, Jr.

Price is in love with Christine, a French girl. He sees her embracing a diplomat at a pre-war embassy soiree. Thinking she is falling for another man, Price joins a squadron of aviators in which each man is trying to remove himself from a dark or unpleasant past, *a la* the French Foreign Legion. The legion is known as "the squadron no man ever quitted alive." Men are sent off on dangerous *mission spéciales*. When a man dies, presumably in triumph, his name is removed from the roster with the swipe of an eraser.

Price is given a mission to take a spy behind German lines. The spy turns out to be Christine, who has been working for French Intelligence all along. She tells Price that she still loves him. He flies Christine to her destination, intending to return in ten days to pick her up. Christine is captured, and when the Germans learn a French pilot will return, use her as bait. Price arrives and is captured. They are both sentenced to die before a firing squad.

Only a surprise bombing raid and landing by planes of the legion saves them from execution. Price and Christine leave for Paris. The legion's commander, well knowing that a woman can be more dangerous than a suicidal mission, silently removes Price's name from the roster.

According to Frank Thompson in his excellent book *Lost Films*, "Gary Cooper and Fay Wray shared a terrific onscreen chemistry that led the studio to publicize the pair as 'Paramount's glorious young lovers.' But Miss Wray's off-screen chemistry was directed at writer John Monk Saunders."

In an interview with William Wellman, Jr., the author asked about this film. "This was a lot closer to my father's heart than *Wings*," said Wellman. "He worked closely with Saunders to write the script." Paramount told Wellman to minimize any footage that was too obviously from the previous film as *Wings* was still on tour. A raid on a German troop train was filmed for *Wings* but never used, and apparently appeared in *Legion*. A few new shots were done between October and November 1927 at the Paramount Studios and Griffith Field. Using an Airco DH.9, Price's landing behind the lines scene was shot on location near Canoga Park.

Wellman was quickly becoming the master of aerial action and deep drama. *Gone With the Wind* producer David O. Selznick described *Legion* as ". . . one of the most focused uses of film to tell a story that I've ever seen. Wellman had the eye of an aviator. He was really a remarkable talent." Unfortunately, there is no way to find out for ourselves, as *Legion* is lost.

The author interviewed Paramount's legendary producer A.C. Lyles, whose tenure with the studio goes back to Jesse Lasky himself. Lyles was very helpful and told the author of his friendships with Buddy Rogers, Richard Arlen and Gary Cooper. When the author asked about *Legion*, Lyles called for his executive assistant to check with the archives to find a copy of the film. Later he admitted there was none.

As Thompson put it, "*Legion of the Condemned's* loss is a truly tragic blow to Hollywood history."

Gary Cooper lifts Fay Wray into a DH.9 in *Legion of the Condemned.*
Collection of William A. Wellman, Jr.

William Wellman Jr. commented, "I'd love to see this film. It was special to my father. I really hope someone finds it someday."

Lilac Time (1928) also starred Gary Cooper as a pilot in the air war against the Germans. The film is far more a love story than a war film. George Fitzmaurice directed this one, as Wellman was working on *Beggars of Life* with Wallace Beery and Richard Arlen. Captain Philip Blythe is a Royal Flying Corps officer just arrived in a squadron. Montana native Cooper is saved from having to manage a British accent by this being another silent film.

Lilac Time takes place at an RFC field in France where the owner of a chateau has offered it as a billet for several pilots. Blythe (Cooper) is engaged to a wealthy English girl but falls in love with the owner's pretty daughter Jeannine (Colleen Moore). Blythe's interfering father and the Germans do their best to stop the romance but in the end they are united.

The filming was done in the hills and valleys between Santa Ana and San Juan Capistrano on the California coast. A passable French chateau and RFC airfield were built for the location shoots. Dick Grace, recovered from his neck injury, had purchased and leased seven Waco Model 10 open-cockpit biplanes for the film. The Waco 10 was widely used for private and commercial short charters around the country. With modifications to the cowling, landing gear and the addition of machine guns, Grace was able to make the Wacos appear as generic RFC fighters. Fictional squadron insignia were the final touch. Grace hired five pilots to fly the planes with him and Ross Cooke, who had worked in *Wings*.

The Wacos were lined up by the chateau, filmed on takeoff, landing, and in formation. Cinematographer Sidney Hickox used the same techniques Perry had perfected on *Wings*. Cameras mounted on the fuselages showed the actors' faces in flight. While *Lilac Time's* air battles are not as dramatic as in *Wings*, they do show how far aviation filming had matured.

Three crash sequences were planned by Grace. He brought a Waco down, flying into the wind, which slowed the plane, and touched down—wheels first, then a wing tip, and then nosed over. The plane flipped over on its back. Grace simply undid his seat harness and climbed down, unhurt.

The second crash landing twisted the Waco around, finally coming to rest in the opposite direction. Grace was bruised in this crash. The last required the Waco to go between two trees and shear off the wings.

Grace was in Los Angeles at the time, so fellow stunt pilot Charles Stoffer did the stunt. But steering the twice-repaired Waco on the ground was not as easy as in the air and Stoffer came too close to the trees on one side. The bracing wires had been removed so the wings would break away easily. The right wing was torn off a few inches from the fuselage and the left wing only lost the tip. The unbalanced fuselage went out of control. Stoffer quickly ducked below the cockpit rim to keep from being killed.

The scene was used for a semi-comic sequence where Jeannine is hiding in a plane and accidentally starts it, careening wildly around the field. She fires the guns and finally ends up crashing between two trees.

Wellman and Buddy Rogers worked together again in the talkie *Young Eagles* (1930). It starred the throaty-voiced Jean Arthur while future Academy Award winner Paul Lukas played a German ace. "My father wasn't really interested in doing *Young Eagles*," said Wellman's son. "But Paramount wanted another airplane film."

Rogers is an American pilot who falls for Arthur while serving in France. He shoots down ace Lukas and captures him. Arthur, a German spy, helps him to escape. But then she is revealed to be an American double agent.

Young Eagles contained what Dick Grace later called the most violent crash he ever did. He flew an aged American Eagle painted with American Air Service insignia. Leo Nomis, another stunt pilot pursued Grace in "German" Waco towards a stream near Thousand Oaks, California. Several cameras were ready to film the crash. With Nomis in pursuit, Grace slid into the shallow bed of the stream and managed to distribute the impact along the wings and landing gear. Suddenly the fuselage twisted while the wings were wrapped around it until the wreckage came to rest on the bank. Grace was unhurt but the crash had been extremely violent.

The German ace's crash was filmed at Van Nuys Metropolitan Airport as Grace brought the plane, this time an American Eagle in German markings, down on wheels and nose. The plane bounced, then flipped on its back and skidded tail-first several hundred feet. Elmer Dyer filmed both crashes. This crash was also used in *The Eagle and the Hawk* (1933).

Wellman wasn't happy with the final cut of the film and asked for his release from Paramount, which was granted. A nitrate print of *Young Eagles* is in storage at the UCLA Film and Television Archives and is not currently being considered for safety stock conversion.

Aviation buff and millionaire Howard Hughes, with virtually unlimited money from the Hughes Tool Company, decided to branch out to motion pictures. Hughes sat through *Wings* several times and was intrigued enough to produce his own air war film under the auspices of his own company, Caddo Productions. *Hell's Angels* would become one of the most chaotic and expensive films ever made. Hughes' hectic management style made the project drag on interminably. He fired two directors, the second of whom snapped at Hughes, "If you think you know so much, why don't you direct it yourself?"

Hughes' intended to make it a silent, since the talkie revolution hadn't yet emerged from *The Jazz Singer* (1927). This would cause a great headache for Hughes later. He purchased a story from Marshall Neilan.

Monte (Ben Lyon) and Roy (James Hall) Rutledge are brothers and students at Oxford. They are frequently at odds over Monte's headstrong antics. While visiting Germany they meet Karl Armstedt, a young German also attending Oxford. Monte is a woman-chasing blade who gets into hot water over a German Countess, married to Baron von Kranz, and hotfoots it back to England. Roy takes on the cuckolded Count in a duel in his brother's stead.

When the war breaks out the brothers join the Royal Flying Corps. Karl is forced to go back to Germany and serve in the military. After training as fighter pilots the brothers attend a ball where Monte meets the coquettish Helen, whom Roy wants. In his usual careless manner Monte accompanies her home, with predictable results.

A Zeppelin attacks London from above the clouds at night. It has orders to target Trafalgar Square. The observer, suspended in a "cloud car" several hundred feet below the airship on a long cable is Karl, feeling regret at having to bomb London. He leads the Captain astray, causing the bombs to fall harmlessly on Hyde Park. Four RFC fighters race into the air to take on the behemoth. Karl is callously cut loose in order to reduce the wind resistance as the Zeppelin tries to escape. Roy and Mnnte's plane is shot down and forced to crash land.

But one fighter rams the Zeppelin, causing it to fall out of the sky in a huge pyre of fire and smoke.

Ben Lyon as the reckless Monte Rutledge in a close-up in *Hell's Angels.*
SDASM Collection

The brothers are sent to France where they again find Helen working in a bar. Monte's courage is questioned by his fellow officers. He impulsively volunteers for a dangerous mission. Roy says he'll go too. The night before the raid Roy finally learns the truth about Helen and Monte. They are to fly a captured Gotha and bomb a German ammunition dump. They are shot down by Baron Manfred von Richthofen's Flying Circus and captured. The German commandant is none other than Count von Kranz, who is less than pleased with the man who made love to his wife.

The Germans believe the RFC flyers have information on a large Allied offensive. Monte is threatened with torture and on the verge of revealing what he knows. But he is shot by his own brother to keep him silent. Then Roy is executed by firing squad. When Monte dies in Roy's arms it has less impact than David's death in *Wings*.

Hughes hired the Norwegian-born Greta Nissen for the role of Helen. She was fine for the silent but later, when Hughes decided to make the film a talkie, her accent was

Stunt pilot Frank Tomick (left) supervised the pilots for *Hell's Angels*. Garland Lincoln (right) provided aircraft for several Great War films.

completely unsuitable. Displaying the talent he later used in finding unknown and buxom stars, Hughes chose the blonde bombshell Jean Harlow for the role.

Hughes took flying lessons at Clover Field in the summer of 1927. Frank Tomick was hired to work on the production. Hughes wanted the aircraft to be as authentic as possible. Tomick and his team scoured the country looking for as many Fokker D.VIIs, Avro 504s, S.E.5s, and Sopwith Camels as possible. They managed to acquire four D.VIIs, but the S.E.5s were proving to be difficult. Avro 504s too were unobtainable. The venerable Curtiss JN-4 superficially resembled the 504. The Kinner Aircraft Company in Glendale worked on the Jennys by trimming the upper wings, installing rotary engines and adding a wheel skid. They ended up with three presentable Avros.

Since Caddo had only four Fokker D.VIIs, Hughes decided to use them on the close shots and use Travel Airs in the long shots. With modifications by Wally Timm, they were virtually indistinguishable from the true Fokkers at a distance. The Travel Airs became known as "Wichita Fokkers" for years afterward.

The Sopwith Camels were Thomas-Morse Scouts with changes to the cowling, tail and wing. Caddo had two S.E.5s and two Sopwith Snipes but they weren't used in the aerial sequences. Hughes had collected more than eighty planes, making him the owner of the world's largest private air force. He told Tomick to find some pilots. When Tomick asked Hughes how much he was willing to pay, the millionaire pointed at several men watching the filming. He said they had all just soloed and would work for nothing just to be in a movie. But he said he'd pay $10 a day for each man. He told Tomick to get the new pilots into the Scouts and have them fly a formation just to see how they would do.

Frank Tomick flies one of Howard Hughes' Fokker D.VIIs in *Hell's Angels*. Travel Air 'Wichita Fokkers' were used for the distant shots. *SDASM Collection*

Tomick didn't think much of the idea and refused to fly with them. The "formation" ended up landing all over the county and required two days to bring all the planes back. Hughes finally relented and Al Wilson, Ross Cooke, Al Johnson, Frank Clarke, Roy Wilson and a former San Francisco cartoonist named Maurice "Loop Loop" Murphy were brought into the fold. Another new name was Paul Mantz, in the first film of a long aviation movie career. Dick Grace was working on *Lilac Time* and wasn't available. Murphy was one of the best Thomas-Morse pilots in the country, but Hughes, in his usual acerbic style, made some disparaging comments about his flying. So Murphy, hot under the collar, had his formation go up and show the millionaire what they could do. It was perfect. Then Murphy buzzed Hughes in a field, so close the man didn't dare stand up. Hughes told Tomick to fire Murphy, but Tomick said Murphy was showing him he was the best.

The Avro training planes were taken to March Field in Riverside for the first aerial sequences. Scenes depicting the antics of green pilots in semi-comic maneuvers were done at March. Hughes, now totally involved in the film, set up Caddo Field in the San Fernando Valley. He also hired Harry Perry, still glowing from his success on *Wings*, as cinematographer. Perry improved on his camera mounts. Elmer Dyer was aerial cameraman.

Bill and Barney Butler built a twenty-seven foot long model of a Zeppelin airship. Originally the model was actually to be filled with helium, but the structure was too heavy for the amount of gas it could hold. The scenes using the model were filmed in a hangar with thick vapor concealing the guide wires. Obtaining precise plans for the miniature and interior was child's play for Hughes. The Zeppelin interiors were built full-scale as was the cloud car. Caddo's sound technicians simulated the heavy thrum of the five Maybach diesels as the Zeppelin flew overhead.

Hughes wanted perfection and the bombing sequences were shot more than a hundred times. The effort paid off. When the bombs fall into Hyde Park, the film does an excellent job of conveying what an actual night bombing raid must have looked like.

There are a few flaws. For instance, the German wartime Zeppelins were not silver as were the later commercial ships, but either gray or dark yellow, and the undersides were often painted black to make them harder to see at night. It was usual for Zeppelins to bomb from above 18,000 feet, which was beyond the altitude of British fighters until the end of 1916. Even so it often took a fighter two hours to reach that altitude.

The sight of several German crewmen saluting the captain who orders them to jump to their deaths is fictional and only intended to increase the drama. The image of the huge burning airship is remarkably dramatic. The mid-air crash of two planes used detailed aluminum models suspended from tracks in the hanger where the Zeppelin scenes were shot.

Hughes seems to have taken Wellman's path to visually interesting aerial sequences. There are plenty of clouds. The "Wichita Fokkers" were filmed taking off from the Flying Circus field. Frank Clarke piloted the plane with the name "Von Bruen" on the side. It is not known who played the part of Baron von Richthofen. The name on the cockpit sill of the Fokker reads: "Rittm. Von Richthofen." *Rittmeister* means "Cavalry Captain," his rank in the Ulan cavalry. However, the Red Baron never flew the Fokker D.VII in combat. It didn't enter front-line service until just days before his death. All but 19 of his eighty kills were made in the Albatros D.III and D.Va.

Hughes learned a lot from Wellman by making the aerial battles dynamic with lots of clouds to provide a background to fly against.
SDASM Collection

There is at least one shot of a squadron passing over toward the viewer which seems to be a negative. The planes are clearly white against a dark sky. Some of the close ups of pilots during combat are shockingly acute when they twist and scream in agony as bullets tear into them. An engine fire in one plane is viewed from the front as the pilot desperately tries to keep from being roasted.

Instead of the Martin MB-2 used in *Wings* for the Gotha bomber, the one-of-a-kind Sikorsky S-29, built by Igor Sikorsky served the same purpose in *Hell's Angels*. Famed pilot Roscoe Turner had bought the big plane in 1926 and leased it to Hughes for *Hell's Angels*. Turner flew it, with his wife in the cockpit, from the east coast to Caddo Field, arriving in March 1928. An open cockpit with a gunner's ring was fitted in front of the actual closed-in cockpit, and other wartime fittings were added. The Sikorsky was painted in generic—and incorrect—German markings. The pilot and mechanic were in the rear cockpit out of sight of the cameras mounted in the front, where Lyon and Hall were seated.

When the Gotha is attacked an engine nacelle catches fire. This was done using a mockup nacelle with a wind machine to fan the flames. Rows of dynamite caps concealed in the hull of the plane near Hall were set behind a sheet of metal to protect the actor from splinters and debris. The effect of seeing Hall cringe from the nearby bullet strikes is extremely realistic. The Gotha's long flaming fall to the ground, trailing a veil of black smoke ends in an actual fatality. The pilot, Al Wilson, was able to bail out of the plane but the mechanic, an eager man named Phil Jones, was unable to get out and died in the impact.

When *Hell's Angels* was released in 1928 as a silent, the audiences greeted it with apathy and disdain. The talkies were already taking over. So Hughes re-shot most of the film with dialogue and added sound effects for the aerial sequences. The result has great impact but is an obvious mix of sound and silent footage. Silent films were shot at sixteen frames per second, and sound at twenty-four. The final result is that the silent footage tends to speed up. It makes the pace clumsy.

Nearly all of the training sequences were cut from the final film and later turned up in Caddo's *Sky Devils* (1933), starring William Boyd, who was soon to be known as Hopalong Cassidy. In fact, considering how much footage was shot, very little was used. For every foot of film in the finished print, there were 249 feet of unused film. Hughes' changes added several months to the project.

Fox Film Corporation produced *The Sky Hawk* (1929). Jack Bardell is an English aristocrat who joins the RFC in the war. But Bardell is in love with his commander's girl. He is sent to France and is partially paralyzed after a mysterious crash. Bardell is labeled a coward and forced to resign. Eventually he regains partial use of his legs and determined to reclaim his honor. With the help of a friend he constructs a working plane from salvaged parts. He arms the plane with machine guns and calls it the "Sky Hawk."

When a Zeppelin raids London Bardell is in the air with his plane, which has been fitted with special stirrups on the rudder pedals. He shoots down the airship, but is also forced to crash-land. The impact from the crash somehow cures him and he is able to walk. His honor is restored.

The film was made on location on the site of Ross Field near Arcadia, California. Fox rented the same balloon hangar Hughes used for his Zeppelin scenes.

First National began work on *Dawn Patrol* in 1929 while Hughes was re-shooting *Hell's Angels* for sound. The script was adapted from a story entitled "The Flight Commander" from the fertile mind of John Monk Saunders.

The up-and-coming director Howard Hawks—who would one day direct dozens of films like *Ceiling Zero* (1936) and *Only Angels Have Wings* (1939) and be nominated for Best Director for *Sergeant York* (1941)—would make *Dawn Patrol* a worthy successor to *Wings*.

Dawn Patrol didn't use the by-then common love triangle plot device. Instead, the film focused on the terrible attrition rate of combat pilots and the stress of command. Richard Barthelmess is Dick Courtney and Douglas Fairbanks, Jr., is his friend Doug Scott. They are commanded by Major Brand, played by Neil Hamilton, who finally made it into the sky after being replaced by Arlen in *Wings*. The hard-nosed Brand is constantly forced to curtail the cavalier attitude of close friends Courtney and Scott. When Brand is promoted and transferred, Courtney is put in command. He finds it much harder to lead than to follow. His friendship with Scott ends when Scott's younger brother, totally unprepared for the Darwinian world of combat, is killed.

The film's dramatic climax finds Scott volunteering for a suicidal one-man mission behind enemy lines. Courtney gets Scott drunk and flies the mission himself. He is killed and Scott now finds himself in command, ready to carry the flame, teaching the new boys to survive.

A full-scale German aerodrome was built in Pico Canyon. The British airfield scenes were shot near Thousand Oaks. Earl Robinson and Leo Nomis, fresh from *Young Eagles*, were on hand for the aerial sequences. The German aircraft were the usual eclectic hodgepodge of post-war types, but two real Pfalz D.VIIs were leased for the film. One of the Pfalzes is now owned by the Museum of Flight in Seattle, Washington. It also appears in the 1938 Errol Flynn remake of this film. The Pfalzes were painted in generic German Air Service colors.

The RFC squadron was again a mix of two Thomas-Morse Scouts, two Travel Air Speedwings, two Orenco Ds and three Garland Lincoln Nieuport 28s painted in RFC schemes.

For the bombing raid scene, small funnel shaped holes were dug in the ground, filled with charges of black powder and lamp black, and covered with dirt. This would cause a nice smoky explosion with little actual destructive power. The sequence nearly ended in disaster, proving that even the best preparation could still fail. A German plane was to blow up from bombs dropped by two British planes. Nomis was flying the lead fighter, followed by Earl Robinson. The explosives were to be set off after Robinson had passed over. After several test flyovers, they were ready. But just as Robinson passed over a German plane it erupted under him. He was caught in the blast. Luckily he was uninjured.

For the effect of a plane exploding while taking off, an old Standard J-1 was put on a track, rigged with a lanyard which would be pulled as the plane left the track and became airborne. The J-1 exploded and fell blazing to the ground. Even Dick Grace wouldn't have tried that one.

The scene where Scott lands to pick up Courtney after he has crashed behind enemy lines was done with one of Garland Lincoln's Nieuport 28s. The first part was with Barthelmess on the lower wing, holding the strut. Then a Swallow was used for the long shot, with a figure painted on the fuselage to look like Courtney hanging on. A Thomas-Morse was used for the crash near French lines. Long troughs for the wheels and tail skid kept the unmanned plane straight until it hit heavy wooden blocks at the end, where it would flip over. But the blocks broke off and the plane continued along the ground, engine running and out of control. Another attempt with heavier blocks did the trick and the plane flipped over right on target.

By 1938, Garland Lincoln's vintage Nieuport 28s had appeared in at least eight films, including *Dawn Patrol* in 1930 and 1938.

Hawks himself appeared in a cameo as a German pilot. A lot of stock footage was generated for sale to other studios or used in other First National films.

While the overly dramatic, even histrionic acting may seem archaic to modern audiences, it was just what the theatergoers of the day expected. Also, most of the actors had spent the greater part of their careers in silent films, where exaggerated facial and hand gestures were typical. *Dawn Patrol* was released in August 1930, two months after the second premiere of *Hell's Angels*. *Patrol* drew better reviews and audience responses than the Hughes film, even though the aerial scenes were not as exciting.

The first release of *Hell's Angels* had been competing against sound, the second against *Dawn Patrol* and *The Sky Hawk*. The entire production cost Hughes more than $3.8 million and the lives of three men. The production had gone on so long that Hollywood wags said they had met a 105-year old man who was the only man alive who remembered when *Hell's Angels* was started.

Hughes rented Grauman's Chinese Theater and turned Hollywood Boulevard into a triumphal parade. Floats carrying replicas of fighter planes passed ranks of searchlights. Speeches by the stars drew nearly half a million people.

Hughes also arranged for simultaneous premieres in New York and tried to persuade Hugo Eckener, director of DELAG, the German Zeppelin Transport Company, to fly the world-famous dirigible *Graf Zeppelin* over the city. Even with a $100,000 offer by Hughes, Eckener declined. In any case he would not have been pleased with how Hughes had portrayed the wartime Zeppelin captains.

Hell's Angels earned about $7 million, at least according to some sources. Noah Dietrich, longtime Hughes business manager, later said the film never recovered its staggering cost. It did, however, raise the bar on aerial cinematography and visual effects, if not plot and acting. What it lacked in depth it made up in action, entertainment and sex—the hallmark of most of Hughes' films. The major studios may not have taken Hughes seriously as a filmmaker but they could not ignore that *Hell's Angels* was a powerful film.

As technology and technique matured only the imagination of the writer was needed for more exciting films. Some films had little box office success, such as *The Last Flight* (1931), with Richard Barthelmess, and *The Lost Squadron* (1932).

Paramount was on a roll and produced *The Eagle and the Hawk* beginning in April 1933. The cast included names soon to be famous, such as Fredric March, Cary Grant and Carole Lombard. John Monk Saunders provided a story which centered on an RFC observer squadron in France. March is Jerry Young, an increasingly depressed and angry pilot who has seen too many friends die. Henry Crocker, (Grant) is assigned as an observer. He carries a chip on his shoulder from being washed out of pilot school by Young. When Young is sent off on leave in London he meets Lombard, who is only listed in the credits as "The Beautiful Lady."

Young returns to the airfield little better than before. Back in combat he shoots down a famous German ace but loses his observer in the battle. The squadron celebrates his victory. But Young has finally cracked from the strain and commits suicide in his quarters. Crocker, upon discovering the dead Young, realizes how dedicated and professional he had been.

Crocker resolves not to let Young's suicide become known. At dawn he loads the body into the pilot's seat of a de Havilland observer plane. He uses the observer's controls and flies to the Front. Once there he turns the machine gun on Young's body, the wings and engine and stays with the plane. Crocker is killed in redemption of his own honor.

The aerial sequences in *The Eagle and the Hawk* are less important than the character development. March's superb acting skills add greatly to his role as the brooding Young. He was still two years from his greatest role of Jean Valjean in *Les Miserables* (1935). Cary Grant, with only a year in movies, makes the resentful Crocker into a memorable character. The cast also boasts Jack Oakie, a sometime comedian who would one day be best known as the bombastic Bacteirian dictator Napaloni in Chaplin's *The Great Dictator* (1940).

The location shooting for *Eagle* may have been done on the same ranch as *Dawn Patrol*, or it may have been on Paramount land near Agoura. The Dick Grace crash from *Young Eagles* appears in *Eagle and the Hawk* in the scene where Young shoots down the German plane. The ground crew tried to match a staged wreck with what appears in the footage from three years before. A few details are different, such as landing gear and engine. Aerial footage from *Wings* and *Dawn Patrol* also appeared, but Frank Tomick flew Thomas-Morse Scouts and de Havillands to film the required new footage. Garland Lincoln leased a Jenny and some Nieuports to Paramount.

Rather than have the actors in actual planes, Paramount used process shots for much of the close-up footage. Previously shot footage or stock shots from *Wings* were projected on a rear screen in front of an airplane mockup with smoke and wind machines. While this served the purpose it is more obviously staged than the actual aerial shots. By the early 1930s the trend towards shortcuts and cheaper illusions was well underway.

RKO's *Ace of Aces* began production in the summer of 1933, just as *The Eagle and the Hawk* was wrapping. *Ace of Aces* was filmed on the RFC airfield location of *Dawn Patrol*. Richard Dix, one of RKO's leading western actors, plays the lead role of Rex Thorne, an American sculptor who wants nothing to do with the dirty business of war. His girlfriend Nancy (Elizabeth Allen) considers it base cowardice. In order to redeem himself to her, Thorne joins the Air Service. In time he not only is an excellent pilot, but shoots down forty-two planes to become the highest scoring ace. But it has changed him into a heartless killer, hated by his squadron mates.

Thorne meets Nancy in Paris. She is now a Red Cross nurse and shocked by the change in him. When a German plane appears over the field to drop a note about an American pilot who landed safely behind German lines, Thorne impulsively jumps into a plane and shoots down the courier, a very young German who didn't defend himself. Thorne is plagued with guilt when the boy dies. Thorne goes back into combat and allows himself to be shot down rather than kill again. He is reunited with Nancy in the hospital, no longer the heartless ace of the skies.

Harry Perry was again in charge of aerial cinematography, with Garland Lincoln, Frank Clarke, and Frank Tomick adding their piloting skills. The Executive Producer of *Ace of Aces* was Merian C. Cooper, the director of *King Kong* and later General Claire Chennault's deputy in China with the Flying Tigers. At least a dozen planes were used including some of the Travel Air "Wichita Fokkers" and five Waco F Models. RKO had two mockup S.E.5s for use in field scenes. Shooting the aerial footage took about two weeks.

Basil Rathbone and Errol Flynn in front of a Thomas-Morse Scout on the set of *Dawn Patrol* in 1938. *Author's Collection*

Warner's remake of *Dawn Patrol* was filmed in 1938, starring Errol Flynn, Basil Rathbone and David Niven. It was hardly distinguishable from the original. If anything can be said in favor of the film it is that the aerial scenes are more a part of the film and the acting has settled down to less histrionic emoting. This might be due to the efforts of director Edmund Goulding, who had worked on *Hell's Angels*. Flynn and Rathbone, already legendary as sword-wielding rivals in *The Adventures of Robin Hood* the same year, were cast as the cocky Courtney and the inflexible Major Brand. Also appearing were frequent Flynn film regulars Donald Crisp and James Burke. All that was missing was Olivia de Havilland.

Leo Nomis worked on the film as an aeronautical supervisor. The aircraft run the gamut of Garland Lincoln's Nieuports and at least one Thomas-Morse Scout. The Nieuports are distinguishable by the wing struts, two having "N" struts and two with "I" struts. Nearly all the aerial footage was from the original First National film. Goulding shot Flynn and Niven in the planes, starting engines and taxiing down the field. The site of the original REC airfield was under housing developments, so the new footage was done at Warner Brothers' Ranch near Calabasas. The planes had been carefully painted to duplicate the originals. The Thomas-Morse was placed in such a way that when Errol Flynn fired a flare into the cockpit it appeared seamlessly as the same plane fired upon by Barthelmess in 1930.

The remake has little to make it stand out against Hawks' original but it does showcase the studios' need to get as much mileage out of new stars and old footage as possible.

Errol Flynn as Dick Courtney on his fatal mission in *Dawn Patrol.*

By 1938 aviation was no longer the fragile and uncertain baby of the 1920s. It was a thriving growth industry with scores of companies competing for the lucrative civil, military and commercial markets. The slow and underpowered wood-and-canvas biplanes were giving way to sleek all-metal monoplanes and powerful engines.

In distant Europe and Asia, the old-world empires of Britain, Germany and Japan were gearing up for another war. While the vast majority if Americans chose to believe the "War to End All Wars" had changed the world for the better, it was growing increasingly apparent that the bad blood remaining in the world was once again coming to a boil.

The War Department encouraged the film industry to make movies about the growing need for air power and generously provided planes, personnel and airfields for use in the films. The intention was to ignite and fan the flames of public support for the air armada (see Chapter Five). The almost quaint stories of antiquated biplanes and their knights of the air were less of a draw than they had been a decade before.

The beginning of the Second World War effectively ended Hollywood's interest in the Great War. When the Great War was mentioned, for the first time as "World War One," it was usually a flashback of an older pilot's experiences in combat.

Not until 1958—thirteen years after Germany's surrender—did the first full-length color motion picture about the "good old days of wooden crates and iron men" reach the screen. That was *Lafayette Escadrille*, directed by William Wellman. After his experiences in France, *Lafayette Escadrille* was a subject close to his heart and within his experience. "It was the one picture I most wanted to make," Wellman said in his biography, "and it was the worst picture I ever made."

William Wellman Jr. (seated in Bleriot) and his father on location at Santa Maria Airport for a scene in *Lafayette Escadrille. Collection of William A. Wellman, Jr.*

The film is semi-autobiographical but only if one looks very hard. Wellman narrates the story. Thad Walker (Tab Hunter) is a reckless young American who gets into trouble with the law and joins the French Air Service to escape the rap. Military discipline fails to curb his impulsive nature. He falls in love with a pretty French girl and runs off with her for several days, much to his commander's frustration. He returns to his squadron and resumes training. The film becomes more about the love affair between the untamed American boy and the sexy French girl than the war.

Wellman originally wanted James Dean for the lead role. "He would have been just what my father wanted," William Wellman, Jr., told the author, "but he was killed before the film was started. So [my father] opted for Paul Newman." But Jack Warner was upset with Newman over matters stemming from *The Silver Chalice* (1954). "Warner told my father that Newman was going to be put on suspension for a few months," said Wellman.

Tab Hunter was given the lead role. Wellman brought in David Janssen, soon to be famous as the falsely accused Dr. Richard Kimble in *The Fugitive* (1963-1967). Janssen would be Walker's wingman and buddy, "Duke" Sinclair. The real Sinclair served in Wellman's own squadron. One young actor from Universal impressed Wellman and was hired for the role of George Moseley. His name was Clint Eastwood.

In one of Hollywood's ironies, William Wellman Jr. plays his own father. Other stars' sons had small roles, including Jody McCrea, son of Joel, and Denny Devine, son of Andy.

A stunning dogfight sequence from the Technicolor *Men With Wings* (see Chapter Three) appears in *Escadrille*. It shows Wellman's magic touch for filming aerial combat. The process shots of Fred MacMurray were replaced with Tab Hunter in the same plane, while William Wellman, Jr., was inserted into the wingman's plane.

What does make the film worth watching for history buffs is Wellman's narration. He explains "Penguins" are planes that don't fly and are used only for learning control on the ground. The plane used in this scene is a replica 1909 Bleriot monoplane. The comic ground chase and wreck are similar to what would later be seen in *Those Magnificent Men in Their Flying Machines* (1965).

Gone were the days when the studios built special airfields and gathered planes from all over the world. *Escadrille* was filmed at Santa Maria Airport north of Los Angeles, using modified structures. Some of Garland Lincoln's well-worn Nieuports were used in the film. The pilots wear French flight helmets, due to Wellman's determination to be as authentic as possible.

The film gives the impression that Americans who joined the escadrille were totally untrained in either basic military discipline or flying. Some sequences are only a way of showing Hunter's bare torso to the young female viewers. In fact, the first combat scenes don't even occur until ninety minutes into the movie.

The Wellmans with the wingless Bleriot 'Penguin' in *Lafayette Escadrille.*
Collection of William A. Wellman, Jr.

The original version of the film, which was to be called *C'est La Guerre*, had Walker dying tragically. But the test audiences were outraged, and Jack Warner ordered three days of additional filming for a re-shoot. In his biography Wellman growled, "That dirty rotten bastard decided—don't laugh—that killing Tab Hunter was impossible."

Escadrille did not live up to Wellman's expectations. One can't help but wonder, if he had been given free rein to make it his way, if it could have been much better. In light of his past work, this would probably have been the case. Thirty-one years after directing *Wings*, "Wild Bill" had reached the end of his patience and walked off the lot. Because of his contract with Warner, Wellman directed only one more film, *Darby's Rangers* with James Garner, in 1958.

Escadrille did achieve one distinction: being included on *Air Classics* magazine's "Worst Films List." Perhaps the poor result led the studios to wait eight years before trying another Great War air movie.

One of the two remaining Garland Lincoln Nieuport 28s used in *Dawn Patrol* is on display at the San Diego Air & Space Museum.
Courtesy Ernie Viskupic, Wingman Photography

One of the most-recognized military decorations in the world is the *Pour le Mérite*. The gold and blue-enameled award was first established as a decoration 'For Merit' to officers in the Prussian Army by Frederick the Great in 1740. Over the next 175 years it was only presented to cavalry and infantry officers—until the advent of air combat. It was then the medal first appeared around the necks of German aces. The first to wear it was Max Immelmann, whose name became synonymous with the "Blue Max." Early in the war any pilot who brought down eight enemy planes received the decoration. But as the number of aces skyrocketed, the German Air Ministry changed it to sixteen kills. That was just as Baron Manfred von Richthofen had downed his eighth plane. Quietly seething, the Red Baron quickly scored another eight kills and earned the Blue Max.

Even in the United States the medal has gained a certain amount of notoriety and the reason may have a lot to do with the 1966 release of *The Blue Max*, starring George Peppard, James Mason and Ursula Andress. The plot centers on Bruno Stachel (Peppard). Stachel is a former infantry corporal who saw his dream and destiny in the sky. He has a chip on his shoulder due to being considered "low-class" by the aristocrat pilots in the German Air Service. When Stachel's first kill is unconfirmed, he lures another British plane close to his own field so he can shoot it down with plenty of witnesses. This does not endear him to his fellow aviators who feel he is a cruel man who does not follow the rules of aerial chivalry.

Stachel is determined to earn the coveted Blue Max. He crashes after inadvertently saving another pilot's life. He later spots that same pilot at an airfield and says, "That's the damn fool who almost got me killed today." A comrade informs Stachel, "He's a friend of mine. Why don't you take it up with him? May I introduce the Baron von Richthofen?"

Baron Manfred von Richthofen's red Fokker as seen in *The Blue Max*. Note the Richthofen crest on the fuselage. The Red Baron while first flying the Albatros and the later Triplane, had many variants on the red scheme, but he probably never put the family crest on his plane.

Stachel turns down a chance to fly in Richthofen's squadron, wanting to be the leading ace in his own squadron rather than follow the best. Stachel falls for Countess Kaeti von Klugermann, the wife of the haughty General Count von Klugermann (Mason). Stachel finally earns his medal and feels on par with the rest of his comrades. The Count learns that Stachel had falsely claimed two kills actually earned by another pilot, now dead. To avoid a scandalous court-martial and get Stachel away from his wife, the Count has Stachel test-fly a new monoplane fighter he knows is unsafe. Stachel is killed testing the plane.

The old love triangle is visible in the film but with a cruel twist as von Klugelmann plots Stachel's death in an "honorable manner." Even Howard Hughes wouldn't have thought of that one.

Although the film takes place in the first half of 1918, the jovial mood of the pilots is somewhat at odds with reality. By then most of the aviators were worn out and prone to depression and heavy drinking.

The photography, visual and sound effects, and especially Jerry Goldsmith's musical score are spectacular. Director Jack Guillermin, later known for big-budget films such as *The Towering Inferno* (1974) brought nearly a dozen stunt pilots and a score of planes to locations in Ireland. The green hills of the Emerald Isle looked much like wartime Imperial Germany, if not the muddy shell-cratered battlefields of the Western Front. Gormanston Aerodrome near Dublin was the German airfield, and locations in Dublin itself were used for Berlin. William Wellman would have hated it. The skies in nearly all the aerial scenes are uniformly gray overcast with no clouds.

George Peppard as the overeager infantryman-turned-ace Bruno Stachel in *The Blue Max*.

Several authentic and replica aircraft were assembled for the film under the technical advice of a group of World War One aviation buffs in Los Angeles. Bitz Flugzeugbau GmbH built two replica Fokker Dr.I Triplanes for the film. One is still in operation in the United States. A half-dozen replica S.E.5s and two Pfalz D.IIIa were used. The S.E.5a fighters are actually Currie Wot 3/4 scale, built by Slingsby Sailplanes Ltd. They are powered by 115-hp Lycoming engines. Three full-scale Fokker D.VII replicas with Gypsy Queen engines and two Fokker Dr.Is also appear. Others are modified de Havilland DH-82 Tiger Moths and Stampe SV.4s. A French-built 1930s Cauldron Luciole serves as both a German and British observation plane.

The "Adler" monoplane Stachel dies in may have been based on a late-war Fokker E.V, which had a reputation for wing failures. In the film the plane is a 1930 Morane-Saulnier 230 Parasol Trainer with a covered front seat.

The stunt pilots were an eclectic bunch, including former Battle of Britain RAF Hurricane veteran Peter Hillwood, who was killed later in the same year. Joan Hughes, MBE, was another of the stunt pilots in *The Blue Max*. During the war she was Britain's youngest female pilot at the age of 17, later a ferry pilot, an instructor and then a test pilot.

Derek Piggot flew a plane under a bridge for the film. He did the stunt twenty times. The Fokker Dr.I's wingspan was about eight feet less than the distance of the span. Piggot aimed for the center by visually aligning poles under and past the span. Guillermin insisted the stunt not be challenged as studio trickery. He placed a herd of sheep in a meadow near the bridge. When Piggot flew close the sheep scattered, at least until the last take. By then the sheep were no longer frightened by the plane and stood still.

The aerial sequences are spectacular. For instance during the dogfights, the camera sees the pilot's view as his guns shake and fire at a distant wheeling plane. It is more effective than even Harry Perry's innovative camera work in the 1920s. The dogfights are very three-dimensional and dynamic as the background pirouettes around the burning airplanes.

When Stachel starts his Pfalz' engine he operates the ailerons, elevators and rudder just as the real pilots did. It helps the audience see how primitive and fragile the old planes were.

Yet the close-up process shots are less than convincing, due to obvious studio lights glinting on the pilots' goggles.

One thing none of the filmmakers from Wellman to Guillermin ever did correctly was to show the effect of whirling rotary engines on the face of the pilots. The engines were lubricated with castor oil which sprayed off the cylinder heads and blew backwards along with the smoke from the guns. Pilots of the era wore scarves to have something to wipe the dirty oil off, not to appear dashing.

Stachel's 'Adler' fighter was a modified 1930 Morane-Saulnier 230 Parasol Trainer.

An amusing note: Karl Michael Vogler, who plays Colonel Otto Heidemann, had just finished another German aviator role, that of the hapless Captain Rumpelstoss in *Magnificent Men.*

Von Richthofen and Brown, released by United Artists in 1971, was the first major motion picture to take on the Red Baron's life and death. The movie tells the story of how a Canadian RFC pilot named Captain Arthur Roy Brown finally downed the highest-scoring German ace.

There is another side to the Red Baron's death. After having scored eighty kills between the summer of 1916 and April 1918, Baron Manfred von Richthofen at 25 years of age was a tired, disillusioned and frustrated veteran. On April 21, 1918, Richthofen was patrolling alone near Vaux-sur-Somme close to Australian lines when he spotted two RFC Sopwith Camels. Lieutenant Wilfrid May was an inexperienced pilot and the Red Baron attacked. But he in turn was set upon by Brown. It wasn't much of a dogfight. Brown was suffering from stomach problems, but he doggedly pursued the red Fokker, keeping it off May's plane.

On the ground the Australians fired hundreds of rifles and several Lewis machine guns at the darting red triplane. Then Richthofen crashed, dead from a single .303 caliber bullet in his chest.

From underneath.

While most historians have little doubt the Australians who finally killed the Red Baron, it was hardly the sensational death expected of the greatest ace who ever lived. Brown had at least thirteen kills to his credit but he was hardly the stuff of legend. He was given credit for the kill.

The controversy continues to this day. Brown's Sopwith and the Australians used the same caliber weapons. In the words of a character in one of John Ford's westerns, "When the legend becomes fact, print the legend."

Roger Corman, who directed horror classics like *Little Shop of Horrors* and *House of Usher*, supervised the filming of *Von Richthofen and Brown*. The story is about the converging lives of the two main characters. The aristocratic hunter Richthofen, played by the handsome John Phillip Law, and the practical, brooding Brown, portrayed by Don Stroud. The film attempts to make Brown a more compelling character, almost as if he and the Red Baron were destined to meet. It is meant to be historical but the screenplay is dull and the acting wooden.

Only the cinematography and aerial scenes keep the film moving as the two protagonist's daily fly into the sky to seek their enemies. The film is stuffed with vignettes of Red Baron legend, including the origin of his red plane and the birth of the famous "Flying Circus."

Nearly all the characters are based on real persons: Ernst Udet, Verner Voss and Lanoe Hawker, to name a few.

Hurd Hatfield, best remembered for *The Picture of Dorian Gray* (1945), portrayed Anthony Fokker, the designer of the famous triplane. Oswald Boelke first saw potential greatness in the young Prussian cavalry officer. When Richthofen needs prompting in the proper skills of dogfighting, Boelke hammers him with his famous "Dicta." Boelke's tactics were so advanced they were used in aerial combat into the Vietnam War.

John Philip Law as the Red Baron on the attack in *von Richthofen and Brown.*

Hermann Goering, long before he became the fat posturing commander of Hitler's Luftwaffe, is seen as an unscrupulous pilot who later takes command of Jasta 11 after Richthofen's death.

As in *The Blue Max*, the locations were largely in Ireland, using the same vintage and replica aircraft. Brown's 209 Squadron actually flew Sopwith Camels, but S.E.5a biplanes were used instead. The same replica Fokker D.VIIs were also used.

In the scene where Boelke was killed the film shows Richthofen as being responsible. But it was another pilot, Erwin Böhme, whose landing gear struck Boelke's wing and caused the fatal crash.

The flying sequences are well done with modern-day versions of Harry Perry's techniques. Much of the dogfighting footage was done with actual planes. However, the machine guns used on both German and British planes fire much too rapidly. For one thing they would have torn the propellers to splinters, interruptor mechanism or not. The sound of zipping bullets and whining ricochets are more suited to a Sam Peckinpah western. Richthofen also has unlimited ammunition.

One of the stunt pilots was Richard Bach, author of *Jonathan Livingston Seagull.*

Five years later Cine Artists Pictures in the United Kingdom threw their hat into the ring. The British motion picture industry had produced some excellent air war films, including *The Dam Busters* (1955) and *The Battle of Britain* (1969). These and other films clearly showed their skill for technical and historical accuracy.

Aces High takes on the subject of the high death toll on young RFC pilots during the war. Peter Firth plays Lt. Stephen Croft, a young officer who joins the RFC. He discovers to his chagrin that his life expectancy is very short. He sees the personal effects of dead pilots removed from his room.

Aces High also starred Malcolm McDowell, trying to avoid typecasting after his role as the sadistic young gang leader Alex in Kubrick's *A Clockwork Orange* (1971). McDowell's Major Gresham is a member of the old school who still believes in chivalry in the skies. He even hosts a party in honor of a German pilot he has downed. Forced to welcome new recruits into the brutal world of aerial combat, he tries not to get too close to them.

Veteran actor Christopher Plummer plays Sinclair, an avuncular friend to the young pilots.

The film shows a lost world of brave men and sacrifice, of young boys learning war's hard lessons. For once, there is little romance other than a side story featuring Croft and his French girlfriend.

Filmed on location at Eton College and Booker Airfield in Buckinghamshire, the film often suffers from the same dreary flat gray that dominated the Irish skies in *The Blue Max.*

Regarding the planes there are a few departures from correctness based on the availability of aircraft. The British S.E.5s were Belgian SV4 Stampe trainers from the 1930s. *Aces High* used four of them, three for flying and one to be burned on the ground.

Cine Artists used some footage from *The Blue Max.* The scene where the observation balloon is destroyed was from the previous film. A scene in which Sinclair and Croft are flying an observer mission, the replica Avro 504 they are in changes to a Cauldron Luciole, also from *The Blue Max.* Apparently using footage from other films didn't die with color photography. Yet even with these minor errors *Aces High* is as excellent a war film as any since *Wings.* It drew good reviews and holds up even today. When it was aired on Canadian television, Arthur Bishop, son of Billy Bishop, the top-scoring British ace, praised the film's technical and historical accuracy.

After 1976 very few films centered on the Great War in the air. *Top Gun* (1986) changed the viewing public's appetite for aerial combat.

At the dawn of the 21st century, Computer Generated Imagery (CGI) sparked a revolution in motion pictures. In the case of air war movies, it was not necessarily a step forward in anything but filmmaking technology.

The first film depicting World War One aviation in the digital arena was *Flyboys* (2006), an American and British production directed by Tony Bill. Ostensibly the story of the Lafayette Escadrille, *Flyboys* was perfect for the secular age of instant gratification and thrill seeking.

Flyboys begins in late 1916 before the United States entered the war. American pilots and the occasional miscreant joined the French Air Service to seek adventure and glory. Blaine Rawlings (James Franco) decides to enlist after seeing a newsreel about the air war. Briggs Lowry joins to escape an abusive father. For the first time in any World War I aviation film an African-American pilot, Eugene Skinner (Abdul Salis), takes to the air to pay France back for allowing him to be a professional athlete.

Veteran aceReed Cassidy (Martin Henderson) becomes their mentor and teacher. He falls for a French girl, who is decidedly worried about his life expectancy.

Soon the pilots enter the violent world of dogfighting. On their first mission to escort bombers the new pilots are savagely attacked by the Black Falcon, the leading German ace. With high losses and a newfound sense of danger the former rookies return to base. The Falcon's comrade, a chivalrous officer named Franz Wolferd, is chagrined at the other pilot's heartless actions.

Cassidy is later mortally wounded by the Falcon, but in his last act rams and destroys a Zeppelin on its way to bomb Paris.

Rawlings is promoted after Cassidy's death. Later, Wolferd is shot down as is Briggs. Briggs shoots himself in the head rather than burn to death in the flaming plane.

Rawlings leads a final mission which pits him against the Black Falcon. Despite having jammed guns, Rawlings manages to shoot the Black Falcon down with his pistol. The rest of the Germans retreat or are shot down. The film ends on a self-justifying note as the characters are related to the actual pilots on whom they are based.

The cinematography and visuals are impressive, even beautiful. Composer Trevor Rabin's moving score is an excellent background for the aerial scenes, evoking emotions and shivers from the audience. Tony Bill had his work cut out for him to make a blockbuster film about a subject most Americans hardly knew or cared about any more.

The movie suffers from some modern film fads. The movie suffers from some modern film fads. Quick cuts and huge pyrotechnics are fine for cop dramas and the *X-Men* films but doesn't mesh well with the more sedate world of 1917. For some reason it seems important that young Americans express excitement with a "Yeeaah!" or "Whoooo!"

The difficulty was in the need to make a film capable of enticing viewers jaded from decades of action, superheroes, ultra-high technology and sleek jet aircraft. Even a CGI Fokker Triplane just can't compete. If the viewer keeps the movie in its correct place, *i.e.*, totally fictional, it's a fun film to watch. But to call it a historical drama is stretching it.

Reed Cassidy is supposedly based on French-born American Raoul Lufbery, the top-scoring ace of the Lafayette Escadrille. The movie was made in the PC-sensitive world, thus the African-American role is the subject of racial prejudice, which is in turn challenged by the "good-guy" Americans. Clichéd vignettes of a pilot shooting himself rather than burn in a crash, or Cassidy ramming a Zeppelin, or when Rawlings has the squadron insignia painted on his plane, would be perfect for a graphic novel. But shooting down a Fokker Triplane with a pistol is ludicrous. One can only imagine how Germans viewed the film—with scorn or laughter.

The airfield scenes were shot at and around RAF Halton near Aylesbury. The same region near Hatfield, Hertfordshire, used for the trench and battle sequences for *Saving Private Ryan* and *Band of Brothers* was used for *Flyboys*. The planes used were Nieuport 17s and Fokker Dr.I Triplanes. None of the Nieuports were from Garland Lincoln's old stock. The few remaining examples are now on display in museums. Four of *Flyboys*' Nieuports were built by Airdrome Aeroplanes of Missouri. The Nieuport flown by Rawlings is a restored original owned by Fantasy of Flight in Florida.

Originally the leading actors were to be filmed while actually flying, but due to a crash this was cut dramatically. Only a few of Rawling's close-ups were done in the air.

While the companies that built the replica planes and the CGI animators did take great pains to recreate the long-vanished relics of the Great War, they left a few gaping holes. They failed when it came to the rotary engine so prevalent in many of the old fighters. The Oberursel and LeRhone engines actually rotated with the propeller, spinning on a common shaft. The engines used in the film are modern radial engines rather than rotary. But to be fair, there is an authentic touch. For the first time the faces of the actors are shown with sooty oil from the engines and gun smoke. Ironically, radial engines do not spray oil. Nearly all the aviation historians the author has spoken with have noted these deficiencies. The omission is more likely the result of thinking the viewing audience wouldn't accept a spinning motor than not being able to duplicate it.

The Lewis machine gun on Cassidy's plane was another modern replica, but the drum magazine does not rotate as in the original.

The German pilots are all flying Fokker Dr.I Triplanes, despite their rarity in the German Air Service. Only 320 were ever built, and they didn't enter service until late in 1917, almost a year after the period depicted in *Flyboys*. But American audiences expected all Germans to fly Triplanes.

Taking this issue further, the Triplanes have Iron Crosses painted on the upper surface of the lower wing, something that was never done in reality. And of course at least one Triplane had to be painted bright red. On the Gotha the Iron Cross is the type painted only on the planes of the Balkan campaign of 1918.

The anti-aircraft artillery firing bursting shells did not exist in 1916.

The filmmakers did take on a Zeppelin raid, but Howard Hughes did a better job of it in 1928, and with far more primitive technology. The Cunard ocean liner *RMS Aquitania* was shown bringing the Americans to France. Contrary to the black hull, white superstructure and red funnels seen in the film, by 1915 most of the big liners had been painted in the camouflage scheme called "Dazzle" in order to conceal them from U-boats.

The CGI used in the film, while able to convey the wildly changing 3-D world of aerial combat, does not have the feel of real airplanes as seen in *Wings*, *Hell's Angels* and *The Blue Max*. It comes across as animated and thin, merely a two-dimensional image. A disturbing trait of the CGI animator is to make everything seem as dynamic and stunning as possible. The CGI planes do maneuvers so violent they would have torn the wings off a real aircraft.

There is a certain irony in that this chapter began with the best—*Wings* in 1927—and ended with the worst almost eighty years later. This chapter is as good a place as any to show the trend Hollywood was taking, from substance to style. The visual effects were the finest that Harry Perry and Elmer Dyer could devise, and obtaining original or modified aircraft was as easy as making a phone call. Tomick, Lincoln, Grace, Clarke and their brethren were the very best in the profession and it came across on the screen. Hollywood will never see their like again.

CHAPTER THREE
The Golden Age of Flight, 1927-1938

The term "Golden Age" can be applied to nearly everything, including Rock 'n' Roll or ocean liners. But in fact the Golden Age of Flight coincided with Hollywood's Golden Age quite well. On every tongue were names like Lindbergh and Bogart, Doolittle and Gable. The Ford Trimotor appeared on almost as many front pages as the stars that flew in them. It was a time of new inventions, scientific progress, and a wild national enthusiasm that would only end with the Stock Market crash of 1929. Even as the nation reeled in the throes of the Great Depression, aviation continued to soar and grow.

This chapter's focus is on many of the films which appeared in the time when Americans were fascinated by flight. The age of the barnstormers was waning and the early scheduled airlines made a flight across the country possible for virtually anyone willing to endure two days' travel and a dozen stops en route. Pilots like Commander Richard Byrd and Wiley Post, Amelia Earhart and Floyd Bennett appeared in the papers and newsreels to show what was possible in the air.

Two years before *Wings* hit the screen *The Air Mail* (1925) was an early silent romance drama. It was produced by Famous Players-Lasky and directed by Irvin Willat, who filmed the nearly fatal collision in *The Grim Game* in 1919. The film starred Warner Baxter and Douglas Fairbanks, Jr. The plot involves a cargo thief turned honest, a girl whose miner father needs a special medicine, and a loyal buddy who wants to be a pilot. It hardly has anything to do with the Air Mail.

The only known print of the film is incomplete in the National Archives. Filmed in Death Valley and near Rhyolite, Nevada, the movie's few aircraft were obtained from Reno and Tonopah. Aerial filming was the province of Frank Clarke, flying the nearly forgotten Catron & Fisk CF-10 Triplane, an early airliner. The only CF-10 that achieved any notoriety was the *Pride of Los Angeles*, which was lost in the disastrous Dole Derby air race from Alameda to Hawaii in 1927.

Air Mail (1932)—not to be confused with the previous film of the same name—starred a young Ralph Bellamy nearly five decades before he appeared as the crafty Randolph Duke in *Trading Places*. Universal hired John Ford, still a relative unknown, to direct the film. It also featured Pat O'Brien and Gloria Stuart, who achieved far greater fame more than sixty years later as the old Rose in James Cameron's blockbuster *Titanic* (1996).

Mike Miller (Bellamy) is the operator of a small airport in the mountains, a regular Air Mail stop. His pilots are determined and brave but the mail run is dangerous. Miller hires cocky pilot Duke Talbot (O'Brien) to fly for him. Dizzy Wilkins, who is the more reliable pilot, dies in a crash. To make matters worse, Duke runs away with Wilkins' widow. Miller is forced to make a mail run by himself and crashes against a mountain. The site is inaccessible and he begins to walk out; but it is Talbot, feeling a new sense of responsibility, who risks his own life to save Miller.

Air Mail has a bit more going for it than the film with the similar name. For one thing it does a credible job, under Ford's direction, to tell something of what the Air Mail pilots had to endure in their duty to get the mail through.

But filming it wasn't much safer, according to Pat O'Brien, in his autobiography *The Wind at My Back*. He relates one scene: "I was supposed to steal a plane [to rescue Miller]. I then jumped into a plane. In most films the camera would cut as soon as I jumped into the plane [and] then a real pilot was filmed taking off and shown in flight. Paul Mantz was doing all the flying. But before we started the scene Jack Ford was chewing his handkerchief, a very characteristic gesture. He said, 'Pat, it would be great if you could take the plane off the ground yourself.'

"I snorted. 'Jack, are you out of your Gaelic mind? I've never even been in a plane let alone flown one of those flying coffins.'

"Mantz said quietly, 'There is an easy solution, Mr. Ford. This is a two-seat plane. Let Pat take it off the ground. I'll be on the floor. Once we get off the ground I'll take the controls.'

"Ford looked at me and said, 'And Mantz isn't even Irish.'

"With a too-casual tone I said, 'If Paul says it can be done I'll do it.'

"We went into action. The cameras rolled. I jumped into the plane as Paul instructed me, I gave it the gas and we actually took off. I've had a lot of scares in my life but this topped them all. Once aloft I looked around. It was pretty exciting. What if Paul had had a stroke while lying on the floor? It was a cheerful thought. I remembered the corny line from *Dawn Patrol.* 'You can't send up boys in planes like that. It's murder.' How true. Cruising around, I figured once a hero was enough. We landed as the crowd applauded. Jack Ford was there and said, 'Pat, we'd better do it again.' I said, 'If you say so, sir.'"

O'Brien's high opinion of Mantz' flying skills—if not his sanity—were increased by the stunt in which Mantz flew through a hangar, the first time the stunt had ever been performed. "Paul did some magnificent, crazy flying in that picture," wrote O'Brien. "On location in Bishop, he flew a plane right through a hangar, one of the most daring feats I've ever seen. I'm surprised Jack Ford wouldn't let me fly that shot. I see *Air Mail* on the late show. When I see that take off I say to myself ,'You were a crazy kid.'"

William A. Wellman, only six years after his success with *Wings* in 1927, was back in the air with *Central Airport*, starring *Dawn Patrol* lead Richard Barthelmess. Once again the love triangle puts the drama into a flying film. Barthelmess as Jim Blaine is a grounded airline pilot and former ace who was blamed for the crash of his airliner years before. Needing work, he joins a small flying circus. He and his younger brother Bud, also an airline pilot, are rivals in the sky and for lady parachute jumper Jill Collins, whom Jim finds hanging from a tree. They fall in love, but Jim is reluctant to carry the relationship further since his profession is dangerous. So Jill and Bud get together. Later, Jim flies out to sea to save Bud after he has crashed, repairing the animosity between them. The story has a great deal of hand-wringing suspense and whimsy.

Central Airport was shot on location at San Francisco, Fresno, Dallas and other airports where viewers will see the large block letters painted on hangar roofs. The film has some of "Wild Bill" Wellman's style in character development. It is essentially a soap opera among barnstormers and daredevils.

Audiences were treated to Fokker and Ford Trimotors, JN-4s and Standard J-1s. Paul Mantz and Elmer Dyer did the aerial camera work, while Frank Tomick flew the planes. Wellman does his signature work in the aerial footage of barnstorming and crashes.

William Wellman, Jr. commented on the film: "I liked *Central Airport.* [My father] told me a couple of things about two scenes that were filmed but never used." When asked about these, the veteran actor replied, "Well, John Wayne, who wasn't famous yet, was just looking for work between westerns was hired to be a pilot in the film. He did this one scene in which a plane crashed. I don't know how it was done, but my father said it was pretty dramatic. Then Wayne was out on the wing helping people out of the plane. But the Legion of Decency or somebody thought it was too violent or objectionable and told Warner to take that crash out."

The Catholic Legion of Decency, formed in 1933, had a set of rules that was far more stringent than the Motion Picture Production Code adopted in 1930. However, Sally Eilers, who plays the female lead Jill, appears in a rather daring slip early in the film, and there is a great deal of steam coming from her physical relationship with Jim. "Anyway," Wellman continued. "The crash itself was taken out. But 21 years later Wayne was doing the same thing in *The High and the Mighty*."

The other deleted sequence from the film involved Humphrey Bogart. "My father met Bogart and his friend Mayo Methot while doing *Central Airport*," said Wellman. "He needed a young couple for a restaurant scene and shot it using them. They weren't married yet. Apparently it too was cut. I've watched that movie several times and I've never seen them. Bogart was totally unknown at that time."

In the early 1930s aviation had not only become big business but was also a subject of much fascination and curiosity by the public. Strange new terms were heard and puzzled over: "stall speed," " wing-loading," " blind flying," " center of gravity," and many more. Some movies used them as major plot devices.

Ceiling Zero is a virtually forgotten Warner drama released in January 1936, starring the increasingly popular team of James Cagney and Pat O'Brien. Directed by Howard Hawks, *Ceiling Zero* tells the story of three ex-military pilots who work for Federal Airlines out of New York. Jake Lee (O'Brien) is the manager of the airline and Tex Clark (Stuart Erwin) is an airmail pilot. The film opens on a dramatic moment as the airline's dispatcher in Newark, New Jersey, is trying to reach an Air Mail pilot who is running out of fuel and unable to find his home field. Below are solid clouds and under that, zero visibility. The engine dies, and the pilot is forced to bail out.

Dizzy Davis (Cagney) is a cocky, pugnacious pilot who wants to work for his old wartime friend Jake. Davis' former employer warns Jake that Davis is unreliable, but Jake hires him as a pilot anyway.

Davis gets off on the wrong foot with his devil-may-care attitude. He finds an immediate attraction to a young woman who works for the airline. He wants to take her out but he is scheduled for a flight to Ohio. Feigning an illness, he asks his friend Tex Clark to take the flight. After landing in Ohio, Tex flies back to Newark. He runs into dense, cold fog, unable to see. His radio is unreliable, but he manages to find the field and crashes into a hangar, sustaining massive burns. He later dies in the hospital. Tex's wife Lou blames Davis for Tex's death. Davis loses his license and Jake, knowing how bad his friend feels, tries to console him. The weather continues to worsen and all flights are cancelled.

Davis, on duty at the airline office, learns that another pilot is unaware of the cancellations. He is ready to fly, but Davis is feeling great guilt and knocks the other man out and takes the flight. The plane is equipped with new but untested de-icing boots meant to prevent ice from forming on the wings and control surfaces.

Jake and his other pilots arrive at the office to learn that Davis is in a heavy snowstorm, giving reports about the de-icing system. He says it isn't working but will continue to describe his observations and recommendations for re-design.

The film ends with Davis dying in a crash, but has regained his honor by helping thousands of other pilots to survive.

Lieutenant Commander Frank "Spig" Wead wrote the screenplay, which was produced by Warner with First National and Cosmopolitan Productions. Virtually the entire film was done at Warner's studio and backlot. There is some stock footage of what may be a 1932 Northrop Gamma in flight, and the canopy mockups appear to be the same design. Paul Mantz did the aerial cinematography while Frank Tomick flew the planes. Tex's crash was very dramatic, accompanied by Lou's hysterical scream.

Ceiling Zero was less successful than the last Cagney and O'Brien aviation film, 1935's *Devil Dogs of the Air* (see Chapter Five). When *Ceiling Zero* was released, de-icing boots, first developed by B.F. Goodrich Rubber in 1923, had become fairly common on many mid-sized and large aircraft. The boots were used extensively during World War II.

MGM brought director Victor Fleming together with writers Frank Wead and Howard Hawks and composer Franz Waxman to produce one of the best pre-war aviation films, *Test Pilot*, in 1938. The lead was Clark Gable, who had reached the pinnacle of his stardom with *It Happened One Night* (1934) and *Mutiny on the Bounty* (1935) behind him. He was less than a year away from his role as Rhett Butler in *Gone With the Wind*, also directed by Fleming. With Gable were Myrna Loy, Spencer Tracy and Lionel Barrymore, all of whom would later star or play supporting roles in other aviation films, although in Loy's case it was the disastrous *Airport 1975* (1974). With such high-powered talent, it's no wonder *Test Pilot* was a box office success and an excellent aviation film.

Jim Lane (Gable) is a swaggering test pilot flying a new racer, the Drake Bullet, on a flight across the country. The plane develops engine trouble and he is forced to land on a farm where he meets Ann (Loy). Love and marriage quickly follow.

Because of his negative attitude about the flight, Jim is fired by boss Howard Drake (Barrymore). Jim accepts a job flying a new experimental racer in the Thompson Trophy Race, which he wins despite an engine fire. Jim is rewarded with the job of testing a new heavy bomber in a high-altitude test flight. He and his friend and mechanic Gunner Morris (Tracy) are flying the bomber when it goes into a spin. Gunner is trapped under sandbag ballast and Jim refuses to bail out. He manages to crash land the plane. He pulls the dying

Gunner from the wreck. Jim realizes the job it taking a toll on Ann and leaves test flying to become an Air Corps instructor.

Budgeted at $2,000,000, *Test Pilot* was the most expensive film since *Hell's Angels*. The plane used for the fictional Drake Bullet was obtained by former World War I pilot Al Menasco from paint magnate Frank Fuller. It was the Seversky SEV-S2 racer, which won the Bendix Trophy in 1937. The SEV design was later adopted as the Army's Seversky P-35 fighter.

Lead actors Spencer Tracy, Clark Gable and Myrna Loy in *Test Pilot*.

The racing sequences were filmed during and after the 1937 Thompson Trophy Races in Cleveland, Ohio. Famed racer Earl Ortman flew the distinctive black-and-yellow Marcoux-Bromberg Special in the racing scenes, standing in as Gable. Technical advisor and cinematographer Paul Mantz used nine camera operators on the ground with nine more in the air. He had cameras mounted in the open doors and windows of planes in flight.

A. Arnold Gillespie, MGM's special effects wizard, was already gaining a reputation for his work by the time he did *Test Pilot*. His later work would include the superb carrier take-off sequences in 1944's *Thirty Seconds over Tokyo* (see Chapter Seven). In *Hollywood Speaks!* by Mike Steen, Gillespie commented on the YB-17 crash scenes: "They [MGM] had made the full-size set of the crashed bomber, and filmed Gable and Tracy crawling out of the wreckage before we shot the miniature of the plane actually crashing. That was a bad thing to do."

The difficulty lay in matching the crash of a miniature with the already wrecked plane. The model would have to end up with exactly the same damage as the full-sized wreck. It required all of Gillespie's skill to make them match "after the fact."

Principal location shooting was done at March Field in Riverside, California. Eager to showcase its newest hardware the Air Corps provided over a hundred aircraft, including twelve of the revolutionary YB-17s, the largest and most advanced bomber in the world. The YB-17 would later be called the "Flying Fortress," a name which the Air Corps took seriously, with disastrous consequences. In 1938 the idea of high-altitude precision bombing was considered to be *the* way to assure victory in any future air war. This eventually happened only after the Air Corps was able to send huge fleets of bombers, protected by fighters to hit strategic targets in Germany (see Chapter Six).

Other aircraft that appeared in *Test Pilot* were the Ryan STA sport monoplane, the Northrop A-17 Nomad attack bomber, and the famous Boeing 247 transport. This aircraft is probably the 247D, designated the C-73 for Army use.

According to Massey Air Museum, also seen was a virtually unknown Harlow PJC-2 cabin monoplane and some B-18 Bolos, the latter being Douglas' entry into the heavy bomber market.

The pilot of the YB-17 offered to take Gable, Tracy and Fleming on a familiarization flight over Catalina. Tracy declined and was called a coward by the macho Gable and Fleming.

Just five years later Clark Gable would be in other B-17s flying over France and Germany as a gunner in the 351st Bomb Group during World War II. He was awarded the Distinguished Flying Cross and the Air Medal.

Test Pilot was a huge box office hit and earned three Academy Award nominations, including Best Picture.

Wellman was not only behind the camera but also producer for Paramount's *Men With Wings* (1938) starring Fred MacMurray and Ray Milland. *Men With Wings* is an action drama that tells the story of early flight as seen by two men and a woman. Walter Abel is Nick Ransom, a reporter turned enthusiastic airplane designer inspired by the Wright Brothers' flight at Kitty Hawk. His little daughter Peggy is friends with Pat Falconer and Scott Barnes. They are all bitten by the airplane bug as Nick tries to best the Wright's feat with fatal consequences.

In an amusing scene reminiscent of the *Little Rascals* Peggy is the "test pilot" for a kite the boys have invented.

As the years go on, Pat (MacMurray) and Scott (Milland) never lose their interest in flying, or in Peggy (Louise Campbell). J.A. Nolan hires Scott to design planes while Pat tests them. Pat, who is arrogant and selfish, loses his job and joins the Army Air Service in France. Peggy falls for the dashing Pat, but Scott is in love with her. After joining Pat in France Peggy marries him. Scott is flying the Air Mail when the new couple comes home.

One of the Travel Air 'Wichita Fokker' D.VII biplanes during the World War I combat sequence of *Men With Wings. Collection of William A. Wellman, Jr.*

The lack of challenge frustrates war ace Pat, so after Peggy gives birth to their daughter, he runs off to fight with the French in Morocco. He comes back a decorated hero, but a leg injury bars him from further active duty with the Air Service. He and Scott form Falconer Airplanes in California, but Pat is still restless and enters the competition to become the first pilot to fly nonstop from New York to Paris.

At the controls of a new plane he is on his way to New York for a long-distance test flight. But in his arrogance he has refused to learn the plane's new instruments and ends up far out to sea beyond New York. After crashing at sea, he is saved in the nick of time by Scott. They land on Long Island just in time to see Lindbergh take off for Paris. "I hope he makes it," Pat says with bitterness in his voice.

A stuntman prepares to jump from a Fokker D.VII mockup for *Men With Wings*. Note the lack of wind on pilots' clothing. *Collection of William A. Wellman, Jr.*

After the Stock Market crash, Scott struggles to keep the business alive. He designs a new bomber for the Army. Pat is killed fighting alongside the Chinese while the new bomber breaks all records. Despite being neglected by her husband, Peggy eulogizes him at the ceremony.

Pat's character is loosely based on Eddie Rickenbacker, who started Eastern Airlines in the 1930s. Nick Ransom may have been based on Gustave Whitehead, who attempted to fly a powered biplane in 1901. A replica of a Whitehead plane appears in an early scene.

The incurably folksy Andy Devine provides comic relief among the tension between Scott and Pat. Pat's obtuse refusal to listen to others was born again with MacMurray's portrayal of the hopelessly thick Professor Brainard in Disney's *The Absent-Minded Professor* (1961).

With Wellman's touch and passion for airplanes, *Men With Wings* has some wonderful vignettes of early aviation. As mentioned in Chapter Two the dogfight sequences were later used in Wellman's last aviation film, *Lafayette Escadrille*. There is even a mention of "wing-warping for lateral control—the keystone of the Wright Brothers' first success.

Aviation legends Alberto Santos-Dumont, Louis Blériot, Eugene Ely and Glenn Curtiss have their moment in *Men With Wings*. Even Cal Rodgers, who flew a modified Wright EX Flyer named the *Vin Fiz* from New York to Pasadena in 50 days, is mentioned with tongue-in-cheek humor. Pat talks about the $25,000 Orteig Prize for flying from New York to Paris. After he is rescued, the film cuts to newsreel footage of the *Spirit of St. Louis* taking off (see Chapter Four).

What makes *Men With Wings* even more compelling is its plethora of renowned and unknown aircraft. Just to name a few: the ubiquitous Curtiss Jenny, reproductions of the SPAD VII and a Lincoln-Flagg LF-1 Nieuport 28. The Fokker D.VII may be one of the "Wichita Fokker" Travel Airs used in *Hell's Angels*. Later planes included the Boeing 247 and P-12, a Lockheed Vega, and a stock Travel Air 2000. Quite a list for one film.

Pat's SPAD bears the markings of Wellman's plane in the Lafayette Flying Corps (see Chapter Two). But twenty-two years after *Wings*, the combat footage lacks the realism of the original film. One wonders if "Wild Bill" had settled for less. The skies are flat, with very few shots of clouds to provide depth. *Men With Wings* did have Paul Mantz and Frank Clarke, however, so it should have been a better film.

Columbia Pictures brought the talents of Howard Hawks and Jules Furthman to create *Only Angels Have Wings* in 1939. Furthman's work included 1935's Academy Award winning *Mutiny on the Bounty*. But he would also write one of the worst aviation films ever made, *Jet Pilot* (1957). Somewhere in between was *Only Angels Have Wings* with Cary Grant, Rita Hayworth and Jean Arthur. The film also starred the lead of the original *Dawn Patrol*, Richard Barthelmess.

The romantic drama focus on Geoff Carter (Grant), chief pilot for a small struggling South American airline that flies over the Andes Mountains. With a disregard for anything but his work, he tries to ignore the amorous antics of Bonnie (Arthur), a piano playing entertainer. Geoff tries to dissuade Bonnie by telling her his job is very dangerous but to no avail.

Enter a married couple, Bat and Judy MacPherson (Barthelmess and Hayworth). Bat is looking for work as a pilot, but Geoff is unwilling to hire him because he once bailed out of a damaged plane, leaving the mechanic to die in the crash. The mechanic was the brother of Kid Dabb (Thomas Mitchell), who works for Geoff.

Judy begs Geoff to hire her husband, and he finally gives in. Bat will have to fly the most dangerous routes. Bat sees the handwriting on the hangar wall: if he dies, no one will care.

An impending government contract beckons to Geoff if he can prove they are able to fly a dangerous new mountain route. Bat and Kid are in a Trimotor, trying to get over the mountain pass in a storm, but the altitude is too much for the plane. When a bird crashes through the windshield and injures Kid, Bat refuses to leave him. He brings the damaged plane back and Kid tells Geoff how Bat stayed with the doomed plane. Bat is welcomed by the other pilots.

Finally Bonnie is ready to give up on Geoff, but with the promise of a new contract that will bring, prosperity he has a change of heart. He offers to toss a coin. Heads, she stays, tails she goes. A sudden improvement in the weather prompts Geoff to jump into his plane before he tosses the coin. Bonnie picks it up to see it is a two-headed coin.

Filmed almost entirely at Columbia Studios, the film makes use of some interesting aircraft, including a Hamilton H-18 Metalplane. The H-18 was the first all-metal plane produced by the Hamilton-Standard Company in 1927. Hamilton Standard may have appeared in more airplane movies from 1930 to 1950 than any other manufacturer. They built the famous variable-pitch propellers seen on nearly every commercial and military aircraft during that period.

Aerial cameraman Elmer Dyer plied his trade from *Wings* in 1927 to *Gallant Journey* in 1946.

A Fokker F-10 doubles as the Ford Trimotor. Several miniatures, the staple of Hollywood for filming dangerous storm scenes, appear in most shots. The hard-working Elmer Dyer acted as aerial cameraman with Paul Mantz.

Geoff is wearing a leather jacket with an Indian head emblem on both front and back. This was the insignia of the 103rd Aero Squadron in France in 1918.

Naval aviator and prolific screenwriter Commander Frank "Spig" Wead wrote his own autobiography as the plot for *The Wings of Eagles* (1957), starring John Wayne as himself. *The Wings of Eagles* tells a colorful and compressed account of Wead's life after World

War I when he was trying to convince the Navy to compete against the Army in races and long-distance flights. The Navy's 1923 Schneider Cup victory and the Army's historic 1924 around-the-world flight are woven into the story while Wead races against Army pilot Captain Herbert Hazard. Wead is partially paralyzed after a fall in his home, which puts him into deep depression until his aviator buddies talk him into being a writer and getting back on his feet. Wead finally succeeds in both and re-enters active duty during World War II.

John Ford, portrayed in by Ward Bond as "John Dodge," directed the MGM production. Using stock wartime footage and pre-war newsreels the movie shows some of the most historic events in early aviation including the Army's 1924 Douglas World Cruisers in flight. Hazard was based on Doolittle, played by Kenneth Tobey.

Wead competed in several races against Doolittle and was instrumental in furthering Naval aviation in that period. He also played a major role in promoting the use of Escort or "Jeep" carriers to supplement the Navy's combatant carrier force.

Colonel John Telles, USMC, was on hand to witness some of the filming aboard the carrier *USS Bennington* (CVA-20). "They put a group of old aircraft for background on the flight deck," Telles explained. "We moved them from the hangar to the flight deck during filming. It was pretty neat to be a part of. But one Corsair wasn't chocked down when the ship made a turn. That plane started rolling faster and faster and we couldn't stop it. The Corsair fell right over the side. No one but us deck crew knew there was no one in the cockpit so there was some confusion."

There were dozens of other films which exemplified the Golden Age of Flight, but most of them had themes better suited to other chapters later in this book.

CHAPTER FOUR

This is Your Life, Hollywood Style: Biographies

When a historical event takes root in the public imagination, the person at the center often finds himself the victim? of a great deal of misinformation and speculation. This is nowhere more true than in Hollywood. "The Dream Factory" never held back in following John Ford's advice to "Print the Legend."

Surprisingly, there has only been one serious major film about the Wright Brothers, possibly because their story wasn't dramatic enough for the movies. The Wrights, with their lifelong mania for secrecy, made it unlikely anyone would ever be able to write a strong screenplay about their lives. That film was 1997's *The Wright Brothers*, a biographical drama released by Millennium Pictures. It did poorly at the box office primarily for the reasons listed above. Late 20th century theater audiences found little to draw their interest. Television might have been a better venue.

But an early air pioneer named John J. Montgomery wound up on the silver screen in 1946 in *Gallant Journey*, starring Glenn Ford. Montgomery is now known as "the father of American gliding" and pioneered several innovative aircraft, both unpowered and powered, from 1884 to 1911.

Columbia's 1946 film, which was directed by William Wellman, was a typical biographical tribute to a forgotten aviation pioneer. *Gallant Journey* begins with some present-day boys playing with toy gliders in a park when they meet an old man who tells them the story of Montgomery. Through flashbacks, Montgomery is seen as a youth full of dreams of flying.

The "Father of American Gliders," John J. Montgomery, circa 1905.

He is ridiculed by all around him. But by the time he reaches adulthood his early successes earn the praise he deserves.

Soon he advances by teaming up with a carnival hot-air balloonist to give his plane a higher altitude to launch. He pays for the experiments out of his own shallow pockets, but after inventing a gold-sifting device, his fortunes grow. Unfortunately, defending the patent in court wipes out his holdings and he finds himself on the brink of bankruptcy. Two Jesuit priests befriend and support Montgomery's work even as many of his friends lose interest.

Regina Cleary (Janet Blair) is smitten with the determined inventor. She believes in him and provides support, even to the point of giving him some silk underwear to repair a damaged wing. Regina stays with Montgomery until the film's climactic and heartbreaking end, when he dies in a glider crash.

The viewers never learn who the old man is at the end of the film. It would be typical Hollywood myth-making for it to be an old Montgomery, long forgotten by history. But the real John. J. Montgomery died in 1911.

Gallant Journey's cinematography captures the exhilaration of gliding above the picturesque California countryside. It was filmed in black-and-white, which weakens what might have been a stunningly beautiful film in Technicolor. The production was filmed on locations in southern and central California. Columbia used modern gliders that resembled the originals, since very few of Montgomery's designs exist. Paul Mantz did the flying, which was filmed by *Wings* veteran Elmer Dyer.

Taken with a grain of salt, *Gallant Journey* does fill in a missing piece of aviation history, and is one of Wellman's better, if least remembered, films.

Gary Cooper, who was long past his young *Mr. Deeds* persona, took on more mature patrician roles in the 1950s, appearing in films such as *High Noon* (1952), *Friendly Persuasion* (1956), and Warner's 1955 film *The Court-Martial of Billy Mitchell.*

Glenn Ford in a scene from Wellman's *Gallant Journey.*

The Court-Martial of Billy Mitchell was a semi-biographical account of an event in the life of General William "Billy" Mitchell, a true legend of American military aviation. The film doesn't have a great deal of flying, but some notable events are related, such as Mitchell's famous 1921 demonstration that airplanes could sink warships. Flying biplane bombers Mitchell and his squadron—which includes a young Darren McGavin—drop heavy aerial bombs on a captured German battleship, the SMS *Ostfriesland.* Mitchell realizes senior Army and Navy officers see air power as a threat, so he deliberately disobeys orders he knows would make the test impossible. He leads his pilots and together they sink the German dreadnought.

Mitchell is exiled behind a desk at Fort Sam Houston while the U.S. Air Service continues to wither on the vine. The loss of the dirigible *USS Shenandoah* (ZR-1) in a storm over Ohio in 1925 further inflames Mitchell's ire. The airship was commanded by a good friend, Commander Zachary Lansdowne. Mitchell makes several inflammatory statements to the press that the Army and Navy are guilty of criminal negligence. He is court-martialed and forced to defend his statements to a military court. Among the senior officers of the court is General Douglas MacArthur, who wants to find a way to get the whole mess over with quietly. But a Senator friend played by Ralph Bellamy—long past his youth in *Air Mail*—defends Mitchell in court.

After a series of setbacks and legal maneuvering, Mitchell is finally able to publicly state his views about the future of air power and the role it will play in future wars. Among

Gary Cooper as Billy Mitchell with a Curtiss JN-4D Jenny.

the historic personalities called upon to testify on his behalf are Henry "Hap" Arnold, Eddie Rickenbacker, Fiorello LaGuardia and Admiral William Sims.

In the end, Mitchell is convicted and he resigns his commission. Dressed in civilian clothes, he looks up into the sky and sees a flight of sleek jest pass over—a harbinger of things to come.

The real Mitchell, whose flamboyant outspokenness often made him a thorn in the side of the infantry-minded Army brass, has long been called "the father of American Air Power." Gary Cooper lacks Mitchell's passion and explosive personality. He was also too tall. He plays the role with a stiffness audiences weren't used to seeing in Cooper. The Mitchell family also disapproved of Cooper, preferring James Cagney for the role.

Elizabeth Montgomery, years before her role as Samantha Stevens on TV's *Bewitched*, made her film debut as Margaret Lansdowne, widow of Zachary. Lansdowne was played by the young Jack Lord, still 13 years from his starring role in *Hawaii Five-O*.

As for reality, the film takes some license, as Hollywood nearly always does with history and biographical subjects. Among the notable examples are the tests to bomb the warships. The planes flown by Mitchell's pilots were in fact Martin MB-2 bombers, rather than the far smaller DH-4s which were incapable of carrying the 2,000 lb. bombs that ultimately sank the *Ostfriesland*. No mention is made of the earlier tests on a submarine, a destroyer,

General William "Billy" Mitchell, the father of the modern air force.

the cruiser *SMS Frankfurt*, or the battleship *USS Indiana*, which was bombed weeks prior to the final test.

Mitchell did make the statements to the press, but he didn't know Lansdowne, who died in the crash of the *Shenandoah*. Mitchell attacked the traditionalist military brass for not protecting pilots, and most of all for failing to look ahead to the future of air power. In that respect the film does well, even to the point of seeing the two Japanese naval officers watching the aerial test with great interest. The US Navy officers are portrayed as being ridiculously obtuse in their opposition to Mitchell's test, and the audience can't help but be supportive of Mitchell breaking the rules.

One of Mitchell's MB-2 bombers scores a hit on the derelict battleship *USS Alabama* on the Chesapeake Bay in September, 1921. *Official U.S. Army photo*

Since the production was done with the benefit of 20/20 historical hindsight, Mitchell's prophecies have more impact to the audience. Nevertheless, *The Court-Martial of Billy Mitchell* failed to have much success in the theaters, and is only remembered for the colorful characterizations of LaGuardia and Rickenbacker's snide comments in court.

The Spirit of St. Louis (1957) was the only full-length biographical drama depicting Charles Lindbergh's solo flight across the Atlantic in 1927. Based on Lindbergh's book of the same name, it follows the preparations up to and during the historic flight.

James Stewart, who turned 19 on the day Lindbergh flew the Atlantic, was profoundly influenced by the feat. It was a role he really wanted to do, but had to literally beg his friend and producer Leland Hayward to convince Jack Warner to let him do the part. Amazingly the slim actor actually went on a diet to fit the role. He was 47 years of age when he played the 25-year old Lindbergh, but he manages it well. This is helped by makeup and cutting the actor's wavy silver hair in Lindbergh's style and dying it a sandy shade of light brown. Stewart had little trouble with Lindbergh's shy, boyish personality. While his voice-over narration helps the plot move along, it's hard for audiences to fit the well-known Stewart drawl into Lindbergh's character. Stewart was not Lindbergh's choice to play himself; Lindbergh preferred Anthony Perkins. The famed pilot was present for some of the filming and was impressed when Stewart, an experienced pilot, automatically tapped the oil temperature gauge during the takeoff scene.

Vignettes of the plane's construction and early flight tests are like watching history being made, and Lindbergh's tenacious attention to detail comes across very well. There are moments of suspense, such as when Lindbergh succumbs to fatigue and falls asleep at the controls only to be awakened by the flash of sunlight from a mirror in his eyes.

A 47-year old James Stewart as the 25-year old Charles Lindbergh with one of the reproduction Ryan NYPs for Warner's *The Spirit of St. Louis.*
Author's Collection

While *Spirit* is a colorful and moving drama it does tend to drag towards the end, while the weary, sleep-deprived Lindbergh attempts to reach his distant goal. As the coast of France comes into view ahead of the spinning propeller, the strains of "La Marseillaise" are heard.

Director Billy Wilder, best known for *Some Like it Hot* and *The Seven-Year Itch*, lent some lightness to the serious drama. Whimsical flashbacks to Lindbergh's early days of flying, while apocryphal, are typical for Billy Wilder films.

An old friend of Lindbergh's, Harlan A. "Bud"' Gurney, portrayed in the film by Murray Hamilton, served as technical advisor. Gurney ensured that Hollywood's legendary talent for dismissing truth for sensation was kept in check.

Filmed on location in San Diego (where the *Spirit of St. Louis* was built), on Long Island and in Ireland and France, the film manages to show the aerial beauty of the land (and water) Lindbergh traversed in 1927.

Aerial supervisor Paul Mantz handled the aerial sequences. Two full-scale flying Ryan NYP (New York to Paris) reproductions were built for the European and U.S. film units. A third plane was used as a cockpit mockup in the studio. All the details were carefully matched to the original aircraft, which now hangs in the Smithsonian's National Air & Space Museum in Washington, D.C. Lindbergh donated the airplane to the museum in 1928.

One of the reproductions had been in the San Diego Aerospace (now Air & Space) Museum, but was destroyed in a fire that swept through the museum in 1978. The second aircraft is now on display at the Missouri Museum in St. Louis.

While the cinematography and attention to technical detail is excellent, the cockpit footage fails to show how tight the interior of the Ryan NYP really is. The author was allowed to sit in the pilot's seat of a reproduction on display in San Diego and was stunned at how cramped it was.

James Stewart as Lindbergh in the climactic Le Bourget landing scene in *The Spirit of St. Louis.* The 1920 Resistal aviator goggles and helmet are the type worn by Lindbergh.

Definitely a film only for aviation aficionados, *Spirit* is one of Stewart's most difficult biographical roles. First screenings of the movie were not positive, so Wilder edited and added several scenes. The entire ending was reshot with a more gripping score by composer Roy Webb and Warner Music Director Ray Heindorf to add cues to the Franz Waxman score.

Costing over $6 million, *Spirit* did poorly at the box office. It was considered one of the reasons Warner went into the red after a successful run of films in the mid-1950s.

When the fate of a famous person is unknown, Hollywood often sacrifices truth on the altar of sensationalism. This is most true in the case of Amelia Earhart's ill-fated 1937 circumnavigation of the world.

Earhart's life and accomplishments were the stuff of legend even before her final flight, but when she and navigator Fred Noonan disappeared in the Pacific Ocean between

New Guinea and Howland Island in July 1937 it ignited a firestorm of speculation and conspiracy theories.

Earhart, who had first gained aviation fame as a mere passenger on a late-1927 flight aboard a Fokker Trimotor from Newfoundland to England, later became the defining aviatrix of the era. She formed the "Ninety-Nines," an exclusive club of woman pilots, championed women's rights and equal employment, was a major advocate of orphans and the disabled, and in between managed to set some impressive aviation records.

The crowning glory of her career was to be a flight around the world at the equator, besting Wiley Post's 1931 and 1933 flights at higher latitudes. She flew a Lockheed 10-E Electra, a twin-engine passenger plane, purchased by her publisher and promoter husband George Palmer Putnam.

Paul Mantz, Amelia Earhart, Harry Manning and Fred Noonan in Oakland, California, on March 17, 1937. This photo was taken the day the four flew to Hawaii for the first east-to-west circumnavigation attempt.

The journey began badly. She crashed in an attempt to take off from Hawaii towards Howland Island. After making repairs, she and Noonan left Los Angeles to fly east. From there they crossed the United States, turned south to Brazil, then headed east over the South Atlantic to Africa. After a harrowing crossing of the Dark Continent, Earhart and Noonan reached India and finally New Guinea. The next leg of the trip would be a dangerous 2,500-mile leap to tiny Howland Island, a miniscule speck in the vast ocean.

On July 2, 1937, Earhart and Noonan, after several frustratingly brief radio calls, disappeared, never to be seen again.

Every crackpot theory swept through the public imagination, from being captured by the Japanese while photographing their bases under FDR's orders to being eaten by cannibals. There was almost no basis for these ideas; and more than likely the Electra, far off course due to mismarked charts and poor radio reception, ran out of fuel and fell from the sky to sink in the depths of the Pacific.

RKO's 1943 fictionalized biography of Earhart, *Flight for Freedom*, was a jingoistic propaganda film that told her disappearance was a result of her spying for the Navy. Much more sensationalistic than realistic, it stars Rosalind Russell as the aviatrix with the fictional name of Tonie Carter. She is involved in steamy love affairs and faces her death with patriotic fervor.

Horace McCoy's screenplay may have been authorized by Putnam and funded by Earhart's friend, aviatrix Jackie Cochrane, wife of Howard Hughes' business partner Floyd Odlum. Carter is dubbed "The Lady Lindbergh," a name Earhart hated. The film came out in the middle of World War II, when anti-Japanese propaganda was eagerly accepted by the public.

Diane Keaton played a humorless Earhart in *Amelia Earhart: The Final Flight* in 1994. The film centered on Earhart's struggles with her fame and her promoter husband's ideas.

With Dutch-born Rutger Hauer as fragile former alcoholic Fred Noonan, *The Final Flight* tells a straightforward, if not compassionate, story of the world-circling flight attempt. Paul Mantz (Paul Guilfoyle) is seen as the pilot who has his hands full trying to train a recalcitrant Earhart to fly the Electra. Even though she had flown her red Lockheed Vega on several record-breaking flights, the twin-engine Model 10 was one of the first multi-engine aircraft she had ever taken up. Her lack of experience leads to the takeoff crash in Hawaii. Noonan is seen as a cushion to her volatile temper while dealing with delays and expenses. While the script does not say that Noonan's past drinking problem was responsible for their disappearance, the audience is left in little doubt that it was a factor.

Since no actual 10-E Electras were then available, the production used a Beechcraft Model 18 that bore a close resemblance to the Electra. Steve Hinton of Planes of Fame Air Museum in Chino, California, flew the Beech in the film. "We had two twin Beeches for that film," said Hinton in an interview with the author. "One was a clunker they used for the crash and whatever, and the other was used for the flying scenes. Back then there weren't too many Electras around. There's a few more today. But it really comes down to what's available in planes and pilots. I don't want to come across the wrong way, but a lot of guys can fly but only a few know how to work with film crews. A lot of times you may have the right airplane but no one checked out on that model who can do the flying and stunts. I could fly the twin Beech for the film."

Hinton explained that a B-25 camera plane was used for the aerial scenes. "I think Skip Evans did the Hawaii crash stunt," said Hinton. The last moments of Earhart and Noonan are poignant as they climb into the darkening sky, clinging to life just a little longer.

The truth has slowly been milked from the legend, and only in the last decade has the story been given some validity.

The most recent Earhart film was simply entitled *Amelia*, and starred Hillary Swank, who came the closest to the real flyer in appearance and character. Produced by Avalon Pictures and directed by *New York, I Love You*'s Mira Nair, the 2009 film is the most accurate telling of the Earhart legend. Nair and screenwriter Anna Hamilton Phelan (*Gorillas in the Mist*, 1988) created a film about an Earhart who is more focused on true love and women's rights than in setting aviation records.

Several original and a few replica planes were used for the film. The bright red Lockheed Vega monoplane Earhart flew on many of her North and South American records was a non-flying mockup. It is now on display at the San Diego Air & Space Museum. The Vega was one of the most reliable and popular monoplanes of the day. Wiley Post's *Winnie Mae* was a Vega.

The Fokker F.VIIb Trimotor *Friendship* was likewise a full-scale replica seen in close-up shots. The interior was carefully recreated down to the last detail. Earhart was touted to the press as the first woman to cross the Atlantic in June 1928, although she was little more than a passenger to pilot Bill Stultz and navigator/mechanic Louis Gordon.

Unlike the previous two films, *Amelia* was able to use a real Electra Model 12A, Serial No. 1208, a nearly identical type to what Earhart flew. Only differing in wingspan, length and a few other details the Electra *Junior* was the property of Joe Shepherd. "Mine was one of the two Electras used in the film," said Shepherd, a retired airline pilot, in a 2010 interview. "The other one was used in the South African scenes. I did all my own flying for the movie." But, he said with a trace of disbelief, "I had to wear a wig and they shaved off my moustache."

Shepherd's highly polished Electra was too shiny for Avalon Pictures. "They had me leave it outside to get rained on and dusty so it looked more correct for a plane working its way around the world," explained Shepherd. For the Hawaii crash, Shepherd said the production found enough Electra parts at Lockheed and aircraft junkyards to assemble a nearly complete plane

"Jimmy Leeward, who owns several planes and races at Reno every year, gave me some tips," Shepherd remembered. "He took me aside and said, 'You gotta guard your plane every minute. Don't take your eyes off it. Those film people are just clueless about airplanes.'"

Shepherd, heeding Leeward's warnings, was there when studio technicians showed up with sheets of aluminum and a big bag of sheet metal screws. "They had this big electric drill. They were going to go up and drill holes all over my plane to fit this metal over the windows. Those guys were just doing their job but they didn't know anything about planes."

Greg Herrick's vintage Ford 4-AT Trimotor C-1077 in flight.
Courtesy Greg Herrick

A restored 1927 Ford 4-AT-10 C-1077 Trimotor appears midway through the movie. Owned by Greg Herrick of Minneapolis, it is the oldest flying metal aircraft in the world. One of the 79 4-ATs built by the Stout Metal Airplane Division of Ford, C-1077 came off the assembly line in 1927. Among the famous pilots who flew C-1077 were Charles Lindbergh and Medal of Honor recipient Floyd Bennett. In March 1929 Amelia Earhart herself also flew the 4-AT seen in the film. "It's had a lot of history in it," Herrick said with pride. Herrick spent almost twenty years restoring the Trimotor, which had been little more than a forgotten carcass abandoned in a Carcross, Yukon, airport.

When asked about *Amelia*, Herrick said, "Avalon contacted me that they needed a Ford Trimotor for this film. I'd heard horror stories about working with the movie industry, so I was leery." Herrick had total control of the aircraft during filming. "Jimmy Leeward was the pilot and James Obawa was the co-pilot and mechanic," Herrick explained. "Most of the flying scenes were done out of Toronto and Hamilton, Ontario."

Hillary Swank in the pilot's seat of Greg Herrick's Ford Trimotor.
Courtesy Greg Herrick

Hillary Swank, who was made to look like Earhart, sat in the venerable "Tin Goose" for several shots. "The film people were great," Herrick said. "But at one point they wanted me to cover up the Ford logo on the side of the plane. I guess they didn't want to make it seem as if they were advertising Ford. But in the end they left it as is."

Herrick was present for the construction of the Fokker and Vega replicas. "I watched them build them. I was just amazed at how perfect they were."

On a sad note, Jimmy Leeward was killed at the 2011 Reno Air Races trials while this book was being written.

Grace McGuire owns the only Lockheed 10-E Electra in the world. "It was three planes up the assembly line from the plane Amelia flew," McGuire, a San Diego resident, explained to the author. "It was built by the same people, by the same tools." There is a strange feeling when one is close to the plane, which is named *Muriel* in honor of Amelia's sister. McGuire knew Muriel very well.

McGuire, who resembles Earhart, hopes to fly the rare Electra to complete the ill-fated 1937 flight. She has made Earhart's life and final flight a quest for truth.

When asked what she thought of the Earhart films, McGuire simply shrugged, "It's Hollywood. They never try to get history right. But the flying and airplane replicas in the last film were very good. And the film didn't follow any of the crackpot theories. I guess the only part I didn't like was how overdone the love affair with Gene Vidal was done."

Avalon Pictures' reproduction Lockheed Vega on display at the San Diego Air & Space Museum. *Courtesy Ernie Viskupic, Wingman Photography*

Amelia is a relatively good film for aviation historians but it suffers from the bane of many 21st century historical dramas: scandal is more interesting than truth or achievements. Even her record-setting feats have little impact on the plot. The old wooden crates from the Golden Age of Flight have little appeal to audiences raised on action and speed. And as in all the Amelia Earhart films, the end is pure speculation. This will continue to be the case until the wreckage of the Electra is found and the truth revealed.

One of the men who followed the "Lindbergh dream" into the skies was a diminutive Texas-born Irish-American named Douglas Corrigan. His early link to aviation was as a welder who worked on the 'Spirit of St. Louis' while employed at the Ryan Aeronautical Company in San Diego. He appears in the famous "graduation photo" of the Ryan team in front of their historic plane. Sixth from the right was the 5'5" red-haired 20-year old Corrigan, looking like a teenager.

Corrigan was determined to do as well as, if not better than Lindbergh, and worked at airports and aircraft companies all over the country, earning enough money to purchase his own plane. In 1933 he was able to buy a well-used 1929 Curtiss Robin monoplane for $310. The Robin's robust construction and forgiving manners made it ideal for many pilots and more than seven hundred were built. Corrigan built and installed extra fuel tanks and bought a used Wright J6-5 165-hp Whirlwind engine.

Working as a mechanic to make ends meet and keep the plane in the air, the cocky Irishman set his sights on his goal. All his friends knew he wanted to fly the Atlantic solo. In 1937 he applied to the Civil Aeronautics Authority (CAA) for permission to fly from New York to London. The CAA didn't think much of the patched-up, shopworn Robin and declined Corrigan's request. They were concerned about the escalating political situation in Europe, but their decision was also influenced by the disappearance of Amelia Earhart less than a year before. They didn't want to deal with another well-publicized aviation death. Corrigan then suggested a flight from Long Beach to New York, with a return non-stop after that. The CAA granted this.

Landing on Long Island after a 27-hour flight with four gallons remaining and only the clothes on his back, Corrigan prepared for the return flight. At dawn on July 17, 1938, with 320 gallons of fuel, a Thermos of coffee and some candy bars, Corrigan took off, heading northeast. His well-wishers waited for him to turn around to the west. But he never did, and 28 hours later he made a bumpy landing in Dublin, Ireland. He swore he'd read the wrong end of the compass needle, a common enough problem in those days. "Honest, I just went the wrong way!" he said.

A legend was born. Instead of being punished for his obvious disregard of the CAA's ruling, Corrigan became an instant hero and celebrity. Americans loved the story of the little guy defying bureaucracy to win against all odds. Everyone knew he was lying, but they loved him for it. Douglas "Wrong Way" Corrigan steadfastly claimed, "That's my story, and I'm sticking to it." He wrote and published his book with that title just a few months later.

Corrigan was an early example of Andy Warhol's "15 minutes of fame" phenomenon. The story was too good not to make into a movie. *The Flying Irishman* was released by RKO in 1939 just eight months after the flight. Corrigan played himself.

In an interview with the reclusive Doug Corrigan, Jr., the author learned some of the backstory regarding the film "The studio was going to use James Cagney to play dad, with the best writers, directors and actors," said Corrigan. "Dad would be the technical advisor. "But then RKO sold out and it became a cheap project. They fired Cagney, they hired cheap writers and a director and second-rate actors. Then they said they wouldn't pay dad the $50,000 [they promised him] unless he played himself."

Douglas "Wrong Way" Corrigan with the Curtiss C-3 Robin he flew to fame across the Atlantic and in *The Flying Irishman*. *SDASM Collection*

Asked how his father had felt about that, Doug Jr. replied, "He wasn't happy about it. He knew he wasn't an actor. But he did it."

It's obvious the film was produced as quickly as possible to capitalize on Corrigan's fame. Using a radio reporter's narrative the film tells Corrigan's story with a little help from screenwriter Dalton Trumbo, who had yet to make his mark on the silver screen. The boyish Corrigan is reasonably good as himself but it is clear he would have done better to stay in an airplane and not in front of a camera. The flying sequences are fun and dynamic. As with most of the acting from the era, the characters are overdramatized.

Released five months before the outbreak of war in Europe, *The Flying Irishman* was a fun, fast-paced, semi-serious retelling of Corrigan's early life and dream of flying. The production was filmed at the Los Angeles Metropolitan Airport and the Culver City Airport. Some shots may have been filmed in the Ryan factory in San Diego, where a Ryan M-2 is seen under construction.

The other star of the film is a Curtiss Robin. Doug Jr. confirmed that it was the actual aircraft his father flew to Ireland. Process and miniatures filled in the aerial shots.

Regarding the whereabouts of the Robin, as of this writing it is in the barn owned by Doug Corrigan, Jr., in California. He is seeking buyers for the crated plane, which has not been on public display since 1988.

As noted in Chapter Two, Howard Hughes was one of aviation's most enigmatic figures. The multimillionaire enthusiastically pursued several lucrative and ill-advised business ventures throughout the 1930s and 1940. Several films have attempted to tell various aspects of Hughes' life. His romances, business dealings, phobias and wealth were detailed on the silver screen with varying degrees of accuracy.

The Aviator (2004), starring *Titanic* star Leonardo DiCaprio, relates Hughes' fascination with aviation in the years prior to and during World War II. Martin Scorsese directed the 170-minute film, which was written by John Logan (*The Last Samurai*, 2003).

Early in the film Hughes is working on his ambitious *Hell's Angels.* Several of the biplanes used were built in full scale. Ironically the production used modern replicas to reproduce what in 1928 were modern replicas of Great War airplanes. When Hughes tries to buttonhole Louis B. Mayer of MGM for the use of some cameras for *Hell's Angels* it is an indicator of what he was facing. The rich kid dabbling in the motion pictures wasn't taken very seriously in Hollywood. It is an interesting opportunity to see how *Hell's Angels* was made, including Hughes' insistence on realism. In a tribute to Wellman, he even insists on "finding some clouds to provide a sense of relative motion."

With Hughes' other ventures into filmmaking and romances to add spice, *The Aviator* is really about his airplanes. The H-1 Racer, the XF-11, the Lockheed Constellation airliner and the huge HK-1 (Hughes/Kaiser) Hercules flying boat known as the "Spruce Goose" are major elements in the film. Nearly all the shots of the graceful Constellation were archival or of static displays.

The Hercules was a truly massive airplane by any standards. Rather than rely exclusively on CGI, Scorsese decided to have flying remote-control miniatures built. Aero Telemetry Systems Inc. of Long Beach, California, built the radio-controlled models of the XF-11 and HK-1 for *The Aviator.* Both could duplicate flight in a way where even CGI would fall short.

Bill Hempel worked for Aero Telemetry as the senior controller on the two models. The author interviewed Hempel by phone in 2010 to learn what it had required to recreate such one-of-a-kind aircraft in flying miniatures. The models were built from scratch, according to Hempel. "The Hercules wingspan was twenty-one feet long," he said. "It weighed 185 pounds, while the XF-11 had a thirty foot wingspan and weighed 485 pounds. It had two 275cc engines for about half a horsepower each. That's a lot of power for a model. These were some of the biggest models ever flown."

Hempel explained, "We were not allowed to test-fly the models prior to filming, since only one of each existed. They were looking for specific shots and once they saw how good the models looked they actually rewrote the shooting script to get more of the models on film. They were really impressed."

Aero Telemetry's detailed radio-controlled Hercules model had a wingspan of 21 feet and weighed 165 pounds. *Courtesy Aero Telemetry, Inc.*

Asked why the production used an "old" technology instead of CGI, Hempel replied, "CGI is really, really expensive, and the studio wanted realism above what CGI could deliver."

The footage of the flying models comes across as real. The Hercules model was flown in Long Beach at the same location where Hughes made his short test of the plane in November 1947. "They brought in these old patrol boats and had them in just the same spot as they appear in the original newsreel footage," said Hempel. He recalled that the Spruce Goose used electric motors. "We could get about eight or nine minutes of footage, then we'd have to bring it down and replace the batteries. With three sets of batteries we could do three flights a day."

Each shot was carefully set up to get the maximum out of the flight. Even though the Hercules was a model Hempel had to use his skills as a pilot to control it. "I'd get the plane in the air and in trim. Most of the time it went fine. But there was one incident where we left it in the water while we changed out the batteries. Then when I ran it up to takeoff again it bounced and was just jumping around and I really had to fight it to get it in the air. Then it pitched straight up, went vertical, and I didn't have any control. It stalled and dove straight at the water, and I was able to recover it before it crashed. It was just going everywhere. That was scary as hell," he said. "People were jumping off the barge and running all over to get away. But I had to stay right there and try to save it."

Once the priceless model was back on the control barge, the explanation for the near disaster became clear. "The plane had taken on some water when we were changing the batteries," said Hempel. When it lifted off, the water fell back to the tail, and when I got it back down all the water went to the nose." After draining and patching the expensive model the crew went back to work, a bit wiser for the experience.

In order to produce the illusion that the model was as big as the 310-foot, 400,000 lb. flying boat, Hempel said he had to fly very close to the cameras to give it a sense of scale. "They wanted to reproduce the original newsreel footage but also shots that had never been done in 1947. In order to get the right scale I had to fly it about twelve feet away so it looked like the huge plane a hundred feet away."

When combined with process and rare newsreel footage, the aerial shots are stunning. The movie's technical accuracy is hard to criticize. For instance, the sleek H-1 Racer replica had to be reverse-engineered by New Deal Studios from archival photos and rare blueprints. Hughes was so secretive most of the original plans were never found. In the film Hughes flies the racer to a new world land speed record of 352 knots, a speed that would hardly eyebrows today. But the photography captures the then-blinding illusion of speed perfectly.

The radical Hughes XF-11 reconnaissance plane was reproduced by Aero Telemetry Inc. With a 30-foot wingspan it weighed 485 pounds and had two 275cc engines.
Courtesy Aero Telemetry, Inc.

The XF-11 prototype reconnaissance plane Hughes called his "Buck Rogers plane" was developed for the Army. For the film an XF-11 was built to 1:4 scale by New Deal Studios with superb detail for close shots. "It had electric motors, smoke generators and the contra-rotating propellers as well," said Hempel.

There is one small error. The U.S. Army Air Force insignia on the XF-11 has the red horizontal stripe that wasn't adopted until 1948, the year after the Air Force became its own branch of the military. The star on the tail boom is canted, rather than upright.

Hughes piloted the XF-11 on its maiden flight on July 7, 1946. An oil leak forced him to bring the plane down on the Los Angeles Country Club Golf Course. During his descent he clipped the roofs of three houses. The model used in the crash sequences was built at a scale of 1:4, as were the homes and surrounding terrain. The miniature was designed to break apart on cue.

The flying sequences are a film ballet with lovely music and neatly filmed cinematography. Scorsese's property department took great pains to create the world of the Golden Age of Flight with stunning realism and in meticulous detail. Four of the miniatures seen in the film are on display at the Evergreen Aviation Museum in McMinnville, Oregon, where the real Spruce Goose resides. Two of the *Hell's Angels* biplanes are also on display at the museum.

What comes across well in *The Aviator* is Hughes' eccentricity when working on his aircraft projects. He was totally involved in the design, construction and testing of the innovative planes—to the detriment of his other ventures. He oversaw every aspect of the birth of what he always hoped would be the defining aircraft of the age. They rarely were, although Hughes' designers had pioneered some remarkable advances in streamlining and speed. For those accomplishments alone the world of aviation owes Howard Hughes a debt of gratitude. His films have earned far less respect, as will be seen in Chapter Nine.

The Aviator was nominated for 11 Academy Awards and took home the Oscar for Best Cinematography. *Flyboys'* Tony Bill might have done better at the 2007 Academy Awards if he had made use of real and model aircraft than computers to create illusions.

Reach for the Sky, released in 1956, was based on the book of the same name by Paul Brickhill, author of *The Great Escape*. It follows the life of Wing Commander Douglas Bader, an RAF fighter pilot who had lost both his legs in a crash in 1931. Bader's career had literally been cut short by the accident, but his assertive and single-minded nature refused to accept defeat. He succeeded in remaining in the RAF, eventually flying Hurricanes and Spitfires in the Battle of Britain. Before he was shot down over France in 1941 Bader defeated twenty-three German planes. He spent the rest of the war in prison camps and was just as driven to escape and return to the sky as he'd been after his crash.

The film stars the talented if two-dimensional actor Kenneth More in the lead role. The prologue states:

Douglas Bader has become a legend in his own life time. His courage was not only an example to those in War but is now a source of inspiration to many in Peace. For dramatic purposes it has been necessary in this film to transpose in time certain events in Douglas Bader's life and also to re-shape some of the characters involved in this story. The Producers apologise to those who may have been affected by any changes or omissions.

It's hard to imagine an American studio doing that.

Squadron Commander Douglas Bader (center) with two pilots of No. 242 Squadron, 1940.

With the period of 1930 to 1945 to cover, *Reach for the Sky* has to compress several of the pivotal events in Bader's life. Highlighted are his crash in a Bristol Bulldog biplane, his long recovery from having both legs amputated, meeting his future wife Thelma, and the struggle to return to active duty. Bader wins the respect of other pilots and becomes the commander of a Hurricane squadron made up of undisciplined Canadians. He later distinguishes himself and reaches the rank of Wing Commander while flying Spitfires. When a mid-air collision brings Bader down he makes a nuisance of himself to the Germans, who are surprisingly accommodating to the legless ace.

Director Lewis Gilbert later worked with Kenneth More on *Sink the Bismarck!* and directed three of the James Bond films. Gilbert made the film enjoyable with little room for criticism. As with most UK-produced war films, *Reach for the Sky* is largely accurate in both history and technical detail. The technical advisor was Group Captain Harry Day, who flew with Bader before the war.

Day and Bader also spent time in the same German POW camp.

Douglas Bader's Hawker Hurricane.

Actors portraying famous personages such as Air Chief Marshal Sir Hugh "Stuffy" Dowding and Air Vice Marshal Trafford Leigh-Mallory put in short but pivotal roles. Interestingly, none of the German officers are named, although Bader met and respected Colonel Adolf Galland, Goering's most effective fighter wing commander.

The production had the full cooperation of the Air Ministry. Most of the flying and ground scenes were filmed on location in Surrey around RAF Kenley. The RAF fighters are real planes, although most of the German fighters and bombers are miniatures, backed up by a wealth of air combat footage. An Avro 504 and an Avro Tutor, correct for the period, appear in the Cranwell training sequences.

The detailed Me-109E miniature makes a hard turn to avoid Bader's Spitfire in *Reach for the Sky.*

Yet a few small errors which arise from the rarity of early-war aircraft are seen. The ten Spitfires provided for the production are late-war Mk XVIs with teardrop canopies and mahogany four-bladed propellers. In fact that model used American Packard Merlin engines.

Interior and process shooting was done at Pinewood Studios. When Bader takes a Hurricane up to show his mettle to the skeptical pilots of No. 242 Squadron, he flies it inverted for a long period of time. It has been pointed out to the author that this was not possible in the early-war Hurricanes with gravity-fed carburetors. The shot is inverted, as can be seen by examination of the clouds and sunlight.

Virginia Bader is Douglas Bader's second cousin, and owns one of the world's finest aviation art galleries in Santa Ana, California. In an interview with the author she stated the film was fairly true to life, but also said that "Douglas never made a penny from it. But it made him a famous man, even so."

At least one of the film's scenes may be apocryphal. Bader had always stated, "No Jerry fighter will ever shoot me down." On August 9, 1941, a collision with an Me-109 over the coast of France ended his combat career. The film toes the line as far as his escape from the falling Spitfire is concerned, but historians generally agree that it wasn't a collision as Bader had always claimed. He was probably shot down. In any event, *Reach for the Sky* follows Bader's side of the story.

Kenneth More as Bader with Supermarine Spitfire in *Reach for the Sky*.
Author's Collection

CHAPTER FIVE

The Approaching Storm

By 1937 Nazi Germany was showing its true colors with aggressive annexation of neighboring countries and a tremendous military build-up, while Japan was waging open war with China. Britain was preparing for the inevitable. American isolationists, led by Charles Lindbergh, were determined to keep the nation out of any foreign wars. In the government and military there were valid concerns about American preparedness. The first hesitant build-up to what would one day become the most powerful military force on Earth had its roots in the uncertain years after 1937.

But Hollywood, ever eager to find box-office appeal, had already produced scores of films with patriotic and militaristic themes. Many were released long before anyone had ever heard of Adolf Hitler.

The isolationists openly accused the studios of fanning war hysteria and antagonizing Germany and Japan. But the Army, Navy, Air Corps, Marines, Merchant Marine and Coast Guard benefited from the films cranked out in the years prior to and during the first months of the war. The movies promoted the role and value of the armed forces to a public that hardly knew the difference between a sailor and a marine.

The millions of young men and women who rallied to the colors after December 7, 1941, were the followers of the thousands who joined the service before the bombs fell on Pearl Harbor.

MGM's silent *The Flying Fleet* (1929) starring *Hell's Angels* lead Ben Lyon told the tale of yet another love triangle with the Navy's aviation service as the backdrop. The film was "Dedicated to the officers and men of naval aviation whose splendid cooperation made this film possible." With that in mind it holds that *The Flying Fleet* might be more than a rehash of a soap-opera romance, but that's what it is. The ending is obvious: after a rivalry over the same girl breaks up the friendship of two aviation cadets, they eventually find a mutual respect in a common goal.

Looking east, aerial view of Naval Air Station San Diego in May 1937 while the Navy was preparing for possible war. On the tarmac are Vought SB2U Vindicator dive bombers of VB-3. Visible at upper center is *USS Ranger* (CV-4). *SDASM Collection*

The Flying Fleet was shot at NAS North Island and NAS Pensacola, and features footage of *USS Langley* (CV-1), America's first carrier. The film's collection of now-rare Navy aircraft includes the Boeing F2B-1, Douglas T2D-1 torpedo bomber and a Consolidated NY-2. The T2D was the forerunner of the more famous TBD Devastator and holds the distinction of being the first twin engine aircraft to launch from a carrier.

Flight was a USMC aviator film, released by Columbia in 1930. A typical military action drama, it was photographed by Elmer Dyer and Paul Perry in San Diego. In the story, Jack Holt is Panama Williams, a veteran Marine flyer. He befriends Lefty Phelps (Ralph Graves), who joins the Marines to become a flyer. Failing to win his wings as the result of a training accident, Lefty becomes a mechanic for Panama as the Marines are sent to Nicaragua. Lefty falls for Elinor (Lila Lee) but backs off when he discovers that Panama is involved with her. When Panama asks Lefty to propose for him, the plan backfires when Elinor falls for Lefty. (It didn't work for Cyrano de Bergerac, either.) After the two men fight, Lefty is lost in the jungle.

Panama flies to find and rescue his friend but is injured and can't fly back. Of course Lefty saves the day, wins his wings and all is well. This is an early Frank Capra film. At this time Capra had yet to develop the style he would later display in *Arsenic and Old Lace* (1944) and *It's a Wonderful Life* (1946).

One of the uncredited roles is of a Marine pilot played by the grandfatherly-looking 36-year old Walter Brennan.

Filmed at the birthplace of Naval Aviation, NAS North Island in San Diego Bay, the movie features the Curtiss OC-2, the first dive/attack bomber used by the Navy and Marine Corps. The OC-2's most famous movie role was in *King Kong* (see Chapter Fourteen). Also appearing in *Flight* is an early Consolidated NY, one of a series of trainers based on the PT-1 Trusty design.

According to critic Leonard Maltin, *Flight* is the "dated story of battling buddies in the USMC flying with some impressive aerial sequences."

Meanwhile, back in the Navy, Wallace Beery went head-to-head with Clark Gable in *Hell Divers* (1931). The story and screenplay were from the fertile mind of Frank Wead. The plot is very complex, primarily about the rivalry of two Chief Petty Officers who are gunners in a dive bomber squadron. Back and forth the story winds its way with on- and off-duty jealousy, one-upmanship and dirty tricks, until the two chiefs find respect and friendship.

Wead's screenplay went through several revisions and additions during pre-production and into the filming schedule as Navy cooperation provided more backdrops to shoot against. The most notable was the carrier *USS Saratoga* (CV-3), filmed while transiting the Panama Canal. Fighter Squadron VF-1B was available for most of the aerial photography, using their 25 Curtiss F8C-4 Falcons. The two-seat attack and observation planes were the backbone of the Navy's and Marine Corps' air arms from 1925 to 1937. The most intriguing sequence is actual 1928 footage of the dirigible *USS Los Angeles* (ZR-3) landing on *Saratoga's* flight deck. (For more on the *Los Angeles*, see Chapter Eleven.)

According to his biographer Warren Harris, Gable underwent several days of training with the pilots who would double him and Beery. Gable wanted to look convincing in close-up. *Hell Divers* began Gable's career-long association with aviation. He played pilots more than any other type of role. It was the perfect he-man occupation for the fanatically heterosexual Gable.

Beery, who was a pilot, insisted on appearing in all but the most dangerous stunts. When Beery's character Windy dies he is buried at sea. Overhead, for the first time on screen, is the soon-to-be famous "Missing Man" formation, flown by RCAF pilots. It was first used by the RAF for the funeral of King George V in 1936 and adopted by the U.S. Air Corps two years later.

Self-centered exhibition pilot Tommy O'Toole (Cagney) faces off against straight-laced Marine Bill Brannigan (Pat O'Brien) in *Devil Dogs of the Air*. The movie was filmed at NAS San Diego.

In 1935 the pendulum swung back to the Marines in *Devil Dogs of the Air* with Warner's first-string Irish team of James Cagney and Pat O'Brien. O'Brien, who had shaken off his reluctance to fly after *Air Mail*, again took the controls as a Marine squadron commander. Lt. Bill Brannigan is a straight-laced Marine officer who has his hands full when an old flying pal, Tommy O'Toole (Cagney), comes to join up. O'Toole, an excellent pilot, has a cavalier attitude that quickly tests Brannigan's patience. O'Toole makes himself hated and resented by the other pilots, and Brannigan is forced to come down hard on him. In the end, O'Toole saves Brannigan's life while realizing the value of teamwork and discipline.

Devil Dogs of the Air is almost a remake of *Here Comes the Navy* (see Chapter Eleven), which also starred O'Brien and Cagney. Lloyd Bacon directed both films, which also starred semi-comic sidekick Frank McHugh.

James Cagney in a studio shot for *Devil Dogs of the Air*.

Devil Dogs was a fun film for fans of the Cagney/O'Brien/McHugh team, but it has more to offer viewers interested in 1930s military hardware. Bacon did the principal photography at NAS North Island in late 1934 with the cooperation of VMA-231 doing most of the flying in their Vought O2U Corsairs. In various shots are seen Loening OL-8 amphibian biplanes, Boeing F4B or P-12 pursuit planes and a Ford Trimotor. O'Toole's plane is a Travel Air D-4000. A Douglas Dolphin amphibian can be seen in the background. But most unusual of all is the one-of-a-kind Curtiss RC-1 Kingburd air transport.

The Army finally made an appearance on screen, in MGM's little-remembered *West Point of the Air* in August 1935. The film starred Wallace Beery, Robert Young and Robert Taylor in his first film role. Shot on location at Randolph Field near San Antonio, Texas, the movie follows Army Air Corps cadets through training, all the while dealing with the ways of love and loyalty. The principal aircraft used for the film were Consolidated PT-4 Trustys, known for being forgiving to new pilots and as one of the ugliest planes that ever flew.

In 1939 Warner Brothers was well ahead of the pack in producing military genre films. One of these was *Wings of the Navy*, again directed by Lloyd Bacon, starring John Payne and George Brent. Naval aviation cadet Jerry Harrington (Payne) goes through training and then graduates from Pensacola to fly PBYs out of San Diego. But his brother Cass Harrington (Brent) works as an aircraft designer. Jerry resigns his commission to fly Cass's newest fighter for the Navy brass. The plane proves to be excellent, and soon Jerry is accepted back into the Navy in time to fly the new plane in a non-stop flight from California to Hawaii.

The movie, with Warner's patented skill for blending drama, romance and patriotism, was virtually a Naval Aviation recruiting film. Bacon and the film crew spent six weeks at NAS Pensacola to shoot footage of cadets being put through their paces. Other than the actors, all of the cadets and training instructors in the film are Navy personnel. The young men learning how to fly SNJs are destined to play a role in the Pacific war just two years away. Five training squadrons provided over 300 aircraft to be used in the production. The familiar NS-1 Stearman and the rare SU-3s—a variant of the O2U Corsair long forgotten by history—are featured in several shots.

Paul Mantz and Elmer Dyer did the aerial work from Mantz' Lockheed Sirius camera ship. From there they went to NAS North Island to film the PBY sequences. The Consolidated PBY-2 was a new aircraft in the Navy and would soon prove invaluable to the nation during the war.

The movie was well-regarded by critics and particularly the Navy Department. The aerial scenes are compelling and must have inspired many young men to consider a career in aviation.

The Navy's Fighting Squadron 6 was featured in MGM's big-budget *Flight Command* (1940) starring Robert Taylor and Walter Pidgeon. Lt. Drake (Taylor) is a Pensacola graduate assigned to fill the billet left by a dead pilot in VF-6 at North Island. At first the confident new pilot is resented by the men in the squadron; but when he saves the life of the commander by using a new blind flying device ha helped develop, he is accepted by his peers.

The plot is basic and familiar but there is nothing simplistic about the aerial work. Shot almost exclusively on Coronado and over San Diego the film is a masterpiece of Navy and MGM cooperation.

Later VF-6 is sent to Pearl Harbor on deployment, and the film crew is allowed to go along. The film offers a rare glimpse of a pre-war *USS Enterprise* (CV-6). The "Big E" was still armed with ineffective 1.1" AA guns, 5"/38 cannon, and water-cooled .50 cal. machine guns. The interior of the carrier and flight deck operations are filmed with as much attention to detail as a training film. VF-6 flew the rugged Grumman F3F-2, the last biplane to be used in the Navy as a front-line fighter. Less than a year later the squadron received new Grumman F4F-2 Wildcats. Many of the pilots seen in the film were in the skies around Midway as part of *Enterprise*'s Air Group 6 on June 4, 1942.

Flight Command was released in December 1940 and was successful in the theaters and reviews. It is a way to see the Navy's fighter squadrons as they were exactly a year away from war.

In the fall of 1940 President Franklin D. Roosevelt had just instituted the Selective Service Act to bring nearly a million men into military service. The RAF had just forced Hitler and Goering to admit that they could not defeat Britain by air. It was clear proof that the Nazis were not invincible. Seeing an opportunity, Paramount moved quickly to produce a film to boost interest in the Army Air Corps. The result was *I Wanted Wings* (1941).

(As will be noted, Elmer Dyer was at the top of the profession in 1940. He again put his talents to work in *I Wanted Wings.*)

Ray Milland, William Holden and Wayne Morris are aviation cadets hoping to win their wings in the Army Air Corps. The film follows them through the rigors of cadet life, pre-flight, basic, and finally advanced training. Along the way they meet blonde bombshell Veronica Lake in her first film role. She immediately comes between Milland and Holden. The story was the brainchild of Beirne Lay, Jr. Lay would go on to pen some of the most memorable aviation stories in the years to come, including 1949's *Twelve O'Clock High,* written with Sy Bartlett.

There is relatively little studio work in the production because director Mitchell Leisen decided to shoot as much live action location footage as possible for maximum effect and realism. At the Army's Flight Training School at Randolph Field, Texas, more than 130 film crew followed Class 40D from the ground into the sky. The Army provided pilots, instructors and maintenance crews for dozens of North American BT-9 and BT-14 Yales, as well as the AT-6 Texans used in the Kelly Field scenes. Some footage from *Test Pilot* (see Chapter Three) of the YB-17s and Northrop A-17 Nomads went into the final cut. Boeing B-17B Flying Fortresses of the 19th Bomb Group were filmed at March Field.

Paul Mantz and Max Conant coordinated the aerial work from Mantz' Lockheed Vega and Orion camera planes. The three lead actors were taken up in AT-6 Texans to learn how to be more authentic on film.

A huge fly-over with a reported 500 Texans appeared in the graduation sequence. The Air Corps' full commitment to the project was underlined by their providing nearly a thousand airplanes in all. *I Wanted Wings* undoubtedly added some percentage points to the Air Corps' recruitment totals in the months to come. Wayne Morris later joined the Navy and became an ace in the Pacific, with seven confirmed victories.

An interesting fact concerns the 19th Bomb Group B-17Bs seen during the March Field sequences. Less than a year later some of the B-17s featured in *I Wanted Wings* took off from Hamilton Field, California, on a flight to Hawaii, where they would refuel before continuing on to Clark Field in the Philippines. They arrived over Oahu on December 7, 1941.

B-17B Flying Fortresses of the 19th Bomb Group at March Field in Riverside, California. These bombers were visible in the background in *I Wanted Wings*.

With the winds of war fast approaching, Hollywood was well on the way to becoming the most effective mass propaganda tool the world had ever known.

Still at the forefront, Warner cranked out several classic military-themed films. *Sergeant York* (1942) with Gary Cooper was to become one of the best recruiting films of the era.

Director Michael Curtiz worked with Frank Wead to produce *Dive Bomber*, a semi-documentary drama about the men who helped to find the solutions to the dangers of high-altitude flying. Lt. Dale Lee, played by Curtiz staple Errol Flynn, is a Navy flight surgeon who has some radical ideas about combating the increasing problem of high-altitude blackouts. He attempts to learn the roots of why dive bomber pilots are dying when they pull out of their dives. Lee runs up against hardnosed squadron commander Joe Blake (Fred MacMurray). Blake resents all flight surgeons and Lee in particular since he is not a pilot. Lee enters flight training, and passes well enough to be taken seriously.

Lee grounds pilot Tim Griffin because he has suffered heart damage from too much high-altitude flying. Blake is angry. But Griffin joins the Ferry Service to fly bombers to England. He is killed on a long flight between San Diego and Seattle, and Lee knows the cause.

Errol Flynn as flight surgeon Lt. Dale Lee in *Dive Bomber* filmed at NAS San Diego.

Blake sees the wisdom in what Lee is trying to do. They cooperate and do tests in pressure chambers. Lee is proven right and designs not only what would later be called a "G-suit" but also a pressure suit to help pilots survive extreme high altitude. Blake climbs into a Vindicator dive bomber to test the suit, but has pushed his body and his luck too far. He dies on the ground. In the end, Lee is invited to fly with the squadron in a graduation flight.

Dive Bomber is as much a recruiting film as a drama. MacMurray, known for his gentle character in television's *My Three Sons* (1960-1972) is surprisingly good as the acerbic Blake. Filmed almost entirely at NAS North Island and on board *Enterprise*, the film was the result of excellent cooperation between Warner Brothers and the Navy.

Since the United States was gearing up for imminent war, the Navy and Marine Corps aviation squadrons were involved in extensive training operations. When Curtiz and his production crew arrived in San Diego for eight weeks of filming they had to work around the training schedule. Curtiz and the aerial unit of Paul Mantz, Frank Clarke and cinematographer Elmer Dyer were ready to capture the formation flying scenes. The result of their efforts: for this Technicolor production, some of the best and most stunning aviation footage ever captured on film. A dozen Navy and Marine squadrons flew every day in front of Dyer's cameras. Two of the aircraft types were Torpedo 3's Douglas TBD Devastators and

Bombing 3's Vought SB2U Vindicators on deployment with *Enterprise*. Less than a year later, both squadrons would be pitted against the Japanese Navy at Midway, with tragic losses among the torpedo crews.

Vought SB2U-1 of VB-3 at NAS San Diego at the time of filming *Dive Bomber*.
Courtesy The Hook *Magazine*

Other squadrons flew Grumman F3Fs. The F3F biplane was the forerunner of the famous F4F Wildcat, the thorn in Japan's side during the first two years of the Pacific war. Among the pilots who flew in the aerial scenes was a then-unknown Lt. Edward "Butch" O'Hare, who would, a few months later, attain fame as the Navy's first ace.

Some planes were painted in pre-war yellow and silver, while others were clad in the early war blue and gray schemes. The SB2U Vindicator, soon to be replaced by the beloved Douglas SBD Dauntless, served the purpose of teaching the Navy's pilots the skill of dive bombing.

Captain Wallace S. "Griff" Griffin (not to be confused with the Lt. Griffin character) is a retired dive bomber pilot of Air Group 19. Griff—who would later gain combat experience in the Curtiss SB2C Helldiver in the Marianas and Philippine Sea Campaigns—trained in Vindicators at NAS Jacksonville in 1943. "Our Vindicators had been brought back from Midway," he recalled. "Several of them had cloth patches over the bullet holes. That was sobering. Those were the worst damned planes to dive in. They had no dive brakes, so you had to drop the landing gear to slow and control the dive. Sometimes the fabric came off the ailerons and elevators."

Captain Wallace S. "Griff" Griffin flew Vindicators in training at Jacksonville, Florida and SB2C Helldivers in combat in the Philippine Sea Campaign, 1944. *Courtesy W.S. Griffin*

An unusual Miles Mohawk appears as the "RAF Fighter" flown by Tim Griffin in his final flight to Seattle.

Some of the film's dialogue about flying raised eyebrows of knowledgeable viewers. For instance, pilots refer to combat at altitudes of 40,000 feet and more as if it were hardly worth mentioning. But in 1941 that altitude was totally unreachable to the Vought Vindicators and Beech 18s seen in the film. Later B-17 Flying Fortresses could reach 35,000 feet, but the Vindicator topped out at 27,000 on a good day. Without superchargers to force oxygen from the rarified air above 30,000 feet into the engine cylinders, the SB2U, indeed none of the aircraft appearing in *Dive Bomber* would ever have reached the soaring 45,000 feet attained by Blake in his final flight.

Since the Navy Department had total say over the content of the script and shooting, the author wondered why such inflated claims were made. But it was possible the Navy wanted to give the future enemy something to think about by claiming American combat aircraft were more than capable of combat operations at 40,000 feet plus. Regarding the technical accuracy of the film, Griff said, "Great flying, but those altitudes were ridiculous."

Early in 1941 producers Jack Warner and Hal B. Wallis were approached by the Royal Canadian Air Force to produce a patriotic film to support the war effort. Michael Curtiz was immediately assigned to take to the skies for *Captains of the Clouds*, released by Warners in February 1942. James Cagney is Brian MacLean, a wild and pugnacious Canadian bush pilot with a reputation for stealing jobs from other pilots, especially Johnny Dutton (Dennis Morgan). Tiny Murphy, played by the colorful Alan Hale, Blimp Lebec (George Tobias) and Scrounger Harris (Reginald Gardiner) are MacLeans's bush pilot rivals.

James Cagney as bush pilot-turned RCAF instructor Brian MacLean in *Captains of the Clouds. Author's Collection*

Dutton, a fair-minded man, makes a dangerous night flight to bring a doctor to an injured MacLean, who feels remorse over his past actions. He knows Dutton's girlfriend Emily (Brenda Marshall) is a domineering social climber who would take the easygoing Dutton away from the life he loves. MacLean marries her, but Dutton is crushed and joins the RCAF to forget.

MacLean, Murphy, Lebec and Harris hear Winston Churchill's radio speech at the start of the Battle of Britain and decide to join the RCAF. Unfortunately, the four eager men are too old for combat. Wanting to do something for the cause, they agree to be trained as instructors. They find Dutton is already an instructor there. Stirring patriotic band music creates a festive air to the training.

MacLean is too undisciplined for the military and washes out. Drunk, he wants revenge. He and the washed-out Tiny buzz the graduation ceremony, which is attended by Air Marshal Billy Bishop himself. But disaster strikes when Tiny is killed after blacking out.

An urgent call goes out for civilian pilots to ferry unarmed Lockheed Hudson bombers to England. MacLean talks his way onto the flight with Scrounger as his navigator. The Hudsons, led by Dutton, have almost reached England when they are attacked by a German fighter. Lebec is killed. Harris is mortally wounded, and MacLean ignores Dutton's orders to remain in formation. "I'm not disobeying orders," says MacLean. "I just can't hear you!" With his excellent piloting skills he rams his damaged bomber into the German plane.

Lockheed Hudson bombers bound for England in the takeoff sequence of *Captains of the Clouds.*

Captains of the Clouds is a strong entry in the patriotic film market. Again the love triangle appears, as well as the archetype of the cocky pilot who has a fatal change of heart to save his comrades. Originally entitled *Bush Pilots*, the screenplay required several revisions before the RCAF approved it. The project quickly gained momentum when James Cagney signed for the lead role. Cagney had just finished another pilot role, playing opposite Bette Davis in *The Bride Came C.O.D.* Originally Clark Gable and Raymond Massey (who actually was a Canadian) were considered.

Cagney, who had already played at least three other cocky men-turned-heroes, was reluctant to do *Captains of the Clouds*. It was in fact his first Technicolor film and the first to show his red hair.

Curtiz and the film crew set off for Canada in July 1941. Having just finished *Dive Bomber* Curtiz went from warm sunny San Diego to the windy, wet North Woods. The early ground and flying sequences were shot around North Bay, Ontario, a small community that still talks about "the time Hollywood came to town." The residents followed the stars and crew around to watch and generally get in the way. Delays due to weather and injuries sustained by Morgan and Cagney further slowed the already overdue filming schedule.

Working from Paul Mantz' Stinson Model A Trimotor, Elmer Dyer filmed the aerial scenes. The pilots, led by *Hell's Angels* veteran Frank Clarke, flew several daytime and nighttime low-level stunts over thick forests and lakes to get the shots Curtiz wanted. Another silent film pioneer, Garland Lincoln, was still in the movie stunt flying business and flew some of the scenes. This was in fact the last movie in which the Associated Motion Picture Pilots (see Chapter One) worked together as a team.

Clarke doubled for Cagney in the Noorduyn Norseman, a Canadian-built single-engine monoplane favored by bush pilots worldwide. Dutton's plane was a Fairchild 71. Two Wacos, an EGC-7 and AGC-8 served as floatplanes.

Top-scoring World War I RFC ace Air Vice Marshal William "Billy" Bishop, who played himself in the graduation scene in *Captains of the Clouds.*

The film crew of 190 personnel left North Bay for the next part of the production, traveling to the RCAF bases at Trenton, Uplands, and Mountain View. The RCAF used the tiny Fleet Finch 16D and North American AT-6 Harvard (the RAF name for the Texan) along with Avro Ansons and Northrop Nomads.

The huge graduation sequence in *Captains of the Clouds* was of an actual RCAF Presentation of Wings Ceremony at RCAF Uplands, Ontario, just as had been done in *I Wanted Wings*. One hundred ten cadets received their wings while a hundred AT-6 Harvards flew overhead.

One of the more interesting characters in the film is not fictional. Air Marshal William A. "Billy" Bishop was the top Canadian ace in the Great War with 72 victories. His role in *Captains* lent authenticity and drama to the film as well as a strong morale boost to Canadians.

Curtiz' crew then moved to RCAF Dartmouth Air Station in Nova Scotia, where the Hudsons were filmed flying 150 miles off the coast. The footage of the pre-dawn takeoff is powerful and realistic. The Hudson was based on the Model 14 Electra, a slightly larger version of the same plane flown by Amelia Earhart. A repainted Hawker Hurricane portrayed the German fighter. With war hysteria at its peak, an alert had to go out to keep the Home Guard from shooting it down.

The story has the "Messerschmitt" attacking the ferry force an hour out of England. The Me-109 was totally incapable of flying that far from its base but Hollywood often chose to overlook reality.

The crew gratefully returned to California in September for final studio work, wrapping in November. Despite the hackneyed plot and romance, the film's aerial scenes are among the best Warner ever produced. The title was taken from a war bond rally speech given by Bishop.

Curtiz was on a roll. After *Dive Bomber* and *Captains*, his next film was *Yankee Doodle Dandy*, followed by his greatest work, *Casablanca*.

William Wellman again brought an aviation story to the screen with Fox's *Thunder Birds* (also known as *Soldiers of the Air*) starring Gene Tierney, John Sutton and Preston Foster. The screenplay is typical Hollywood fare: Young British cadet Peter Stackhouse (Sutton) fights airsickness while trying to prove himself to his veteran American instructor Steve Britt (Foster) who happens to be a friend of Peter's late father. The basis for the plot was the Army's program for training Chinese, American and British cadets for overseas service. Wellman's touch along with Paul Mantz' experience made the aerial cinematography worth watching.

The flight line at Falcon Field in Mesa, Arizona for *Thunder Birds*. AT-6 and BT-13 trainers in view. *Collection of William A. Wellman, Jr.*

Lest the reader assume that only men could be pilots in this period, we conclude this chapter by discussing *Ladies Courageous*, starring the beautiful Loretta Young and the plucky Geraldine Fitzgerald. Roberta Harper (Young) commands the fledgling Women's Auxiliary Ferrying Squadron (WAFS),), which ferries planes from the factories to military airfields.

Roberta knows there is some prejudice and concern about the WAFS' ability to fly long missions, so she is under pressure to prove that her female aviators are just as capable as the male pilots. Roberta's sister Vergie (Fitzgerald) is an ambitious glory seeker who makes Roberta's life even more difficult.

WAFS pilot Nadine courts Alex Anderson, who is betrothed to flyer Jill. Superstitious pilot Gerry Vail approaches her 100th mission with worry since her barnstorming father and brother were killed on their 100th exhibition flight. Roberta calms Gerry by saying she'd already flown her 100th mission.

The WAFS receive their first overseas delivery to a secret South Pacific base. The mission is canceled when Virgie deliberately crashes her plane during a military review to garner headlines. Her ego is hit hard when she sees her husband being taken to Leavenworth for desertion. Roberta, whose own husband is listed as missing in action, washes Virgie out of the WAFS. Roberta resigns, but Vergie steals a plane to fly to Washington and clear things up. Vergie crashes on takeoff.

Finally the Army accepts the WAFS into their ranks as the Women's Air Service Pilots (WASP). Their first mission is to deliver planes to the South Pacific. Roberta learns her husband is safe and they are reunited.

This is much more an aerial soap opera than a serious aviation drama. The women, particularly Loretta Young, appear as though they spend all their time in the beauty parlor between flights and histrionic displays of drama. Turnabout was fair play as two beautiful women dueled for one man—lucky devil.

Universal had the full cooperation of the USAAF in producing the film based on the Virginia Spencer Cowles novel. John Rawlins, who was best known for Saturday morning *Dick Tracy* films, directed what was called the "official motion picture story of the WAFS."

Shot almost exclusively at Long Beach Army Air Force Base, the film has some dramatic flying scenes. Sixth Ferry Group Squadron Commander Barbara London and five pilots did most of the flying but still managed to tend to their regular duties. Even before the cameras, the WAFS had something to prove to the male-dominated aviation world.

The WAFS and the later WASPS were a critical boost to the war effort by taking over the job of ferrying planes from male pilots who were needed for combat service. The WAFS had a long and trying climb to prove themselves, but noted aviatrixes such as Jackie Cochran and Nancy Love were the driving force that made it into a reality.

The author interviewed one former WASP who declined to be identified. "I served through all of 1944 from North American Aviation in California, flying B-25s and AT-6 Texans," she said. "I was proud of what we did. All of us were. I saw that movie just after it came out. We were excited at first, but it made us look like a bunch of drama queens with perfect makeup and hairdos. Just junk, is all it was."

CHAPTER SIX

The War in the Air: Europe

On September 1, 1939, Germany invaded Poland—only the first nation to fall under the Nazi Blitzkrieg. But even as Hitler's legions swept virtually unchallenged over Eastern Europe, a glimmer of hope was holding fast in the west. France and Britain were poised to resist. While France would fall in the summer of 1940, Britain held on, forever changing the world's opinion of "underdogs" and "fighting for a hopeless cause."

The RAF was fully prepared not only to resist but also fling the Germans back into the sea. By the fall of 1940 a new hero was born in the skies over Britain: the RAF fighter pilot.

Scores of war and aviation films—some accurate, some apocryphal, but all compelling—were released within months of the start of the war.

The first film was about the birth of the beloved Supermarine Spitfire, deservedly considered the most famous and beautiful plane ever built. And it, along with the Hawker Hurricane, was the instrument of the Luftwaffe's downfall in 1940. *Spitfire* (1942) was released by the appropriately named British Aviation Pictures Ltd. Originally called *The First of the Few*, the film begins during September 1940 as German bombers are striking London. Squadron Leader Geoffrey Crisp (David Niven) tells other pilots the story of the Spitfire's birth. As a friend of the late Reginald J. Mitchell, Crisp relates the Mitchell's struggles to convince a parsimonious Air Ministry of the need for a fast new fighter. Mitchell is played by Leslie Howard, star of *Gone With the Wind* and *The Petrified Forest*. With little effort the gentle, soft-spoken Howard makes Mitchell a fragile but heroic figure.

The scourge of the Luftwaffe during the Battle of Britain, the beloved Supermarine Spitfire inspired a movie about its origins.

Mitchell is dying of cancer and is desperate to see his dream take flight. He designed several Schneider Trophy-winning seaplanes and earned the respect of the staid Air Ministry. A visit to Germany brings him in contact with Willy Messerschmitt, designer of the Spitfire's future rival, and several Luftwaffe generals. Mitchell is shocked to learn the Germans are no longer abiding by the terms of the Treaty of Versailles and are in fact aggressively building an air force.

Mitchell convinces the head of Rolls-Royce to design a new engine, then drives himself to total exhaustion to make the plane a reality. An Air Ministry official tells Mitchell, "We'll need it in twelve months. That's all the time we can give you." Mitchell, with a sad smile, says, "You shall have it in eight. Because that's all the time I can give *you*." The film wraps with Mitchell's death as the Spitfire, now part of Britain's defense, takes to the skies.

A German attack ends Crisp's story and he leads his pilots into the sky. After the Germans are slaughtered Crisp gazes wistfully into the heavens and says, "They can't take the Spitfires, Mitch. They can't take 'em."

The willowy Howard bears little resemblance to Mitchell, who was a robust and athletic man. A sad irony is that Howard himself had less than a year to live. He died in a KLM DC-3 when it was shot down by a German plane over the Bay of Biscay in June 1943.

Mitchell never visited Germany or met Messerschmitt. Geoffrey Crisp is a montage of two pilots, "Mutt" Summers and Vickers test pilot Jeffery Quill. Quill appears in the film as a Spitfire pilot.

Some Battle of Britain pilots have roles in the opening and closing scenes. Group Captain Brian Kingcombe, DSO DFC earned eight victories. Squadron Leader Tony Bartley, DFC also had eight kills.

In the film Mitchell created the name "Spitfire" but in reality he was told what Supermarine planned to call the new fighter. Mitchell is said to have sighed, "That's just the sort of bloody silly name they'd choose."

Spitfire has a great deal to offer the aviation-loving viewer, including rare archival footage of several planes, including the Supermarine S4 taking off from Southampton and in flight. The original footage is long lost. Much of the combat footage is real, taken from gun-camera film and other sources during the Battle of Britain. *Spitfire* was released while RAF Spitfires were actively engaging German planes over France.

The Battle of Britain (1969) was directed by Guy Hamilton, best known for several of the James Bond films. Twenty-nine years after the actual event it tells the story of Fighter Command's titanic efforts to hold off the Luftwaffe and prevent a German invasion. An all-star cast, excellent cinematography, technical accuracy and lots of airplanes make the film a true classic.

Shot on location in Britain, Spain and France, the film begins just as France is about to fall. Air Chief Marshal Sir Hugh "Stuffy" Dowding, played with great dignity by Lawrence Olivier, informs the Prime Minister that there is no further point in sending valuable men and planes to fight on the Continent. They must be saved for home defense.

A number of characters and situations are introduced, running the gamut of crusty impatient veterans and green newcomers to dedicated flight controllers and dry-humored air base commanders. Failed Stuka raids on RAF radar stations portend the coming battle, while the men and women of RAF Fighter Command under the leadership of Air Vice Marshal Keith Park (Trevor Howard) work out the tactics to foil

A detailed radio-controlled miniature of a Hawker Hurricane used in *The Battle of Britain.*

the Germans. A great deal of technical information is fed to the audience, including the disposition of the fighter bases and how the alert is sounded.

The early bombing raids attract small groups of fighters into the sky to take on hoards of Heinkel He-111 bombers. As the battle continues more of the men are drained by fatigue from constant fighting. The German pilots are at first enthusiastic but are soon depressed by their heavy losses.

When the Luftwaffe responds to a British raid on Berlin, the tide turns in favor of Fighter Command. By bombing London the Germans are no longer in effective range of their fighters and are vulnerable to Spitfires and Hurricanes of 12 Group, farther north. September 15, 1940, is the great day, when hundreds of bombers and whole wings of RAF fighters swarm over England. The sky rains burning German planes. At the end, the German invasion force is seen tossing their equipment into piles and climbing onto trucks. The threat is over. Winston Churchill's words, "Never in the field of human conflict was so much owed by so many to so few," begin the end credits.

The film is truly epic in scope. The author interviewed Geoff Simpson, a trustee of the Battle of Britain Memorial Trust. He corresponded with several surviving veterans on the author's behalf and said the general consensus it that the film is accurate in most respects, if not in actual characters. Simpson went on to say, "The depiction of squadron dispersal and coordination was correctly done, as is the growing fatigue of the pilots. Some license was taken as in the scene where the bomber crashes in London while the RAF pilot comes down under his parachute. But they are real events."

All the British scenes were shot on or near the actual airfields used in 1940. RAF Duxford, North Weald, Debden and Hawkinge were used for the dispersal and airfield scenes. RAF Bentley Priory, home of Fighter Command, was also opened for location filming.

Over a dozen British and German technical advisors worked on the movie. "Ginger" Lacey was a Battle of Britain legend and triple ace, and General Adolf Galland was one of Goering's top wing commanders with 103 victories. The long list of advisors assured the film would be accurate, both technically and historically.

Former Luftwaffe fighter commander Adolf Galland served as one of the dozen technical advisors for *The Battle of Britain.*

Unlike most American air war films, this one pays more than lip service to the need for radio discipline in combat. The RAF pilots are downright laconic in the cockpit. Michael Caine, even as he vectors his flight towards the Germans, seems on the verge of boredom.

As for the aircraft, let us start with the Germans. Thirty-two Heinkel He-111s, called the CASA 2.111, were obtained from the Spanish Air Force. In fact, one of them had been Francisco Franco's personal transport. No Dornier Do-17, Junkers Ju-88 or Me-110 twin-engine bombers were available.

Spanish Air Force CASA 2.111s were repainted as Luftwaffe He-111 bombers for the production.

For the Stuka attack on the radar masts, an original Ju-87 was deemed too expensive to restore to flying condition. Instead a pair of Percival Proctors were modified to resemble the Stuka, and called "Protukas." In addition, 27 Hispano Aviacion 1112 Bochon fighters were modified for the movie to resemble Me-109Es. Ironically nearly all the German planes used Rolls-Royce Merlin engines.

The production was able to find seven later model Spitfires, but only one Spitfire MkI and one MkIIa were available. The MkII had seen combat in the actual battle. The planes were painted in period schemes, with some modifications to canopies, wingtips and other features. Three flyable and three non-flying Hurricanes were also used. Large-scale radio-controlled models exploded and crashed on the beaches or in the water. Battle footage was filmed in flight.

A brightly-painted B-25 Mitchell was used as the primary camera ship. The garish scheme served to help fighter pilots to more quickly line up their approach. Bad weather and overcast caused Hamilton to move the production to Spain for clearer skies.

One of the two Percival Proctors modified as Ju-87 Stukas. The distinctive gull-winged aircraft were dubbed 'Protukas' by the production crew.

One character of note is that of Squadron Leader Evans, played by W.G. Foxley, who had been an RAF navigator. He was badly burned in a 1944 crash attempting to save another airman. Evans was based on the late Tom Cleave, a fighter pilot who also served as technical advisor.

At the start of the German offensive, Group Captain Baker, played by *Reach for the Sky's* Kenneth More, is reprimanding Section Officer Maggie Harvey about using her gas mask case as a handbag. He fails to notice the bombs falling in the far background. It's excellently done with the sound arriving a few moments after the blast. An aerial shot shows the bombers dropping their payload on the field. The blasts are just what a 50kg bomb would have created.

Field Marshal Hermann Goering is portrayed as an overstuffed, bombastic martinet with more medals than a South American dictator. He alternately berates and coddles his pilots, asking what they need to defeat the RAF. One pilot, who was based on Adolf Galland, responds, "Ein geschwader von Spitfires"—a squadron of Spitfires. Needless to say Herr Goering wasn't amused.

At least three American films about Americans fighting for the RAF were produced prior to December 1941. Bearing in mind the large percentage of Jewish movie moguls it's not surprising how many studios relentlessly kept the heat on Hitler. American audiences were fascinated with a new generation of Yanks dueling in the skies over Britain, just as William Wellman and his comrades had done in 1917.

The garishly-painted B-25 camera plane used in *The Battle of Britain* allowed the pilots to line up their attack approaches quickly for filming.

Twentieth Century Fox was the first to throw its hat into the ring in support of England. *A Yank in the RAF* (1941) featured two of the top stars of the time: handsome, dark-eyed Tyrone Power and curvaceous Betty Grable, whose photo would soon grace many a G.I. footlocker.

Power is Tim Baker, a ferry pilot who meets his old flame in London. She coaxes the cocky pilot to make a difference in the war against Germany. He joins the RAF, and after a long sequence of training begins flying missions over France. He shows total confidence in his abilities but lacks team spirit, which does not endear him to his fellow pilots. Eventually the sacrifices of his comrades convinces Baker how much his work is needed and he becomes the total RAF pilot, loyal and brave to the cause.

Fox was able to obtain a wealth of combat footage from the Air Ministry, eager to assist any film to help gain American support. The studio was also permitted to send director Henry King and his cameramen to film RAF bases and operations for background footage. King spent weeks looking for places in California resembling Dover, France and Holland.

The studio built several full-scale mockups and smaller scale models of Spitfires, Messerschmitts and Hudsons. Employees at the Lockheed plant in Burbank, California, played RAF mechanics in the film.

King's own plane was used as the camera ship to shoot aerial footage of ferrying Hudson bombers and training. Although all the combat footage is real, the majority of the battle sequences were created in the Fox studios. Special effects wizards Fred Sersen and his team used lenses with a 1:1 ratio to provide an effective full-scale appearance to the rear-projection footage.

The evacuation of Dunkirk was filmed at Point Mugu on the California coast.

An original ending had Power being killed, but Darryl Zanuck was persuaded by the British to change it. The British feared that Americans would assume Yanks were doomed to die in the effort. A new ending was shot before the film's September 1941 release.

Colonel Steve Pisanos, the "Flying Greek," served in No. 71 Eagle Squadron in the RAF before joining the USAAF to fly Thunderbolts and Mustangs. He became a double ace and went on to be a test pilot. *Author's Collection*

The author interviewed Colonel Steve Pisanos, who before joining the USAAF and becoming a P-51 Mustang ace with the 4th Fighter Group had been in RAF No. 71 Eagle Squadron. Pisanos, known as "The Flying Greek" and author of the book of the same name, served in the Eagle Squadron in the summer of 1940 until September 1942 when he joined the USAAF.

"The Tyrone Power movie was technically accurate," Pisanos said. "I really enjoyed it." When asked about some of the details the 93-year old ace related his training as being close to what is in the film. "I was trained in the Harvards over here, but when I got to England I was in the Miles Master in an Advanced Training Unit, an ATU. Then I went into Hurricanes and Spitfires."

A Yank in the RAF was a huge success for Fox and for the war effort. To this day it remains a romance and war classic. It was followed the same year by *International Squadron*, produced by Hal Wallis and directed by Louis Seiler. *International Squadron* starred Ronald Reagan as a ferry pilot bringing Hudson bombers to Britain.

The screenplay has a lot of *A Yank in the RAF* in it. Warner Brothers, in an attempt to beat Fox to the punch, used whatever aircraft and locations could be obtained quickly and at low cost. Airfields and aircraft from around the Los Angeles basin were used for the film. An eclectic collection of airplanes, including three Ryan STAs, a Boeing 100, a Brown B3 Racer and a Travel Air, were cobbled together to serve as the RAF's top fighters. The resulting film is far below Warners' usual standards. Shot at Van Nuys and Alhambra Airports, the film had little to offer audiences.

Darryl Zanuck threatened a lawsuit if *International Squadron* was released before *A Yank in the RAF*. Warners held off until October 1941—barely two months before America's entry into the war.

Universal produced *Eagle Squadron*, the worst of the three American films that celebrated the RAF. Released in 1942, *Eagle Squadron*—whose screenplay was adapted from a story by *Horatio Hornblower* author C.S. Forester—has Robert Stack as a young and impassioned American joining the RAF Eagle Squadron. Stack resents the blasé attitude of his fellow fliers, believing them to be uncaring and heartless. But in time Stack comes to realize that the RAF pilots are dedicated to their job and do care about the men they fly with. He volunteers to undertake a hazardous mission in France to steal a Messerschmitt fighter and bring it back to Britain. The plot is hackneyed and thin.

Ernest Schoenstack, best known as producer of *King Kong*, spent six weeks in Britain filming Eagle Squadron bases and operations for background footage. The majority of the flying was done in the studio with mockups and models.

Regarding *Eagle Squadron*, Pisanos said, "We really disapproved of that film. I didn't like it at all. In fact when the film was being shown in London we were told not to even go to the theater."

America's entry into the war necessitated the creation of an aerial armada never seen before or since. Thousands of planes and hundreds of thousands of airmen and ground crew swelled the British Isles, North Africa and the Mediterranean to bring the fight to the skies over Europe.

It was a learning experience for the Yanks. Their confidence was bolstered by advanced weaponry, but the tactics were far from settled. USAAF doctrine was based on the perceived accuracy of the famed Norden bombsight to hit targets from 20,000 feet of altitude. In practice it proved to be a very difficult task. The British openly criticized the policy as suicidal.

But beginning in late 1942 American bombing raids over France were conducted in daylight, first with scores, then hundreds and eventually thousands of B-17s, B-24s, B-25s, B-26s and A-20s. General Ira. C. Eaker, commander of the 8th Bomber Command, doggedly persisted in promoting daylight bombing despite heavy losses. Aircrew morale was low. Enter Colonel Frank A. Armstrong, former commander of the 97th Bomb Group, the first B-17 group in England. Armstrong was sent to the "hard luck" 306th Group, which had experienced the highest rate of aircraft losses and the lowest tonnage of bombs delivered on target. Armstrong arrived at Thurleigh to whip the 306th into shape and forge them into a highly effective unit. He led them on the very first raid into Germany.

This was the origin for *Twelve O'clock High*, released in 1949. Writers Beirne Lay, Jr., and Sy Bartlett had both seen combat with the 8th Air Force and wrote what is considered the best air war film ever made.

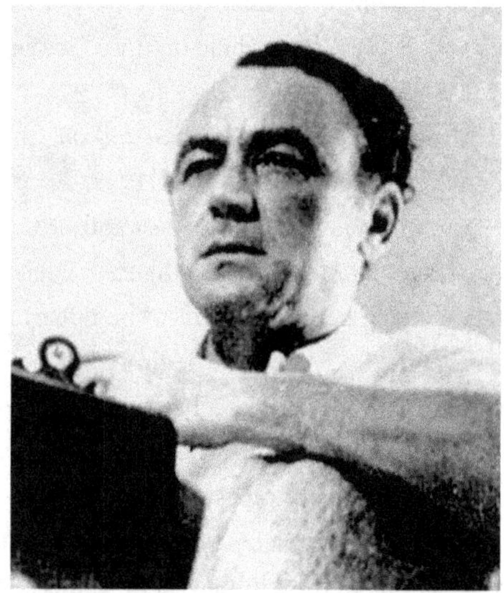

Beirne Lay, Jr. and Sy Bartlettt wrote the screenplay for *12 O'Clock High* and other films. Both men served in the USAAF during the war.

The movie opens in 1948 with Harvey Stovall, played with wonderful warmth by Dean Jagger, in London. Spotting a Toby mug in a shop window, he buys it and takes a trip down memory lane to the village of Archbury, where his old unit, the 918th Bomb Group, was based. The audience is taken back to 1942, the first year of the USAAF daylight bombing campaign. The 918th Group has been suffering fearful losses to German attacks, and morale is dangerously low. Colonel Keith Davenport (Gary Merrill) cares deeply for his men and allows them to lose the combat edge they so need to fight and survive in the air.

General Frank Savage (Gregory Peck) is ordered by General Pritchard to relieve Davenport and take over the 918th. Savage relentlessly trains the men and boosts their morale. He demotes poor officers and promotes good ones. He comes down hard on Lt. Colonel Ben Gately (Hugh Marlowe), whom Savage sees as a lazy coward. Savage forces

Gately to take command of a "deadbeat" crew of the worst men in the group. Gately's plane is named *Leper Colony.*

Stovall, the group's adjutant, is a sounding board for Savage's policies and progress.

Eventually even the hard-nosed Savage succumbs to the strain and grows to love his men, which leads to his own psychological breakdown at a critical moment.

Twelve O'clock High, while not an action war film, is nevertheless a classic. Henry King worked real magic on the movie, eliciting some of the best characterizations ever done from a cast of superb actors. The production was filmed on location in Florida and Alabama over a six-week period in early 1949. At Eglin AFB in Florida the studio built Quonset huts, a briefing room, a control tower and administration buildings to 8th AF specifications. The early scenes where Stovall returns to Archbury were filmed at the abandoned Ozark Field in Alabama, where the overgrown and decrepit condition was perfect for the post-war sequences. Ozark, which Henry King stated "was more English than any other field I have seen in that country," also possessed wartime dark-surfaced runways and taxiways. After the weeds and overgrown brush was removed, Ozark Field served for the takeoff and landing sequences.

Gregory Peck as General Frank Savage in *12 O'Clock High.* The flight gear he wears is actually of a type not issued to bomber crews until 1944, nearly two years after the period depicted in the film.
Courtesy Bruce Orriss

The Air Force cooperated fully on the project, providing twelve B-17Fs. Several had been used as radio-controlled drones in the Bikini Atoll atom bomb tests and still showed traces of radioactivity. The crews could only work in them for short times and they had to be periodically washed down. The aircraft were painted with the markings and insignia of the 91st Bomb Group with the "triangle A" emblem on the tail.

The belly landing in the opening wartime sequence was flown by Paul Mantz. He had to slide into a line of bell tents and come to a stop as close to King's cameras as possible. The four throttles were fitted with a welded rod to allow Mantz to perform a two-man job.

Most of the combat sequences were done in the Fox studio with full-scale mockups. The mockup in which Gregory Peck is seen was built with a radial engine and propeller just outside the left window to provide visible spinning blade tips.

In an interview with B-17 pilot Ed Davidson, who flew with the 96th Group in 1943-44, the author asked about the realism of the film. Davidson replied, "*Twelve O'clock High* is the best bomber movie there is. It doesn't have much combat but the sounds, the feel of the action, is perfect. I think it's a great film in every way."

Davidson isn't alone. While interviewing combat crews for this book the author found in nearly every case universal praise for the film. One B-17 gunner commented, "Those .50 caliber machine guns sound like solid thumps, just as the real guns did."

Gregory Peck in the pilot's seat of 'Picadilly Lily,' the full-scale B-17 nose mockup. Note the spinning propeller which added a high element of realism to the sequence. *Courtesy Bruce Orriss*

A few anachronisms are seen in the combat footage. A German fighter is played by a Republic P-47D Thunderbolt, seen in a three-quarter view.

Twelve O'clock High is often used in military leadership courses at the U.S. Naval Academy at Annapolis, according to Captain Dick Evert, a retired Naval aviator. The movie earned several Academy Award nominations and a Best Supporting Actor Oscar for Dean Jagger.

While most air war movies attempted to convey what it was like to fly bombers in combat, they generally fall short in three respects: the brute power of roaring engines, shaking airframes, and the cramped interior. Having been fortunate enough to ride in a B-17, the author realized how inadequately film reproduces reality.

The noise of four powerful Wright Cyclone engines is a force, not a sound, as it permeates the airframe. The plane shakes and shudders with none of the smoothness we have all come to expect on a commercial airliner. Conversation is virtually impossible. A B-17 looks like a huge plane from the ground, but negotiating the interior from the tail to nose is like threading a needle. The bomb bay catwalk is only eight inches wide, set between two angled racks. Only by expelling all breath was the author, at a burly 250 pounds, able to squeeze through. Yet in most movies the crew runs through the plane as if they were four-year olds.

The next film in our historical chronology is *Memphis Belle* (1990). The movie opens on the day before the *Belle's* crew is to fly its 25th and last mission. Colonel Harriman (David Strathairn) is caught between concern for his crews and the badgering of callous public relations officer Derringer (John Lithgow).

96th Bomb Group B-17 pilot Edwin Davidson during advance flight training in 1943.
Courtesy Ed Davidson

Belle's Captain Dennis Dearborn, played by rising star Matthew Modine, is a serious officer only concerned with the mission. The crew is an eclectic bunch of dramatic personalities, from a self-professed ladies' man to a former whorehouse piano player, from an Irish Catholic dreamer to a cocky co-pilot. The ten crewmembers have five antagonistic pairings, which during the course of the film neatly resolve their mutual issues.

Their target is Bremen, known as "flak city." The mission goes badly with a heavy smokescreen forcing the group to come around and approach the target again. *Belle's* navigator, sure he is doomed, tries to force the bombardier to jettison the load so they can return to base. The co-pilot desperately wants to shoot down a German fighter and takes over the tail guns. He hits an Me-109, but it careens out of control and slices through the fuselage of another B-17 crewed by rookies.

While the *Belle* is away, Derringer, concerned only with publicity, is taken to task by Harriman, who forces him to read several letters from the families of dead crewmen. Derringer realizes how fragile the young lives are.

The ball turret gunner, played by *Rudy* star Sean Astin, who had been teasing the flight engineer about being a virgin, is nearly killed when his turret is shot to pieces. The engineer pulls him from the shredded turret. The waist gunners have their own personal issues.

Sean Astin as ball turret gunner Sgt. Richard "Rascal" Moore in *Memphis Belle. Author's Collection*

Finally they are once again on the bomb run and successfully hit the target. The radioman is seriously wounded, and an engine catches fire after being hit by flak. Only a desperate dive by the pilots extinguishes the flames. Then the right wheel refuses to extend. The flight engineer has to manually lower it. In a tense build-up, the *Belle* narrowly escapes destruction when the wheel locks down a mere second before touchdown. After landing, the crew celebrates.

The plot is totally fictional. The real *Memphis Belle*, a 91st Group B-17F out of Bassingbourn, England, was the first plane whose crew flew the required twenty-five missions to complete a combat tour. Their last mission was in May 1943 over Lorient, France, and not nearly as hairy as depicted in the movie.

Robert Morgan, the *Belle's* pilot, said of the film that more happened in that one mission than could have happened if he'd flown another fifty missions. The real *Belle's* nose art was less extravagant than appears on film—just simple block letters. But that wouldn't have looked as good on the posters.

The original crew of the 'Memphis Belle' in 1943. Left to right: Top turret gunner Harold Loch, ball gunner Cecil Scott, radio operator Robert Hanson, co-pilot Jim Vernis, pilot Robert Morgan, navigator Chuck Leighton, tail gunner John Quinlan, waist gunner Tony Nastal, bombardier Vince Evans and waist gunner Bill Winchell. Several of the crew were on hand to provide technical assistance to the actors during filming in England.

Yet while largely apocryphal *Memphis Belle* is the *Das Boot* of bomber movies. It conveys how frightening aerial combat was. Being trapped in an aluminum tube more than four miles above a hostile country and watching other planes torn to bits and falling to earth is something no airman could ever forget.

Interior and effects filming was done at Pinewood Studios. An unused RAF base at Binbrook in Lincolnshire was the location for the ground and flying scenes. Other exterior sequences were done in Duxford.

Five B-17s were collected from the U.S. and Europe. All but one of the Fortresses were B-17G models with the chin turret removed. B-17G *Sally B,* owned by the B-17 Preservation Trust in England, played several planes. The sole F model, N17W, is owned by Seattle's Museum of Flight. Dan Hagedorn, the museum's curator, told the author the plane is now restored to perfect wartime condition, with every detail as perfect as can be. "When someone walks into our B-17F they are stepping into history," said Hagedorn.

The elaborate nose art on B-17G 'Sally B' for the filming of *Memphis Belle*. Compare this with the actual nose are in the crew photo.

Seven P-51Ds were gathered for the film, despite that there were no 51Ds in England in May 1943. Three veteran HA 1112 Bochons used in The *Battle of Britain* appeared as 109s.

Famed aviation writer Bruce Orriss, known for his love of the B-17, was one of the production's technical advisors. He worked with the intention of making sure the film historically and technically toed the line. The B-17s were not only painted correctly but "weathered and battle-worn" with chips and scrapes from combat. Orriss also worked on assembling original or reproduction flight gear. Fleece-lined leather suits, oxygen masks, helmets, Mae West life preservers and other paraphernalia were as correct as possible. Several "billboard" mockups were placed in the background. Some ten-foot wingspan radio-controlled models moved in the foreground while the real planes were in the background.

Most of the aerial photography was shot from the B-25 camera ship *Dolly*, formerly owned by Tallmanz Aviation and now by Aces High. A modified Grumman TBM Avenger served as another camera ship, and cameras were mounted in some of the Mustangs as well. *Memphis Belle* used real Browning machine guns.

Orriss and Tommy Garcia, another B-17 buff and restorer, worked with Pinewood Studios to perfect the interior of a 1943 B-17F. They worked from 8 a.m. to midnight for weeks. Garcia coached the actors how to operate the guns and speak while wearing oxygen masks. In the sequence in which D.B. Sweeney as the flight engineer has to crank down the landing gear, Garcia said wartime B-17s had emergency cables to allow the doors to fall open. The script was modified to have Sweeney trip the cables and nearly fall out. A full-scale mockup with ball turret was built twenty feet above the sound stage floor for underside photography. Spent blank cartridges rained down on the heads of the production crew so less harmful rubber cartridges ware substituted.

Ball turret gunner Ed Silverstone had this to say about *Memphis Belle*: "I thought it was very accurate, as far as the ball turret goes. It was just like that. Cramped and isolated. And that's what flak was like. The plane shook like hell. All you could do was wait it out and pray."

Silverstone commented on the young age of the crew. "I was nineteen when I flew in the 100th. All the guys were young, even the officers. There was a sign on our Officers Club door that said something like, 'Any officer below the rank of Colonel must bring his mother along,'" he laughed.

There's a curious statement made by Val the bombardier (Billy Zane six years before his role as Cal Hockley in *Titanic*) when the crew is trying to help Danny, the wounded radio operator. Knowing that he can't do anything, Val suggests putting a parachute on Danny and pushing him out to be picked up by the Germans on the ground. Val says, "Another crew did it. This guy lost an arm."

Val is referring to *Twelve O'clock High*, when a bomber crewman tells Dean Jagger he put a chute on a wounded top turret gunner and pushed him out to be taken by the Germans to a hospital. That happened to a 92nd Group plane, *Ruthie II*, on a raid over Hannover in July 1943. The top turret gunner, Tyre Weaver , was hit by a 20mm shell from an Fw-190 which blew off his left arm at the shoulder. Navigator Keith Koske knew Weaver wouldn't survive until they reached base, so Koske helped Weaver into the forward hatch. After tumbling out of the plane, Weaver was able to pull his ripcord and was picked up by German troops and taken to a hospital. He later let his comrades know he was in Stalag Luft IV.

Boeing B-17F N17W was used for 'C-Cup' in *Memphis Belle*. This aircraft, after undergoing more than sevneteen years of painstaking work, has been restored to original 1943 condition and is on display at Seattle's Museum of Flight.

The author interviewed Sean Astin, who played Sgt. Richard "Rascal" Moore, the lothario of the crew. When asked about the filming and what it meant to him, Astin replied, "My initial impression of being in the B-17 was that it was a lot smaller than I thought. Crawling through the fuselage was terribly claustrophobic."

Astin and the other actors were able to talk to the survivors of the original crew. "Eight of the original crew came over to England and we spent some time together," said Astin. "One night in particular at a pub, everybody drinking lots of English ale, they regaled us with stories of their experiences. Their stories were funny and harrowing. Our performances were made vivid because of our extraordinary opportunity to spend time with them."

During the filming one of the French B-17s, *Baby Ruth*, crashed on takeoff after losing directional control and clipping a wing on a tree. The gear collapsed. Amazingly the crash was nearly identical to one created by the special effects department for the film. "[The B-17] split in two in the crash," Astin explained. "Nobody was killed, thank God, but a column of thick and dense smoke went up into the sky."

"Getting to fly in formation with a couple of other B-17s and Mustangs and Messerschmitts screaming around us is one of the greatest things I've ever done in my life,"

Astin said. *Memphis Belle*, while fictional, is as close as Hollywood is ever likely to get to what it was like to fly a B-17 in combat.

Columbia's *The War Lover* (1962) took on the touchy topic of a man who sees war as a grand game. B-17 pilot Captain Buzz Rickson (Steve McQueen) has a zeal for combat and a belief in his own invincibility. His co-pilot, Ed Boland (Robert Wagner), is less sanguine about war and sees his commander as a heartless killer. During a raid, Rickson disobeys orders to return to base when heavy cloud cover is reported over the target. He continues on and drops his bombs over Kiel.

After flying twenty-three missions with no injuries, Rickman is convinced he can't be killed. But he also fears what it will be like when he can't kill Germans any more. On their next mission over Leipzig, the plane is seriously hit and Rickman has to deal with several wounded men. Over the Channel he orders his crew to bail out while he tries to save the crippled plane. Rickson, still fighting to stay in control, flies the B-17 straight into the White Cliffs of Dover.

The screenplay for *The War Lover* was based on a novel by John Hershey. The aerial sequences are spectacular, the drama compelling and the climax stunning. For the production three B-17s were ferried to England. One of the pilots was acclaimed writer Martin Caidin, who later wrote *Marooned* and *Cyborg*, the book that inspired the TV series *The Six Million Dollar Man*. Two Fortresses were coastal rescue planes and needed extensive reconfiguration with turrets and other wartime gear.

The production was done in black-and-white to make use of stock combat footage and shots from previous movies. The Paul Mantz belly-landing scene from *Twelve O'clock High* appears in *War Lover*. Location shooting was done at RAF Bovington in Hertfordshire and RAF Manston in Kent. Sound stage and effects work were done at Shepperton Studios.

According to the author's interviews with 8th AF veterans this film correctly depicts briefings and preflight checks. Rickson talks to his ground crew chief and asks about specific items like low manifold pressure, oil and fuel load, just as a real pilot would. The two men also review details about the bomb load—information that a pilot would need to correctly trim the plane's center of gravity.

Director Phillip Leacock's cameras captured several interesting angles of takeoff. Puffs of exhaust from the engines, flaps lowering, an underside shot of the landing gear coming up and a shot from through the windshield add to the film's unique cinematography. A clear shot of a propeller being feathered appears during the Leipzig raid.

Yet there is too much open radio chatter. Former 301st Bomb Group radio operator Frank Sexton told the author proper procedure was to keep off the radio at all times. "Only emergency communications were permitted," Sexton said. "All that chatter would have earned a serious rebuke from group."

During a raid over Kiel, the sound of the exploding bombs is clearly heard. "Never heard a single bomb burst in my entire twenty-five missions," said 100th Group ball turret gunner Ed Silverstone. "It's just too loud in the plane and you're too high up."

One of the gunners is portrayed by Michael Crawford, destined for fame as the lead in Andrew Lloyd Webber's stage musical *Phantom of the Opera* in 1986.

In 1948 MGM released *Command Decision*. General Casey Dennis (Clark Gable) takes drastic steps to send bombers to destroy factories where the new Lanz-Wolf jet fighter is built. Bomber Command's Major General Kane (Walter Pidgeon) fights Dennis' fanatical determination to attack the factories despite huge projected losses. Dennis knows that unless the Lanz-Wolf is stopped it will take the lives of many more men later on.

The two antagonists square off to make a decision that will affect the course of the war and the lives of hundreds of young airmen. Seen to be too radical in his long-range theories, Dennis is relieved of command. But his successor, Brigadier General Garnet, played by *Beau Geste* star Brian Donlevy, soon takes up Dennis' torch and carries on. The raid does destroy the factories, ultimately saves the lives of many more airmen. Dennis is vindicated.

Director Sam Wood, who did sterling work on *For Whom the Bell Tolls* and *Pride of the Yankees*, was able to get the most from the talents of Gable, Pidgeon and Brian Donlevy.

The production was primarily filmed at March Air Force Base, and one scene was done at San Fernando Valley Airport beside two B-17s. Gable had been filmed flying the first YB-17 in *Test Pilot* and flown Fortresses in combat during the war. In *Command Decision* he had come full circle, back to March and the B-17 for a final time.

Clark Gable as a gunner in the 351st Bomb Group in England.

MGM's Victor Fleming and writer Dalton Trumbo created *A Guy Named Joe* (1943), starring Spencer Tracy, Irene Dunne and Van Johnson. The plot follows a cocky and argumentative B-25 pilot named Pete Sandidge (Tracy) who is in love with WASP ferry pilot Dorinda (Dunne). Pete has flown several harrowing missions against Germany, so Colonel "Nails" Kilpatrick, played by the crusty, nasal-voiced James Gleason, feels Sandidge needs a break from combat and orders him to Scotland. Dorinda urges Pete to take an instructor billet in the States instead. Pete agrees but takes on one more mission with his best friend Al Yackey (Ward Bond).

After bombing a German carrier, and sustaining damage to his aircraft, Pete orders the crew to bail out. He then crashes his plane into the ship. Pete finds himself in a strange netherworld of clouds and people he knows to be dead. He is introduced to "The General," played by the granddaddy of all film heavies, Lionel Barrymore himself. Pete is assigned to be a guardian angel to Ted Randall (Johnson), a new, nervous cadet.

Spencer Tracy as reckless B-25 pilot-turned guardian angel Pete Sandidge in *A Guy Named Joe*.

Ted meets Dorinda, who soon falls for him. Ted is then sent to the South Pacific to fly P-38s. Pete, who resented the new romance, has a change of heart. When Dorinda learns her new love is going to fly a dangerous mission to destroy a Japanese ammunition dump she takes a plane and flies it instead, destroying the target. It's the traditional love triangle with a new twist. *A Guy Named Joe* is a true classic.

In the opening scenes, while Sandidge lands at his base, there are children waiting around for him as if he were Santa Claus in Army khaki. Don Defore, who would later be famous as "Mr. B" from television's *Hazel*, is one of the P-38 pilots. Future *Pink Panther* series director Blake Edwards has an uncredited role as a pilot.

Nearly all the flying sequences were filmed in rear-projection behind mockups at MGM studios, using authentic training and flying footage. It's a rare opportunity to see Lockheed P-38s in flight. Since the studio had no actual combat footage, they used the talents of special effects wizard A. Arnold Gillespie to create the action sequences in miniature on the backlot.

Pete's B-25 attack on the German carrier was one of Gillespie's gems. While the smoke streaming from the plane is too slow, the bombing and subsequent fiery crash are very realistic.

The Kriegsmarine aircraft carrier *Graf Zeppelin* never saw service.

The P-38E came from Drew Field in Florida. It only had electric motors but with appropriate sound effects served for filming.

Major Edward Hillary was technical advisor, having had extensive experience in AAF operations as a P-40, P-39 and later P-38 squadron commander in the Pacific. General Henry A. "Hap" Arnold, commanding general of the Army Air Forces, visited the Culver City studios during production.

The role of "The General" is supposedly based on the father of American air power, General William "Billy" Mitchell.

After appearing as Han Solo in *Star Wars*, Harrison Ford starred in *Hanover Street* in 1979 with Lesley-Anne Down. The film is little more than a sappy love story set against the backdrop of the air war. Ford is Lt. David Haloran, a B-25 pilot who meets a British nurse in an air raid shelter. They fall in love, but she has failed to mention she is married to a British agent. After David is shot down he returns to England and later accepts a dangerous intelligence flight over France. His passenger is his lover's husband.

Hanover Street isn't much but it does have some acceptable B-25 sequences. The musical score was written by acclaimed composer John Barry, who wrote the scores for *Somewhere in Time*, *Out of Africa*, and many James Bond films.

The 8th Air Force had no B-25 groups in combat during the war, but writer and director Peter Hyams collected five B-25 Mitchell bombers and had them flown to RAF Bovington for the film. The five planes were given fictitious group markings. They were christened with overly contrived names like *Gorgeous George*, *Marvelous Miriam*, *Amazing Amanda* and *Brenda's Boys*. Aerial sequences were shot at and around RAF Little Rissington. EMI Elstree Studios served for the cockpit and special effects footage. The film, which fared badly at the box office, was preceded and followed by huge hits for Harrison Ford: *Star Wars* (1977) and *Raiders of the Lost Ark* (1981).

The RAF still held onto the tried-and-true Spitfires, Hurricanes, Halifaxes and Wellingtons, but quickly surpassed the Battle of Britain-era hardware with a series of fast, high-performance aircraft. Among them were the Avro Lancaster and de Havilland Mosquito. These bombers were used in three highly popular and exciting films in the years following the war.

One of the most memorable air war films, produced by Associated British Film Corporation, was *The Dam Busters* (1955). It tells the highly accurate account of when RAF Bomber Command sent nineteen Avro Lancaster four-engine bombers of No. 617 Squadron to bomb three major German dams in the Ruhr Valley in May 1943. The Lancasters each carried one revolutionary "skipping" 9,250 lb. bomb slung under the modified bomb bay. The bomb was spun up to 500 rpm; and when it was released at exactly 230 knots at sixty feet over the water, it would skip over the surface, finally sinking along the thick concrete face of the dam. At a depth of 30 feet the bomb would detonate and cause a "water hammer" effect to breach the dam.

Eccentric genius Barnes Wallis, who designed the dam-busting "Upkeep" bomb for RAF Bomber Command.

Wing Commander Guy Gibson led No. 617 Squadron on the daring raid. After weeks of training in Wales the squadron flew the low-level night mission to the Möhne, Eder and Sorpe dams. After dozens of attempts and flying into fierce flak, the Lancasters managed to hit and breach the Möhne and Eder dams, and damaged the Sorpe. Eight bombers were lost and 53 crewmen killed. The raid caused severe damage to German industry in the Ruhr Valley.

Paul Brickhill's book *The Dam Busters* was the catalyst for Associated to produce the film. The production relied heavily on the book, which when written in 1951 had to avoid revealing classified information about the bomb.

The "Upkeep" bomb used on the actual raid. In the film the bombs were nearly spherical, rather than cylindrical.

Two respected British actors played key roles in the film. Richard Todd, who had been a paratrooper with the British 6th Airborne on D-Day, was Gibson; and Michael Redgrave, father of Lynn and Vanessa, was cast as the affable and eccentric genius Barnes Wallis.

Wallis is testing a theory to hit and destroy a major dam, previously thought an impossible target. Using small spring-fired balls on a long pond, he proves that a bomb, spun and dropped at just the right altitude and speed and distance, could sink beside a dam and breach it. The Air Ministry and Bomber Command are skeptical but agree to let Wallis test the concept with real aircraft on small-scale dams. Wallis proves his theory and full-scale production of the bombs begins. The deadline for the raid is only two months off.

A "bomb aimer" uses his "coat hangar" bombsight in *The Dam Busters*.

Gibson is ordered to take a select group of experienced crews to begin training in low-level night flying. When the full-sized bombs are found to break up on impact with the water, Wallis goes into deep despair, but redesigns the casing and shape of the weapon. Further obstacles are encountered when it proves difficult to ensure the exact altitude of sixty feet for bomb release. Gibson devises a clever system of using small spotlights on the lower fuselage of the Lancasters to converge at the required altitude.

The crews are briefed on their targets and take off, headed south towards the Ruhr. Gibson's section of nine aircraft heads for the Möhne dam and attacks, losing some of his planes. The first bombs fail to breach the stout concrete.

Back in England, Wallis and the other Air Ministry officials wait to learn the outcome. As each failed attack is radioed back, their gloom deepens.

Then three bombs strike perfectly in the water and the face of the dam breaks open, causing millions of tons of water to cascade through the breach. The mission is a success.

Director Michael Anderson worked closely with Brickhill and Group Captain J.N.H. Whitworth to create an accurate and compelling film of the training and execution of the raid. Four original Avro B.VII bombers were provided by the RAF and modified for the production. The bombers were flown by RAF Canberra pilots, who found the low-level flying an exciting change from their normal duties. The huge Lancasters, which appear ungainly and even ugly on the ground, became graceful in flight.

The Derwent Valley in Derbyshire, where much of the training for the actual raid was done, served for the Ruhr Valley sequences. Other shots were done over the English coastline. Actual footage of a Mosquito dropping the 1,200 lb. "Highball" bomb over water was inserted. No. 617 Squadron's base RAF Scampton appeared in some sequences, but most of the principal ground footage was done at RAF Henswell to the north.

Anderson made good use of moonlight for much of the low-level footage. The images of black Lancasters flying over the Channel are extremely realistic. The camera plane stays with the bombers through the diving turns and attack runs, lending an even more visceral feeling of being there. There is a stark and simple reality in many UK-produced war films, and *The Dam Busters* ranks among the best. Wallis' revolutionary goal carries the story from beginning to end, even more so than the combat sequences.

Richard Todd during the attack sequences in *The Dam Busters*. Unlike most American bomber movies, the actors communicated with the headsets on, which added a high degree of authenticity to the film.

The only weak point in the action footage occurs when the dams have been breached by the bombs. Even though large-scale models were built and destroyed, the actual explosions were simulated by matte masks. A huge rising blast shape erupts from the dam while the image of an obviously unmatched cloudy blast is inserted into the mask. The flak tracers and some aerial explosions are hand-animated. Yet it doesn't hurt the film in any way.

The names of the crews and pilots are true to history, and the names of their planes are also accurate. For instance, Gibson's plane is called *G for George*.

While the film is largely accurate historically, some details were changed. Wallis was not the originator of the plan to hit the Ruhr dams. They had been considered prime targets even before the war had started. The real bombs, codenamed "Upkeep," were actually cylindrical in shape, but the RAF wanted to keep certain details of the weapons classified so the bombs in *The Dam Busters* were nearly spherical. The sequence where Gibson is in a theater and conceives the idea of using spotlights is fictional. In reality, Gibson had gone to the Ministry of Air Production for the solution, which they had pioneered for RAF Coastal Command. One shot of a plane crashing into a hillside was not in the original release. The footage of a B-17 Flying Fortress came from Warner Bros.

Wing Commander Guy Gibson, who led nineteen Avro Lancasters of No. 617 Squadron into Germany to bomb three Ruhr Valley dams.

According to Geoff Simpson of the Battle of Britain Memorial Trust, "The film made Gibson appear more approachable than he really was. Richard Todd wrote in a private letter dated June 8, 1995,

'Gibson was a born leader of men but not entirely popular with those who served with him, since he was quite cold and calculating and inclined to be very cocky.'"

Simpson continued, "The film gives the impression that all the crews were handpicked. We now know that this was far from the case." The crews of the nineteen bombers were chosen for the job as a unit.

The Dam Busters premiered in London on May 17, 1955, the twelfth anniversary of the raid. Gibson was not there to see it. He had been killed in the crash of a Mosquito in September 1944.

A curious postscript emerged when George Lucas, while doing rough cuts on one of his own productions, used clips from *The Dam Busters*. Several shots, including the briefing, three-plane elements peeling off to their targets and even the tight banks made as the Lancasters slid into their attack runs all have an eerie familiarity to fans of *Star Wars*. Lucas matched many of the camera angles in the Rebel attack on the Death Star.

Total Film Magazine voted *The Dam Busters* as the 43rd Greatest British Film of All Time in 2004.

The Merlin-powered plywood DH.98 Mosquito, known with affection as the "bamboo bomber," was the fastest aircraft until the emergence of jets in 1944. The Mosquito was used as a bomber, low-level ground attack fighter, long-range photo-reconnaissance and night fighter.

633 Squadron, a U.S./UK production by Mirisch, released by United Artists in 1964, starred the up-and-coming male lead Cliff Robertson a year after his portrayal of Lt. John F. Kennedy in *PT-109*. *633 Squadron* centers on an aggressive squadron of Mosquito crews in 1944. Based on the book by Frederick E. Smith, the story follows Wing Commander Roy Grant (Robertson) who has led the squadron on a series of successful raids all over Germany. Grant is an ex-RAF Eagle Squadron pilot who chose to remain in the UK when the U.S. entered the war. But when the squadron is assigned to hit a heavily defended rocket fuel factory far up a fjord, they have bitten off more than they can chew.

Mirisch contract player George Chakiris, who had gained fame for his role in *West Side Story* (1961), is Lt. Erik Bergman, a Norwegian guerilla officer who has informed Bomber Command of the existence of the fuel plant. The vital target is set under the overhang of a massive cliff, making normal high-altitude bombing impossible. So the intrepid 633 Squadron is given the dangerous job of attacking the site. Bergman returns to Norway to run guerilla operations to destroy the German flak batteries ringing the fuel plant, but he is captured by the Gestapo. Since Bergman knows too much, Air Vice Marshal Davis, played by the taciturn character actor Harry Andrews, orders Grant to destroy Gestapo headquarters before they torture Bergman into telling what he knows. Grant is successful and kills Bergman; but Davis, still worried, moves the date for the raid up to the next day. Grant hits the target under murderous flak and on a nearly impossible attack run. The aircrews destroy the fuel plant at the cost of every single plane in the squadron.

The film was directed by Walter Grauman, known for suspenseful television dramas like *Peter Gunn* and *Steve Canyon*. Grauman was a veteran of more than fifty B-25 missions during the war, so he knew what combat looked and felt like.

The plot requires some suspension of disbelief. The fuel plant is supposedly "bomb proofed" and impervious to aerial bombardment. But the overhanging cliff is vulnerable to being struck by "special" bombs, resulting in a collapse which will destroy the factory.

633 Squadron was the first major film to be shot in the color Panavision widescreen process. No combat footage could be used, because all the color footage shot during the war predated the Panavision anamorphic camera system. Mirisch collected several RAF and German aircraft for the production; the small group of planes was known as the "Mirisch Air Force." Eight TT35 Mosquitoes were obtained with the cooperation of the Air Ministry.

Modified to appear as the FB Mk VI fighter-bomber version, five were flyable, while the remainder were used in ground sequences. A crash scene used differing camera angles to give the illusion of more than one crash. No. TA639 is now on display at the RAF Museum in Cosford, Shropshire.

Cliff Robertson as Wing Commander Roy Grant in *633 Squadron*. *Courtesy Cliff Robertson*

Cliff Robertson, an avid pilot and aficionado of wartime aircraft, added some amusing elements to the production. "I was a pilot but they knew how much I wanted to own a Mosquito and wouldn't let me near one alone," Robertson explained in a 2010 interview with the author. The veteran actor, who owned a Spitfire Mk IX that he flew for more than twenty years, said, "Mirisch was able to find eight Mosquitoes. But if they'd waited just another two weeks, those planes would have been burned for scrap or given to museums. That's how close it was."

Robertson related a staged crash scene. "A very sad scene was when they showed a Mosquito crashing into a truck. A stuntman pulled the pyrotechnics wires as it hit the truck. It caught fire and that poor plane burned for about eight hours. I watched it die."

The German "Me-109s" were the same four-place Me-108 "Taifuns" seen in *The Longest Day* and other postwar films (see Chapter Fourteen). The B-25 camera ship actually appears in the film as the plane flying Bergman to Norway.

Primary shooting was done at various RAF bases in Hertfordshire and MGM British Studios. The Norwegian fjord scenes were done in Scottish lochs.

"There was one scene right at the end," Robertson said, "where the survivors of the crash all stand up in unison. It looks a little silly."

The film did well at the box office in the United States, and rated No. 11 on Channel 4's "100 Greatest War Films of All Time."

Five years later, another U.S./UK collaboration hit the theaters with the sound of growling Mosquitoes. *Mosquito Squadron*, an Oakmont and United Artists production, featured Glasgow-born David McCallum. His boyish good looks had won him great acclaim for his role as the "good Russian" Illya Kuryakin in the TV series *The Man from U.N.C.L.E.* from 1964 to 1968.

Once again a squadron of Mosquitoes is called upon to hit a secret German Luftwaffe testing base in France. McCallum plays Squadron Leader Quint Munroe, who has his hands full with his pilots, missions and a guilt complex caused by the presumed death of his closest friend Scotty while attacking a V-1 site in France.

Munroe is nearly killed in a photo-reconnaissance mission over France and then assigned a daring low-level mission against a fortified chateau with a revolutionary bouncing bomb called a "Highball." The chateau is where several French resistance fighters and Allied prisoners are being used as human shields to protect a secret underground Luftwaffe facility for the development of new weapons. Among the prisoners is Scotty, who has lost his memory. Munroe slams the bomb into the outside wall of the chateau in order to help the prisoners escape, but is shot down as he pulls away. Scotty fails to remember Munroe, but rallies by sacrificing himself in front of a German tank, allowing Munroe to escape, whereupon he and the other survivors of the raid are later picked up by submarine.

The plot has some familiar points from *633 Squadron*, of which it is often referred to as a sequel, and uses some of the same aircraft from the earlier film. As in *633 Squadron*, the targets are related to the V-1 rockets, the main character is less than thrilled with the assignment, and the Gestapo captures the guerilla leader.

Only five of the rare Mosquitoes were still available since *633 Squadron* five years earlier. The production also used many of the same RAF airbases for the filming, including Bovington and Little Rissington. The chateau seen in the film was an English manor house near Farnborough.

The acting is done well; but as with nearly every war film of the era, makes more than necessary use of pyrotechnics. Huge fireballs erupt with every bomb blast, as if the target were a fuel or napalm dump. Only recently have filmmakers learned to accept that real explosions are more flash and bang than fire.

The "Highball" bouncing bomb was an actual weapon, developed by Barnes Wallis. The Highball was a 1,200 lb. bomb with 600 lbs. of explosive filler. Two Highballs could be carried by a single Mosquito. The bombs were designed to be spun to about 800 rpm to impart a "skipping" motion towards a reinforced target.

The Mosquito's best side is seen in both this and *633 Squadron,* with several swift and low passes in nearly every scene to show the graceful lines of the "Wooden Wonder."

Director Boris Sagal, whose credits included television shows such as *The Man from U.N.C.L.E.* and *Dr. Kildare,* was the driving force behind the film's high-pitched suspense and action. Ironically, Sagal, who had worked with Vic Morrow in *Combat!* and on two *Twilight Zone* episodes, died in nearly the same tragic way that took Morrow's life during the filming of *Twilight Zone: The Movie* in 1982. Morrow was killed along with two children when a crashing helicopter struck him with its spinning blades. While directing a television movie, *World War III*, that same year, Sagal stepped out of a helicopter and accidentally walked into the spinning tail rotor.

DH98 Mosquito used in *Mosquito Squadron*. Their use in the movies saved several of them within weeks of being burned as scrap.

In an interview with David McCallum the author was surprised to learn that much of the cockpit dialogue in *633 Squadron* was ad-libbed. "Oh yes," said McCallum, "Nicky Henson, a wonderful actor who was my bombardier in the film, and I sat in the cockpit mockup. We made up all our dialogue with great British aplomb.

'I hope you brought your driving licence with you.'

'Why?'

'Because if you fly this thing any lower you're going to need it!' Some of them made it into the movie."

As for being in the actual aircraft, the *NCIS* regular related one moment. "I was in the cockpit, and under instructions from someone hiding behind me, actually taxied the plane.

I tell you, those big Rolls-Royce Merlins are simply awesome. Those propeller blades are within a few inches of the window. It was pretty terrifying."

Fighter Squadron, a color action drama released in 1948, starred Robert Stack and Warner contract player Edmund O'Brien. *Fighter Squadron* follows the mid-1944 missions and off-duty life of the 17th Fighter Group in England. It was written by Seton Miller, whose credits included *Dawn Patrol* and *The Adventures of Robin Hood.* The film was Warner Bros.' first major post-war air combat production. Miller's screenplay is a clichéd and not always believable mix of drama, action and whimsy. Miller used many *Dawn Patrol* elements, and it doesn't require much scrutiny to see the similarities.

The film centers on the old and new pilots of a P-47 Thunderbolt unit during bomber escort missions over France and Germany. Major Ed Hardin (O'Brien), a former Flying Tiger, is a top-scoring ace with a rebellious streak. The hard-nosed "by-the-book" General Gilbert refuses to let the pilots drop their wing tanks when attacked by German fighters, or to fly below 18,000 feet.

Hardin openly challenges Gilbert's shortsighted policies. When Hardin finds he is to be given command of the group, he resists, but finally accepts when he realizes he will at last be able to employ some of his own tactical theories.

The other pilots, including the cocky Stu Hamilton (Robert Stack), learn that Hardin wants the pilots to be allowed to fly "on the deck" to attack ground targets. He also wants the authority to drop tanks when they are attacked. Hardin goes over Gilbert's head to Major General Mike McCready, in whom he finds a sympathetic ear.

Hamilton wants to get married but Hardin feels he won't be focused on getting the job done. But Hamilton goes ahead with the wedding. Hardin wants to transfer Hamilton, but allows him to fly with the group on one last mission. Hamilton is shot down, and as his crippled Thunderbolt falls out of the sky he radios, "You were right. I thought about Ann."

D-Day looms and Hardin finally convinces the high command to permit low-level strafing attacks and dropping of wing tanks, allowing the P-47s to fight German planes. Hardin is shot down and believed killed on D-Day; but his successor, Duke Chapell, takes over with Hardin's trailblazing policies.

Interwoven into the plot is a silly running gag about Sergeant Dolan, a wisecracking lothario con man who uses black cats—considered very bad luck—as a way of getting off the base to woo several English girls. When Dolan is finally recognized by a photo in a magazine article he is put in the stockade. His "not as dumb as he appears" lackey is given his stripes.

Acclaimed director Raoul Walsh, best known for stunning films like *The Roaring Twenties* (1939) and *High Sierra* (1941), gave *Fighter Squadron* its best elements. Another plus was Max Steiner's alternately dramatic and lighthearted score.

The production was filmed primarily at Oscoda Army Air Force Base in Michigan. In May 1948 Walsh and the company of 115 began filming at Oscoda, a wooded and hilly region near Lake Huron that resembled both England and mainland Europe. Lake Huron filled the role of the English Channel.

With the cooperation of the Air National Guard, the states of Tennessee, Georgia and North Carolina provided pilots and sixteen P-47Ds. The planes were repainted to match the markings of the 57th Fighter Group. Paul Mantz worked with the pilots on all the aerial sequences from his B-25 camera plane. Two technical advisors, 56th Group ace Major Joe Perry and 4th Group ace Major Leroy Gover, provided Walsh with the historical and technical accuracy he wanted. Stock color combat footage from the Army Air Force 1947 documentary *Thunderbolt* was combined with the live footage to create a full-length production.

The Republic P-47, known as the "Jug," was one of the most successful fighter-bombers in the war. Powered by a huge turbo-supercharged 2,000 hp. Pratt & Whitney R-2800 Twin Wasp 18-cylinder radial engine, the Thunderbolt could fly better above 25,000 feet than any fighter. With eight .50 caliber Browning machine guns the Jugs were perfect for ground attack and infantry support missions.

Jack Larson as Lt. "Shorty" Kirk in his first film role in *Fighter Squadron*. *Courtesy Jack Larson*

As in the film, the policy of low level ground attack was hotly debated throughout 1943 and finally adopted by Lt. General James Doolittle after he took command of the 8th Air Force in January 1944.

In the film's opening sequences the group arrives back on base after a mission with two damaged planes. The crippled P-47s are directed to land first—a standard policy in the Air Force, according to Col. Pisanos of the 4th Fighter Group. "Most of the fighter bases had twin runways, so the crippled planes were brought in first," he explained. "We adopted that from the RAF."

Also seen in the early shots was a B-17G leased from Mantz. Hardin's plane is damaged and out of ammunition. He is invited to fly under a B-17 for protection from German fighters, a reversal of roles for bomber and escort. The dialogue is typically American jargon:

Bomber pilot: "Hey little friend, we're the bomber passing a Thunderbolt."

Hardin: "You call that junk heap a bomber?"

Bomber pilot: "Your tail is drooping, peashooter."

Hardin: "My cylinders are shot off, I'm running on a built-in eggbeater."

Three Me-109s dive for the attack. The bomber pilot urges Hardin to run but he says he doesn't have the fuel.

Bomber pilot: "Get under our wing. We'll try and cover you."

After a series of attacks, the bomber is hit.

Bomber pilot: "Cannon shot in the wing. You all right, Thunderbolt?"

Hardin: "Yeah. But it's letting the sun in on me."

All but one of the Germans are shot down and the remaining plane peels away.

Bomber pilot: "You can come up for air, Thunderbolt. The third one's running home to tell Adolf."

Hardin: "Thanks for the umbrella."

Bomber pilot: "Well we gotta return the favor. You guys have helped us plenty."

The shot required pilot Joe Perry to fly at very close quarters to the huge bomber. The German fighters were actually P-51D Mustangs of the California Air National Guard, filmed near Van Nuys after the Michigan location shooting was completed in June 1948. The Mustang resembled the Me-109 and so were painted using water-based paint in Luftwaffe markings. Four P-47s were brought to California for the dogfighting sequences.

The studio process shots were the result of nearly twenty years of aviation film experience, resulting in very dynamic motion shots. The actors had been instructed how to move the control sticks to give the highest realism to the action.

Robert Stack, who would eventually make a name for himself in aviation films, as Captain Stu Hamilton in *Fighter Squadron.*

Hamilton lands behind enemy lines to rescue a downed Hardin, who climbs into the tight cockpit with Hamilton on his lap.

Hamilton: "Comfy, Ed?"

"You gotta lose some weight," is Hardin's laconic reply.

This was based on an actual incident during a Berlin mission on March 18, 1945 when Lt. George Green of the 4th landed his P-51 near a German air base to pick up Major Pierce McKennon.

Still the clichéd dialogue weakens the film with the American pilots trading wisecracks and jokes. One man happily sings "I've been working on the railroad" as he tears a locomotive apart with his guns. "All that chatter would never have been tolerated," said Pisanos. "Not even the hotdog pilots were that talkative in combat. The radio was very quiet except for calling out German fighters. We listened a lot more than talked."

Another item of note is the long bursts the pilots fire at ground or aerial targets. The eight machine guns in a P-47 carried a total of 3,200 rounds. At the maximum rate of fire (between 600-800 rounds per minute) the ammo lasted only about 32 seconds. Hardin and his men never seem to grasp this fact, but that's Hollywood.

Major Leroy Gover was flying a P-47 for one of the ground attack sequences. Flying low, he was enveloped by a pyrotechnics blast prematurely triggered by a technician. Neither Gover nor the plane were affected by the explosion, but the event was eerily reminiscent of the near death of Earl Robinson during the filming of *Dawn Patrol* in 1930 (see Chapter Two). The shot made it into the film and proved one of the most stunning scenes.

The combat sequences are well done and exciting, and even the advent of CGI hasn't done much to improve on it. Because of the limitations imposed by stock footage, some inconsistencies emerge. Not all the P-47s have the same paint scheme. Some are natural metal with black stripes while others are olive drab with white stripes. Group markings are also varied.

Among the rookie pilots assigned to the group is "Shorty" Kirk, played by the young Jack Larson in his first film role. Larson was later best known as Jimmy Olsen in *The Adventures of Superman* (1952-1958). His first appearance in the film has him with Hardin and Chappell. He is very nervous about combat.

"To tell you the truth, I'm scared," he admits in a small voice.

Hardin: "You'll do better than you think. That's an order."

After Kirk leaves, Hardin turns to Chappell. "Were you ever that young?"

Chappell snorts. "I was born an old man."

Larson provided a great deal of interesting background information for this book. "*Fighter Squadron* was my baptism in film," he recalled. "I was nervous. Mr. Walsh had a reputation for being hard on actors. But he just let me do what felt right."

"Warner had one of the greatest wardrobe departments and did everything with accuracy," Larson said. "They made a full set of perfect uniforms for me. Mr. Walsh had me in uniform every day, to keep me in character. On the first day I was to work, the assistant director called to me and said, 'Okay, go out there.' All the planes were on the field and I ran out there, all excited. I don't know how it happened but I ran straight into the rudder of a P-47. Right on the edge, just BAM! and I knocked myself out."

Edmond O'Brien and Jack Larson with P-47 Thunderbolt on location in Oscoda, Michigan, for *Fighter Squadron.* Courtesy Jack Larson

The new actor woke up to see the crew hovering over him with worried looks on their faces. "I needed a lot of stitches," continued Larson. "It took about a week and then I got my chance. The actor who really befriended me was John Rodney, who played Colonel Brickley. He really took me under his wing, a wonderful man."

One scene that did not make it into the final version of the film involved Kirk mistakenly pulling the cord for his seat life raft in the cockpit. "It was quite a complicated sequence," Larson said, "with this life raft expanding under me and me screaming for help. In fact it was a bit dangerous. I might have been trapped in there and suffocated. They finally got it done, but never used it. They screened it at the wrap party."

Larson commented on what it was like to be around the Thunderbolts: "I was shown how to climb into the cockpit and what to do, but it was pretty overwhelming. When we started those engines it just took over all my senses. I was very moved by being around those huge planes and the patriotism of the event. But that's me," Larson said with a chuckle. "I get really emotional about things like that. I cry at card tricks."

One of Larson's most memorable scenes occurred when he has returned from his first mission with a victory over a German plane. The crew chief paints a black swastika on his P-47. Kirk, woozy with adrenaline, grins at the symbol. "Can't they make it bigger?" he asks.

The reviews for *Fighter Squadron* were mixed, primarily focusing on the clichés and obvious fighter pilot stereotypes. Robert Stack's opinion of the film was likewise negative, Larson said. "He called it a Technicolor turkey."

Far to the south in the Mediterranean Theater of Operations, a new fighter group was garnering headlines. After completing primary and advanced flight training in Alabama and Texas, they were ferried to North Africa, and then to the new 15th Air Force in Italy. There they gained a reluctant respect from fighter and bomber groups for their flying skill, tenacity and courage.

They were the African-American pilots of the first all-black fighter group to see combat. The 332nd Fighter Group—consisting of the 99th, 100th, 301st and 302nd Squadrons—was on the hot seat to prove itself. The story of the Tuskegee Airmen, as they came to be known, was a long struggle against racism and a hostile bureaucracy.

The first group of pilots to receive wings and Air Corps commissions was the 99th Pursuit Squadron in April 1943. They were shortly followed by other squadrons and sent to North Africa. The crews had little success in proving themselves, as many of their missions were of moderate value and even less notoriety, but in time the 332nd came to show their stuff in combat. Their story was told, after a fashion, in the 1995 television movie *The Tuskegee Airmen*, starring Lawrence Fishburne, Malcolm-Jamal Warner, Cuba Gooding Jr, and Andre Braugher.

The film is a fictionalized account of the first squadrons to see combat. Directed by Robert Markowitz, who had a long string of television movies behind him, the production used a fair amount of dramatic license among the history.

Cadet Hannibal Lee (Fishburne) and several other African Americans from all over the country meet in Tuskegee, Alabama, to begin training. Lee is an ardent foe of segregation. Among the cadets is Walter Peoples III, a hotshot who is a discipline problem and is told he will not continue the training. Shattered by the disgrace, he takes a plane up to dive it into the ground in a spectacular suicide.

First Lady Eleanor Roosevelt arrives for an inspection and asks Lee to take her up in an AT-6. After several trials and tribulations the cadets receive their wings and deploy to North Africa as the 99th Pursuit Squadron. Still fighting the old racial attitudes, they are restricted to ground attack missions. Lee takes a flight of pilots on a mission when they see a group of German fighters. Leroy Cappy (Warner) attacks, shooting down a German plane. Cappy is hit by another German and dies in a crash.

Meanwhile the House Armed Services Committee convenes a meeting to determine if the "Tuskegee Experiment" should continue. Critics, led by "good old boy" Senator Conyers (John Lithgow), claim that "Negroes are incapable of handling complex machinery and will not fight."

A pair of P-51D Mustangs in HBO's *Tuskegee Airmen.*

Lt. Col. Benjamin O. Davis (Andre Braugher) passionately and effectively defends his men. Two new squadrons join the 99th to create the all-black 332nd Fighter Group. Deployed to Italy as bomber escort, the group begins real front-line combat. Lee and Billy Roberts (Cuba Gooding Jr.) sink a German destroyer. Lee is awarded the Distinguished Flying Cross and promoted to captain. He tells his ground crew chief to paint the tail of all his planes bright red.

On their next mission, the group escorts bombers over Berlin. Because of their success in taking on German fighters, bomber crews start requesting that the "Red Tails" escort them. The film wraps with an accounting of the Tuskegee Airmens' accomplishments and citations for bravery.

The brainchild of 99th Fighter Squadron veteran Robert Williams, the story took several years, numerous changes and some compromises to reach the screen. Location filming took place near Ft. Smith, Arkansas, and used the same barracks seen in *Biloxi Blues* (1988) with Matthew Broderick. [Coincidentally, Broderick had played Col. Robert Gould Shaw, the commander of the first all-black infantry regiment in the Civil War, in *Glory* (1989), which also starred Braugher.]

More exterior work was done at Juliette, Georgia and Muskogee, Oklahoma. A collection of basic and advanced trainers such as PT-17 Stearmans and AT-6 Texans were assembled for the early sequences. At least five P-51D Mustangs, painted with the garish red tails, were used. To make it appear as there were more planes than the production actually possessed, the film crew borrowed a trick from *Memphis Belle* by having several silhouette aircraft placed in the background. In addition, some authentic gun camera footage was added. The gun camera film of Lee and Roberts' attack on a German destroyer is wartime combat footage of a Japanese destroyer being sunk by 20mm cannon fire, probably by a P-38 in the Pacific near Rabaul. Clips from *Memphis Belle*, *The Battle of Britain* and other air war films filled in where needed.

The 99th flew P-40 Warhawks, P-39 Airacobras and P-47 Thunderbolts before being issued the P-51B Mustang. This is not mentioned in the film, as it would have complicated the plot. Audiences not familiar with wartime fighters would have been confused at the variety of planes. Also, obtaining flyable Warhawks and Airacobras in sufficient numbers would have been impossible.

The author interviewed Dr. Roscoe Brown, a veteran of the 100th Fighter Squadron about his opinions of the film. Brown, who commanded the 100th in 1944, also holds the rare distinction of being one of the few pilots to have shot down a German Me-262 jet fighter. "Bob Williams was creating a script for a movie about the airmen in the late 1980s," recalled Brown. "But at that time no studio wanted to do a film about black airmen. But Bob finally managed to sell it to HBO."

Asked about his opinion of the film, Brown commented, "A group of Tuskegee Airmen were treated to a preview, and on the whole we were pleased, even though the film had some errors. No one ever committed suicide in training. The 99th flew P-51Bs, not D models."

First Lady Eleanor Roosevelt's visit to Tuskegee took place in March 1941, not after the 99th graduated, as seen in the film.

One scene depicted an AT-6 with engine trouble having to land on a country road. A largely black chain gang is working in a nearby field under armed guard when the plane, along with the others in the flight, come to a stop and the pilots step out. The prisoners and guards are astonished at what they see: "They's colored flyers!"

"That really happened," said Brown. "One flight did have to land near a prison camp."

Regarding the combat and flying sequences, Brown commented, "At least half of our missions were escorting B-24 Liberators, but the film only focuses on the B-17s. We never talked that much in combat," Brown said with a laugh. "We were too busy and it was totally against radio discipline."

Brown also cleared up one of the legends of the 332nd. "To my knowledge no bomber group ever requested us to fly escort for them. We were given the assignments because we stayed with the bombers and did our job. That was all."

Another myth regarding the group centered on the oft-repeated claim that no bombers escorted by the 332nd were lost to enemy fighters. This is incorrect, as U.S. Air Force records attest. At least 25 bombers were lost to enemy action while being escorted by the 332nd Fighter Group. This—while a far cry from the claim of none at all—is still a remarkable record and much better than the record of all-white fighter groups in the 8th and 15th Air Forces. It must also be remembered that "enemy action" also means flak, which fighters are unable to counteract.

A closing comment by Brown capped the interview very well: "Thirty-two pilots were captured by the Germans. And one pilot said he was better treated by the Germans than he was by the whites back in America."

George Lucas began work on a Tuskegee Airmen movie project in 1988, intending to make a film centering on the combat experiences of the 332nd Group. The result was *Red Tails*, released in 2012. Brown, who worked closely with Lucas on the production as a technical advisor, said,

"We went over to Prague in the Czech Republic. I spent about two weeks working on the film, viewing rushes and making recommendations. Lucas did have about eight or ten P-51s and a couple of B-17s over there. They used a former MiG base and built World War II Quonset huts and base facilities, tents, a control tower and all the facilities. The place looked just like an airbase in Italy in 1944."

Lucasfilm used a wealth of footage of pilots entering and leaving the planes, taxiing, taking off and landing, and flying in formation.

Lt. Roscoe Brown while serving in the 100th Fighter Squadron, 332nd Fighter Group in Italy. Brown flew 88 missions and was awarded the Distinguished Flying Cross.

Brown's recommendations influenced the set design, including the muddy runways and parking areas covered in pierced-steel matting.

While working on the screenplay with co-writers John Ridley and Aaron McGruder, Lucas was given access to the Tuskegee Airmen's logbooks, and several of the mission sequences make use of this resource. "Lucas wanted the combat scenes done digitally," Brown continued. "And he wanted it done right."

Unlike Michael Bay's take on the story of *Pearl Harbor* (see Chapter Seven), for *Red Tails* Lucas and director Anthony Hemingway used CGI to enhance the story instead of showing the most mind-twisting action possible. Lucas spent months studying actual aerial combat footage and other war movies to familiarize himself with how aircraft really behaved. The CGI aircraft in *Red Tails* are superbly detailed, and the aerial sequences are done in a way that looks amazingly like actual combat footage. It is very hard to spot the computer's touch. Huge formations of bombers spread their wings across the sky with remarkable realism, and the aerial view of the Allied landing at Anzio in January 1944 is awesome.

For the first time, the cockpit interiors are tight and realistic with a break from the usual camera angle shot from the pilot's left or right front. In *Red Tails* the camera is directly in front of the pilot.

Small but important details are almost hidden in the production: Arming the guns before combat, the effects of fuel leaks on a burning plane, and the sound of machine guns versus cannon give added weight to the film's realism. For the first time since *Command Decision*, the Me-262 jet comes to the screen. As swift as the Mustangs are, the Luftwaffe jet makes them look sluggish, and the effect of four 20mm cannon on the American bombers is shocking.

Engine noise however, is very low, allowing the pilots to converse in nearly conversational tones, both in the fighters and bombers. And Lucas couldn't help but put a small *Star Wars* touch into *Red Tails*: bullets zipping past sound just a bit too much like TIE fighter cannon.

Red Tails is chronologically the most recent film in this book, completing the century of aviation movies. But there are plenty of planes and films to go.

CHAPTER SEVEN

The War in the Air: The Pacific

Halfway around the world from the events in Europe was another war—one defined by vast expanses of ocean and sweltering heat. Wake, Midway, Bataan, Guadalcanal, Port Morseby, Rabaul, Tarawa, Iwo Jima and a hundred other places most Americans would have been hard-pressed to find on a map were thrust into the headlines on a daily basis.

The Pacific war's roots began in 1937 when Japan, under the guise of self-defense, invaded mainland China with the ultimate aim of conquest and exploitation of natural resources. From 1940 until mid-1942, Japan seemed unstoppable. And no one believed this more than the Japanese.

For America the Pacific war began on a warm Sunday morning in December 1941 when six Japanese aircraft carriers launched more than 350 planes to attack American Army, Navy and Marine facilities on Oahu. From the moment the people of the United States heard of the "Day of Infamy," nothing would ever be the same. American blood had been shed and American nationalism had been challenged.

Weeks after the fires had died and the last body buried, Hollywood was cranking out the films to inspire, inflame and invigorate people to support and fight the war.

Most of the war films since *Wings* portrayed the Germans as cultured but evil skulking monocle-wearing buffoons. Likewise, after Pearl Harbor the Japanese were portrayed as short, bucktoothed, bespectacled monkeys with no regard for human life. The studios were under no obligation to show the Japanese military as anything but subhuman monsters, and the films produced well into the 1950s reflected this. Respected Chinese and Korean actors were given roles as sneering killers in khaki uniforms. To the American public, there was little difference between the Asian races.

This was apparent in two movies depicting the work of the Flying Tigers in China. The American Volunteer Group (AVG) was made up of American civilian and military pilots who volunteered to become mercenaries for General Chiang Kai-shek's Nationalist Air Force in 1941. President Roosevelt signed the bill authorizing the AVG in April 1941, and in a very short time pilots and ground crew took 100 Curtiss P-40B Tomahawk fighters to China to set up operations against the Japanese.

In time, the controversial unit led by former Air Corps Captain Claire L. Chennault began to show their stuff in the skies over the Far East. The Tigers soon gained a reputation as skilled if unconventional fighters whose kill ratio of 220 to 16 was higher than that of the RAF against Germany. After Pearl Harbor the Tigers continued to fight for China, earning bounties for every Japanese plane shot down. Eventually most of the Tigers joined the new 5th Air Force.

John Wayne (left) with John Carroll in a publicity pose for *Flying Tigers*.

In 1942 Republic Pictures capitalized on the legend of the Tigers with John Wayne as Captain Jim "Pappy" Gordon, a hard-nosed but compassionate AVG commander with more than his share of stress. Gordon's job is to do was much damage to the Japanese as possible while keeping his pilots alive. His pilots are "gung ho" for shooting down Japanese planes, but they also know the value of teamwork.

This changes when an old friend of Gordon's, Woody Jason, played with great vigor by John Carroll, arrives in a white linen suit and pith helmet. Gordon, knowing Woody's skill as a pilot, allows him to join. Woody is eager to win some of the bounty money and takes a P-40 up—without permission—to show what he can do.

Unfortunately, the plane is unarmed, and Woody finds himself in a jam. Only Gordon's intervention saves Woody's tail.

Later Woody causes the death of "Hap" Davis (Paul Kelly) and is ostracized by the Tigers. When Gordon volunteers to take an old transport full of high explosives to bomb a railroad bridge, Woody takes over. Gordon orders him out but Woody says he needs to make up for what he did. After bombing the bridge, the plane is hit by enemy fire. Gordon bails out but realizes Woody is still in the plane, diving in a suicide attack on the train. Woody dies heroically.

The story is merely a remake of movies like *Captains of the Clouds*. John Wayne, who had already gained fame as one of Republic's best "he-man" leading men, began a long career portraying war heroes with *Flying Tigers*. Co-written by Kenneth Gamet and Barry Trivers, whose *International Squadron* (1941) failed to hit the mark, the film has no connection to the real AVG beyond the title. Using typically "Chinese" music in the score and blatantly racist portrayals of Asians, the film was as politically incorrect as it was possible to be in 1942. Among other events in the story, Japanese pilots mercilessly strafe a pilot while he dangles helplessly from his parachute.

Filmed on ranchland near Studio City, Republic created a reasonable facsimile of an AVG base, complete with headquarters, barracks, medical facilities and an airstrip. Wartime needs prevented Republic from acquiring real P-40Bs so seven wooden mockups were constructed. Two replicas were fitted with Curtiss OX-5 60-hp engines—the same type used in the Jenny—for taxiing shots. The others had powerful electric engines to spin the propellers during engine run-ups.

Early in the film Gordon's Chinese crew chief complains about the bullet holes in the plane. Gordon, with perhaps a bit of tongue-in-cheek humor, dryly replies, "Termites."

Clarence 'Ace' Braguunier and Robert King, who worked for Paul Mantz, supervised the construction and operation of the P-40s. Since the P-40 was in operational service in every theater of the war, the War Department insisted the instruments not be shown. The panels seen in the interior shots were fakes.

Real P-40s were filmed at Curtiss' factory in Buffalo, New York. They were repainted with the "shark mouth" motif and flown by Curtiss pilots. Republic also used detailed miniatures built by the famed Lydecker Brothers special-effects team for the aerial sequences. Much of the miniature footage was done in New Mexico, where the Lydeckers were able to make use of cloud formations, something Wellman had pioneered in *Wings*. The twin-engine transport flown by Gordon and Woody is a Capelis XC-12, a failed design built in 1933 (see Chapter Nine).

Paul Kelly with John Wayne as Jim Gordon in Republic's *Flying Tigers*. Wartime security forced the studio to build several wooden P-40s with Curtiss OX-5 engines for the production. When Gordon returns from a mission with bullet holes in the plane, he blames them on termites. *Author's Collection*

Flying Tigers was a huge success, breaking all of Republic's box office records for 1942. American audiences were happy to see "evidence" of the United States fighting back against the Rising Sun and neither knew nor cared that the film was as far from reality as possible.

The next major film to tell the AVG story was Warner's 1945 production *God is My Co-pilot*, the story of Colonel Robert L. Scott, who joined the Tigers in 1942. Based on the bestselling book of the same name, the film stars Warner contract player Dennis Morgan.

As a boy growing up in rural Georgia, Scott is fascinated with flying and later joins the Air Corps. Prior to the war he works as an Air Mail pilot, but December 7 finds him as an instructor in California. He wants to go into combat, but at 34 years of age he is considered too old. Unbeaten, Scott wrangles his way into the war by flying C-47s from India over the "Hump" to China and Chennault's Flying Tigers. He makes friends with an ebullient Irish Catholic missionary, Big Mike Harrigan (Alan Hale).

Scott meets Chennault in Kunming, and begs the General to let him join the Flying Tigers. The wily Chennault (Raymond Massey) tells Scott that the Tigers are mercenaries paid by the Chinese government. Finally Scott convinces Chennault to give him a P-40. He quickly becomes a "one-man air force" by single-handedly attacking Japanese troops along the Burma Road. Scott's chief rival in the air is "Tokyo Joe," an American-educated fighter pilot with a wicked sense of humor and several kills.

Col Robert L. Scott after his time with the Flying Tigers.

But with the U.S. now at war, the original AVG pilots are disbanding. The day the Tigers are to return home the local Japanese radio mocks them. Chennault, now a USAAF General, asks his men to stay long enough to attack Hong Kong on July 4. The Tigers agree and Scott leads one of the squadrons. Tokyo Joe (Chinese-American actor Richard Loo) and Scott meet in the skies over Hong Kong. Scott is victorious after using a radical maneuver of dropping his flaps and slowing, which makes Joe fly past and into Scott's bullets.

Scott's plane is damaged and he is forced to bail out over the jungle. Then he is informed that he has a blood disease and the doctors won't let him fly. He desperately prays to a god he hardly believes in and is told by Chennault of a brand-new P-40 waiting for him to take on the next mission. The film ends with Scott hearing Big Mike's words of faith in his mind.

Unlike *Flying Tigers*, *God is My Co-Pilot* is largely factual, to a degree. Real names are used. Chennault accurately explains how the simple but highly effective early warning system works. The attack on Hong Kong took place, but was actually flown on October 25, 1942. Scott by that time had 19 victories. The story about Scott painting the spinner on his P-40 different colors was also true; and although the Japanese didn't believe there were more AVG squadrons as the film suggests, it did cause some confusion. Big Mike, Tokyo Joe and several other characters are added for color, but much of the film can be taken at face value.

Scott was one of the most highly decorated and top-scoring pilots in the China-Burma-India (CBI) Theater of Operations. The boyishly charming Dennis Morgan does a credible job with the role, earning the audience's respect and support. Many adult male viewers understood Scott's determination to get into the fight.

Dennis Morgan as Robert Scott with Alan Hale as "Big Mike" Harrigan seated in a very roomy P-43 Lancer mockup in *God is My Co-Pilot.*
Author's Collection

The P-40s seen in the film are a conglomeration of Republic's *Flying Tiger* castoffs and two additional aircraft from a USAAF reclamation depot in San Diego. The Kunming sequences were shot at the Warner Bros. Ranch, while Luke Auxiliary Airfield near Phoenix, Arizona, was the location for most of the aerial shots. Those used twenty-five P-40s of the AAF Training Command. As many as twenty B-25 Mitchells were also used for the Hong Kong raid. The Japanese Zeros were AT-6 Texans painted in both camouflage and gray schemes. Scott flies a rare Republic P-43 Lancer over the mountains with Big Mike in the back seat.

For a time Warner Bros. commanded one of the largest privately-owned air forces. Stunt pilots Frank Nolta and *Wings* veteran Frank Clarke, then a Major in the USAAF, did much of the flying. Scott himself recreated many of his famous dogfights. Early in the filming, an AT-6 collided with a B-25 during a head-on pass. The AT-6 pilot failed to stay with the element leader and didn't turn in time. Instead it struck the bomber, cutting off its wings. The B-25 fell to earth, trailing smoke and debris. Three men died in the B-25 and two in the Texan.

The aerial camera work is excellent, especially during takeoff when the P-40s leave the runway and the camera plane follows them into the air.

As in most American air war movies, the aircraft interiors are far too roomy. There is plenty of elbow room in the P-40, and even the Zero's cockpit is like a flying Barcalounger. Tokyo Joe spends a lot of time chatting up his Yankee opponents on a hand-held microphone (instead of holding the throttle), taunting them before attacking. Scott trades the wily Japanese pilot barb for barb until the final moment as Joe is suddenly faced with his own doom.

When the film premiered in Scott's hometown of Macon, Georgia, it drew strong praise. *God is My Co-Pilot* was the last of Warner's overtly patriotic wartime films produced during a long and successful run. It would be another three years before the propellers turned again in *Fighter Squadron* (see Chapter Six).

Warner's 1943 production, *Air Force*, starred the up-and-coming bad boy of films, John Garfield. The movie tells the story of the crew of a B-17 Flying Fortress after it leaves California on December 6 and finds itself smack in the middle of the Pearl Harbor attack.

The *Mary Ann* is one of twelve 19th Bomb Group B-17Cs being sent to the Philippines. The crew is an eclectic band of handsome pilots, grizzled crew chiefs and hotheaded gunners. Joe Winocki (Garfield) is fed up with the Air Force and has no intention of staying in after his hitch is up. He has few allies in the crew, especially Sergeant White (Harry Carey), who has a son in the Philippines. The pilot is "Irish" Quincannon (John Ridgely) while George Tobias, an old Warner semi-comic regular, portrays a crew chief who has a dog named "Mr. Moto."

After surviving the attack, the crew is informed they are to be refueled and fly on to embattled Wake Island. With little time to rest, the plane is once again on the way to Clark Field in Manila. The crew feels the tension building as they approach the war, wondering how combat will be. They arrive at Clark Field, still burning from a recent attack. White is eager to find his son, a fighter pilot. But Lt. White had been killed in combat.

The *Mary Ann* sinks three Japanese ships in a desperate attack. Quincannon is mortally wounded but Winocki manages to bring the crippled B-17 in for a belly landing. The crew struggle to get her airworthy again for another mission against a Japanese invasion fleet headed towards Australia. With only minutes to spare, they get her in the air as Japanese troops overrun the field.

A photo of the B-17C 'Mary Ann' used in *Air Force* during filming in Florida.

The battle-scarred Fortress leads a tiny force of bombers to hit the enemy fleet in the Battle of the Coral Sea. After the *Mary Ann* finally dies in a crash landing, the crew joins the rapidly dwindling Allied army.

In March 1942 General "Hap" Arnold approached an old friend, Howard Hawks, a former military pilot. Arnold urged Hawks and Warner to produce an honest air war film. The USAAF would provide the aircraft, personnel and facilities for the film, despite the rapidly growing need for these assets in the war. With Arnold's blessing the film could only be called *Air Force.*

Warner Bros. budgeted nearly $3,000,000 for the production and was provided with the combat records of the 19th Group for research information. Production began with the climactic Battle of the Coral Sea, filmed in the Santa Barbara Channel with detailed 40-foot miniatures of Japanese warships.

Paramount leased the B-17 mockup used in *I Wanted Wings* to Warner for the process shots in the studio. For an early attempt at showing the gunners shooting at the Zeros, the action is intense and realistic. For the flying sequences, Hawks moved the production to Drew Army Air Field near Tampa, Florida, which stood in for the Philippines.

The bombed-out fields of Hickam and Clark were recreated on swampland near Drew Field. Many of the ground sequences were shot at night or in low light to add to the funereal atmosphere.

Ten B-17s were acquired with the cooperation of AAF liaison Theon Coulter and Sam Triffy. Two B-17s playing the part of the *Mary Ann* were B-17Bs #38-584 and 39-10. After filming they were reassigned to training duty until they were scrapped in 1946.

Drew Field provided several training Bell P-39 Airacobras, P-43 Lancers and a few Curtiss P-40C Tomahawks. The Japanese bombers were Martin B-26 Marauders from the 397th Bomb Group. The P-43s were painted as Japanese fighters. Paul Mantz supervised the aerial sequences with the help of cameraman Elmer Dyer.

Military and civilian authorities in the Tampa Bay area were warned in advance of the "Japanese" aircraft in the sky. Hawks, who was much like Wellman in his determination to get the job done, often made things difficult for the AAF pilots in the film. When the runway lights failed during a nighttime approach, it was only the quick thinking of a young James Wong Howe, Hawks' director of photography, who ordered flares placed on the runway to allow the B-17s to land. Hawks just kept on filming.

Triffy was nearly killed when a P-43 he was flying could not lower its landing gear. While he was finally able to get the gear down, Hawks later said he would have preferred a belly landing in front of the cameras.

Air Force was a gritty and honest drama set in the first uncertain and desperate weeks after Pearl Harbor. Scenes of dying women and children, of merciless Japanese troops and bombed-out airfields were intended to inflame the righteous might of the American people, to quote Roosevelt.

When models were shown landing or taking off, the wires were hidden by foreground foliage along the runways. It was one of the few weaknesses in 1940s-era special effects.

As for historical accuracy, Warner took some license with the facts. None of the B-17s that arrived over Oahu on December 7 reached Clark Field. The B-17s already based there fought a desperate battle to stem the Japanese tide until retreating to Australia.

One item of note is the sawing off of the bomber's tail to fit a tail gun. This field modification was done before the newer B-17Es, which did have tail guns, reached the western Pacific.

The attack on Japanese shipping was loosely based on the exploits of Captain Colin P. Kelly, who was credited with sinking the Japanese battleship *Haruna* with a B-17 on December 10, 1941. Kelly did not hit nor sink the *Haruna*, which was not in the Philippines, but his plane was the first B-17 to be shot down in the war.

Air Force remains one of Warner's best air war films, earning Oscar nominations for writing, effects and cinematography, and winning the Oscar for Best Film Editing.

The Japanese attack on Pearl Harbor has enshrined December 7, 1941, in the hearts and collective memories of the American people. After a rapid build-up of political, economic, cultural and military tensions, the Japanese sent the First Air Fleet to destroy the U.S. Pacific Fleet as well as Army and Marine air bases in Hawaii. After attaining almost total surprise, the Japanese withdrew to leave eight battleships and nine other ships sunk, hundreds of aircraft destroyed on the ground and over 3,500 Americans dead. That the attack had been carried out before a formal declaration of war had been delivered to the U.S. was one of the factors that inflamed Americans to fight and destroy the Japanese.

In 1968, twenty-seven years after the moment the first bombs fell on Battleship Row, Darryl F. Zanuck went out on a very long limb to produce the costliest, biggest and most wide-ranging war movie ever filmed. *Tora!* Tora! *Tora!*—made in the turbulent years of yet another war, Vietnam—was a very risky venture for Zanuck. Yet *Tora!* became the standard by which all following war films were measured.

As a detailed account from both American and Japanese perspectives of the events leading up to and including the attack on Oahu, *Tora! Tora! Tora!* is truly epic in scope and vision. The film has been the subject of scores of articles, books and documentaries, so the author will only focus on the aviation aspects of the production.

In order to recreate an entire Japanese air armada of 353 planes, twelve B-17s, several PBYs, scores of P-40s and a single Stearman, Fox had to build everything from scratch. The advent of Panavision, which used anamorphic lenses had almost rendered the millions of feet of wartime footage unusable, although as will be seen, it still turned up in later films. Since the events of December 7 existed only in grainy black-and-white newsreels, director Richard Fleischer used them as visual references.

Fox needed three years to prepare and eight months to film the massive project with a budget of $25,000,000. Elmo Williams, one of Fox's most successful producers, secured permission from the Department of Defense to film at the Pearl Harbor Navy Yard, the anchorages along NAS Ford Island, at NAS Kaneohe Bay, Hickam Air Base and several other locations. Although nearly three decades had passed since the attack, some things hadn't changed. There were bullet holes in the Ford Island runways, and the hangars at Kaneohe Bay still bore evidence of repair after the attack.

Thirty North American AT-6 Texans and Vultee BT-13 Valiants were modified in Long Beach with extended fuselages and wings, rebuilt tails, new canopies, three-bladed propellers and wheel spats. The final result was twelve A6M Zeros, nine D3A Val dive bombers and nine B5N Kate torpedo bombers. Twenty-one more AT-6s retired from the Japanese Air Self-Defense Force were modified for carrier deck scenes filmed in Japan. Fox acquired more than forty other planes including five flyable and five grounded PBY Catalinas, two flyable

The superbly filmed take off sequence aboard the *USS Yorktown* off the California coast for *Tora! Tora! Tora!*

P-40N Warhawks and five B-17 Flying Fortresses. Twenty-seven fiberglass P-40 mockups were built for the Wheeler and Hickam Field sequences.

A full-scale *Akagi*, flagship of the Japanese carrier force, and the battleship *Nagato* were constructed for the Japanese side of the project on the shores of Kagoshima Bay in Kyushu, Japan. To ensure technical accuracy, one of the advisors was Minoru Genda, who had planned the actual Pearl Harbor attack in 1941.

Captain George Watkins was chief pilot during the California sequences, which involved launching the planes from a carrier. One of the men the Navy assigned to the production as a lead pilot was Commander Dean "Diz" Laird. Laird was a Hellcat veteran with five Japanese victories during service in the Pacific. In an interview with the author, Laird commented on the experience of flying the "Japanese" aircraft: "George Watkins, whom we called 'Gorgeous George,' needed pilots with experience flying 'tail-draggers' in formation."

When Laird saw the "Japanese" planes, he was impressed. "For the Kates they cut off the AT-6 engine, added about three feet in front of the cockpit and replaced the engine. Then they cut the fuselage behind the cockpit and put on a BT-13 tail. With a long canopy it looked really good. A concrete-filled torpedo about ten feet long was hung under the fuselage. It weighed a ton," he laughed.

"The Kates had the AT-6 engine," continued Laird, "so we had to fly them at almost full throttle to cruise at 105 knots." The BT-13 Vals were fitted with wheel spats and a modified tail. "Watkins met all us pilots at Long Beach and said to me, 'I want you to lead the dive bombers down to North Island.'"

The uncannily authentic appearance of the Zeros, Vals and Kates was borne out when they arrived over San Diego. "While flying them down to North Island," Laird said, "we flew them right over the Coronado golf course." On the course that day were retired Admirals Max Leslie and Elliott Buckmaster. Leslie had been commander of Bombing Squadron 3 at the Battle of Midway while Buckmaster had been *Yorktown*'s captain.

"I was told later that when we flew over the course," Laird smiled, "Buckmaster turned to Leslie and said, 'Jesus, Max, I thought we shot all those sons of bitches down!'"

The planes were moved down to the dock and loaded aboard the second *USS Yorktown* (CV-10). Off the coast of California, Fleischer recreated the historic predawn launch of the strike force. *Yorktown's* modern "non-skid" flight deck was overlaid with a false bow and wooden planking to appear as the *Akagi*. When combined with the Japanese film unit's footage of the miniature and full-scale *Akagi*, the effect was perfect.

Laird's Val was first to launch. He and Watkins led the thirty planes into the skies without a single problem. The planes were then ferried to Hawaii.

Retired Air Force Lt. Colonel Arthur Wildern was the chief pilot for the Pearl Harbor attack sequences. He led a team of forty-seven off-duty and retired Navy, Marine, Army, Air Force and Air National Guard pilots who flew the Japanese and American aircraft.

When Williams and Fleischer first approached Wildern, who had been a fighter-bomber pilot in the Army during World War II and had participated in the sinking of a German cruiser in Brest Harbor, he told them he was the man for the job. He personally picked the men to recreate the attack and defense. The pilots had to have extensive close formation skills as they would be flying the planes in tight quarters and at extreme low-level over active Navy and Air Force facilities.

Among those pilots was Dean Laird. "Jack Canary called me and asked me to come out and fly for the film," Laird said. He and his fellow pilots logged more than 4,000 hours in the air while they bombed Pearl Harbor. For weeks Pearl rocked with the noise of roaring radial engines and explosions. "It was run just as if we were planning a real strike," Laird said. "A forward air controller worked with the cameramen to tell us when to come in on a run or do a re-take. For most of the shots there were only three planes, just Art and myself and a young Marine who had just come back from Vietnam. We wore Japanese flight jackets and brown leather helmets with fur lining."

"I was in one of the Kates during the first attack on Battleship Row," Laird remembered. "We came in low, banked and headed in. Of course there weren't any ships. That came later. But it was incredible. I also dropped bombs on the fantail of one of the destroyers. A stuntman was supposed to be blown off with the explosion. I hit it perfectly."

Jack Canary was killed when his Val lost control and dove into the ground.

Japanese actor Takahiro Tamura in a Kate torpedo bomber mockup in the role of Lt. Commander Mitsuo Fuchida as the attack force approaches Pearl Harbor.

The efforts of the pilots generated more than 35 hours of combat footage, using more than a ton of explosives and 120,000 gallons of diesel fuel for the pyrotechnics. After principal photography, Fox returned to Los Angeles for six weeks of backlot, miniatures and process shots.

Some details are worth mentioning. During the predawn takeoff, steam can be seen spewing from a point on the forward flight deck. This was Japanese practice to help pilots judge the wind direction. The early-morning orange sunrise reflects off the canopies while blue flames pulse from the radial engine exhausts.

Just minutes before the attack, a lone yellow N2S Stearman is flying over Oahu when the instructor and student pilot find themselves surrounded by the oncoming wave of torpedo bombers and fighters bound for Pearl Harbor. This actually happened. The pilot was Cordelia

Fort, a WASP working as a civilian instructor. Her plane was an Interstate Cadet monoplane. She took the controls from the student when she saw the Japanese planes nearby, although they didn't surround her as in the film.

Lieutenants Ken Taylor and George Welch were not the only Army pilots to make it into the air that day; actually 17 were able to do so. Taylor was credited with four kills and Welch with two.

One of the lengthened and modified AT-6 Texans in its role as a Nakajima B5N Kate torpedo bomber used in *Tora! Tora! Tora!*

Laird related an amusing anecdote about the two pilots who owned the P-40s. "One day they were called in by the director and parked about a hundred feet from the line of fake P-40s. When they went inside the hangar, I commented on how perfect the fakes looked. I said to my Navy buddies, 'Hey, that gives me an idea. Let's switch one of the fakes and park the real one in the line.' We did it. Then these guys come out and one jumps into his plane and the other one jumps in, and of course, there's no seat. He just falls in. Then he climbs out and walks all around the plane. We're on the ground laughing our heads off. Then he screams at us, 'Okay, who took my fucking plane!'"

A D3A Val dive bomber which began as a Vultee BT-13 Valiant. This aircraft is owned by Ken Laird of Pennsylvania. *Courtesy Ken Laird*

Lt. Dean "Diz" Laird of VF-171 in 1949. Laird was one of the lead pilots of the Japanese planes during the filming of *Tora! Tora! Tora! Courtesy Dean Laird*

There is a remarkable and unscripted sequence in the scene in which the Zeros are strafing the parked P-40s. A radio-controlled fiberglass P-40 with a working 1,100 hp engine was to roll along behind the parked fighters, get hit by strafing fire and crash. But the stunt coordinators lost control of the speeding mockup, which careened into the line of planes, causing total havoc. The stuntmen visible in the shot aren't acting; they're running for their lives.

One of the most famous scenes from *Tora! Tora! Tora!* as the B-17 slides into a one-wheeled belly landing during the attack.

Two Curtiss P-40E Warhawks, playing the part of Army P-40C Tomahawks, prepare to take off and attack the Japanese bombers.

The five B-17s seen in the film were all either F or G models, the latter with the chin turret removed. No B-17C or D models still existed.

According to Laird, the famous "wheels-up" landing was not planned. "The pilot radioed he had landing gear problems and the director told him to orbit the field until they could get five cameras set up," Laird explained. "Then he came in, smooth as glass, and touched down. Just perfect."

Aviation Chief Ordnanceman John Finn the day he received the Medal of Honor for his actions at NAS Kaneohe Bay on December 7, 1941. *Author's Collection*

The attack on the PBY base at NAS Kaneohe Bay shows a man using a .50 caliber water-cooled machine gun to shoot back at the low-flying planes. This was ACOM (Aviation Chief Ordnanceman) John W. Finn of Patrol Squadron 14. Finn was rousted from bed that morning to drive to the hangars and take up a heavy gun in defense of his base. Finn was wounded over a dozen times from 20mm shrapnel and was credited with shooting down two attacking planes.

The author knew Finn well before his death at age 100 in May 2010. In an interview at his home in Pine Valley, California, Finn recounted the events of that day and how they were recreated in the movie. "They got it pretty close," Finn said with a grin. "The kid playing me was in just the right spot between the hangars and shooting back like hell! That's what I had, a big, heavy .50 caliber. But I didn't have any sandbag revetments around me. My boys in VP-14 were bringing out belts of ammo so I could keep on shooting at the Japs."

Finn received the Medal of Honor for his deeds on December 7, and until his death was the oldest living MOH recipient and the only survivor of the six who received the honor for December 7.

"I liked that movie," Finn said with his characteristic candidness. "It brought back a lot of memories."

Of the Japanese planes in the film, most later turned up in private collections. One of the Vals is owned by Ken Laird (no relation to Dean Laird) of Pennsylvania. Others are owned and operated by various units of the CAF. Several have appeared in dozens of later films and television shows. *Tora! Tora! Tora!* footage found its way into *Midway* (1976), *The Final Countdown* (1980) and *Pearl Harbor* (2001). Imitation is the sincerest form of flattery, as will be seen in the next entry.

The final result of three years of work and a huge amount of money shows in the finished film. *Tora! Tora! Tora!* is as close as anyone will ever get to what it really looked like on December 7th.

With Hollywood's ever-growing mania to remake old films it was no real surprise when in 2001 *Pearl Harbor* was released by Touchstone Pictures. The film is a milestone in big-budget extravaganzas, utilizing the most advanced Computer-Generated Imagery (CGI) then available. The final result, while extravagant and awesome, is far more style than substance.

Pearl Harbor is about as historically accurate as a Tom & Jerry cartoon. Set against the backdrop of the Battle of Britain, the Pearl Harbor attack and the Doolittle Raid, the plot is an almost cruelly sappy love story based on the tired old love triangle. The movie was directed by Michael Bay, whose credits included the action-packed *Armageddon* (1998) and the later *Transformers* films. It's not hard to see why *Pearl Harbor* turned out as it did.

Rafe and Danny are two hotshot pilots in the USAAF. Close friends, they have a bond in the sky that stems from their rural Tennessee childhood. Rafe (Ben Affleck) falls in love with Army nurse Evelyn. He is under the command of Jimmy Doolittle (Alec Baldwin) and joins the RAF Eagle Squadron while Danny (Josh Hartnett) remains in the U.S. Rafe is shot down and presumed dead. Danny and Evelyn fall for one another while they are assigned to Hawaii. Rafe shows up alive and fights Danny over Evelyn. On December 7, Hawaiian shirts and all, they fly two P-40s from their small auxiliary field to fight the Japanese.

Doolittle recruits Rafe and Danny for a bombing raid on Tokyo. In a B-25 they take off from the *Hornet* to bomb Japan. They crash-land in China. When Japanese soldiers approach, Danny, knowing that Evelyn loved Rafe first, is mortally wounded saving his friend.

Rafe marries Evelyn and raises Danny's son as his own.

Short historical vignettes are inserted in the film. The Japanese plan to attack Pearl Harbor, Admiral Kimmel's frustrated efforts to protect his fleet, and FDR's half-hearted diplomatic maneuverings add some "authenticity" to the film. Japanese drum music telescopes the build-ups to the attack like a *Reader's Digest* version of *Tora! Tora! Tora!* All in all, *Pearl Harbor* lacked substance and was very short on credibility.

Several real aircraft were used in the film, supplied from various sources, including Chino's Planes of Fame Air Museum. Chief pilot Steve Hinton told the author about the museum's role in *Pearl Harbor*. "That was a good project," Hinton said. "At Badminton, west of London, we collected four Spitfires and Hurricanes and a few mockup Spitfires. We had our own Spanish 109, too. Some of the footage was done near the White Cliffs of Dover. We did about two days of filming with the Spitfires and Me-109."

The RAF sequence, using real aircraft, is good to the point of being believable.

Regarding the Hawaii sequences, Hinton described the work to get the various planes to the islands: "The planes were shrink-wrapped and placed on a barge at North Island in San Diego. We had two Kates, two Vals, three Zeros and a B-25." Also included were three P-40Ns and one P-40E. "We flew the hell out of those planes, putting in 500 hours in the six weeks we were there," Hinton continued. "We flew down between sets, in dogfights, in formation, tail chase, down runways. The movie has CGI, but it's mostly flying."

As mentioned, *Pearl Harbor* marks one of the first attempts to use CGI to recreate what had always been done with real aircraft, mockups and miniatures. Bay's penchant for action films came to the fore, putting the fighters into maneuvers that would tear a real plane apart and kill the pilot. Flying between buildings and under power lines, twisting and turning in impossible aerobatics were just a normal day at the office for the CGI pilots of *Pearl Harbor*.

When asked about the plethora of CGI used in the film, Hinton commented, "Bay would ask us, 'Can we do this?' and I'd either say yes or no. There were some things that had to be done with CGI, such as flying too close to the ground or between buildings, things that were not possible given the limitations of the area. But we did as much for real as we could. Then they took it and added all the CGI stuff later. Maybe three planes were in the air and the rest were added in the studio."

The Doolittle Raid sequence was primarily done aboard the *USS Lexington* Museum in Corpus Christi, Texas. "We took three B-25s down there," Hinton recalled. "That was an exciting takeoff because the ship was moored and not moving. We launched towards the sea. After running the engines up and releasing the brakes, once we were moving we were committed," he laughed. "Fly or swim." With no bomb load and just enough fuel to take off and land, the takeoff was relatively easy.

Rafe and Danny's dialogue is pure 21st-century cockiness, and hardly how real pilots would have behaved while their base, nation and comrades were being savaged by an enemy force.

To do justice to the many glaring historical shortcomings would require far more space than this chapter permits, but a few things need to be mentioned. For instance, the Japanese attack force takes off in broad daylight and attack at near noon. Jimmy Doolittle didn't recruit fighter pilots for the secret mission; instead he chose the 17th Bomb Group based in the northwest.

Bay's wardrobe department must have been patting themselves on the back for having the correct 17th BG shoulder patch on Rafe and Danny. Their characters are loosely based on P-40 pilots Taylor and Welch but that's as far as the resemblance goes.

Last but not least, the attack on Pearl Harbor resulted in the sinking and severe damage of far more than the explosion of *USS Arizona* and the overturning of the *USS Oklahoma*. Nowhere in this "historical drama" is there mention of Kaneohe Bay, the *USS West Virginia, USS Nevada, USS Tennessee, USS Maryland* or the other 12 ships which disappeared under the onslaught of Japanese bombs and torpedoes. Over 3,500 American military and civilians died and yet all that Michael Bay and his team focuses on are the *Arizona* and *Oklahoma*.

During pre-production, a noted aviation historian was allowed to view the screenplay. He commented, "You know, you have three movies here. Battle of Britain, Pearl Harbor and the Doolittle Raid." He was informed, "It's really just a love story set against a wartime background."

That says it all, but the film's advertising mentions nothing about a love story. Instead the ads touted *Pearl Harbor* as a historical drama. The theater trailer taglines were "December 7, 1941—it was a Sunday morning..." and "Experience the event that changed the world." Love story? *USA Today* said "[*Pearl Harbor*] is one of the wimpiest wartime romances ever filmed."

The late Roger Ebert had this to say: "The film has been directed without grace, vision, originality, and although you may walk out quoting lines of dialog, it will not be because you admire them. There is no sense of history, strategy or context." Bay protested Ebert's critique, insisting that the director and his team had done meticulous research. Yet when Danny is bore-sighting his fighter's guns, he says, "Tap in number 6," indicating the P-40 had six wing guns. The P-40B only had four.

David Thatcher, a surviving Doolittle Raider, commented, "I saw that movie for the first and last time in a sneak preview on board a carrier. There were about fifty Pearl Harbor survivors there. They all said that 'It wasn't like that.' I hated it. All the Raiders would have hated it."

John Finn had said it best: "The less said about that movie the better."

In January 1942 Captain Francis Low conceived the idea of launching Army medium bombers from a carrier. Low took the idea to Admiral Ernest J. King, who bumped it up to Roosevelt. In a remarkably short time Aviation Project No. 1 was born. Famed aviation pioneer Lt. Col. Jimmy Doolittle was chosen to lead it.

The 17th Bomb Group (Medium) was asked to volunteer for an important mission. Every single crewman of the twenty-three B-25s volunteered and flew to Eglin Field in a remote region of Florida. From there they learned to fly their 10-ton bombers off a runway in less than 500 feet—an amazing feat in itself. A few weeks later they flew to NAS Alameda near Oakland, California. There they found the brand-new *USS Hornet* (CV-8) waiting to hoist their planes aboard.

Not until the *Hornet* was well out to sea were they informed of their target: Tokyo. Six hundred miles from the enemy coast, a Japanese picket boat spotted the incoming force and radioed a warning. Two hundred miles short of their intended launch point, the bombers were loaded with bombs, extra fuel and as much goodwill and support as *Hornet's* crew could provide.

Led by Doolittle, one at a time the big B-25s—whose 67-foot wingspans allowed only six feet of clearance from the carrier's island superstructure—rolled along a pair of painted lines on the flight deck and clawed their way into the lightening sky. The date was April 18, 1942.

The flight to Japan and on to bases in China would be over 1,500 miles. Doolittle knew there was little chance of all the planes reaching the safety of Chinese-controlled airfields at night. After several hours, during which each plane and crew were totally on their own, the Raiders reached their targets and bombed Japan. Little real damage was inflicted but even so, the raid was a great morale boost for the American public and a sharp reminder to the Imperial General Staff of Japan's vulnerability.

Of 16 bombers, 15 either crash-landed in China or off the coast. Eight Raiders were taken prisoner by the vengeful Japanese, three of them were executed and one died of malnutrition and abuse. Most of the airmen returned to the states months or even years later, to find themselves decorated heroes.

The miniature of Tokyo used for the studio bombing sequences was built by Donald Jahraus, under the supervision of A. Arnold Gilliespie.

MGM publicized the Doolittle Raid in what is still considered to be the best aviation war movie ever made. *Thirty Seconds Over Tokyo* (1944) was based on the best-selling wartime book by Capt. Ted Lawson, who piloted Plane 7, *The Ruptured Duck*. The movie starred Van Johnson and Spencer Tracy a year after their teaming in *A Guy Named Joe*. The film tells a lightly varnished account of one of the most daring bombing raids of the war. Filmed in early 1944, while many of the Raiders were still out of the country or in prison camps, the film makes excellent use of the cooperative relationship that had grown between the studios and War Department.

The movie follows the 17th Bomb Group, and most directly Lawson's crew. Lawson's wife Ellen, played by the perky Phyllis Thaxter, arrives to be with her husband in Florida while he struggles to learn to lift his big plane off in fewer than 500 feet. Tracy, as a compassionate and efficient Doolittle, makes a few cameo appearances during training.

After their planes are hoisted aboard the *Hornet*, the airmen try to learn their way through the bewildering maze of corridors and compartments. When the Japanese detect the task force, all hell breaks loose, and the American planes are forced to take off in the morning, meaning they will arrive in China at night. Lawson's *Duck* follows Doolittle into the air and heads for Tokyo. There they find the city alerted and burning from ordnance dropped by the previous six bombers. After dropping their bombs on Tokyo, Lawson and his co-pilot Davenport know their chances of reaching an airfield in China are slim. The *Duck* runs out of fuel just as they reach the Chinese coastline and it crashes in the surf. The crew suffers heavy injuries.

Rescued by Chinese guerillas, the battered B-25 crew reaches the temporary safety of a hospital, where Lawson's badly torn leg is amputated. They hear of two other crews being captured by the Japanese. With the help of their Chinese friends, the crew of the *Ruptured Duck* manage to avoid the enemy patrols and eventually reach the United States.

Bruce Orriss, in his superb book *When Hollywood Ruled the Skies*, stated, "MGM's production of *Thirty Seconds Over Tokyo* achieved a realism unprecedented in a wartime studio production." Filming at Hurlburt, Eglin and Peel airfields in Florida, director Mervyn LeRoy worked closely with Lawson and c Dalton Trumbo to make the story of the raid come to life on film. With the cooperation of the War Department, MGM was able to secure the use of a dozen B-25Cs and their crews from a training squadron.

Lt. Winston Green of the 336th Training Squadron was a pilot for the production. It was his job to lift the heavy Mitchells off a runway that had the outline of a carrier deck painted on it—in fewer than 700 feet. In reality, the Raiders were trained to do it in fewer than 500 feet, but their B-25s had been stripped of extra guns and equipment. The B-25s used in the film were heavier.

After a long run-up to full power with brakes set and flaps extended, the bombers strained almost to the point of shaking apart. Upon releasing the brakes they fairly leaped into the air, often scraping the tail skid in the process. On film it looks extremely realistic and dramatic. Major Dean Davenport, Lawson's co-pilot, was technical advisor.

In March the production moved to Stage 15 at MGM, where a 130-foot section of *Hornet's* flight deck had been recreated. Three B-25s were used for footage of engine start-up and deck scenes. A 60-foot model of *Hornet* was set in MGM's 300-foot exterior tank. On board were sixteen 1/12th scale B-25s with working engines built by master modeler A. Arnold Gillespie, who had won an Oscar for MGM's *Mutiny on the Bounty* (1932). Gillespie's team simulated the movement of the carrier in the tank by pushing the water past the hull while pitching and rolling it at the same time. The six-foot B-25 radio-controlled models moved along a suspended wire into the air. With newsreel and live-action footage spliced in, the sequence is almost too perfect to be taken as studio effects.

The author was treated to a ride in the CAF's veteran B-25, *Maid in the Shade*, early in 2011. MGM's recreation of being inside a Mitchell is perfect, noise and all.

The second unit for *Thirty Seconds Over Tokyo* worked in the San Francisco Bay Area, filming the Tokyo bombing sequences from more of the B-25s. Using areas of Oakland that resembled Tokyo, the bombers flew at low-level over the water to 1,000 feet altitude while explosions, smoke and flame pots were ignited on cue. Most of the filming was done from a B-24 fitted with camera mounts in all the gun positions for maximum angles. These sequences were filmed only a short distance from where the real raid began on the runway and docks of Alameda. Shortly after the final bombing footage was completed, the studio learned of a real fire in East Oakland and contracted Capt. James Davis to fly two B-25s fitted with 16mm cameras to obtain footage of the fires while the planes flew over.

The acting is pure 1940s-era hyperbole. Johnson's acting tends towards overreacting, but in one scene, as he stops the *Duck* in Alameda, an officer asks him, "Everything okay on your ship?"

Lawson, knowing he has some mechanical problems, says in a very unconvincing tone, "Why, uh...yes, sir, yes sir!"

The film premiered in November 1944. It was nominated for two Academy Awards, one of which was given to Gillespie for Special Effects.

Sergeant David Thatcher is a Montana native who was gunner and flight engineer aboard Lawson's plane. As of this writing, David Thatcher was 90 years of age and was one of only five surviving Doolittle Raiders. In an interview with the author, Thatcher talked about his impression of the film. "I was in North Africa and had returned just as the film was being made," he said. "I was based in Santa Monica for a couple of weeks and met many of the actors and crew."

Asked about his opinion of the film, Thatcher said, "It pretty well followed the book, but there were a few things that weren't correct. We had a 120-gallon collapsible rubber fuel tank between the top of the bomb bay and the overhead," he explained. "We didn't use that gas until after we left Japan. Until that was empty I wasn't able to crawl forward to talk to Lawson and Davenport like they show in the film."

Robert Walker with the man he portrayed in *Thirty Seconds Over Tokyo*, Sgt. David Thatcher of Ted Lawson's 'Ruptured Duck.' Thatcher returned to the U.S. just as filming was ending and met the cast.
Author's Collection

Thatcher, who was the only crewmember able to walk after it crashed in China, had gone out to the plane in the surf to retrieve whatever they could use. "It wasn't until daybreak that I could see the damage. The front of the plane was smashed flat right back to the wing. It's a wonder any of the officers survived." As for Robert Walker's portrayal of himself, Thatcher said, "He had me down pretty good."

The sequences of the Eglin training garnered a comment: "They did it as well as we did in 1942—almost," Thatcher added with a chuckle.

Thirty Seconds Over Tokyo set a standard which has rarely been matched and never really surpassed. The Doolittle Raid sparked extreme reactions in Japan, prompting the General Staff to devise a major operation to attack and destroy the U.S. Pacific Fleet's carriers. This led to the Battle of the Coral Sea and in June, the attack on Midway.

One of the most interesting Pacific war films was Fox's *Wing and a Prayer* in 1944, starring Don Ameche and Dana Andrews. With Midway as its climax, the film follows the crew of an unnamed aircraft carrier tasked with decoying the Japanese. Commander Ed Moulton's (Andrews) rookie torpedo squadron causes no end of frustration for Air Wing Commander Bing Harper (Ameche). The captain, played by the grandfatherly Charles Bickford, has orders to avoid battle while allowing the ship to seen all over the Pacific.

Meanwhile morale aboard the carrier plummets. A pilot who loves his wife dearly is killed. A loudmouth who bragged he would personally sink a Japanese carrier brings shame on the squadron by disobeying orders. A movie star's crew is comprised of an underage gunner and a too-old radioman. A Navy Cross winner named Cunningham is unable to face combat.

A. Arnold Gillespie, the miniatures wizard of *Thirty Seconds Over Tokyo* and several other aviation movies.

Finally the captain reveals their true mission: to make the Japanese think the navy is scattered all over the ocean, leaving Midway ripe for the picking. They charge into battle with the Japanese fleet. Cunningham flies his plane into an oncoming torpedo, saving the ship. The movie star's crew gets lost in the fog. Moulton begs Harper to break radio silence but the strict Harper refuses. It is only when his plane crashes into the sea that Harper reveals that he cares deeply for every man in his air group.

Directed by Henry Hathaway, who would later direct *True Grit* (1969) and *How the West Was Won* (1962), *Wing and a Prayer* was written by Jerome Cady. He later wrote the suspenseful *Call Northside 777* in 1948.

Even though it is a fictional account of the Battle of Midway, *Wing and a Prayer* contains some excellent aerial sequences. Hathaway and three camera operators spent seven weeks aboard the *USS Yorktown* (CV-10) during her shakedown cruise in the Caribbean. Hathaway was able to get more than 50,000 feet of film covering every aspect of carrier operations for use in studio process shots. There is compelling footage of arming, fueling and spotting planes, run-up, takeoff and landing. All of the footage had to be approved by the War Department because they depicted current U.S. Navy carrier operations.

Several Curtiss SB2C Helldivers, Grumman F6F Hellcats and TBF Avengers were provided for filming on a large carrier deck mockup on the Fox backlot. The aerial battle scenes were filmed on Stage 9 and on the Fox lake with miniatures of ships and planes, combined with process shots, stock wartime footage and some impressive camera trickery.

Of note is the lateral hangar deck catapult used by Cunningham in his suicidal dive on the torpedo. The catapult was fitted on *Yorktown*-class carriers. They took up valuable hangar deck space better utilized for extra aircraft. They were rarely used in combat and after Midway were removed from *Enterprise* and *Hornet.*

What *Wing* lacks in reality it makes up for in character development and dialogue. Life and death aboard a carrier in wartime are given great attention. After being shot down, a crew desperately try to escape their sinking plane but are strafed by the ruthless Japanese while the ship's crew hears it all on the P.A. system.

Dana Andrews and Don Ameche wait for a missing plane in *Wing and a Prayer.*

The unpopularity of the Vietnam War made the early 1970s a bad time for war films. It wasn't until 1976 that a major war movie was produced.

Charlton Heston, one of Universal's top stars after the release of *Airport 1975* (see Chapter Eight), was cast as a naval aviator in the big-budget *Midway*. Based on a book by Donald Sanford, *Midway* is a mostly factual account of the most pivotal victory of the Pacific War.

In late May 1942, with the odds hugely stacked against them, a small task force of U.S. carriers, cruisers and destroyers sailed from Pearl Harbor to defend the tiny atoll of Midway from a massive Japanese attack and invasion. The Japanese force numbered over a hundred ships, including four carriers and eleven battleships. But due to superb cryptanalysis, intelligence and tactics (and a good deal of luck), the outnumbered American force managed to be in the right place at the right time to sink the carriers *Akagi, Kaga, Hiryu* and *Soryu* on June 4.

Commander Joseph J. Rochefort, the man whose team provided the crucial intelligence information that helped the U.S. Pacific Fleet to defeat the Japanese at Midway.

Heston is Captain Matt Garth, an intelligence officer working under Admiral Chester W. Nimitz, the Commander-in-Chief of the Pacific Fleet (CINCPAC). Garth is estranged from his son, Tom, a new ensign assigned to a fighter squadron. Tom is in love with a Japanese-American girl.

Thanks to some code-breaking wizardry, Naval code department chief Joe Rochefort finds the clue to Japanese intentions in the Pacific. Garth passes it on to Nimitz, credibly portrayed by patrician, white-haired Henry Fonda, and kicks off a chain of events that leads to a confrontation with the huge Japanese force near Midway Island. A carrier force led by Admirals Ray Spruance (Glenn Ford) and Jack Fletcher (Robert Webber) positions itself at the rendezvous known as "Point Luck'" to head off the enemy carriers.

Henry Fonda as Admiral Chester W. Nimitz with Cliff Robertson as Commander Jessop in *Midway.*

Back and forth the film carries the unfolding events, from the first alert by PBY Catalinas to the attacks on the island. The tragic suicide attempts by the doomed torpedo squadrons leave only a single survivor; while Admiral Chuichi Nagumo, commander of the carrier force, tries to cope with ever-increasing opposition from land and sea aircraft. Then American luck changes when the dive bombers appear high in the sky over the Japanese force and in five cataclysmic minutes destroy three carriers. The last Japanese flattop manages to launch a force to hit *USS Yorktown*, which is fatally damaged. *Enterprise* and *Hornet* send more dive bombers, led by Matt Garth, to hit the last Japanese carrier.

After reconciling with his son, Garth dies as he tries to land his damaged plane aboard the *Hornet*. In a way the audience was cheated because he was killed without a satisfying conclusion to the father-and-son soap opera they were forced to watch for two hours.

Captain Matt Garth, (Charlton Heston) questions slovenly code breaking genius Commander Joseph Rochefort (Hal Holbrook) in *Midway*.

The events leading up to and including the battle are seen from both the Japanese and American perspectives, as was done in *Tora! Tora! Tora!* six years before. In this case, however, the Japanese are American actors speaking English. *Midway* attempts to recreate the epic scale and realism of Fox's film, with far less effectiveness.

Director Jack Smight, who directed *Airport 1975*, did as good a job with the subject and screenplay as could be expected, considering the limited World War II-era hardware available. Frank Pines, who worked for Tallmantz Aviation on *The Great Waldo Pepper* (see Chapter Twelve), gathered a few authentic warbirds for the production. Two Grumman F4F-4s stood in for the planes of three squadrons, and a single PBY-5A Catalina played twelve different aircraft. A few retread *Tora! Tora! Tora!* Zeros, Kates and Vals appeared in carrier deck shots. A non-flying SBD Dauntless and F4F were used for cockpit process shots in the studio. A North American SNJ was modified to look like the cockpit of a Douglas Devastator. On Universal's Sound Stage 22 the production made use of sections of the scrapped *USS Hancock* for some flight deck and interior sequences.

Stock footage of Vought SB2U Vindicators from 1941's *Dive Bomber* appeared as both dive and torpedo bombers in *Midway. Courtesy* The Hook *Magazine*

Cast members of Universal's *Midway* pose before a vintage SBD Dauntless on board *USS Lexington* in the Gulf of Mexico.

Midway could have been titled *Tora 2!* as so much of the aerial and ground attack footage was liberally borrowed from that film. Many of the Hickam Field, Kaneohe Bay and Ford Island footage appeared as Midway's Sand and Eastern Islands. Even the one-wheeled B-17 landing was spliced in. Not content with using only footage from *Tora!*, Universal also took scenes from 1956's *Away All Boats* and even *The Battle of Britain*. Spitfires appear in some shots.

Ironically, scenes from the best air war film of all time were used to bolster one of the worst: The opening sequences of the Doolittle Raid are sepia-toned shots culled from *Thirty Seconds Over Tokyo*.

The use of more than the usual amount of stock footage adds to confusion. The Vought SB2U Vindicators in echelon formation from *Dive Bomber* are seen behind the cockpit mockup of the SBD Dauntless, TBD Devastator and F4F Wildcat. While the average viewer might not know the difference between an F4F and F6F, Universal's assumption that any blue plane with white stars will serve any purpose removes whatever credibility *Midway* might have had. For instance, Tom Garth's crash landing on the carrier is a much-used shot of a Hellcat crash from 1944. Matt Garth takes off in a Dauntless, flies with Vindicators in the background, dives for an attack in a Helldiver and crashes in a Korean War Grumman F9F Panther jet. It seems he must have perfected mid-air transfers in *Airport 1975* (see Chapter Eight). To mask the inadequacies of the process back-projections, nearly all the cockpit mockups are shown in heavy clouds.

One of the film's major weaknesses is the overuse of superimposed captions to identify ships. Captions for "Carrier Hiryu," "USS Yorktown," and PBY search plane "*Strawberry 5*" appear with maddening frequency, as if the audience were unable to figure these things out for themselves. Granted, the battle of Midway was a complex and fast-paced engagement with several events happening at once, necessitating some explanation in the script. But relying on the captions shows a lack of good writing. Even when Ensign George Gay, the sole survivor of Torpedo 8, is rescued, a caption informs the audience who he is.

Sink the Bismarck! (1960) also concerned a complex naval battle but excellent screenwriting helped the audience follow the chain of events. In an interview with the author shortly before his death, Cliff Robertson admitted he had been allowed to write his own lines for the role of Commander Jessop. "I think it was the best dialogue in the movie," he said candidly. "Some of the other stuff is just too heavy-handed and melodramatic."

For a macho over-actor like Heston, the role of a Naval officer is too plebian, especially for someone who chatted with God in *The Ten Commandments* (1956). Hal Holbrook's whimsical portrayal of a slovenly "aw shucks" Rochefort is not much of a compliment to a brilliant officer.

Filmed on location at Fort MacArthur in San Pedro, California, and at NAS Pensacola, Florida, much of the aircraft carrier deck and interior shots were done on board the *USS Lexington* (CV-16) while it was on a training cruise in the Gulf of Mexico. *Lex* portrayed all three of the U.S. vessels in the film, and more than one Japanese carrier. The *Lexington* had an angled flight desk for jet operations, a glaring difference from the straight decks of World War II vessels. In order to make *Lex* appear "foreign" the footage was flipped so the island superstructure was seen on the port (left) side of the ship. George Gay served as a technical advisor to the production.

A number of historical mistakes appear in the film. For one thing no Japanese pilot—deliberately or otherwise—flew his plane into the *Yorktown* in a Kamikaze-style attack. That was pure Hollywood.

Task Force, a 1949 Warner release, tells a dramatic history of the Pacific War. The film opens with Admiral Jonathan Scott (Gary Cooper) preparing to retire. In a narrative voice-over Scott flashes back to his stint on board the *USS Langley* (CV-1) in San Diego Bay in 1925. Scott joins a small band of young aviators as they learn by trial and error the dangerous business of carrier aviation. His commanding officer is Pete Richard, played by Cooper film staple Walter Brennan. Pete has his hands full keeping his young protégée out of trouble, but Pete's efforts fail miserably when at an embassy soiree Scott offends a Japanese envoy. Scott is sent to the Panama Canal for a cooling-off period. Meanwhile Naval air power is gaining in strength and prestige with the launching of *USS Lexington* (CV-2) and *USS Saratoga* (CV-3) and the development of advanced aircraft. Scott finally has his chance to fly with the fleet and weds Mary, played by the original soccer mom Jane Wyatt years before her *Father Knows Best* role.

The Scotts find themselves in Hawaii on a quiet Sunday morning in December 1941. After the attack, Scott sails out on *Enterprise* to help locate and attack the Japanese fleet. The build-up to Midway has Scott as Air Group Commander aboard *Yorktown* with Pete Richard. Scott eventually wins command of his own carrier as the war moves towards the invasion of Okinawa. There Scott's carrier is heavily damaged and is forced to return to the mainland as the war ends. The battle-scarred warship enters New York Harbor, with the Statue of Liberty seen through gaping holes in her hull. Scott reads the announcement of V-J Day to his crew. The scene returns to the present. As Scott steps onto the dock he is welcomed by Mary and Pete as a flight of sleek jets roars overhead.

The ending eerily foreshadows two future films, *The Court-Martial of Billy Mitchell* and *The Gallant Hours* (1960). Both have ending sequences that contain elements of *Task Force*, right down to futuristic jets in the sky and the Admiral's Barge with a retired warrior in civilian clothes.

Gary Cooper Naval aviation pioneer Lt. Commander Scott in *Task Force.*

Written and Directed by Delmar Daves, who wrote the screenplay for *Petrified Forest*, *Task Force* blends history with a pseudo-romantic drama to make the evolution of Naval aviation into a part of the film's allure.

Originally intending to use the millions of feet of wartime stock footage of the carrier war, Daves appealed to the Navy Department to allow his crew to film aboard a carrier. He was given permission to film aboard *USS Antietam* (CV-35) and the escort carrier *USS Bairoko* (CVE-115), both based in San Diego. The diminutive *Bairoko* served as the *USS Langley*, while *Antietam* served as the *Yorktown*, *Saratoga*, *Hornet* and *Franklin*, Scott's ship at the climax of the film.

Air Group 14 provided plenty of opportunity to film Hellcats and Avengers while the *Antietam* steamed along the California coast. A single SBD Dauntless was brought on board as a prop, along with Paul Mantz' modified Boeing 100/F4B which doubled as an F8C Helldiver. Mantz did the flying for a pivotal scene that depicted the first takeoff from the *Langley* in 1922, using a de Havilland DH-4 modified to resemble a Vought VE-7 Bluebird. With cleverly simulated newsreel footage, the scene is a very convincing representation of an aviation milestone.

Since much of the early military stock footage was in black and white, Daves filmed the first part of the movie in that format, then switched to color to make use of color wartime footage.

One of the more poignant sequences is of the doomed TBD Devastators as they take off to be massacred at Midway. The scenes are shown in correct chronological order as the war progresses with more advanced planes, rather than using the usual one-plane-looks-like-any-other method so often seen in war films.

The escort carrier *USS Bairoko* was modified to appear as the first carrier *USS Langley* for *Task Force*. The ship was filmed in San Diego Bay and at sea for the early sequences.

Scott's ship is referred to as *Clipper*, but it is clearly the *USS Franklin* (CV-15), which was severely damaged by a Kamikaze strike on March 19, 1945, during the Okinawa invasion. Over 1,200 of her crew were killed and wounded. She sailed to New York for repairs under her own power and became known as "The Ship That Wouldn't Die."

Pete Richards could be said to be Captain Marc Mitscher, who was one of the pioneers of early Naval aviation. The closest any of the actors comes to an actual historical figure is Bruce Bennett as McCluskey. Clarence Wade McCluskey commanded *Enterprise's* Air Group 6 at Midway. Cooper does well with the role of Scott, although it is necessary to suspend disbelief that the 47-year old actor could appear youthful in the early scenes. In his narration he sounds like Lou Gehrig giving his "I consider myself to be the luckiest man on the face of the Earth" speech from *The Pride of the Yankees* (1942).

The love story between Scott and Mary does not interfere with the pace of the movie.

The film's technical advisor was a former Navy fighter squadron commander, S.G. Mitchell, who served at Midway on *USS Hornet*. Mitchell's work with Daves is one primary reason for the production's technical accuracy. What makes *Task Force* worth watching is the incredible wartime footage that dramatizes a bygone era.

Three films emerged in 1943 and 1944 that told the story of how airmen were trained before going off to war. The first of these was Paramount's *Aerial Gunner*, starring *Wings* lead Richard Arlen. The film is all in flashback as Sgt. John Davis (Arlen) relates how only he and one other gunner survived a mission in the Pacific. John has an old enemy from his youth, Foxy Pattis (Chester Morris).

John is sent to the Air Force's Aerial Gunnery School in Harlingen, Texas, where he finds Foxy is his instructor. Foxy, still holding a grudge that John's father was responsible for the death of his own father, vows to make sure John will not graduate. The rivalry continues even when John saves Foxy's life during a ground firing test.

Sandy Lunt (Jimmy Lydon) tries to be a peacemaker but only gives the two men something else to fight over: his sister Peggy. Sandy, who has pushed himself hard to avenge his father who was killed at Pearl Harbor, dies after his gun goes wild and damages the trainer he is in. Peggy had already consented to marry Foxy but blames him for Sandy's death. The tables are turned when John, who excelled despite Foxy's interference, is given a commission and sent to fly bombers in the Pacific. Foxy is assigned as one of John's gunners.

John tries to encourage his crew to work together as a team. They fly off on a mission to bomb a Japanese island, and their bomber is damaged by Zeros. John and his co-pilot manage to land on another part of the island so his crew chief "Gadget" Blain (Dick Purcell) can repair the engines. John and Foxy fight off advancing Japanese troops with their machine guns as Gadget repairs the plane so they can take off. But Foxy refuses to leave knowing that Peggy is in love with John. He fights off the enemy troops long enough for John and Gadget to take off and escape. Accompanied by a spirited version of "Off we go, into the wild blue yonder," the dedication declares, "This is the story of the aerial gunner..." This may have been Paramount's intention, but the film is really just another convoluted love triangle about two men unable to work out their differences until one dies a martyr.

The production was filmed on location at the Gunnery School at Harlingen, Texas. There the actors were put through the same training as the gunner cadets, up to and including firing at targets in the air. It must have been a thrill for Arlen, twenty-six years after he'd dueled "Kellerman's Flying Circus." Arlen was 44 years old when he did *Aerial Gunner*, while Morris was 42, both rather old for basic training.

The Air Force provided the school's AT-6 Texans and Beechcraft AT-11s for the production. The AT-11 trainer was based on the Beechcraft 18 twin-engine transport. For once, the bombers were Consolidated B-24 Liberators rather than the ever-present B-17s. While not as attractive as the B-17, the B-24 was the other side of the Army Air Force heavy bomber coin. The B-24 could carry more bombs, fly higher, faster and farther than the B-17. More Liberators were built than any other U.S. combat aircraft—nearly 19,000 in all.

The second film purported to be "the story of... " training was RKO's *Bombardier* (1943). The lead was Pat O'Brien, who couldn't stay away from airplanes despite his experience with John Ford in *Air Mail.* O'Brien is Major Chick Davis, who is determined to prove that bombardiers trained on the new American bombsight will soon make the critical difference in strategic air warfare. Chick's old friend and adversary Captain Buck Oliver (Randolph Scott) argues that the difference will be made by dive bombers to hit targets on a dime. A duel of bombing techniques proves Davis right and he is given command of a new bombardier training school in New Mexico. Davis arrives with his best sergeant, Archie Dixon (Barton MacLane), to shepherd the new cadets into qualified bombardiers.

The old rivalry between Davis and Oliver heats up over a civilian woman secretary and the issue of whether the graduated cadets will become sergeants or officers. Davis pushes hard for the War Department to have the bombardiers commissioned as lieutenants. He has his hands full with these issues along with some of his cadets, who suffer from fear, airsickness, inability to learn the complexities of the bombsight, or an overactive libido. One cadet tells Davis he was approached by a spy to provide details of the bombsight. Davis arranges a trap and they capture the spy.

Eventually the first class graduates just as the Japanese attack Pearl Harbor. Davis is promoted to Colonel and put in command of a bomb group in the Pacific. Naturally Oliver and many of his graduates are in the same group as they take off for a night mission to bomb Nagoya, Japan. Oliver is in the lead ship to drop incendiaries on the target, but he is shot down before he can release his load. Captured and tortured, Oliver escapes and drives a truck through the target area, setting fires and illuminating the target for Davis' planes as they arrive overhead. The target is destroyed and Oliver is killed.

RKO worked with the War Department and the Army Air Force on *Bombardier*. John Twist's screenplay went through several revisions to keep pace with the war in Europe and Asia. Director Richard Wallace, who was known for romance dramas, took his film crew to Kirtland Army Air Base in Albuquerque, New Mexico, in October 1942. Virtually all the men seen in the film with the exception of the actors were air cadets undergoing training.

Midlands, Texas, was the location for the bombing of Nagoya, Japan. Ironically, Midlands is the home base of the Commemorative Air Force (CAF). Future directors Robert Wise (*The Hindenburg*) and Robert Aldrich (*Flight of the Phoenix*) were part of the filming unit.

The aircraft filmed are B-17E and B-17F Flying Fortresses, along with Douglas B-18 Bolos, developed from the venerable DC-2 airliner. Most of the B-18s deployed in the Pacific were destroyed on the ground in the first Japanese attacks.

The actual Norden computing bombsight is never seen or mentioned by name, as it was still considered top secret during the war. However, post-war examination of Nazi documents proved the Germans not only knew about it but also copied an early version before the U.S. even saw combat.

The author interviewed two USAAF bombardiers regarding the famed Norden. Lt. Lynn Tipton was in the 493rd Bomb Group. "Looking into the sight you're on a straight vertical line, that's your course," said Tipton. "A second line crosses that line. When the target passed under the second line, that's when you hit the bomb release."

Lt. Joe Armanini flew twenty-five missions with the famous "Bloody Hundredth" Group. "It was a very easy bombsight to operate, very accurate," he said. "You either went with the wind or against the wind, but if you had a crosswind, that's when the bombing was off. If all the settings were done correctly there was almost no way you could miss. We were told to destroy the Norden if we were forced down. They took its secrecy very seriously."

One of the first bomb groups to receive training at Kirtland was the 19th. As mentioned in Chapter Five, the 19th was sent to the Philippines via Hawaii on December 7, 1941. Brigadier General Eugene Eubank, former C.O. of the 19th, introduced the film. Davis is based on Col. John Ryan, who commanded the school at Kirtland.

Twentieth Century Fox's *Winged Victory* (1944) was directed by *Gone With the Wind* veteran George Cukor and starred Edmond O'Brien. Six eager young men join the Army Air Force to become pilots and are followed through basic training, flight training and into combat. Only four of the six earn their wings after one is killed in a training crash and another washes out to become a gunner. When the new officers meet up with their crew, they are presented with a brand-new B-24H. Their excitement takes over as the crew tries several silly and clever names, including *The Big-Chested Angel*, before agreeing on *Winged Victory*.

Christmas services in the Pacific are interrupted by a Japanese air raid. The bombers scramble. The entire episode is viewed from the ground with little understanding of what is happening in the skies. *Victory* arrives late over the field, damaged and with wounded aboard. The landing is violent and brings the audience to an understanding of how quickly fate can change lives in war. The ending is left to the imagination.

Winged Victory holds a special distinction as being one of only two major motion pictures to use B-24 Liberators. The young recruits spend a lot more time singing off-key than training, but are soon subjected to a bewildering, fast-paced series of tests and classes. All the officers in the film are real AAF instructors, as evidenced by their rapid-fire dialogue. Virtually every aspect of preflight, basic and advanced flight instruction is exactly what AAF cadets were put through.

The Army provided over a dozen technical advisors in everything from physical training to aerial combat for the production. Dozens of Vultee BT-13 trainers and several B-24 bombers were supplied. Filming took place at an Army airfield in Santa Ana and Camp Pendleton Marine Base in California. Screenwriter Moss Hart adds overly patriotic and maudlin sentiment to the plot in a way that would have warmed George M. Cohan's heart.

The Consolidated B-24 Liberator wasn't as popular or attractive as the B-17, but it could fly farther and faster with a bigger bomb load than the Fortress. The B-24 was seen in relatively few air war movies other than *Winged Victory*.

Winged Victory was the debut of several fine actors, most notably Gary Merrill, later to star in *Twelve O'clock High,* as well as *Invasion of the Body Snatchers*' Kevin McCarthy. George Reeves, later to be known as television's Superman, has a role. Edmond O'Brien, who was a Sergeant in the Army Air Force, later went on to star as a P-47 ace in *Fighter Squadron* (1948). Red Buttons was a Marine Corps corporal. In fact all 300 members of the cast were active duty military personnel.

The death of one of the cadets is a somber reminder that more young men die in training accidents than in combat. In more than sixty pilot and aircrew interviews the author has yet to find a man who didn't lose friends in flight training.

A mediocre 1952 Monogram release entitled *Flat Top* stars Sterling Hayden and Richard Carlson. Hayden is Collier, a CAG aboard *USS Princeton*, cruising off the Korean coast in 1952. While watching air operations he recalls being aboard the same ship just before the Philippines Campaign in late 1944. In a flashback he takes charge of a new squadron of undisciplined pilots who resent his by-the-book methods. But in time they realize he has their safety and success at heart and go on to become outstanding pilots in retaking the Philippines.

Filmed on board the light carrier *USS Princeton* (CVL-23) while on deployment to Korea, most of the men seen in the film are of Air Group 19, all combat veterans. A lot of previously unused combat footage of F4U-4 Corsairs was interspersed with live action work shot aboard the carrier. The film's plot doesn't offer much to the viewer but the aerial and combat footage is well worth watching.

As mentioned in Chapter Five, Captain Wallace "Griff" Griffin was a dive bomber pilot in Air Group 19 flying off *USS Lexington* (CV-16) during the battle of the Philippine Sea. He commented, "All that old combat footage really showed what it was like to fly in battle." Griff later transferred to fly Corsairs and had this to say about them: "Those Corsairs are just beautiful planes. I loved to fly them."

Dawn Patrol's old storyline reappeared when John Wayne climbed into a Grumman F6F Hellcat for RKO's 1951 release, *Flying Leathernecks*. Directed by Nicholas Ray, who would do *Rebel Without a Cause* four years later, the production was filmed in Technicolor.

Major Dan Kirby (Wayne) arrives in Hawaii to take command of an undisciplined Marine F4F squadron bound for the Solomon Islands and Guadalcanal. Kirby's job is to whip them into shape in order to fight off the determined Japanese forces attacking the islands almost daily. His second-in-command, Carl Griffin played by taciturn Robert Ryan, outwardly supports Kirby's hardnosed discipline and leadership, but privately resents him.

After several hairy missions in which the Marines give as good as they take, they are given new F4U Corsairs for the final drive to push the Japanese out of the Pacific. In the end the squadron is turned over to Griffin, who realizes Kirby had been an excellent commander all along.

The screenplay was written by James Edward Grant and Kenneth Gamet. Grant had written several Wayne films, including *Sands of Iwo Jima* (1949). Gamet was the writer for *Flying Tigers* in 1942. With those writers and his old friend Ray, it was no wonder John Wayne came off best in the final result.

John Wayne diving in his F6F Hellcat after a Japanese Zero in *Flying Leathernecks*.

Grant and Gamet rolled out a very old plot and added some World War II touches. *Leathernecks* tends to drag during much of the character and plot development, but in the air the film has few equals.

However, the film falls short in the use of F6F Hellcats, which first reached the Pacific in mid-1943, after the Guadalcanal Campaign had ended in a Japanese defeat. During the Marines, Army and Navy's three-month defense of that tiny island the Grumman Wildcat was the primary front-line fighter. A few Bell P-39 Airacobras and P-40 Warhawks filled in the gaps, but no Hellcats flew over the island during the period the film takes place.

Kirby's role is probably based on Captain John Lucien Smith, commander of VMF-223 on Guadalcanal. Smith had 19 victories over the Japanese during his time in the Pacific.

Filmed entirely on location at Camp Pendleton and El Toro Marine bases in California, the film also makes great use of color wartime footage. Tons of sand and ground coral were used to cover the Camp Pendleton runway alongside a complete 1942-era airfield set. To further disguise the arid southern California region, hundreds of palm trees and jungle foliage were planted around the location. More than forty Marine fighters from two training squadrons were brought in from El Toro Marine Air Base in Lake Forest, California. Also on the set was Paul Mantz with his B-25 camera ship to film all the aerial sequences.

The author interviewed Colonel Dean Caswell, USMC, about his participation as a pilot in *Flying Leathernecks.* Caswell flew Corsairs in VMF-221 in the Pacific in 1944 and early 1945. Staging off *USS Bunker Hill* (CV-17) he shot down seven Kamikazes in a single day. For the film, Caswell flew AT-6 "Zeros" for the film. "I had about 260 hours in the AT-6 so I could do whatever Paul Mantz wanted," said Caswell. "Short of actually getting myself killed, that is!"

"One day I was being shot down by John Wayne," continued Caswell. "Mantz was in that B-25. He had me stand on my tail, pointed straight up, kick it over into a snap roll, turn on the smoke generator, then fall in a spin. I was spinning right at the ground. Then I was to pull out just over the ground. I did it just right. But then Mantz started yelling that he wanted me to pull out *inside* the trees!"

The intention was to have the plane disappear in the trees and cut to a shot of an explosion. "I did it again and again and Mantz kept telling me, 'No, go lower, lower!' I finally got so low I came back with branches in my antenna wires. Mantz saw that and said, 'That's fine.'"

Despite Mantz' insistence on the nearly suicidal stunt, Caswell and the aerial coordinator got along well. "He scared hell out of me," said Caswell, "but he did the same things he told us to do. I liked him and I know he liked me."

As in all John Wayne films the Japanese came off the loser. "They always lost the fight," Caswell said, laughing. "One of the Corsair pilots got behind me and I swear he was really trying to shoot me down. I guess every "Meatball" he saw was still the enemy."

Caswell related that some of Wayne's off-camera parties were fantastic. "I danced with Maureen O'Hara, met Bing Crosby, Bob Hope, Jack Benny, Red Skelton, a whole bunch of stars." Wayne took Caswell under his wing, so to speak. "He wanted to be a Marine so much he couldn't stand it," Caswell said. "One Marine officer gave Wayne his USMC ring and he wore that thing like it was his own."

The Navy's patrol planes were given some screen time in MGM's *High Barbaree* (1947) starring Van Johnson and Cameron Mitchell. From a story by Charles Nordhoff and James Norman Hall, the plot follows a PBY Catalina crew, led by Lt. Brooke (Johnson) after they are damaged in a depth-charging attack on a Japanese submarine. Only Brooke and his navigator, Lt. Moore, (Mitchell) survive the forced landing in enemy waters. The film flashes back to Brooke's past, with his girlfriend, played by the throaty-voiced June Allyson.

Less a combat movie than a drama about men struggling to survive the elements in hostile waters, interlaced with an overly drawn-out love story, *High Barbaree* does have some interesting flying sequences. Nordhoff and Hall were well versed in writing about men lost at sea. They had been the authors of *Mutiny on the Bounty* and its companion book *Men Against the Sea* in 1934.

For the production, director Jack Conway—whose career went back more than twenty-five years—asked the Navy to provide two PBYs. The Navy re-commissioned two of the patrol planes. They were filmed on land, on the water and in flight around NAS North Island and off the coast of Coronado. Process shots were done on MGM's sound stages. The combat and flying sequences were first-rate, up to MGM's standards, but beyond that the film loses its focus and steam.

While the Marines, Army and Navy were slugging their way up the Pacific, island by island to within reach of Japan, another campaign was taking place back in the States. It was a new, ultra-secret project that would not only contribute to the ending of the war, but would literally change the world. The development of the Atomic Bomb, code-named the "Manhattan Project," was the War Department's all-out effort to end the war without an invasion of the Japanese home islands.

This book is not the place to debate the wisdom or folly of using the Atom Bomb on Japan, but the last entries in this chapter cover two movies which made the entire enterprise into a jingoistic, flag-waving justification for the act.

The Beginning or the End (1947), starring Brian Donlevy as a convincing General Leslie R. Groves, was MGM's first shot at the subject. With a few fictional characters and some amazing special effects, the film deserves mention here. The B-29 sequences were either USAAF stock footage or MGM studio mockups and process shots. A B-29 fuselage section served for most of the close-ups of the *Enola Gay* and other planes.

With no existing film of the actual Hiroshima blast, A. Arnold Gillespie managed a fairly convincing effect. An opaque white dye was poured into a large tank of water and glycerin, and filmed at high speed. Then the shot was reversed and projected against a sky and land background. It looked so good that the Air Force later requisitioned it for some of their training films.

Other factual events were recreated in the movie, providing very credible backgrounds for the story, but the film was quickly forgotten.

Above and Beyond (1952), written by Beirne Lay, Jr., and Norman Panama, takes the audience behind-the-scenes of "Operation Silverplate," the USAAF's role in the atom bomb project. Robert Taylor as Lt. Col Paul Tibbets, is transferred from a B-17 Group in Europe to wring the bugs out of the fire-prone B-29 Superfortress. Then he is offered the job of organizing and leading the new 509th Composite Group for a highly secret mission.

Tibbets is assisted by security chief Major Bud Uanna (James Whitmore), who is to find and stamp out all security leaks and loose talk. Lucey Tibbets (Eleanor Parker), who narrates the film, arrives at Wendover Field in Utah to be with her husband. But she has no idea what he is doing. She can't accept how much of him the job takes and it causes no end of frustration and marital discord.

Robert Taylor (right) as Colonel Paul Tibbets confers with a crewman in *Above and Beyond.*

Tibbets assembles his team of experts, airmen and scientists to perfect the bomb casing and the method of delivery. Several failed attempts to achieve a perfect drop only add to his stress. Then the group flies to Tinian in the Marianas, where they prepare for the big mission—still secret to all but a few high officers.

On the morning of August 6, 1945, Tibbets lifts the heavily-loaded B-29 he christened *Enola Gay* off the runway and turns north, headed for Japan. Once the plane is airborne weaponeer Deak Parsons arms the bomb and Tibbets tells his crew what they are carrying.

The vagaries of weather determine that Hiroshima will be the target. Tibbets flies the Superfortress over the doomed city and bombardier Thomas Ferebee releases the bomb. Tibbets yanks the B-29 into a tight turn as the sky turns an incandescent white. Watching the huge mushroom cloud rise over the burning city, Tibbets is awestruck by what he and his team have done.

Above and Beyond remains one of the best and most accurate versions of the Atom Bomb story. The newly established United States Air Force, having gained its independence from the Army, wanted to publicize its role in winning the war and cooperated with MGM. General Curtis E. LeMay, leader of Strategic Air Command, appeared in the film played by the future Thurston Howell III Jim Backus and gave the production his full backing. The Air Force provided three technical advisors, all of whom had experience with the B-29 or had served in the 509th. The same B-29 fuselage section from the earlier film was used for *Above and Beyond* at the Culver City studios. Eight B-29s were provided from Davis-Monthan AFB near Tucson, Arizona, where all of the Wendover and Tinian sequences were filmed. Paul Mantz and his B-25 were there to film the flying and bombing scenes.

A few inaccuracies can be noted. Even though *Enola Gay* left Tinian at 2:45 a.m. the movie has the plane lifting off in broad daylight. The bomb seen in the film as "Little Boy" was not an accurate representation of the weapon. When it falls from the B-29's bomb bay, it is actually footage of a Barnes Wallis 12,000 lb. "Tallboy" used by the RAF. The mushroom cloud footage from *The Beginning or the End* found its way into *Above and Beyond.*

The nose section of Boeing B-29 Superfortress 42-65401 that appeared as 'Enola Gay' in *Above and Beyond* and *Enola Gay* is now on display at the Stockton Field Aviation Museum in Stockton, California.

While technically and historically accurate, as far as national security would allow, the film slows when Tibbets and his wife share the screen in a tedious series of tender and tense moments. Their marital discord, which did happen but not at the time of his work on "Silverplate," was actually supported by LeMay to illustrate the truth about the Air Force's commitment to Duty, Honor, Country. Robert Taylor, who was known in Hollywood as "The Perfect Profile," was hardly a dead ringer for the boyish Tibbets.

The role of Major General Brent was done by Larry Keating, who often played patrician scientists as in *When Worlds Collide* (1951). The role is based on General Uzal Ent, commander of the 2nd Air Force, the man who chose Tibbets for the job.

The Japanese are never seen as people, only as a generic target city.

Released in January 1953, while the Korean War was in full swing, the film does offer a small note of humanity when Tibbets is interviewed by the press after returning from the raid. "Colonel," says a reporter, "I represent a news service that's read by sixteen million Americans. You just dropped a bomb that killed eighty thousand people. I just want to know how you feel about it."

Tibbets, showing his contempt replies, "How did *they* feel about it?"

Above and Beyond was only one of three films covering the Manhattan Project. In 1980 a television drama starring Patrick Duffy as Tibbets entitled *Enola Gay* told a more "politically correct" version of the story. *Enola Gay* made use of the only two flying B-29s: the CAF's *Fifi* and the American Air Museum's *Fertile Myrtle*. A third non-flying B-29 from Pima, Arizona, was also used. Together the three old warplanes were taken to Davis-Monthan AFB for the ground and flying scenes.

Thus ended the Pacific War, but as will be seen air warfare had a long way to go.

CHAPTER EIGHT

Drama and Disaster: Airliners

For most Americans the airplane isn't a weapon of war. Millions of people have come to take the airliner for granted as a means of fast, if not always timely, transportation. Since the dawn of commercial airlines in the mid-1920s, the aircraft have grown larger, faster, more comfortable and sophisticated.

With hardly a thought passengers entrust their lives to people they have never met and know nothing about: air traffic controllers, ground crew, mechanics, pilots, engineers, flight attendants and the thousand others who designed, built and maintain the plane they have boarded. With each passing year stricter regulations and a more cost-conscious airline industry have made travel by air more of a hassle than an adventure. The terrifying events of 9/11 and subsequent increased security measures have added a sobering element to the idea that "getting there is half the fun."

Some airliner films are pure drama but most focus in some way on the potential for disaster. Unfortunately for the audience, some of these films were disasters in more ways than one.

In 1936 First National released *China Clipper*, a fictional drama of the first transpacific airline to use flying boats. Dave Logan (Pat O'Brien) runs an airline between Washington, D.C., and Philadelphia. He wants to expand the company's reach, but he has serious financial problems that force his backers to sell out. Logan becomes hard and ruthless, alienating everyone. He joins his old friend Hap Stuart (Humphrey Bogart) to fly a Ford Trimotor on a risky Key West-to-Havana mail run, which quickly expands to cover the Caribbean and South America.

Theater one-sheet for *China Clipper.*

Logan's ambition drives away even Hap, who tells him, "You used to be regular, now you're not even human. You're letting your job turn you into a heel with a cast-iron heart. You got a swell gang here. They made this airline, not you." Logan angrily punches Hap, who quits and leaves. Logan is working hard on a venture to use a new and unproven flying boat designed by his elderly father on a transpacific line. Logan coins the phrase "China Clipper" for the new aircraft.

Government regulations put more pressure on Logan, and he continues to push everybody to their limits. Hap returns, encouraged by Logan's bold plan of assuring pilots they have a career with the airline. Logan's father works himself to death to give Logan the plane he wants.

Amid much fanfare the first huge flying boat lifts off with Hap at the controls. The plane wings its way over the Pacific, from Honolulu to Midway to Manila, into the teeth of a typhoon, and finally arrives in China.

Directed by Ray Enright (whose work included several westerns) and written by Frank Wead, *China Clipper* is a fictional dramatization of the most ambitious airline goal ever dreamed. As Logan correctly put it: "A four-engine flying boat with an average cruising speed of 160 knots at 60 percent horsepower, with a full load range of 3,500 miles. Thirty-six passengers and 24 sleeping passengers, 2,000 pounds of mail or express, with a crew of six. That plane will have a gross weight fully loaded of 26 tons, and we expect it to take off on three of its motors."

The Martin MB-130, workhorse of the Pan-American China Clippers.

From 1935 to just prior to World War II, Martin M-130 and later Boeing 314 four-engine flying boats flew from the United States to various Asian cities. Interestingly, the navigator on the inaugural flight of Pan-American Airways' *China Clipper* in November 1935 was Fred Noonan. Noonan was lost in July 1937 with Amelia Earhart.

The film is a veiled advertisement for what was once one of the greatest airlines in the world.

Bogart was reaching his career peak, having just finished the role of Duke Mantee in *The Petrified Forest.* The normally gentle O'Brien plays a driven, thoughtless, even mean dreamer, which turned many fans off the film after its August 1936 release.

Enright made extensive use of stock footage of the M-130 flying boat at anchor, takeoff, in flight and landing. Some actual cabin and cockpit footage was also used but mockups based on photos served for most interior scenes. Even tiny Midway Island has a small appearance six years before it became a target for the Japanese Navy.

One of the better RKO airline films was 1939's *Five Came Back.* With a troupe of character actors, the film follows a race against death for eleven passengers and crew of a small South American transport after it crashes in the jungle. Aboard the plane are the competent and unflappable pilots, a bodyguard hired to escort a gangster's five-year old son, a chorus girl with a heart of gold hidden under an acerbic shell, a police officer escorting a condemned prisoner, a young couple, and a kindly old anthropologist and his wife. Together they find themselves in real danger after being forced down in a storm. The airplane can be fixed but it will take time, and the increasingly insistent drumming of unseen cannibal natives heralds a certain and terrifying fate.

The eclectic band of survivors work and quarrel with each other. Ellis, who is engaged to be married to Alice, is a belligerent drunk and is taken to task by Brooks, the pilot. Chorus girl Peggy (Lucille Ball) feels motherly affection for little Tommy, who doesn't know his gangster daddy has been killed. Tommy's bodyguard Pete, played by the less than avuncular Allen Jenkins, dies when he encounters the natives. The prisoner Vasquez is befriended by Professor and Mrs. Spengler, played by the epitome of old-English charm, C. Aubrey Smith and Elisabeth Risdon, who find in him a surrogate son. John Carradine is a bellicose cop who also falls victim to the cannibals.

Brooks and his co-pilot Joe have finally finished repairing the plane. The dwindling group clears enough jungle to allow a takeoff. The bad news is that the plane can only carry five of the nine survivors. Vasquez, who has nothing to lose, uses the gun he took from Pete's body to choose who will leave and who will stay. Peggy, Tommy, Brooks, Joe and Alice are to go. Ellis challenges Vasquez and dies. The Spenglers willingly remain behind, earning the respect of the saved. As the plane gathers momentum and lifts off into the night sky, the native drumming ceases. Professor Spengler urges Vasquez to kill them to save them from a horrible fate. Knowing he has only two bullets, Vasquez calmly shoots them and faces his own doom.

Written by Jerome Cady, who wrote *A Wing and a Prayer* (1944), the plot and interaction between characters is the best example of what was later done, with less effectiveness, in *Lifeboat* (1944) and *The Poseidon Adventure* (1972).

The single 1933 Capelis XC-12 twin-engine transport was a failed attempt by a Greek restaurant owner named Socrates Capelis to enter the commercial airline market. The plane's unusual design had a low wing with high-set engines and a triple tail with bi-level stabilizers. After only a few flights, the XC-12 was grounded as a safety hazard.

The one-of-a-kind Capelis XC-12 transport used for ground scenes in *Five Came Back*. This same plane was also used in Republic's *Flying Tigers* (see Chapter Seven). *SDASM Collection*

For the next decade the Capelis and models of it appeared in over a dozen other films and serials by RKO, Republic, Universal, Fox and Monogram, including 1942's The *Flying Tigers*.

The plane was placed in the RKO soundstage, which was dressed with the usual heavy jungle foliage. During the crash-landing and takeoff shots, the large model was towed by wires along a cleared strip between foreground and background trees to conceal the guide wires.

Some of Cady's best work went into the dialogue between the Spenglers and Vasquez, portrayed by the Maltese-born Joseph Calleia, who was most often cast as Italians, Spaniards and Mexicans in several action films.

According to some *Star Trek* fan sites, the film was an inspiration for S. Bar David and Oliver Crawford's story for the classic *Star Trek* episode *The Galileo Seven*, in which several crewmembers are stranded on a planet with hostile indigenous tribes.

World War II pushed most of the airline-related film projects on the back burner. But after the guns fell silent it wasn't long before a few minor and major productions emerged about airline and transport subjects. Hollywood was slow to catch on to how quickly the public was taking to flying from place to place in early Douglas and Boeing aircraft.

Daredevils of the Clouds (1948) was released by Republic and directed by George Blair. Blair was later best known for science fiction and adventure serials, and this is reflected in *Daredevils*. American Terry O'Rourke (Robert Livingston) owns a small airline in Canada. Times are hard and O'Rourke, a former military pilot, is struggling to keep from losing his shirt.

Canada's often rough weather and rugged terrain causes no end of problems, making passenger and cargo transport a constant juggling act of compromises. A big American airline is trying to buy out O'Rourke, but he thinks that the price is far too low.

A crooked pilot plans to parachute from his plane which is carrying a shipment of gold. The crashed plane will be looted by the pilot's cronies. But a loyal employee learns of this and sabotages the parachute. The pilot jumps to his death. Meanwhile O'Rourke and pilot Kay Cameron (Mae Clarke) take off to find the wreck and hunt down the thieves. After a short but suspenseful chase, they find the thieves, recover the gold and are rewarded, thus saving O'Rourke's airline.

The film is only 60 minutes long, and the plot is simple and predictable: the "little guy struggling against the odds to survive" with an airliner twist. Clarke's most notable film appearance was having a grapefruit shoved in her face by James Cagney in *The Public Enemy* seventeen years earlier. The gold theft and pursuit was later recreated in *Cliffhanger* (1993) with Sylvester Stallone.

James Stewart as the self-absorbed Theodore Honey talking to Marlene Dietrich as actress Monica Teasdale in 1951's *No Highway in the Sky. Author's Collection*

No Highway in the Sky (1951) was James Stewart's first aviation-themed postwar film. Theodore Honey (Stewart) is an almost comically absent-minded American scientist working for an aeronautical establishment in England. He is obsessed with proving the theory of metal fatigue in the Rutland Reindeer, an aircraft in worldwide commercial service. A series of mysterious crashes compels Honey's employers to send him to Labrador to investigate the wreckage. It is only when Honey realizes he is aboard a Reindeer with far more than the safe level of flight hours does he see the human side of the danger.

Kenneth More is a wisecracking co-pilot who counteracts Stewart's determinedly focused goal of stopping the plane. Glynnis Johns (as a compassionate stewardess) and Marlene Dietrich (as a Garbo-esque film star whom Honey tries to protect) add a potential but never-realized love triangle to the story. The two women try to protect the childlike Honey from the wrath of passengers after he deliberately damages the plane to prevent it from flying on to its doom.

The production was filmed in Denham Studios, Bucknghamshire. German-born Director Henry Koster had worked with Stewart on *Harvey* (1950) and was nominated for an Academy Award for 1947's *The Bishop's Wife*. The film was based on Nevil Shute's novel *No Highway.*

The fictional Rutland Reindeer was in fact a radically modified Handley-Page Halifax bomber of World War II. A variant of the Halifax was the HP.70 Halton, converted as a civilian transport. After fitting on a distinctive tail, swept wings, engine nacelles and a new nose, the Reindeer was born. A detailed miniature was used for the takeoff sequences. The takeoff scene used the model against an unconvincing matte, as the plane jumped and wobbled in the frame. Interestingly, Honey's theory of metal fatigue was proven true following numerous crashes of Britain's finest jet airliner, the de Havilland Comet, in 1954. *No Highway*, a relatively unknown comedy-drama, is worth watching as an early disaster film.

The fictional 'Rutland Reindeer' that appeared in *No Highway in the Sky* was in fact a very radically modified Handley-Page HP.70 Helton transport, a variant of the venerable Halifax bomber of World War II.

Some of the details of engines and wing can be seen on the Reindeer.

William Wellman directed Ernest K. Gann's first major screenplay, *Island in the Sky*, in 1953 with John Wayne and Lloyd Nolan. Gann had been a pilot with American Airlines and later flew several harrowing missions in C-47s and C-54s over the Himalayas during the war.

Co-produced by John Wayne and Robert Fellows, the Warner production follows Captain Dooley (Wayne), an airline pilot contracted to fly for the Army Air Transport Service to Europe via Labrador, Greenland and Iceland. Dooley leads the crew of a Douglas C-47 Skytrain as they struggle to survive an emergency landing near a frozen lake on the Quebec-Labrador border. Bad weather and navigational error make the odds of rescue very low. Temperatures drop to minus 40 degrees below zero. The rescuers are searching, desperate to find the downed airmen before time runs out. Tension, quarrels and wrong turns further lower the odds of success. Finally Dooley and his men are found and rescued.

The voiceover narration was done by Wellman himself. He would perform the same duty in his last air film, *Lafayette Escadrille* in 1958.

John Wayne, Sean McClory, Jimmy Lydon, Wally Cassel and director William Wellman on location in Truckee, California for *Island in the Sky*. Note 'crashed' DC-3 in the background, *Island in the Sky. Collection of William A. Wellman, Jr.*

Gann based the story on his own experiences during a search for the crew of a downed plane in 1943. The action and plot are hard-bitten, even raw, according to critics who applauded the film's realism. Wayne leads a cast of stars and character actors, including cowboy actors James Arness, Andy Devine, Paul Fix and "Daniel Boone" Fess Parker. Also two former child actors, Darryl Hickman, who played Winfield in *The Grapes of Wrath* (1940), and Carl "Alfalfa" Switzer appear as airmen. Switzer would be murdered six years after the film's release.

The California Forestry Service assisted the production by cutting trees for a runway at Donner Lake in the Sierra Nevada Mountains near Truckee, California. A C-47 was flown in and "damaged" to appear as the crashed transport. Weather conditions during the January to March 1953 location shooting were harsh. The ground scenes were shot with little need for visual effects, other than the use of wind machines and simulated snow. As for the aerial shots of the C-47 being laden with ice and the final crash-landing, they are pure vintage Wellman. It would be easy to see Dick Grace at the controls.

A totally unbelievable sequence occurs when Dooley's co-pilot Frank opens the right cockpit window and sticks his head out to see ahead. Outside it is at least twenty below zero with a 100-knot airstream. The entire aircraft is one solid blanket of ice. Not only is Frank unaffected by the frozen air on his face, but he is also able to talk to Dooley in a normal voice, and doesn't even lose his hat.

While *Island* bears some striking similarities to 1964's *Fate is the Hunter*, both films are considered aviation classics.

The next of Gann's stories was *The High and the Mighty* (1954). Once again John Wayne, as co-producer, was the male lead. Gann's screenplay told the story of the passengers and crew of an airliner flying from Honolulu to San Francisco. Midway through the flight, the plane experiences severe engine trouble, which also causes a loss of fuel. The pilot, John Sullivan (Robert Stack), is convinced the plane will have to be ditched in the ocean, and that many of the passengers will die. His co-pilot Dan Roman (Wayne) is equally sure they can make land before the fuel runs out. Roman is old for a co-pilot; his experience goes back to the First World War and barnstorming, then flying bombers in World War II. He survived a crash just after the war which tragically took the lives of all on board, including his wife and son.

The tension builds to a fever pitch in the cabin, on the flight deck and in San Francisco as the plane's crew struggles to reach land. With two of the four engines out of fuel and the gauges reading nearly empty, Sullivan and Roman manage to milk a few more miles from the plane and make a suspenseful landing with dry tanks.

The High and the Mighty was the first real major airline disaster film, preceding the *Airport* series by almost twenty years. It had all the elements of the later movies, including passengers and crew with major personal problems. Paul Fix and Carl Switzer again appear in small roles, as does William Campbell, who later made a name for himself as the Klingon

Captain Koloth in *Star Trek* episode *The Trouble With Tribbles* in 1967. Another featured player is Phil Harris, the longtime wisecracking bandleader on the Jack Benny radio program.

Business tycoons, old rivals with a grudge, little boys traveling alone, nervous first time flyers, and bickering spouses all add to the tension and the tedium. Not a well-adjusted person in the lot. The dialogue might have made a reviewer think the movie was an overly complicated, weepy soap opera on an airliner that just happens to be in danger of crashing into the sea. When Roman goes back to tell the passengers of the danger it's more of a chat about how to ditch successfully, complete with jokes and tears. An interesting note is that the stewardess hands out the life vests from a box.

Jack Warner didn't believe movie audiences would accept a full-length film set inside an airliner. Wellman used every trick in the book to pull a dramatic story out of actors forced to wait inside a fully furnished airline cabin for hours on end. Instead of the large bulky CinemaScope cameras then in use for most epic films, Wellman used an anamorphic lens on a standard 35mm camera to provide a wide-angle vision of the aircraft cabin. With the help of experienced cinematographer William H. Clothier, who worked with Wellman on *Island*, Wellman managed to convey the cramped confines of the cabin while not making the audience feel claustrophobic.

Young Mike Wellman, son of the director with his screen father on the set of *The High and the Mighty*. Note repainted Transocean Airlines C-54 in the background. *Collection of William A. Wellman, Jr.*

The aircraft used for the ground shots was a former military C-54 transport that in 1953 was operated by the California-based Transocean Airlines. The airline's chief pilot Bill Keating did the stunt flying for the production. Keating was asked by Wellman to do several landings, each one closer to the runway threshold than the one before it, to get the most dramatic shot possible. On Keating's final attempt he hit the runway lights with his nose gear.

A second C-54 with wing and engine damage was used for the final sequences filmed at Glendale's Grand Central Airport. Oakland Airport served as Honolulu's airport for the engine start-up, taxiing and takeoff scenes. A large-scale model was filmed against backdrops for the sequences of the damaged plane. A rare Coast Guard B-17/PB-1G "Dumbo" patrol plane followed the airliner.

William Wellman, Jr., related anecdotes about the film's shooting, including a story about Wayne attempting to take over as director. "My father yelled at Wayne and said, 'Look, you come back here behind the camera and do my job, and you're going to look just as ridiculous doing it as I would be going out there with that screwy voice and that fairy walk being Duke Wayne.'" That apparently ended the matter and added another page to "Wild Bill" Wellman's legend. "That really happened," Wellman, Jr., said, laughing.

"Except for the fact that it's about an airplane," continued Wellman, "it's not the sort of picture my father was used to making. It's a soap opera. My father said it was *Grand Hotel* with wings. The actors didn't like it, because they could be filming someone in the front seats and the people in the back had to stay there in character, for take after take."

The film's impact on audiences was varied but very positive; *The High and the Mighty* was the basis for nearly every disaster film to come, including *The Towering Inferno* (1974).

The third in the Gann aviation trilogy, as it were, was 1964's *Fate is the Hunter*, starring Glenn Ford and Rod Taylor. Ford, whose last flying role was in Wellman's *Gallant Journey*, has graduated from gliders to airliners. He is airline executive Sam McBane. He is the last friend of Jack Savage (Taylor), a pilot who was accused of causing the death of 53 passengers in a plane crash. The investigation concluded that Savage had been drinking.

McBane believes his friend did not cause the crash and tries to prove it. He is beset by bureaucratic apathy and officials who want the matter dropped. But McBane perseveres and finally forces an impartial investigation that recreates the events leading up to the crash. The investigation finds that a spilled cup of coffee had shorted out some instrumentation, leading Savage to believe that an engine had caught fire, thus causing the accident. Savage is cleared.

The story was also based on Gann's experiences. Unlike *High and the Mighty*, this film centers on the aftermath of a crash and the subsequent guilt, repercussions and investigation to learn the truth. It has many of the elements of a National Transportation Safety Board (NTSB) investigation, including a recreation of the events leaving to the crash.

Wellman did not direct this film, frustrated by Warner's poor treatment of *Lafayette Escadrille.* Instead Ralph Nelson was given charge of the production. Nelson had already directed *Lilies of the Field* in 1963 and *Father Goose* a year later. He would go on to direct Cliff Robertson in his Academy Award performance of *Charly* in 1968. Able to evoke strong suspense and emotion from his actors, Nelson did so with Ford and Taylor.

No aircraft manufacturer was willing to provide a real, flyable plane for the film. Douglas apparently insisted that their DC-7B not even be recognizable. Two DC-7Bs were cannibalized and fitted with parts from at least one Boeing 707 to create a jet for the movie's ground and crash sequences. The wings were taken off the DC-7B and remounted to make it appear as if they were swept back. The nose of a 707, along with a long spike, was added. Other modifications completed the " Consolidated Airways" aircraft. The runway, taxiway and tarmac were constructed on the Fox backlot.

The film drew mixed reviews, and a dissatisfied Gann reportedly asked that his name be removed from the credits. The film wasn't totally forgotten, though. The sixth episode of the television series *JAG*,—entitled *Pilot Error* (1995)—made several references to *Fate is the Hunter*.

Paramount's 1957 production of *Zero Hour!* had little effect on the genre of airline disaster films, but it cropped up in an unusual place twenty-three years later. Starring Dana Andrews and beauty Linda Darnell, *Zero Hour!* tells the saga of an airliner whose crew is incapacitated by spoiled food. The tension builds while the passengers cope with their impending doom and the airline executives and controllers try to find a solution.

Paul Mantz' favorite North American B-25 N1203 camera plane in the 1950s. The modified Mitchell was used in dozens of aviation films after the war.

The story was adapted from a 1956 Canadian Broadcast Corporation play entitled *Flight Into Danger* by Arthur Hailey, Jr., who would later go on to write some of the *Airport* films in the 1970s. Interestingly this film's lasting claim to fame is how it cropped up in a comedy film 23 years later. Paramount purchased the rights to the story for the Zucker and Abraham's madcap comedy *Airplane!*, released in 1980. Even the main character Ted Stryker returns, this time in the form of Robert Hays. (For more on this film see Chapter Twelve.)

Collisions between aircraft had been happening since the Wright Brothers first took to the sky, but it wasn't until 1960's *The Crowded Sky* that a major film concerned an airline collision. Director Joseph Pevney would go on to direct television's *Star Trek* two years later. Oscar winner Charles Schnee wrote the screenplay based on a novel by Hank Searls.

The Crowded Sky is a drama about an impending collision of a Navy jet fighter and an airliner. The fighter is flown by Commander Dale Heath, played by future *FBI* lead Efrem Zimbalist, Jr. Heath was involved in a mid-air collision over El Toro, killing three other men. He is flying an F-80 from NAS North Island to Washington, D.C., with a sailor named McVey (teen heartthrob Troy Donahue) as passenger. Also in the air is a Trans State Airlines DC-6 headed to Los Angeles. The pilot is again Dana Andrews as Dick Barnett.

1950s teen heartthrob Troy Donahue climbs into a T-33 in *The Crowded Sky*.
Courtesy Efrem Zimbalist, Jr.

On board are a collection of passengers and crew with a lot of problems. Barnett and his co-pilot Mike Rule are old enemies. A series of mental voice-overs and flashbacks relate the tortured stories of the crew and most of the passengers. The tension builds while the two aircraft grow ever closer.

Heath is dealing with a balky radio. "It's a crowded sky," he says to McVey. "Planes flying without ATC tally up over 2,000 near misses a year. A near miss is two planes missing by"—he holds up his right hand with thumb and forefinger an inch apart—"that much."

Finally the two planes are fast approaching one another. In his last act, Heath makes sure McVey ejects while Heath sacrifices himself. In a blindingly fast encounter the jet slices into the DC-3's belly. While their lives hang in the balance, the passengers all come to the inevitable self-realization and epiphanies that change their lives. In the end the airliner makes an emergency landing.

In an interview with Zimbalist, the author learned some of the actor's thoughts on the film. "It was pure drama," said Zimbalist, "not like the action films that came along later. Lots of flashbacks and personal stories."

Efrem Zimbalist as Air Force pilot Dale Heath with Donahue in the back seat of the T-33 mockup. Zimbalist said he found it difficult to act while not being able to see the face of the other actor. *Courtesy Efrem Zimbalist, Jr.*

National Airlines leased a Douglas DC-6 airliner to Warner. It was painted in the fictional 'Trans State Airlines' colors. National provided pilots for the aerial sequences.

While the passengers are settling in, the engines are heard to start up, rattling and sputtering. This would be very disconcerting to anyone not familiar with flying radial-engine aircraft today, but in the late 1950s none of the passengers takes notice. The sound of engines was much more evident. Minor technical details add authenticity to the script, as when Barnett is told the fuel mixture is too rich on the Number 2 engine. He tells the flight engineer to check the exhaust flame color, an old pilots' trick.

The crash landing is spectacular as huge flames erupt from the burning engine.

The Lockheed F-80 Shooting Star was provided by the Navy but painted in NASA colors. "We did dozens of takes of Troy and I getting in that plane," Zimbalist said. "It's a very small cockpit and we got very sweaty. Makeup had to keep re-doing our faces to keep us looking like we'd just shown up for the flight."

Zimbalist commented on the process shots: "I had to do scenes with Troy even though we weren't facing each other. That was a new experience." He watched some of the miniature work being filmed. "I was fascinated by how they filmed those models to look like great big airplanes. When you watch it being done you think, 'That looks fake.' But then you see it on the screen and it looks so real."

Turnabout was fair play for Zimbalist and Andrews when Universal began a new era in big-budget disaster films with *Airport 1975,* the second, (some say first) in a series of all-star, suspenseful airline films. The movie opens with appropriately dramatic music written by John Cacavas, best known for suspense and horror films. Columbia Airline Flight 409 pilot Stacy (Zimbalist) is flying a 747 to Los Angeles. As the plane with its human cargo is over the Rocky Mountains, a private pilot, Scott Freeman, (Dana Andrews) is on a nearly convergent course with the airliner. Freeman suffers a heart attack, causing his Beechcraft Bonanza to careen out of control.

Suddenly, Stacy looks up through the windshield to see the Baron headed straight for them. After a stunning, shattering impact, in which the co-pilot is blown out of the plane through a huge hole in the flight deck, the wounded Stacy manages to put the jumbo jet on autopilot. Chief Stewardess Nancy Pryor (Karen Black) takes control of the 747 while they weave through the towering peaks of the Rocky Mountains. She is talked through the flight by Denver ATC, but Joe Patroni, the hard-bitten staple of the *Airport* films portrayed by the hulking and compassionate George Kennedy, knows that talking Nancy down to a safe landing in Salt Lake City is impossible.

Alan Murdock (Charlton Heston) will supervise a mid-air transfer from an Air Force CH-53 Stallion to enter the 747 and save the day. Murdock and Nancy are old flames, further adding to the dramatic interplay. After a failed attempt that results in the death of an Air Force officer, Murdock makes the transfer and takes over the plane. Nancy, who has become a heroine to the passengers, finally goes back to the cabin, clearly the worse for wear, and informs them the chief pilot is aboard and flying the plane.

After a tension-filled approach to Salt Lake Airport Murdock finally stops the huge 747. He exhales mightily, "Ladies and gentlemen, thank you for flying Columbia Airlines."

Zimbalist laughed at the ironic coincidence of the collision. "It took Dana Andrews fourteen years to get back at me."

Unlike Douglas with *Fate is the Hunter*, Boeing had no problem with Universal using their 747 for the film, which was directed by Jack Smight, whose credits included several television police dramas. The 747, registration N9675, was a 747-123 operated by American Airlines—hence the red, white and blue stripes on the hull. Renting the plane cost $30,000 per day, so Universal managed to get most of the aerial shots in two days. The close-up "damaged" 747 was a full-scale mockup of the flight deck area on a Universal soundstage, using powerful wind machines to simulate the 190 knot slipstream.

On this point the author interviewed retired American Airlines 747 pilot Bob Simon. Simon is now the Wing Commander of Air Group One of the Confederate Air Force in San Diego. "If something had punched that big a hole in an airliner," he said, "the noise would be so loud conversation would be lost. And the wind would be so fierce it would be impossible to move around the flight deck."

The shots of the damaged airliner show a simulated hole, but the angle never shows it directly. The mid-air transfer sequences were filmed over the Wasatch Mountains of Utah with the 747 and a CH-53. One of the movie's weak points is the need to suspend disbelief to accept the plot. A Sikorsky CH-53 Stallion's top speed is just barely able to match the stall speed of a 747 at low altitude.

Simon, who like most pilots admits he has never witnessed a mid-air transfer, had this to say: "They were flying at about 190 knots," he said. "To put a man out on a tether would be suicide. If you even put your hand outside a plane's window at 100 knots it's like hitting a brick wall."

Despite these shortcomings, the aerial shots of the huge 747 flying through the peaks of the Wasatch Range are magnificent. The Beechcraft used in the film was in fact destroyed in a real mid-air collision with a Cessna over California in 1989.

Charlton Heston, to be convincing in his role, spent hours on American Airlines' 747 simulator in Fort Worth, Texas. By contrast, Zimbalist told the author he asked the film's technical advisor Captain Donald McBain what he should do while flying the 747. "He just told me, 'Nothing. This plane practically flies itself; you don't have to do anything.'"

George Kennedy plays the same role in all the *Airport* films, that of Joe Patroni. When questioned about the damage to the 747 he replies dryly, "Oh, not a great deal, there's just a big hone in it where the pilots usually sit!"

A dramatic scene from Universal's *Airport 1975* as the CH-53 Stallion releases a tether to deliver an Air Force pilot to the damaged 747. The sequence was filmed in less than two days to keep rental costs for the 747 down. *Author's Collection*

As in *The High and the Mighty* and *The Crowded Sky* the passengers run the gamut of what would very soon be the staple of disaster film characters. Drunks, first-time flyers, jokers, hysterics, belligerents, know-it-all kids, sick children, singing nuns, old actresses, doctors, couples with marital problems and more. To lend pathos to the suspense, a young girl with kidney disease faces imminent death if she fails to reach the donor hospital in Los Angeles in time. The girl, played with almost overbearing sweetness, is sixteen-year old Linda Blair, just two years after she puked pea soup in *The Exorcist*.

Just as the plane comes to a stop in Salt Lake, Linda is informed that a donor kidney of the right type just happens to be waiting for her and she will be saved. No loose ends there.

Silent film actress Gloria Swanson is the most appealing character, as she is playing herself. She makes one interesting and factual comment: "In 1917 I flew with Cecil B. DeMille from Hollywood nonstop to Pasadena."

The idea of a stewardess flying a plane wasn't born with this film. Exactly nineteen years previously Doris Day played a stewardess who flew a DC-6 to a safe landing in MGM's *Julie*.

Airport 1975 has won its place in two important books: *The Fifty Worst Films of All Time (And How They Got That Way)* and *The 100 Most Enjoyably Bad Movies Ever Made*.

As to the matter of Andrews and Zimbalist appearing together in two aircraft collision movies, rather than a totally unbelievable coincidence, it is more likely the work of a casting director with a sense of humor.

The films that followed were less credible and stretched audience patience to the breaking point. Academy Award winning sound effects editor Peter Berkos said, "Universal was number one at being number two." The next installment in Universal's commitment to disasters after the epic *Earthquake* (1974)—also starring Heston—was *Airport '77*, or as it was sometimes known in Hollywood, "*Airport* meets *The Poseidon Adventure*." This time the jumbo jet is privately owned by a wealthy art collector, and the passengers are rich friends and associates. The jet is carrying a priceless cargo of art treasures when it is hijacked by art thieves posing as crewmembers. The hijacking goes horribly awry when, at low altitude, the aircraft strikes an oil rig, careens into the ocean and sinks.

Because the 747 is so well-built the passengers and crew are able to survive in the submerged cabin. A huge Navy search ensues, and soon the plane is discovered in shallow water. After several mishaps and failed attempts, the Navy manages to raise the sunken jet and rescue the most deserving of the passengers. None of the truly reprehensible characters survive in this Universal morality play.

The film showcases not only the Boeing's remarkable sturdiness but also the Navy's superb search-and-rescue capability. While this could technically be called James Stewart's last aviation film, it hardly deserves the appellation.

The next *Airport* film used the more advanced Supersonic Transport (SST) as the doomed vehicle. The plot of *Concorde: Airport '79* centers on a millionaire defense contractor who uses his company's missile technology to kill his girlfriend, who is on board an SST en route from New York to Moscow. (Read it again, but it doesn't get any better.)

The film makes use of the seventh Concorde built, which first flew in January 1975. Universal leased the aircraft from Aerospatiale for the duration of principal ground and aerial filming. This same aircraft later served Air France from 1980 until July 25, 2000, when it crashed at Charles DeGaulle Airport, killing all aboard.

Onboard the Concorde are several actors whose careers gave them few options in the late 1970s: Charo, Avery Schreiber, John Davidson, Susan Blakely, Sylvia Kristel, Eddie Albert, and Jimmy "J.J." Walker. This was Martha Raye's last film.

The ridiculous plot and mawkish characters made *Airport '79* more of a joke than an action-adventure. It was literally laughed off the screen at the initial screening for Universal personnel and media. Universal opted out of the airline disaster business after the *Concorde*.

Movie audiences had expected that each new film in a series would have more thrills and more advanced technology. By 1983 no one would have gone to see just another 747 doomed to crash. Based on a bestseller by Thomas H. Block, *Starflight: The Plane That*

Couldn't Land (1983) was presented as a made-for-television movie. Block's original book was entitled *Orbit*, but that was too tame for television.

Lee Majors, long past his fame as Steve Austin in *The Six Million Dollar Man*, is Captain Cody Brooks, the pilot of a revolutionary hypersonic airliner that whisks passengers from New York to London in just four hours. The aircraft is intended to enter near-orbit in a long parabolic arc.

After the usual bunch of rich, self-absorbed and colorful passengers—including the aircraft's designer—have boarded, Starflight One lifts off for its maiden flight. Then things go awry as a malfunction in the rocket controls fails to shut down, forcing the airliner with its fragile human cargo into orbit. Things go south very fast between commercial breaks as the crew and Starflight Control realize the plane is stuck in orbit. Even after the rockets are repaired, there is no way for the aircraft to re-enter Earth's atmosphere without a heat shield. The passengers and crew are doomed to die either from eventual asphyxiation or as a blazing meteorite traveling at 17,000 miles per hour.

NASA sends up a Space Shuttle to assist; and by using a long umbilical tunnel, manages to gather several passengers into the payload bay. But fate strikes again and several people are killed.

Level-headed Josh Gilliam, the aircraft designer, played by *Barney Miller* star Hal Linden, is moved to the Shuttle in a sealed coffin to be returned to Earth and find a way to save the Starflight. The idea is literally out of this world, as he and his team frantically devise using the Shuttle to act as a heat shield in front of the de-orbiting Starflight. It's risky, but Brooks and his crew manage to pull it off, bringing the huge jet down safely.

The acting is terrible and Lee Majors does this film no favors. Even the presence of Ray Milland, the only real "star" on the flight, was of little help. There are plot holes big enough to fly a Star Destroyer through, according to one reviewer.

This was NASA's only appearance in a disaster film, and they come off looking pretty good by their heroic efforts in pushing the Shuttle turnaround time of three launches in a mere thirty hours. *Columbia*, the only Shuttle then in service, is shown landing at Edwards AFB in California, which would make a Cape Canaveral liftoff a few hours later impossible. All the stock footage of *Columbia* is seen with the white-painted main fuel tank. There was no technical advisor on the production, possibly because he would have walked off the job in disgust and disbelief.

Star Wars veteran John Dykstra created the Starflight One miniature as a cutting-edge design based on actual concepts of a hypersonic aircraft. The "aerial" sequences are visually spectacular, and the special effects of weightlessness are fairly convincing. According to one studio source, a converted 707 fitted with some of the Starflight interiors were flown in several parabolic arcs to provide the film crew and actors with twenty seconds of weightlessness.

This was the same method used by Ron Howard for 1995's *Apollo 13* and by HBO for *From the Earth to the Moon* (1998).

But other than that, the film has little to offer but something to watch between bathroom breaks. This was the last gasp of the *Airport* genre, having gone as far as possible into the realm of flight without taking a ride to another planet.

CHAPTER NINE

Blowtorches on Film – The Jets Take Over

During the last two years of World War II American airmen encountered new German secret weapons in the forms of the Messerschmitt Me-262 jet and the rocket-powered Me-163 Komet. They were a serious new threat to the massed bomber formations.

Fewer than two years after the war the first films about the new jets were streaking across the screen. Test pilots wore the mantle of "single combat heroes" in the skies during the post-war years.

The most unusual post-war jet film put gangster actor Humphrey Bogart in the cockpit of a radical new jet plane built by his old *Action in the North Atlantic* co-star Raymond Massey. *Chain Lightning,* released in 1950, is the fictional story of former B-17 pilot Matt Brennan (Bogart) joining forces with hard-nosed millionaire aircraft designer Leland Willis (Massey) to test the new Willis JA-3 supersonic jet fighter.

Brennan finds his old wartime flame Jo Holloway (Eleanor Parker) working for Willis. He tells Willis that the jet can fly nonstop from Nome, Alaska, to Washington, D.C., via the North Pole. Willis knows the flight would impress the Air Force. Another friend of Brennan's, test pilot Carl Troxell (Richard Whorf), wants to design the JA-4 with an ejection seat, but Brennan is unconvinced the idea will work.

Brennan flies the JA-3 from Nome to Washington and earns a substantial bonus, enabling him to marry Jo. But when he learns that Carl had been killed testing the JA-4 with the ejection seat Brennan does a demonstration flight in front of Air Force officials and utilizes the ejection seat on purpose, proving the jet's safety.

Chain Lightning is not a typical Bogie film. He is out of place in a cockpit even though he had flown the China Clipper in 1936 for Pat O'Brien. The hard-driven, callous Leland Willis is clearly based on Howard Hughes, who had already gained a reputation as a millionaire who built revolutionary planes he expected the government to buy.

Warner contracted with Paul Mantz as aerial coordinator to build a full-scale mockup of the Willis JA-3 for ground sequences. Using a derelict Bell P-39 Airacobra fuselage as the core, the jet's hull is sleek with a needle nose, just as American audiences would expect in 1950. An 80-foot miniature also appeared in several aerial shots. Even though the JA is a jet, it has no air intake for the engines.

Noted military aviation historian and author Colonel Walter Boyne.

Some footage was shot on location at what was then Muroc Army Air Base (now Edwards AFB). Many of the ground shots were done at Van Nuys Airport. Warner had to wait several months after finishing principal photography until the Air Force approved their use of stock test flight footage for the film. The Me-163 Komet rocket fighter turns up in the wartime sequences. Mantz flew his B-17F.

Colonel Walter Boyne, a highly renowned aviation writer and historian, generously consented to being interviewed for this book. He said, "It's inexcusable to have Humphrey Bogart as a pilot; he was still playing his role in *Casablanca*. The interior shots [in the] flying scenes were standard Hollywood hokum, with altimeters unwinding. It doesn't really make the cut for re-watching as the aircraft and flying scenes are not worth suffering through the hackneyed plot."

The Sound Barrier (1952), released in the United States as *Breaking the Sound Barrier*, starred Ralph Richardson. It told the story of how a British aircraft manufacturer broke the sound barrier using a radical new aircraft. Even though the plane is technically capable of exceeding Mach 1, test pilot Tony Garthwaite (Nigel Patrick) is killed when his controls freeze at the critical moment. All seems hopeless until another pilot, Philip Peel (John

Justin)—knowing he has nothing to lose—instead pushes forward on the control stick. This is the critical moment and his plane streaks through Mach 1 without a bump.

The movie's plot is totally fanciful but the suspense is very compelling. Produced by London Film Productions and directed by David Lean, the movie leads the audience to believe it has just seen history take place. Lean's later film credits included blockbusters like *Lawrence of Arabia* (1962), *Doctor Zhivago* (1965) and *A Passage to India* (1984). He cut his directorial teeth on *Sound Barrier* in the art of suspenseful drama.

The aircraft used in the film to portray the fictional "Prometheus" is a Vickers-Supermarine Swift, a jet fighter that first saw service with the RAF in 1949. The Swift's top speed was just under Mach 1; it was incapable of going supersonic, even in a dive.

Three other notable planes appear in the film: the venerable Spitfire, a de Havilland Vampire jet fighter and the de Havilland Comet, the first jet airliner. The Comet appears in a film that depicts a time prior to the airplane's debut. Just two years after the film's release two Comets broke up in mid-air, killing all on board (see Chapter Eight).

Garthwaite flies the Vampire, a unique twin-tailed jet on a non-stop flight from England to India—something that the Vampire could only do with at least three fuel stops.

Garthwaite flies a de Havilland Vampire from England to India non-stop in *Breaking the Sound Barrier*, a flight which would require at least three fuel stops.

Lean chartered one of the last flying Avro Lancaster bombers to use as a camera ship during the flying sequences. But due to an oxygen failure, some of the film crew became unconscious until the Lancaster reached a lower altitude. Lean then opted for a twin-engine

Vickers Valetta transport. Most of the flying scenes were filmed at the Vickers Aerodrome at Chilbolton at Nether Wallop, Hampshire.

When the film was released in the U.S. Chuck Yeager was invited to the premiere. He had every reason to believe the film was based on his own exploits with the Bell X-1 in October 1947, but was surprised to learn it was fictional. He nevertheless enjoyed the show, and as he reached the lobby of the theater, heard media attendees muttering, "So where was Uncle Sam?' and "Why didn't we do it first?" Yeager tried to explain that the United States was first to go supersonic and that he was the man who'd done it. According to his autobiography, Yeager might have saved his breath. Even Secretary of the Air Force Thomas Finletter believed the film's version. He asked Yeager if he had reversed the controls at the moment of transonic flight. "No, sir," Yeager told him. "If I'd tried that, they would've found the X-1's nose poking out of the ground in China."

The Supermarine Swift used in *Breaking the Sound Barrier*. The aircraft was incapable of the speed necessary to break Mach 1.

Screenwriter Terence Rattigan wrote the story based on newspaper accounts of test pilot Geoffery de Havilland, Jr., Scion of the famous aviation family, de Havilland was testing a tailless research plane, the DH.108 Swallow, in an attempt to break the sound barrier. While executing a steep dive on September 25, 1946, he was killed when the plane suffered a catastrophic break-up. If he had succeeded in breaking Mach 1 he would have beaten the United States by more than a year.

Test pilots again took to the skies in 1956's *Toward the Unknown*, an almost-forgotten film starring William Holden. *Unknown* has some similarities to *Chain Lightning* in that a former combat pilot goes to work as a test pilot and runs into an old flame.

Major Lincoln Bond (Holden) is a Korean War ace who had been captured by the North Koreans. After more than a year of torture, he was forced to sign a confession. Bond goes to

Edwards AFB for work as a test pilot, but General Banner (Lloyd Nolan) is not convinced Bond is trustworthy and blocks his appointment. Banner finally allows Bond to fly routine support and chase missions for other pilots. Bond soon flies the new Gilbert XF-120 fighter, which the Air Force is considering accepting for production. The plane is structurally unsound and Bond tries to convince Banner. But Gilbert and Banner don't believe Bond's claim.

After Bond saves Banner when the former is in danger of crashing after his drogue chute deploys prematurely, they learn to trust one another. Bond is given the coveted assignment to fly the new X-2 rocket plane. Banner wants to fly it himself but Bond, without orders, takes the plane to full power, which throws it out of control. He barely survives the bailout, leaving Banner to realize flight test is for the younger men.

Toward the Unknown, produced by Holden's short-lived Toluca Productions was almost exclusively filmed at Edwards AFB, home of the Air Force Flight Test Center. One of the best scenes filmed with process mock-ups and in miniature, shows Bond flying his F-92 chase plane directly behind Banner's XF-120. The 120's chute has deployed, making the aircraft virtually impossible to fly. Bond pushes the wingtip tank of his plane right into the center of the chute, forcing it to collapse and allowing Banner to land safely.

William Holden as test pilot Major Lincoln Bond in *Towards the Unknown*.

Leon Frewin is a historian at Yanks Air Museum in Chino, California. In 1956 Frewin was an airman at Edwards. "I was there when they filmed the opening sequence with the crashed F-92," he said. "A bunch of us airmen dug a big trench and put the F-92 in it so it would appear as if it had bellied in. We were supposed to run past a fire and rescue the pilot but most of us ended up on the cutting room floor."

Asked about the planes appearing in the film, Frewin said, "That movie has more USAF hardware than any film I ever saw." The film features a host of early jet age aircraft, including the Martin XB-51 ground-attack bomber, which played the role of the Gilbert XF-120. The XB-51 was not accepted by the Air Force for production and as such this film is one of the only ways to see it in flight. The Bell X-2 rocket plane—successor to the X-1 and X-1A—also appears along with the rapier-like X-3 Stiletto and the Navy's Douglas D-558-2 Skyrocket in which Scott Crossfield broke Mach 2 in 1953.

The experimental Martin XB-51 ground attack bomber used as the fictional Gilbert XF-120 in *Towards the Unknown. Official USAF photo*

The early 1950s were called the Golden Age of military aviation, or the "Blowtorch Era." Scores of new fighter, bomber, transport, helicopter, reconnaissance and attack designs came and went at Edwards in a never-ending parade. The film is a virtual inventory of what the USAF was testing and flying in 1956. The Convair C-131 Samaritan and F-102 Delta Dagger, Douglas' B-66 Destroyer, Lockheed F-94 Starfire and F-86 Sabre are seen in flight and on the ground. A rare Boeing YKB-29T, the tanker version of the Superfortress, fuels the F-100 Super Sabre and F-101 Voodoo.

The Air Force was testing "zero length takeoffs" using rocket sleds while *Unknown* was filming. An EF-84G Thunderjet is seen testing the system. A look at the background revealed the B-47 Stratojet, Beech C-45 Expeditor, the huge B-36 Peacemaker and the B-45 Tornado. Audiences were further treated to an early demonstration by the Air Force Thunderbirds in their F-84 Thunderstreaks.

Colonel Boyne gives *Toward the Unknown* high marks. "This picture was made by the airplanes that appeared in it and is worth seeing just for the XB-51," he commented. "The scenes of Edwards are well worthwhile."

Originally the roles of Bond and Banner were to be played by Gregory Peck and Clark Gable. Holden, who had just played a Navy pilot shot down over Korea in *The Bridges at Toko-Ri*, became friends with Lt. Colonel Frank Everest, Jr., who flew the X-2 in several flights. Everest was one of the film's technical advisors.

The role of General Banner is probably based on General Albert Boyd, the head of flight test at Wright-Patterson Air Force Base in Ohio. Boyd was much like Banner, acerbic and efficient. He also insisted on doing a lot of his own flying.

Edwards AFB in the Golden Age. Noted test pilots, left to right: Chuck Yeager, E. G. Russell, Fred Ascani, J. S. Holtoner, Jack Ridley and Art 'Kit' Murray. Planes, left to right, front to rear: X-4, XF-92, T-28, T-33, F-84F, F-86D, F-89, F-94C, B-47, B-45, KC-97 and B-36. *SDASM Collection*

Toward the Unknown is better than the usual aviation/drama/romance film and it's worth staying up to watch on Turner Classics.

Howard Hughes was back in the motion picture business when the Jet Age began. Long over his sour memories of *Hell's Angels* Hughes decided to make a film about the jet planes. The film was *Jet Pilot* (1957). Hughes had not mellowed much since 1930. Under the direction of Josef von Sternberg, whose work included 1935's *Crime and Punishment*, principal photography began in December 1948 and ended three months later. But then Hughes took control of the footage. *Hell's Angels* had taken an unprecedented three years to reach the theaters, but *Jet Pilot* managed to double that. The story of an American Air Force pilot falling in love with a Soviet woman was a hard sell in 1952. The increasing hysteria against Communists, Senator Joe McCarthy's hearings, the Hollywood Black List, and the Rosenberg Trial made RKO hold the film on the shelf for six years, by which time Hughes had sold RKO to Universal. By the time audiences saw the finished product, the former state-of-the-art aircraft were outdated and obsolete.

John Wayne as Air Force pilot Jim Shannon in a T-33 Shooting Star for Howard Hughes' *Jet Pilot.*

The script was written by Jules Furthman, who had penned the screenplays for *To Have and Have Not* (1944) and *The Big Sleep* (1946). *Jet Pilot* wasn't up to those standards. But it is vintage Hughes: an unbelievable plot, high budget overruns and spectacular aerial photography.

Col. Jim Shannon (John Wayne) is ordered to play host to defecting Soviet pilot Anna Orief, played by the pretty Janet Leigh three yeas before her shower with Norman Bates in *Psycho.* Of course Shannon falls in love with Anna and marries her in order to keep her from being deported to the USSR.

Shannon sneaks her into a T-33 and takes her to Siberia. He isn't impressed with what he sees in the workers' paradise, but handles it with his usual aplomb. After a long series of unbelievably casual interrogations the Soviets convince Shannon to test their version of the "parasite" fighter. Anna helps her husband escape to the States, bringing the story full circle.

Even though Shannon had defected and wrecked a USAF fighter he is back in uniform at the end of the film.

The genre for this film is "drama," but it should have been "fantasy" or "comedy." American and Soviet Air Force audiences must have spent more time laughing than watching the film. Wayne's six-foot-four frame is a bit tight in the cockpit of an F-86. The author interviewed retired Colonel Ralph Parr, an F-86 ace in the Korean War. Parr said, "Well, it would have been a tight fit, but he could have made it. Barely." Regarding the film in general, Parr remarked, "It's a better movie for the planes than the story. It's just too ridiculous."

Despite the film being set circa 1950 the uniforms are Army brown rather than Air Force blue. It's even more of an anachronism when seen in 1957.

The film was shot on location at George Air Force Base in Victorville and Edwards Air Force Base. Eager to promote itself the Air Force willingly offered assistance in base facilities, aircraft and personnel.

The Bell X-1 rocket plane used to break the Sound Barrier in 1947.
The X-1 made its last flight in *Jet Pilot* with Chuck Yeager at the controls, as a Soviet parasite fighter before being donated to the Smithsonian.
Official USAF photo

Major Charles E. "Chuck" Yeager, the man who just a year before had broken the Sound Barrier in the Bell X-1, was ordered to do some of the flying in *Jet Pilot*. Being the naturally adventurous type Yeager had at first been thrilled at the prospect but was eventually disappointed. "I never saw Duke or Janet Leigh," he wrote in his autobiography. "The Air Force volunteered yours truly to do all the dangerous flying. I spent all my time at 15,000 feet being filmed by Paul Mantz in a B-25 camera plane." Von Sternberg said, 'We need the kind of balls-out flying that only you can do, Chuck.' I flew for free in an F-86, doing stunts that would've cost them a fortune if I were a professional stunt pilot. They asked me to dive into the overcast inverted at 12,000 feet with another pilot on my tail, then pull out down on the deck. I dove too steeply, reaching .92 Mach straight down and when I pulled out, I came back too hard on the elevator and the damned thing ripped right off my tail, taking with it about a third of my horizontal stabilizer."

Yeager's wingman saw how low he was when the tail tore off and assumed Yeager had crashed.

Hollywood beauty Janet Leigh as Soviet Air Force test pilot Olga "Anna" Orlief. Note that the uniform is intended to impress 1950s male viewers.

The Bell X-1 was used as the Soviet parasite fighter dropped from a B-50 Superfortress. The wings and stabilizers were painted white. With Yeager at the controls, it was the last flight of the famed rocket plane.

The huge B-36 Peacemaker was seen with its 20mm turrets extended.

The Soviet base scenes were shot at George Air Force Base in Victorville, California. RKO set designers managed to build and modify structures to appear very primitive, as the American public expected of the backward Russians. The Soviet Yak-12 fighters were Lockheed T-33 Shooting Stars, painted to alter their silhouettes. Shannon said, "It looks like a Soviet version of our T-33." When Janet Leigh exits the plane and removes her helmet, she looks as if she just came from the beauty salon. Shannon delivers one of the great lines in film history: "A woman."

In deference to the male-dominated sexual attitudes of the 1950s, just as she opens the front to reveal an impressive bosom, a jet screams over with a wolf whistle. As she is about to remove her sweater—under which is only a bra—Shannon stops her, and the jet sound is a disappointed "Whew!" Leigh's uniform fits well enough to be on the cover of *Vanity Fair*.

John Wayne hasn't lost his penchant for chatter in the cockpit. Whether in an F-86, an F6F or a P-40, he still has a lot to say.

Some obvious miniatures are used, as when the two Sabres seen from overhead switch positions.

Walter Boyne said, "Like *Hell's Angels*, this movie is watchable only if you hold your nose when the airplanes are not flying. John Wayne as a test pilot in love with a Russian lady pilot is absurd, but it does allow some interesting in-flight scenes. On the whole, a rung above *Chain Lightning*, but not by much."

The Navy cooperated in the making of two films in 1954. Both were filmed on board the aircraft carrier *USS Oriskany* (CV-34). Both films were written by James Michener and used the same Grumman F9F Panther squadron. These were Paramount's *The Bridges at Toko-Ri*, starring William Holden and Fredric March and MGM's *Men of the Fighting Lady* with Van Johnson and Walter Pidgeon.

Michener wrote "The Forgotten Heroes of Korea" for The *Saturday Evening Post* as the basis for *Toko-Ri*. A reluctant Navy fighter pilot has been pulled back into service to fight in the skies over Korea. Lt. Harry Brubaker (Holden) has deep concerns and doubts about the war. The carrier group commander, Admiral Tarrant (March), is a father figure to Brubaker and the other pilots. Mike Forney (Mickey Rooney) and Nestor Gamidge (Earl Holliman) are a helicopter crew who pull Brubaker from the freezing waters of the Sea of Japan after he has ditched. Forney, a pugnacious short-tempered Irishman, sports a green silk top hat and scarf while flying.

Mickey Rooney and Earl Holliman as the trouble-prone helicopter crew in *The Bridges at Toko-Ri.* Rooney spent his off-screen time on board *USS Oriskany* entertaining the ship's crew.

Ordered to attack heavily-defended railroad bridges in North Korea, Brubaker is sure the attack will come to no good and result in his death. Brubaker is hit by anti-aircraft fire and forced to belly land. Forney and Gamidge are called to pull him out but their helicopter is disabled. In a gripping and shocking finale, Brubaker, Forney and Gamidge are all killed in a muddy Korean irrigation ditch.

Holden had only agreed to do the film if Paramount would keep Michener's original ending, rather than a happier one. This may be due to Holden's younger brother Robert Beedle, a Naval aviator, being killed in combat during World War II.

USS Oriskany in Yokosuka Naval Base Japan in 1953. Note Douglas A4D Skyraiders on flight deck.

The Navy's cooperation included providing 19 ships—nearly a full task force—off the coast of Japan. VF-192, the "Golden Dragons," were part of Air Group 19 during the filming of *Toko-Ri* and *Fighting Lady*. The squadron flew the Grumman F9F-2 Panther.

The Commander, Air Group 19 (CAG) on board the *USS Oriskany* was James D. "Jig Dog" Ramage. Jig, as he prefers to be called, is retired and living in Coronado, California. In an interview about the making of *Toko-Ri* while he was CAG, Jig described some amusing memories and technical observations. "When the film crew and cast came on board in Japan, I met Holden, March and Rooney and showed them around," he said. "Holden was amazed by how the pilots could go up every day and fly missions. I was very impressed with him. Rooney was great. He entertained the crew night after night with song and dance, jokes, just great stuff."

In one sequence while the carrier was docking at Yokosuka Naval Base, the Douglas AD-1 Skyriaders are used to "windmill" the ship into the dock. Contrary to what the film shows of the CAG protesting, Ramage said windmilling was a common enough practice. "I never had any objections to it at all while I was CAG."

Grumman F9F Panther in flight. The Panther was a fighter and was almost never used on bombing missions during the Korean War.

The author also interviewed Capt. Rex Warden, a Panther pilot and veteran of eighty strike missions over Korea. Warden commented on the accuracy of the shipboard and flying scenes: "The approach and landing are perfect. The scene where they put up the barrier to stop the plane looks like a training film, it's so perfect."

"The LSO's (Landing Signal Officers) had a difficult job," Warden said. "We called them 'Paddles.' Sometimes they had to dive into the net to avoid a wingtip." As for Brubaker's ditching, Warden said, "It's always dangerous. I've never seen a ditching that smooth. One wing always touches and the plane cartwheels. But the part where Holden is being hoisted up is done just right."

"I never had to ditch, thank God," said Jig Ramage. "Life expectancy in those cold waters was less than twenty minutes. The helicopter crews had to move fast to get the men out of the water and back to the ship."

The helicopter Forney flies is a Sikorsky H-5, used for rescue missions during the Korean War. The Technicolor aerial and ship sequences are beyond par, filmed from camera planes and on board the ship. The interior cockpit shots were done with excellent rear projection at Paramount, adding realistic sound and visual effects.

Holden learned how to taxi a Panther in order to provide realistic close-ups. The combat scenes were superbly filmed in both miniature and on location. The hairy low-level attacks on the bridges are festooned with tracers and smoke interlacing the sky around the fighters.

Warden said, "In reality the ADs, the Skyraiders, were used to bomb bridges and other land targets. They carried much more ordnance than the fighters, which provided cover for the ADs. They strafed the enemy on the ground, but sometimes it only seemed to make them mad," he chuckled. In the film the Panthers fly down the valley to drop their bombs on the bridges. "It's not done that way," said Warden. "The attack planes always flew along the bridge not at right angles. You'd never hit anything that way. That's Hollywood's doing."

Several characters were based on men Michener met while aboard *USS Valley Forge* (CV-45) in 1952. Tarrant was based on John Perry of Carrier Division 1, while Brubaker's character—and particularly the circumstances of his death—were loosely taken from an incident involving Ensign Marvin Broomhead. The February 8, 1952, attack on railroad bridges over the Yalu River forced Broomhead to ditch his plane. Early reports stated that Broomhead and the helicopter crew had been killed by Communist troops. In reality, however, they had been captured.

Captain James "Jig Dog" Ramage, Commander, Air Wing aboard *USS Oriskany* during the filming of *The Bridges at Toko-Ri.*

Toko-Ri took the Oscar for Special Effects at the 28th Academy Awards.

"The Case of the Blind Pilot" was published in the November 29, 1951, *Saturday Evening Post*, written by Commander Harry Burns. It concerned a pilot who had received a serious head wounds during an attack and lost his sight. Another pilot stayed close by and talked the blinded pilot down to a belly landing on an emergency field. This was the basis for the film *Men of the Fighting Lady.* Author James Michener (Louis Calhern) boards the *USS Valley Forge* to interview the ship's doctor (Walter Pidgeon) about an incident in combat.

The avuncular doctor narrates the story. The film's plot is a series of vignettes about life and death aboard a carrier. Ensign Ken Schechter (Dewey Martin) is blinded in a raid and Lt. (jg) Howard Thayer (Van Johnson) talks him down. A great deal of suspense is built up as Thayer talks Schechter into an approach on the carrier. Schechter keeps blacking out and is sure it won't work. But Thayer refuses to let him die and coaxes him into every delicate move, "flying" Schechter's plane for him. Schechter brings his cripple in to a rocky but survivable landing.

Former F6F Hellcat ace Dewey Martin with Van Johnson
in *Men of the Fighting Lady.*

Both Schechter and Thayer are real persons. While the story is basically true, a few details were changed. The planes flown in the real mission were Douglas AD-1 Skyraiders. Thayer didn't talk Schechter back to the ship; instead Thayer kept the wounded pilot flying more than 100 miles to belly land on an emergency field.

Dewey Martin had been an F6F Hellcat pilot off *USS Intrepid* in World War II. The author asked him about the film. "I was under contract to MGM," the 89-year old Martin said. "Since I had been a Navy pilot in the Pacific they signed me to do the movie. The film crew and the ship's crew did such a good job that it was just like I'd gone back into the Navy." Martin went on to say, "The operations on the flight deck and in combat are just what I recall."

When asked about the blind pilot scenes, Martin responded, "Well, they did all that in the studio, long after we left the *Oriskany*. It took days to get all the footage of me in the cockpit with the back projection of the other plane above me. It was hot in that suit and helmet in the studio, I can tell you," he grinned.

Much of the aerial and rear-projection footage appears to be leftover from *Toko-Ri*. It's hard to say for sure since the ship and squadron was the same.

Men of the Fighting Lady contains a deeply emotional note of sorrow for lost pilots and the futility of war. The pilots are watching a home movie sent by their families. The movie shows the wife and children of a pilot who was just killed, wishing him a Merry Christmas. The young boy is Jerry Mathers, soon to be famous as Beaver Cleaver.

The shot of Dodson's fatal crash in his Panther was footage of an actual crash aboard *USS Midway* (CV-41) on June 23, 1951. The pilot, George Duncan, was slightly injured. The same footage appears at the end of *Midway* (1976) as the fatal crash of a Dauntless flown by Charlton Heston.

Cast members of MGM's *Men of the Fighting Lady* on board the *USS Oriskany*. *Author's Collection*

After returning to the states upon completion of their deployment, VF-192 changed their name to "The World Famous Golden Dragons."

James Stewart was back in the sky in *Strategic Air Command* (1955). The extravagant Technicolor production by director Anthony Mann and writer Beirne Lay, Jr., exposes a world hardly imagined by Americans. Released in the first decade of the Cold War, *Command* centered on former B-29 pilot turned professional baseball player Robert "Dutch" Holland.

Dutch is married to America's sweetheart, June Allyson, with her husky voice and Donna Reed dresses. Dutch is ordered to go on active duty in the new Strategic Air Command for twenty-one months. At first Dutch is resentful but in time feels a sense of duty to the job, the men and the planes.

A Grumman F9F Panther of VF-192, the "World Famous Golden Dragons" on *USS Oriskany's* catapult. This aircraft was used as Lt. Harry Brubaker's plane in *The Bridges at Toko-Ri.*

Harry Morgan portrays a veteran Sergeant who shows Dutch through the interior of a huge B-36 bomber. "What do you think of her, Colonel?" he asks.

"She's a battleship!" Dutch replies.

Dutch soon becomes so dedicated to SAC he puts his work ahead of his family, and drives himself to near exhaustion to complete a full deployment of a B-47 wing to Japan. An injury during a crash eventually grounds Dutch. In the final shot he wistfully gazes into the sky as a wing of brand-new Boeing B-47 Stratojets fly over, protecting America and keeping the peace.

Stewart had matured from the fresh-faced Lieutenant of the USAAF documentary *Winning Your Wings* thirteen years before. Stewart was in fact a Colonel in the USAF Reserve. He wears the uniform well and plays the role with the comfort of familiarity.

Frank Lovejoy, a veteran television and western actor, is perfectly cast as a cigar-chomping hard-nosed SAC commander General Hawkes. It takes little effort to realize the character is liberally borrowed from the real-life General Curtis E. LeMay, who must have grinned at the fictionalized version of himself. When Hawkes is smoking a cigar near a plane being refueled, a ground crewman mutters to Dutch, "The General's cigar, sir. Doesn't the General know the aircraft might explode?"

A huge Convair B-36 Peacemaker from Carswell AFB. The ten-engine bomber was touted as having "Six turning and four burning." *Official USAF photo*

Dutch, with grave certainty, says, "It wouldn't dare."

Lovejoy played his role so well that when he went into a base administration office the duty airmen all stood and saluted him. Lovejoy laughed. "Take it easy, I'm not the real thing." When Stewart came in they stayed in their seats. Stewart said, "Fellas, I *am* the real thing."

Carswell Air Force Base in Texas, home of the 7th Bomb Wing, was the location for most of the ground and flying sequences. The aircraft exterior and interior scenes are so technically detailed and spectacular that a copy of the film must have made it to the Soviet Union to be studied by Red Air Force intelligence officers.

The author interviewed retired Major General Chris Adams, who worked under LeMay. Adams is described as a walking encyclopedia of SAC history. "Sure the film had a lot of footage of our hardware," Adams said. "But we wanted the Soviets to see what we had. One word: deterrence. That was the purpose of LeMay supporting the film."

"Fellas, I *am* the real thing," At the time of filming *Strategic Air Command*, James Stewart was a Colonel in the USAF Reserve.

In an age before the horrors of total nuclear war were understood viewers were amused by the film's whimsical tone. In a scene showing how SAC bomber crews train, an officer asks, "You mean New York City's just been bombed by a bomber that they didn't see or hear?"

"Sure," another officer says flippantly. "We've been bombing cities every day and every night all over the U.S. Just people don't know it."

Adams commented, "Of course they didn't carry any bombs. Denver was a favorite target. I bombed Houston and Dallas many times."

There's a message in the film today's audiences would find hard to sympathize with. Dutch returns from a long flight to meet his new baby daughter. After holding the tiny new life in his hands, he tells his wife about the new B-47 jet bomber he would be flying. "Sally, this is the most wonderful thing you can imagine," he says.

Strategic Air Command's B-36 No. 5734 prior to takeoff at Carswell AFB in Texas.

The ironically named B-36 Peacemaker is seen in several flights both real and in miniature. Director of Photography William Daniels was responsible for the beautiful cinematography.

Major Walter Douglas is a retired B-36 co-pilot. In a phone interview he said he had been at Carswell AFB when the movie was being filmed. "I watched as Paul Mantz in his B-25 camera plane followed the B-36 into the air," recalled Douglas. "He had that plane right off the port wingtip and stayed with it all the way until they had the footage they needed." Douglas admitted that he was impressed by the final film. "It really made the B-36 look good," he said. "That was a lot of airplane and the movie did a good job of it."

The B-36 crash in Greenland was based on an actual crash in Newfoundland that had occurred a few years earlier. Adams said, "The B-36 was one of the most forgiving airplanes I ever flew. It would probably have kept the crew alive in the crash seen in the film."

For the later B-47 Stratojet sequences Paramount made good use of Air Force footage of aerial refueling. Dutch is tired and unwilling to bandy civilities with the C-97 tanker crew.

"What'll you have, Ethyl or Regular?"

"Ah, whatever you got! Just fill her up."

U.S. Air Force training footage of a Boeing B-47 Stratojet being refueled from a KC-97 tanker was used in *Strategic Air Command*.

The B-47 cockpit mockup used for *Strategic Air Command* is on display at the March Field Air Museum in Riverside County, California.

When Dutch is trying to land in bad weather at Kadena AFB in Okinawa, the camera shoots from over his shoulder to peer through the windshield, being swept by a single wiper. The cockpit mockup is now on display at the March Field Museum in Riverside, California.

Strategic Air Command was a box office success, netting more than $6.5 million.

On the tails of *Command* was another bomber film entitled *Bombers B-52,* starring future *Streets of San Francisco* lead Karl Malden and future *FBI* agent Efrem Zimbalist, Jr.

Theater one-sheet for *Bombers B-52.*

The film was not the superbly written and filmed recruiting draw of *Command.* It used SAC's massive Boeing B-52 Stratofortress as a backdrop for a battle of wits between a handsome playboy pilot and a career sergeant. Master Sergeant Chuck Brennan's (Malden) pretty daughter Lois (Natalie Wood) is being romantically pursued by Colonel Jim Herlihy (Zimbalist). The Air Force is Brennan's career and life, but he is also a devoted husband and father. Herlihy tries to appease Chuck but is unable to convince the sergeant that his intentions are honorable. While this is going on, the new B-52 is coming into service and the Air Force needs Chuck's expertise. Herlihy is ordered to back off from Lois in order to keep Chuck from retiring.

A fire aboard a new B-52 over a remote area forces the crew to bail out. Chuck remains on board to try and save the ship but he finally jumps, landing far from rescue. He is found by Herlihy. Chuck no longer protests the budding romance.

Directed by Gordon Douglas, the film was shot on location at March AFB and Castle AFB in Merced, California. The Stratofortress was brand-new at the time and the USAF was happy to showcase the newest hardware. Because the main character was a dedicated career sergeant *Time Magazine* called the movie a "$1.4 million want ad for Air Force technicians."

The author interviewed Zimbalist regarding the film. The actor remembered that he was awed by the huge bombers and the men who flew them. "A pilot took me up on a flight and I was just amazed at the complexity," he said. "When we were on the runway he told me I could steer it over to the parking area." Zimbalist expressed fear at being told to maneuver the 300-ton bomber. "I said, 'I can't do that!' But the pilot said, 'Relax, just steer it like a car. There's the wheel, and there's the brake.' So I did. The smoothness was amazing," he said with a chuckle. "That enormous machine handled like a bicycle." Zimbalist didn't receive much instruction about how to appear experienced at the controls. "I just sat there and did what they told me."

A new Boeing B-52 Stratofortress at Castle AFB in Merced, California. The B-52 was the newest strategic bomber in the USAF inventory and the Department of Defense was eager to showcase the huge aircraft.

General Adams had his own opinions of *Bombers B-52*. "It was not much of a film, not like *Strategic Air Command*." Adams said it was more of a drama and about these two guys bumping heads. But it did have some nice and fairly accurate B-52 ground and flying sequences.

Warner hadn't lost its ability to twist reality with *The McConnell Story* (1955). It is a highly dramatized biography of the life and career of Joseph J. "Mac" McConnell, Jr. the highest-scoring jet ace during the Korean War. With Alan Ladd in the title role the plot takes great liberties with the truth. In fact other than the number of McConnell's combat victories the entire film makes his life into a rather silly love story. The film also stars June Allyson as McConnell's wife "Butch." Mac's best friend is Ty Whitman, played by the talented James Whitmore.

A tired Joe McConnell, played by Alan Ladd in Warner's *The McConnell Story*.

Gordon Douglas, who had just finished directing Whitmore and giant mutant ants in *Them!*, molded Ted Sherdeman's story to appeal to 1955 audiences. The film opens with a patriotic speech by a USAF General who says with a straight face, "This is not fiction." The film follows McConnell as he washes out of Army Medical School and then pilot training to become a bomber navigator during World War II. Along the way he meets Butch, who wins his heart. He wins hers despite his being in trouble with the MPs most of the time. After taking a desk job to please Butch, McConnell yearns for the sky. Ty, who is a jet instructor, gets Mac back into training. Eventually McConnell makes it through pilot training and gets his wings. Ty says to Mac as he climbs into his first jet, "Go on, Tiger. You own the sky."

Then Mac goes off to Korea, where he distinguishes himself as a top ace. When he returns to the States he becomes a test pilot for new jets. As America's top ace he is given a house in Apple Valley, California. Butch is deeply concerned for his safety but he is heedless. Then fate takes a turn for the worst and Mac is killed. Ty finally convinces Butch that Mac died for a good cause.

There are a few major discrepancies in the filming. Mac was a B-24 navigator, but Warner put him in a B-17G. During one harrowing mission the crew sees a German rocket plane, the Me-163 Komet. The crew refers to it as a "jet." The shot of the Komet is actual combat footage of the rocket slicing past a bomber. A great deal of Korean War combat footage is inserted with the flying done by USAF pilots from George Air Force Base.

Alan Ladd, who was at the zenith of his acting career, plays the role of the taciturn, headstrong McConnell well, but it's hard to warm up to the character. His cocky attitude was most often the root of all his problems. As for Butch, the author interviewed a pilot who had flown with McConnell, but didn't wish to be named for this quote. The pilot said, "Butch was no June Allyson. She wasn't a lady, either."

McConnell was killed on August 25, 1954, while testing the new F-86H, a nuclear-capable version of the Sabre. After a malfunction, he lost control and impacted the desert floor at Edwards Air Force Base. One of the investigating officers was Chuck Yeager, who recreated the last flight, proving that it had been equipment malfunction. The film's final scene was written to reflect this.

Captain Joseph McConnell, Jr.
top-scoring jet ace of the Korean War.

The skies over Korea were again the venue for *The Hunters*. Released by Fox in 1958 it is a raw account of life and death in the air. But again, just as in dozens of previous films, the *femme fatale* and the cocky pilots rear their tedious heads. Robert Mitchum is Major "Iceman" Saville, a confident World War II fighter ace. Saville is second-in-command of an F-86 Sabre squadron in Korea under Colonel "Dutch" Imil, played by Richard Egan,

Saville has to ride herd on two pilots in particular: the young, cocky and handsome Lt. Pell (Robert Wagner) and Lt. Abbott (Lee Phillips), a good pilot who is too eager to prove himself. During a dogfight the brash Pell abandons his element leader, Lt. Corona, to go after a MiG. Corona is killed and Saville tries to get rid of Pell, but Imil tells him that Pell will grow up soon enough.

Abbott's wife, while asking Saville to help her husband, falls in love with him. Abbott, learning of the budding affair between his wife and Saville, goes to him and offers up his wife in return for a one-on-one crack at "Casey Jones," the top North Korean ace. Saville refuses, but fate takes over. In a battle far behind enemy lines Abbott goes against the MiG-15 ace and is wounded and shot down. Saville, who feels responsible, shoots down the MiG and ditches his Sabre near Abbott's parachute. Together they try to evade North Korean patrols while Pell strafes the enemy troops. Pell is also downed.

After a series of encounters with friendly Korean farmers and enemy troops the men eventually return to their base. Abbott is repatriated home, where he asks his wife for forgiveness.

With some of the love triangle elements of *Hannover Street*, the film also resembles *Dawn Patrol* and *The Eagle and the Hawk* (see Chapter Two) as well as *The Flying Leathernecks* (see Chapter Seven). Dick Powell, who also directed Mitchum in the submarine drama *The Enemy Below* in 1957, used extensive stock combat footage for this film. The F-86s are part of an operational squadron and most of the aerial sequences were done over Arizona, Nevada and California. Powell was provided with a new C-130 Hercules transport as the camera plane—one of the rare times a B-25 wasn't used. Florida's Palm Beach AFB served for ground shots. The North Korean MiG-15s are Republic F-84 Thunderstreaks painted with communist markings.

Walter Boyne commented, "The movie is blessed with great aerial photography and made before Hollywood hated the military so that it is still patriotic. The U.S. is still the 'good guy.' Air Force cooperation permitted using the swept wing version of the F-84 as the MiG-15. The original novel was written by James Salter, an F-86 pilot with a MiG [kill] to his credit. I suspect he was disappointed with the final film."

Critical reaction to the film was mostly negative, citing the banal and unbelievable love triangle as the problem. But critic Mark Hansen credited the film's extraordinary aerial cinematography.

Colonel Ralph Parr, USAF, Korean War F-86 Sabre ace. Parr, who provided excellent background material for this book, commented that *The Hunters* was one of the best air war films about the Korean War, "even if the plot wasn't much to talk about." *Courtesy Ralph Parr*

Meanwhile, back at Edwards AFB, another test pilot was screaming into the blue onboard a rocket plane on film. This was United Artists' *X-15* (1961) starring a young Charles Bronson. Richard Donner, who would later direct the *Lethal Weapon* series, brought the film crew out to the hot baking flats of Edwards to film a movie about the pilots who rode the black X-15 rocket to the edge of space.

Lt. Colonel Lee Brandon (Bronson) is one of three X-15 pilots working to iron out the myriad technical problems with the new aircraft. Stress and fatigue are reflected in their relationships with wives and girlfriends. Several setbacks, including a ground engine explosion, plague the program. But in the end the X-15, after being dropped from its B-52 mothership, streaks like a black arrow into the dark blue skies over Edwards.

Not much of a plot. But the aerial sequences—kindly provided by the Air Force—are spectacular. The tagline is, "Actually Filmed in Space!"

Writer Tony Lazzarino originally intended to build the film around the successful Bell X-2 flights, but the Pentagon suggested the new X-15 would make a better subject. At the time of the film's release in December 1961—as the entire nation was focused on the astronauts of Project Mercury—the Air Force was developing the first true "spacecraft." The North American X-15 was the most advanced rocket plane up to that time and was designed to take pilots to altitudes of more than fifty miles at speeds above 4,000 miles per hour. Among the men who flew the sleek rocket were Joe Walker, Shuttle pilot Joe Engle and Apollo 11 commander Neil Armstrong.

The film uses dramatic stock footage to showcase what the Air Force was doing in the upper reaches of the atmosphere. Fifty miles had been designated "space," and anyone who flew above it was given the coveted title of "astronaut." The film was an Air Force propaganda effort to show that a man who flew the X-15 was an astronaut and had full control of the spacecraft from launch to landing, unlike the Mercury astronauts who were, to use a derogatory term, "spam in a can." Lazzarino had considered *Exit, Time of Departure* and *Beyond the Unknown* as titles. The first two were too bland and misleading, while the third was too close to the Holden film.

Charles Bronson as Lt. Colonel Lee Brandon, X-15 test pilot.

Principal photography was done at Edwards during the summer of 1960, with detailed assistance by the Pentagon, Air Force and NASA, who oversaw the program. Besides the X-15, other notable aircraft seen are Lockheed F-104 Starfighters and F-100 Super Sabres, one of which is shown in actual crash footage.

Some scenes are well worth watching for the aviation buff. An engine explosion on the ground is almost shocking to watch, while seeing the black rocket slung under the huge B-52's wing in flight is an awesome sight. There is very little miniature work in this film. Nearly all of it, other than the process cockpit shots, is real.

An amazing phenomenon began in 1983 with the release of *The Right Stuff*, a dramatization of Tom Wolfe's account of the early days of test flight and manned space flight. Wolfe's book was brought to the screen by Philip Kaufman, director of the 1978 remake of *Invasion of the Body Snatchers*. The phenomenon was the reawakening of public interest in the Mercury Seven astronauts.

It bears remembering that *The Right Stuff* was an apocryphal story with a great deal of literary license. And this translated well into a movie with more than its share of the "legend over truth." *The Right Stuff* is about as historically accurate as an Abbott & Costello comedy. A folksy narration by Levon Helm, who plays flight engineer Jack Ridley, helps to set the stage.

The film begins with Ridley describing the dangerous attempts to break the sound barrier with the Bell X-1. Chuck Yeager (Sam Shepard) is first seen in Pancho's Happy Bottom Riding Club on the edge of Muroc Air Base in the Mojave Desert. Yeager just happens to be there for no apparent reason, and so is his wife Glennis (Barbara Hershey). When the current Bell test pilot, Chalmers "Slick" Goodlin demands an exorbitant fee for breaking the barrier, the Army turns to Yeager.

"That guy over there. Yeager. Some kind of war hero. Shot down five Germans in one day."

In reality Yeager was doing advanced flight testing for the Army at Wright-Patterson AFB in Ohio, under the aegis of General Albert Boyd. Boyd chose Yeager and Bob Hoover as pilots, Ridley as engineer, and Major Bob Cardenas as the B-29 pilot and project manager.

In the film Yeager has his famous accident while horseback riding with Glennis and breaks his ribs. He takes Ridley aside and asks for help. "I don't want it getting around or they'll find someone else to fly the goddamn thing," he says.

In an interview with retired Brigadier General Cardenas, the author asked about this. Cardenas, a highly skilled engineer and former B-24 combat pilot and head of the Bomber Test Division, said, "Two nights before the ninth powered flight, in which Chuck broke the sound barrier, I received a call from a doctor who told me he had just worked on Yeager's broken ribs and thought I should know about it.

Sam Shepard and General Chuck Yeager with the 'Glamorous Glennis' X-1 mockup on location at Edwards AFB in *The Right Stuff.*

The next day I talked to Ridley and he thought he could come up with a way of helping Chuck close the X-1 hatch."

Jack Ridley did devise the broom handle solution. But the scene in which he went into the hangar and asked Mr. Russell to let him saw off about a foot of the broom he was using to sweep the floor was an insult to Jack Russell, one of the X-1 rocket technicians.

Captain Chuck Yeager and Jack Ridley at Muroc Air Base in 1947 during the Sound Barrier flights. Unlike the 'sidekick' role in *The Right Stuff*, Ridley was one of the best aeronautical engineers and test pilots in the Air Force.

Cardenas had to make the decision of whether to go with Yeager or put in Bob Hoover instead. He had always considered Hoover, a former P-51 pilot and POW, to be a better "stick-and-rudder" man than Yeager. "If I used Hoover I'd have to give him a few powered flights so he'd be ready for the big one," said Cardenas. "But General Boyd had said he wanted the project done safe but brief. I went with Yeager."

Jack Ridley was one of the most brilliant engineers in the Air Force. But his character is just a recurring sidekick to Yeager, doing little more than dispensing Beeman's Gum.

In *The Right Stuff* Glennis is present as the X-1 is loaded onto the B-29 Superfortress. *Glamorous Glennis* is prominent on the orange nose. Glennis was actually in West Virginia living with her husband's family at the time.

Accompanied by stirring music and dramatic cinematography, Yeager breaks the barrier.

Edwards Air Force Base was used for most of the X-1 and later flight sequences. The X-1 aerial shots were done using models as the FAA refused the Ladd Company to allow the full-scale mockup to be dropped from *Fifi*, the CAF's B-29. Guide wires and internal rockets were used. The technique was developed at Republic Pictures in the 1940s and 1950s by the Lydecker Brothers. More than 40 models were made for the film by USFX Studios. The Douglas D-558-2 Skyrocket was the Navy's answer to the X-1A. The plane used in the brief flyover and newsreels is a modified Hawker Hunter.

Later in the film two comic lackeys (Jeff Goldblum and Harry Shearer) inform President Eisenhower the Soviets have launched a satellite into orbit. With blatantly mocking satire the government takes on the project of getting a man into space before the Soviets. Yeager himself appears briefly in a cameo during the scene in which the two men are at Pancho's.

He asks Shearer, "Hey, y'all want a glass of whiskey?" Shearer replies, "I'd like a Coke. In a clean glass."

Al Shepard (Scott Glenn) is approached on an aircraft carrier by Goldblum and Shearer, who are hopelessly seasick. They tell Shepard, "We're going up against the Russians all the way. It's got the highest priority." Shepard grins. "Sounds dangerous," he says. "Count me in."

In reality NASA contacted 133 test pilots to report for the first briefings at the Dolly Madison House on Lafayette Square in Washington, D.C. No pilot was approached in person, but that wouldn't be dramatic enough for Kaufman.

Colonel Robert Cardenas, project manager for the X-1 Sound Barrier tests. Cardenas was the pilot of the B-29 which dropped the X-1.

The main characters in the film are more caricatures than actual portrayals. John Glenn is even more a pious boy scout than in real life. Gordo Cooper is a reckless and cocky "hot dog." Kaufman even takes a gratuitous jab at Vice President Lyndon Johnson, who throws a tantrum when he is denied access to Annie Glenn during a delay in her husband's flight. Johnson was a strong supporter of the program and close friends with the Glenns.

The chief German scientist is never named but is assumed to be Dr. Werner von Braun. Von Braun was never involved with the spacecraft design and did not play a role in John Glenn's famed orbital drama.

But the worst characterization is of Virgil I. "Gus" Grissom, (Fred Ward). Grissom was an experienced fighter pilot in Korea, a skilled test pilot and excellent engineer. During an examination of the new spacecraft by the astronauts, Grissom wants to know why a hatch with explosive bolts for emergency egress was not installed. Actually it had been but this was an example of the setup to sink Grissom in the film. During the recovery of Grissom's spacecraft in the sea off Bermuda the hatch blew off. Gus had to scramble out or drown. He was picked up but the capsule sank in 17,000 feet of water. He was taken aboard the recovery ship and examined. As seen in the film he is shaking, nervous and very defensive. The audience is left with a view of Grissom as a cowardly loser who panicked at the crucial moment.

A further stab is taken at Gus by a technician saying, "We've had hatches on planes for ten years. They've been subjected to heat, water, shaking and dropped from a height of 100 feet onto concrete. And not one of them has ever 'just blown.'"

No ambiguity there. But it's also false.

The real tragedy is Grissom's fate and the role the blown hatch played in it. NASA did extensive tests on the explosive hatches and learned they could indeed blow without warning. When gearing up for the Apollo program, NASA had the spacecraft's contractor, North American Aviation, design a hatch that had to be manually unbolted and opened. On January 28, 1967, Gus Grissom, Ed White and Roger Chaffee were inside the Apollo 1 Command Module for an extended test of the systems. They were sealed in, and the spacecraft was pressurized with 100% oxygen. A spark ignited flammable materials. White attempted to open the hatch. He needed ninety seconds. The astronauts were dead of smoke inhalation in fifteen seconds.

The tragic irony is that since Grissom had been proven right—that the hatch could blow without warning—NASA insisted on a new hatch design. And three men died.

The Mercury launch and flight sequences in *The Right Stuff* are superb and very accurate, especially Glenn's re-entry. Again the weakness is the grand dramatic license taken with history. Yeager's final appearance in the film involves a 1962 record-setting flight while he was Commandant at the USAF Aerospace Research Pilot School at Edwards. He attempted to break the 114,000-foot altitude record set by the Soviet Union. He used a modified Lockheed NF-104 Starfighter. Contrary to the film's portrayal, Yeager didn't "steal" the plane. Jack Ridley is there to dispense Beemans gum but in reality he had been dead since 1957. The Starfighter is a rare aircraft in film, and seeing one in flight is something to enjoy. The film aircraft was an F-104G which lacked the external rocket booster on Yeager's NF-104.

"I think I see a plane over here with my name on it." Sam Shepard as Chuck Yeager with the Lockheed F-104G Starfighter.

The ejection sequence is accurately shown, if a bit confusing. Yeager's seat rig had an explosive charge to blast it out of the plane. While he was falling alongside the seat it struck him with the still-glowing end and broke open his helmet. The sudden blast of air and molten debris burned his face and hands severely. Yeager survived, but while filming *The Right Stuff* stuntman Joseph Svec died after losing consciousness from smoke inhalation and failed to pull his ripcord.

Bill Conti's powerful score adds a strong patriotic feeling to the movie.

All in all, only *The Right Stuff's* aerial sequences have any value. If the movie is taken as a fictional dramatization of historical events it holds up but should not be taken seriously. The one thing the film can be commended for was its effect on the American public. After the October 1983 release of *The Right Stuff*, the astronauts and Yeager in particular found themselves in the spotlight again. Suddenly astronauts most Americans had forgotten or ignored for nearly twenty years were again heroes and sought out for public appearances and autographs. The author counted himself among those who were profoundly affected by the story, and it has not faded to this day. In a way *The Right Stuff* was the early origin of this book.

Because of the lack of Vietnam air war films, other than several Marine Corps and Army dramas that feature the ubiquitous Bell UH-1 Hueys (see Chapter Eleven), *Flight of the Intruder* (1991) is the only one that fits the bill. Director John Milius (*The Rough Riders,* 1997) worked closely with the Navy and the screenwriters to do justice to author and former A-6 driver Stephen Coonts' bestselling book.

To put the story into a nutshell, Lt. Jake Grafton (Brad Johnson) and his bomber/navigator Lt. McPherson are on a single-aircraft low-level mission over the Gulf of Tonkin to bomb a suspected NVA truck park. The target turns out to be no more than trees, a wasted mission. Evading NVA anti-aircraft fire on the deck, McPherson is mortally wounded. After a rough landing on their carrier, Jake learns his friend is dead. During an emotional debriefing with his squadron commander, Frank Camparelli (Danny Glover), Jake is told to move on and write to his friend's wife.

Lt. Commander 'Tiger' Cole (Willem Dafoe) arrives to work with Camparelli. Jake, meanwhile, flies to Subic Bay in the Philippines and meets a friend of McPherson's wife, who is also the widow of a Naval aviator. A fight in a bar with some belligerent merchant sailors makes Jake even angrier about the loss of his best friend on a useless mission. He returns to the ship.

Jake and Cole are sent on a mission to use anti-radar missiles and bombs to attack the SAM sites outside the city of Hanoi and have a violent scrap with a North Vietnamese MiG-17. Jake, feeling a need to strike back against the policy of leaving Hanoi alone, suggests they bomb the city. Cole refuses.

Brad Johnson, Danny Glover and Willem Dafoe with an A-6 Intruder of VA-165 on board *USS Independence. Author's Collection*

The next mission puts them in the air with Lt. Boxman's plane, which is shot down by SAMs. North Vietnamese television proudly displays the wreckage of Boxman's plane. Like all the other aviators, Cole is enraged and consents to Jake's idea of bombing Hanoi's "SAM City," which is off-limits by national policy.

Their next mission is to hit a power plant with ten bombs. Dropping only two bombs, they fly to SAM City with the other eight. A fault in their fire control system and a near miss from a SAM force them to fly over the target twice before they are able to bomb and destroy the SAM installation. Upon their return to the carrier Jake and Cole are informed they will be court-martialed at Subic Bay. But the opening of Operation Linebacker II—the U.S. aerial bombing campaign against North Vietnamese targets—helps the Navy to cover up the impromptu mission. The crewmen are grounded while the rest of the air group attacks SAM installations around Hanoi.

Camparelli is shot down, loses his bomber/navigator, and other planes of the squadron are hit by enemy fire. Jake and Cole fly to attack the anti-aircraft guns that shot down Camparelli, but they too are hit and forced to eject. They are separated. Cole is on foot, running from NVA soldiers, while Jake meets up with Camparelli. Cole is mortally wounded but tells Jake by radio he is clear and unhurt. A strike by AD-1 Skyraiders swoops in and Cole orders them to bomb the NVA troops at his location. He is killed in the strike, giving Jake and Camparelli time to get away. They are found by an HH-1 Jolly Green Giant helicopter in the woods. After a harrowing, narrow escape they return to the ship. Camparelli is promoted to Captain and Jake, at last free of his demons, wants to stay with him.

The heartbreaking death of young men, useless missions, revenge, a merciless enemy and heroic sacrifices all play a part in the film. It may have been too much for one movie and led to some of the criticism generated after the January 1991 release.

The Navy provided the aircraft carrier *USS Independence* (CVN-62) for the principal photography during November 1989, at a reported cost to Paramount of $1,000,000 per day. VA-165's A-6E Intruders were also provided for the deck, launch and most of the aerial sequences, which were backed up by process and miniature footage. Also appearing in various shots are Vought A-7 Corsair attack bombers, Douglas AD-1 Skyraiders, McDonnell Douglas F-4 Phantom IIs and a Grumman C-2 Greyhound transport. The Phantoms were on loan from Air National Guard units. An actual MiG-17 Fresco was obtained from a private collection. The city of Hanoi seen in the film was a 1:160 scale detailed model.

Stephen Coonts wrote the book based on his own experiences in the Navy during the war. The Navy and Air Force fought the air war over Vietnam with one hand behind their backs, and there were no illusions among the pilots and aircrews that they weren't being allowed to fight the way they were trained. Hanoi, the capital of North Vietnam and its surroundings were off-limits, while the NVA had free rein to do whatever they wanted. Many of the targets they were assigned were either of low value or totally useless.

This was the root of Coonts' novel about an unauthorized mission to attack the heart of SAM City. Linebacker II in December of 1972 was the United States' last major attempt to weaken the North Vietnamese resolve by targeting tactical and strategic sites. But in the end it was no more effective than Goering's attempts to break the British in the summer of 1940.

The author interviewed Navy A-6 veterans Charles Beauchesne and John Stubbs regarding their opinions of the film. Both aviators had seen extensive combat in Vietnam and knew many of the men on whom Coonts based characters in his book. Captain Charles Beauchesne served 28 years in the Navy. During Vietnam VA-52, Nightriders of CAW-11 flew off *USS Kitty Hawk* (CV-63). "Coonts' novel concentrated on the bombing of North Vietnam in the spring of 1972. At that time it was very intense," Beauchesne said. "The NVA had had four years to reinforce their SAM defenses around Haiphong Harbor and Hanoi."

Captain Charles Beauchesne, who flew A-6 Intruders on missions over North Vietnam during the time depicted in *Flight of the Intruder*.

When asked about the film's depiction of bombing trees for no gain, the veteran aviator said, "What was ultimately frustrating is that we were sent on single night strikes to targets that had no value but [were located] in very high threat areas. We were essentially being sent to keep the NVA SAM crews up all night and ruin their morale."

Beauchesne had one positive comment on the film's depiction of combat: "I saw the movie for the first time while attending a squadron reunion. And when they lit off that SAM at Jake Grafton's plane, it just lifted me about six inches off my chair. It looked so real my heart went from zero to sixty in a second. I had a salvo of three SAMs come at me as I was coming off a strike on Haiphong and that's just what it looks like."

But the anti-aircraft artillery (AAA) was almost never in front of an attacking aircraft. "The Triple A was always behind me," said Beauchesne. "I used to turn my four rear-view mirrors down so I wasn't distracted by the lights. In the movie these guys are jinking back and forth and up and down to avoid the Triple A ahead of them. The NVA were not able to aim ahead of us."

Lt. John Stubbs was a pilot in VA-115 off *USS Midway* (CV-41) in 1971-72. "There was way too much joking in the cockpit, said Stubbs. "In reality the crews were much more serious. They depended on one another not only for their lives, but also to complete the mission. The on-board computers back then were state-of-the-art, but they were still prone to malfunctions, as in what happened to Cole and Grafton. They had to work together without all that joking."

"The attack on Hanoi's 'SAM City' was too low," continued Stubbs. "We almost never flew at 200 feet at night. And the SAMs were not going to get you at that altitude. There was too much light during the night in the film. In reality when you fly at night you're flying in ink. Just black. We lost some crews that just flew into the ground." MiGs were not a factor, especially at night. Stubbs admits he never saw a MiG in his entire tour.

In the film Grafton and McPherson go to hit a truck park only to bomb trees. "I personally made a lot of little trees out of big trees," Stubbs laughed. "Quite frankly the target designation was atrocious. "We spent days planning missions, unlike how it is shown in the movie," he said. "The actual combat is very, very brief. In the film it went on much too long."

The death of McPherson, it was based on the real-life Lt. Ray Donnelly, according to both Stubbs and Beauchesne. "Ray was my usual B/N," said Stubbs, "but I was on leave and he flew with Lt. Mike McCormick. When they landed, Ray was dead already. It was very somber when they pulled him out of the cockpit."

Danny Glover, Willem Dafoe and Brad Johnson added to the box office appeal, but critical reviews were mostly negative. Some errors in continuity and ineffective special effects further weakened the film's technical success.

A Grumman A-6 Intruder armed for ground attack The A-6 could carry a larger bomb load than a B-17 Flying Fortress. They are still used by the Navy even today.

CHAPTER TEN

Faster, Louder, More Money: Action Films

The unpopularity of the Vietnam War put the armed services in a bad light even a half-decade after the last troops had returned home. From the late 1970s into the 1980s the Department of Defense was hard at work on improving its public image with big-budget recruitment campaigns. Slogans such as "The Army—Be All You Can Be," "The Few, the Proud, the Marines," and "Aim High—Air Force" were carefully planned to improve the public perception of the armed services. With the economic recession of the era, many young men and women entered the military as a way to get a job and an education.

One of the most sure-fire ways the military had at its disposal to boost its image was through the ever-growing popularity of the movies and, to a lesser extent, television. With much the same eagerness that the Army showed in working with Paramount in 1927 for *Wings*, the Navy and Air Force sought to use movies to show they were the good guys. In a few years a new genre of high-budget action films emerged, including the *Rambo*, *Mad Max* and *Terminator* series, which catapulted Sylvester Stallone, Mel Gibson and Arnold Schwarzenegger into super-stardom. They were examples of the rapidly growing craze for more "bangs for your box-office buck."

While not necessarily "war movies" in the traditional sense these films made liberal use of military hardware such as machine guns, rockets and anything that would make big explosions. The public—for the most part those under thirty yeas of age—were quick to forget the "baby-killer" image of the armed forces in favor of watching tons of high explosives and hundreds of rounds of ammunition decimate a town or drug-smuggling operation on screen. More often than not the enemy consisted of international crime lords, drug smuggling cartels or fictitious Middle East dictators. Both Hollywood and the Department of Defense eventually got what they wanted: respectively, profits and prestige.

Based on a best-selling book by Martin Caidin, *The Final Countdown* (1980) was the first of many military-themed action movies during this period. *Countdown*'s plot was about a modern nuclear-powered aircraft carrier being drawn by a mysterious force into a time warp and emerging the day before the Japanese attack on Pearl Harbor.

Starring Kirk Douglas as a competent and personable captain, James Farentino as the Commander, Air Group (CAG) and military historian, and Martin Sheen as a protagonist Defense Department representative, the film follows a wholly improbable plot. *USS Nimitz* (CVN-68) finds itself in a position to stop an attack that had happened nearly forty years before. The audience is drawn into the story, despite the incongruity. A pair of patrolling Grumman F-14 Tomcats see two A6M Zeros strafing and destroying an unarmed yacht carrying a crusty senator and his secretary. Realizing the Zeros will soon discover the *Nimitz*, the captain orders them shot down. The Tomcats use their superior speed and weapons to shoot down the Japanese planes with ease.

The survivors from the senator's yacht are rescued by a helicopter and taken back to the ship. They are totally unable to comprehend what is happening. The surviving Japanese pilot manages to get a gun while being interrogated and kills two members of the Marine detachment. In a desperate attempt to gain control of the situation and prevent more killing the captain orders the CAG to reveal what he knows about the Pearl Harbor attack. The astonished pilot drops his guard and is shot.

After the *Nimitz* launches a strike force to sink the unsuspecting Japanese fleet and stop the attack, the time storm returns and pulls the carrier back to 1980. In the end a few things have been left behind. The CAG and the senator's secretary remain in 1941 to later appear at the end as the elderly owners of the company that built the ship in the first place.

Yes it's ridiculous, but *The Final Countdown* was a box-office success. No attempt was made to explain the phenomenon that caused the time warp. It's almost a minor point in the ever-complex series of clues to what the crew find themselves in.

The U.S. Navy cooperated in the filming, providing full access to the *Nimitz* for the production. Interwoven into the story are a series of vignettes showing carrier operations including jet takeoffs, landings, helicopter rescue and mid-air refueling. It's no accident. *Countdown* is a recruiting film. Not many of the intended audience ware likely to fear being pulled into a time warp.

The production was made while the *Nimitz* was in the Atlantic. Stock footage of *USS Kitty Hawk* (CV-63) was used for the Pearl Harbor sequence. The location shots were done at NAS Key West, Florida.

F-14 Tomcat of VF-84, the 'Jolly Rogers' that went back in time to take on the Japanese fleet in *The Final Countdown.*

The acting and screenplay work well at moving the story along at an ever-more rapid pace. It's easy to imagine how the 1941-era civilians view the amazing hardware of jets and helicopters. The fighter pilots of VF-84, "The Jolly Rogers," have some fun by engaging in a dogfight with the Zeros in order to prevent them from killing the yacht's helpless survivors. The audience is pulled to the edge of their seats, knowing that at some point the powerful F-14s will have to destroy the primitive fighters. The image of the two jets screaming towards the camera in their determination to shoot down the Japanese planes sends a shot of righteous patriotic adrenaline through the audience.

The Executive Officer of VF-84, Commander Rich "Fox" Ferrell, did the stunning falling-at-the-sea shot while filming with the Zeros. He came very close to the surface of the ocean and the "scream" heard in the soundtrack is mixed from the jet sound and that of his wife's scream when she viewed the rushes. The Zeros had their throttles to maximum to stay in the shot with the alarmingly throttled-back Tomcats. In what has to be the most one-sided aerial engagement in history, the Tomcats bring the Zeros down with cannon and missiles in less than thirty seconds.

Ever since the film's release there has been an ongoing debate among aviation buffs as to how the F-14 would do in combat against the Zero. It might seem blindingly obvious, yet it's not that clear, based on interviews with Tomcat pilots. Captain Rick "Wigs" Ludwig, former C.O. of the Fighter Weapons School "Top Gun" at NAS Miramar, said, "The Tomcat would eat the Zero alive. In speed, firepower, acceleration, no contest. Just don't try to fight in the Zero's environment. Don't try to turn inside him. The Zero would be gone before you could line up your shot. But if you're outside his environment, he's dead."

The duel between the AT-6 Texan 'Zeroes' and the F-14 Tomcats in *The Final Countdown* was one of the most compelling, if brief, aerial engagements ever seen on film.

The A6M Zero's maneuverability at low-altitude was exemplary. The F-14 would have to duel with the Zero from at least two or three miles away. Capt. Dick Evert, who commanded VF-211 and flew Tomcats in both VF-24 and VF-124, agrees. "An F-14, with its wing-loading and power, will not turn inside a Zero," he said. "It would far 'outzoom' it, but in terms of getting a missile shot at a Zero it would need a lot of stand-off distance. But turning inside and staying with it, no way."

As to whether a heat-seeking AIM-9 Sidewinder missile could hit a radial-engine Zero, both Evert and Ludwig agree the old engine would probably have put out enough heat at full power for a Sidewinder to lock on.

A few inconsistencies emerge in the film without doing much damage. For instance, one of *Nimitz*' aircraft returns from a photo reconnaissance flight over Pearl Harbor on December 6. The photos seen in the film were actually taken by Japanese pilots on December 7 during the attack. When the CAG (Farentino) details the upcoming raid, he names the six carriers as the *Tongi, Tongna, Shokaku, Zuikaku, Hiryu,* and *Soryu*. Except for the first two—which were in fact the *Akagi* and *Kaga*—he was correct. The author was not able to find any reason for the strange discrepancy. Interestingly the closed captioning does get it right.

The Zeros are modified AT-6 Texans. The extras and some speaking roles are active-duty ship's personnel. They give it their all but it's obvious they should remain in the Navy and not pursue a career in acting. In the scenes when the ship is drawn back into the present, footage from *Tora! Tora! Tora!* was used to depict the Japanese attack, along with radio news clips.

Two years after *Countdown* premiered, Clint Eastwood, who was feeling his directorial oats after a series of successes, released *Firefox*. Based on a novel by Craig Thomas, the movie centers around Mitchell Gant, a former Vietnam War fighter pilot who has withdrawn from the world and any contact with the military. He suffers from PTSD and memories of his imprisonment by Viet Cong troops.

British MI-5 and the CIA collude to bring Gant back from the wilderness to steal a top-secret Soviet super fighter. The MiG-31 Firefox is the fastest, most advanced and dangerous threat to NATO that ever existed. The Firefox has ultra-sophisticated thought-control technology and is invisible to radar. Gant is forced to travel to Moscow under an assumed identity, make contact with western spies and penetrate the Soviet airfield where the plane is being readied for testing. Along the way several people are killed in their support of Gant's mission, which further causes him to regret being involved. Then he assaults the real pilot, climbs into one of the two flight-ready Firefoxes and takes off just as the Soviet General Secretary arrives for the flight test.

The futuristic MiG-31 Firefox miniature was built by famed model maker Gregory Jien, whose work included models for *Star Wars* and *Blue Thunder*.

The Red Air Force tries to overtake and stop Gant but their own technology and his experience foils them. After a daring refueling from a U.S. submarine on an ice floe in the Arctic Gant thinks he has escaped. But the second Firefox, flown by the pilot he left alive, shows up and the two billion-Ruble fighters begin a suspenseful and blindingly fast duel to the death. In the last second, just as all seems lost, Gant is able to fire missiles from the rear of his plane and destroys the Russian. Flying into the sunset, Gant heads for home.

As an action film *Firefox* does have a great deal to offer. But even though it deals with a more pedestrian situation, *i.e.*, stealing an enemy plane, it's far less believable than *Final Countdown*. The acting is overly contrived with clichéd lines and overdrawn characters. Eastwood as Gant would have done better to stay behind the camera or drop the idea entirely. There is very little for the viewer to relate to, other than a hope that Gant will be able to succeed in foiling the minions and tyrants of the Evil Empire. Gant's constant uncommunicative manner and the blatantly stereotypical cultured Russian dialogue only serve to slow the film's pace.

But not in the sky. The Firefox, in both miniature and full-scale, is a truly evil-looking monster, appearing as what the next generation Soviet fighter would be. Twin rudders, chiseled nose, canards and drooping wings heavy with ordnance convey menacing intent. The audience is thrilled to see the black plane take off and streak into the skies. A series of shots showing the aircraft shrieking by in a blur or flying low over the water with walls of white spray shoot up behind it are awe-inspiring to the audiences of 1982. Yet it seems woefully amateurish in today's CGI era.

The final battle between "good" and "evil" is hard to support. The viewer is supposed to root for the American but it's hard not to feel compassion for the Russian, who was just doing his job when he was cold-cocked by Gant. The Russian dies in the attempt to stop the stolen Firefox, while Gant, still sullen, takes his prize to his masters. The hypersonic jets engage in a harrowing chase down meandering ice canyons—in a warped echo of the Death Star trench—and over snowy landscapes. Tracer cannon fire spits past Gant's Firefox, causing the viewer to wonder why he is never hit by the man with more experience in the plane.

Firefox is not much of a film, and hardly a star in Eastwood's portfolio.

A year later Columbia did what *Firefox* failed to do by making an aircraft into the star of a film. In this case the hero was a helicopter. *Blue Thunder's* high technology and fast action would have fit well in this chapter, but the reader will find it in Chapter Eleven among the other helicopter movies.

In January 1986 a "sleeper" film reached the theaters. *Iron Eagle* tweaked the public interest in jet planes and hot pilots with a wholly improbable story and little military cooperation. TriStar's *Iron Eagle*, from a story by *The Boys in Company C* director Sidney J.

Furie, follows the teenaged son of an Air Force pilot who is shot down and imprisoned by a ruthless Middle Eastern dictator. Doug Masters, played by the 20-year old Jason Gedrick, is a member of a group of teenaged Air Force brats called the Young Eagles. Doug is a skilled pilot who is told by his father, Col. Ted Masters, to grow up and show some responsibility. Colonel Masters, played with real skill by former San Diego stand-up comedian Tim Thomerson, is shot down and taken prisoner by the leader of an unnamed Middle Eastern nation.

When Doug and his friends learn that Col. Masters will be executed in three days' time Doug runs to a no-nonsense fighter pilot for help to get his father out of "that shithole." The Oscar-winning actor Louis Gossett, Jr., plays Col "Chappy" Sinclair. Chappy, after learning no serious attempt beyond ineffective diplomatic means will save his fellow Air Force officer, agrees to help Doug and his friends. By using the unique talents of the Young Eagles Chappy and Doug secure two F-16Cs, weapons, fuel, intelligence and weather data for an unauthorized rescue mission. Doug proves he is capable of flying the F-16 and with Chappy's guidance, they fly to the airbase where Doug's father is being held.

Louis Gossett Jr. and Jason Gedrick planning their audacious rescue raid in the 1986 hit *Iron Eagle*.

A series of fights with enemy "MiGs" and anti-aircraft missiles cause Chappy's plane to go down, leaving Doug to go it alone. But with a tape of Chappy's instructions Doug destroys the enemy flight line and defenses. Doug demands that Col. Masters be released and driven to the field or he will destroy their refineries and other vital installations. The enemy finally gives in, and Col. Masters climbs into the plane to find his own son in command. The dictator is not pleased and flies his own jet to shoot down the American infidel but ends up as a flaming ball of debris under Doug's cannon.

Doug returns to face a court of inquiry and finds Chappy alive. Chappy helps not only to defuse the Air Force's intent to prosecute Doug but also to give the teenager an appointment to the U.S. Air Force Academy.

As action movies go, *Iron Eagle* is hard to beat. As for reality and plausibility, it's impossible to accept. It's every red-blooded American boy's dream of taking a fighter plane and blasting hell out of a "bad guy" on a grand scale. But in order for the audience to stay in the theaters they have to suspend disbelief to nothingness. The boys and girls of the Young Eagles run roughshod over their fathers, obtaining secret intelligence information, photos, weapons, mid-air refueling and anything else Doug and Chappy need to fly over to Africa and weak havoc, all with successful impunity, of course. A hard-rock soundtrack ensures most of the viewers will be from 15-25 years of age and gain an undeserved scorn of military discipline.

An Israeli Kfir fighter of the type used as enemy MiGs in *Iron Eagle*.

The Air Force, seeing how the screenplay made a mockery of their security, decided not to provide any base facilities or aircraft. Therefore the entire film was shot on location in Camarillo, California, and in Israel. All the American air base sequences with F-16s and "enemy" MiGs were done using Israeli Air Force aircraft. The "MiGs" were in fact Israeli

Aircraft Industries Kfir fighters, provided for the production. The national insignia are fictitious.

It doesn't take a rocket scientist to guess that the country where Col. Masters is being held is Libya, although it is never named. When the film was being made, Libya was *the* quintessential Middle Eastern evil nation. On April 15, just three months after *Iron Eagle* reached the theaters, 18 USAF F-111 fighter-bombers bombed Tripoli in retaliation for a Libyan-sponsored terrorist bombing of a Berlin nightclub.

The leader of the fictitious nation is too-obviously based on Col. Muammar Ghaddafi, and is overacted at that. As with all film heavies from foreign countries the leader uses better diction than an Oxford literature professor, with tiresome repetitious threats.

As long as the audience shrugs its collective shoulders and lets the film take over, it's a fun movie to watch.

When the author interviewed Louis Gossett, Jr., regarding his role as Chappy, the actor said, "It was a fantasy, a real fantasy. I have a lot of respect for the Israeli Air Force. We did it there because it was the only country that had F-16s and planes that could be MiGs. But what was incredible, was that while we were on the base in Israel, we would be working and suddenly we'd have to stop filming because they needed the planes to bomb something," he said with a grin. "Then they'd bring the planes back and we'd go out and film some more."

Gossett admitted, "Chappy's character is created from what I did in *An Officer and a Gentleman*. There's a connection there." While filming the *Iron Eagle* movies, Gossett said, "There was a fear inside me, because me and machines don't get along. Equipment always failed me and I had to be in all these fast jets and stuff. I heard Tom Cruise had to clean up his cockpit because he lost it," Gossett laughed. "I was given advice not to have breakfast before a flight. I only had a very light dinner the night before. So when we're in the air I can feel the G-forces moving the food around in there. I got out a bit unsteady but I made it. The pilot said, 'Hey, you didn't lose it. Congratulations.' Then I went into the bathroom and threw up."

Right on the heels of *Iron Eagle*, which spawned two sequels, came the mother of all military aviation action films, Tony Scott's blockbuster *Top Gun*. Top Gun, as the Navy's Fighter Weapons School was commonly called, had been established in 1968 when the skill of the Navy's fighter pilots had degraded to the point where their kill ratio had dropped from a Korean War high of 17-to-1 to a miserable 3-to-1. American Navy pilots had lost the skill of dogfighting in favor of using missiles. The new school was a spectacular success, and when Top Gun graduates began fighting in the skies over Vietnam the kill ratio quadrupled to a respectable 12-to-1.

The Navy Fighter Weapons School (NFWS) at NAS Miramar (now Marine Corps Air Station) in San Diego, the home of Top Gun in the 1980s.

There has been a great deal written about the film and its impact on American popular culture. Capt. Rick Ludwig, who commanded the Top Gun Fighter Weapons School at Miramar in 1987 after the film's release, told the author, "I was getting ready to move to San Diego for my assignment at Miramar when my wife and I decided to go and see this movie, which had just been released. I guess my first reaction was 'Oh my gosh. My job is going to change.'"

While *The Final Countdown* had been a science fiction film with some actual carrier operations thrown in, *Top Gun* was a dramatized portrayal of the world and personality of Navy fighter jocks. Lt. Pete "Maverick" Mitchell, yet another hotshot pilot, is played by one of Hollywood's most successful hunk stars, Tom Cruise. Maverick has something to prove, since his father, a Navy Phantom pilot, had been killed during the Vietnam War and been accused of bad conduct. Maverick's RIO, or Radar Intercept Officer, is Goose, played by the affable *ER* star Anthony Edwards. Goose is married and has his hands full keeping Maverick under control.

While on deployment in the Indian Ocean, Mav and Goose are involved in a test of wills with several fighters from an unnamed Middle Eastern country. Maverick comports himself well and he and Goose are sent to Miramar for training at the prestigious Top Gun, where they will learn with the best of the best to become proficient at Air Combat Maneuvering (ACM). Along the way they meet Iceman and Slider (Val Kilmer and Rick Rossovich), rivals for the Top Gun trophy.

Maverick's love interest is "Charlie," a sexy civilian contractor who teaches the Top Gun students about enemy aircraft performance. Maverick is eager to show her some of his own performance, and they soon fall in love.

Maverick's instructors and fellow classmates are frequently frustrated by his cavalier attitude to the training, earning him several rebukes and scorn. When Goose is killed trying to eject during a flat spin over the ocean, Maverick is thrown into despair and self-doubt.

Top Gun's commander, Viper, is played by the former Duke Forrest of 1970's *M*A*S*H*, Tom Skerritt. Viper takes Maverick aside and says he understands the younger man's drive to prove himself. Viper had been on the mission that had taken the life of Maverick's father, and he explains that it was because of a violation of international law by the Navy that the senior Mitchell had been made the scapegoat. He was actually a hero but it would never be made public.

Maverick graduates from Top Gun, but does not earn the trophy, which is won instead by Iceman. The aviators return to the Med where they learn of a tense situation with the same Middle Eastern forces as before. An encounter with enemy fighters starts out small but quickly expands to a serious and hostile dogfight. Iceman is in trouble and calls for help. Maverick and his new RIO race to the scene and save Iceman while shooting down several of the enemy planes. Maverick finally puts his demons behind him and eventually returns to Miramar as a Top Gun instructor.

The story has many, if not most, of the elements of countless aviation war movies since *Wings*. A hotshot pilot with an attitude, a doomed sidekick, a sexy love interest, a rival who later reconciles with the main character, who at last finds peace with what had been driving him. Only one man is in love with the woman, but two rivals for her affection must have been considered by writers Jim Cash and Jack Epps, Jr. The character of "Charlie" was a late alteration to the script and cast. Scott had been resigned to having Maverick meet a cute girl who would not be able to interact on an intellectual level. But Christine Fox, who was a civilian employee of the Center for Naval Analysis, a specialist in air superiority, provided the basis for the character of "Charlie." That was a very serendipitous encounter.

The movie has a lot of inaccuracies in the plot and training but what it does very well is showcase the ethos, the mystique, of the Navy's fighter pilots. All the men in the movie are young, fit, handsome, and athletic— in short, hunks. Even the volleyball game unfolds like a *Playgirl* video. Producer Jerry Bruckheimer said, "The pilots who attend Top Gun are a combination of Olympic athletes and rock 'n' roll stars. We immediately saw a movie."

The Navy cooperated with the production, providing full access to NAS (now Marine Corps Air Station) Miramar, the Naval Training Center in San Diego and the carriers *USS Enterprise* (CVN-65) and *USS Ranger* (CV-61). Also added was the expertise of Captain (now Rear Admiral) Pete "Viper" Pettigrew, who provided technical advice to the production. Pettigrew was one of the elite, a Naval aviator who had shot down a MiG-21 in May 1972 over North Vietnam.

The opening sequences of the film, accompanied by stirring rock music, show flight operations on an aircraft carrier flight deck. It was done with such skill that the audience was immediately pulled into the action. Filmed on board the *Enterprise* 100 miles off the southern California coast, the sequence used the carrier's current Air Group of VF-114 "Aardvarks" and VF-213 "The Black Lions," several of whose aircraft had fictitious squadron insignia painted on the rudders. Maverick's squadron featured a diving eagle, and Iceman's plane sported a closed fist holding a lightning bolt.

Paramount had to pay an average of $7,000 per hour for fuel and the use of the planes during shooting. For the opening sequence Tony Scott wanted to film the carrier flight operations with the sun backlighting the aircraft. But during one shot the *Enterprise* changed course, thus ruining Scott's shot. He asked the commanding officer if the ship could be put back on the original course, but the captain said it would cost $25,000 to turn the ship around. Scott immediately wrote a check and gave it to the captain to get another five minutes of footage. That at least wasn't taxpayer money.

An F-14 is silhouetted by the predawn sun in the memorable opening sequence of *Top Gun.* Director Tony Scott had to write a check for $25,000 to the *USS Enterprise's* captain to turn the ship around to get five more minutes of footage.

The flying sequences showed the dynamic and high-speed world of modern aerial combat in a way that amazed even experienced Tomcat pilots. Tomcats of VF-1 "Wolfpack," VF-51 "Screaming Eagles" and the A-4 Skyhawks of Top Gun's "Aggressors" were provided for the filming at Miramar. The "MiG" fighters were Northrop F-5 Tigers, painted black with fictitious insignia. Lt. Commander Robert "Rat" Willard coordinated most of the pilots and military flying for the production, while doing more flying than anyone else.

Capt. C. J. "Heater" Heatley, an instructor at Top Gun who flew Tomcats in VF-124, worked on the film as both an extra and aerial cinematographer. "I did some of the flying that appears in the film," Heatley said. "I did a lot of the air-to-air photography of the combat from the cockpit, in the back seat with a Panaflex camera in my hands."

Much of the aerial footage was done from a Learjet camera ship owned and operated by Clay Lacy. Lacy, whose work included *Firefox* and *The Right Stuff* and would later involve *Flight of the Intruder*, had three computer-controlled cameras mounted at points on the Lear's top and bottom fuselage in addition to another mounted in the nose. This allowed full capture of the subject in flight.

In the modern arena of air combat, it is no longer possible to film several planes in a dogfight as was done for decades. Jet fighters make turns over two or three miles and often fight at a distance of several miles. The airspeed will put a jet in and out of camera range in a second. So Scott, Lacy and Willard had to work on how to film several jets in close air combat. Hundreds of fast passes, turns, dives, fly-bys and other maneuvers were filmed in order to combine them into a comprehensible dogfight. "Often two fighters won't be close enough to see more than a small silhouette," said Rick Ludwig.

Repainted Northrop F-5 Tigers portrayed the fictional MiG-28 fighters in *Top Gun.* Note the American AIM-9 Sidewinder heat-seeking missile on the wingtip.

Filmed in the era before CGI became commonplace, *Top Gun's* aerial footage is excellent. The only miniatures in the production were blown up or on fire. "The flying scenes were just phenomenal," said Ludwig. "The way they choreographed the flying with the music was fantastic. I never saw flying like they did in that movie," said the fighter pilot with 28 years of service. "They did things with an F-14 that just isn't done."

Some of Maverick's maneuvers are pure Hollywood. When he and Goose fly inverted over an enemy MiG in the early part of the film, both canopies are seen in the shot. "That's impossible," Ludwig protested. "The rudders would have been overlapping. I've never seen anybody fly canopy-to-canopy like that, not even the Blue Angels." The veteran fighter pilot wasn't finished: "And that full aileron roll Mav did when they were being fired upon, there's no reason for it. I don't think they needed to put any of that stuff in. Do one high-speed fly-by of a tower, I don't care who you are, you're done with your career. Period."

Heatley commented on how Scott took license with reality. "That aileron roll Tom Cruise does, that's just not done. No aviator in his right mind would do that."

Tony Scott also took great liberties with the aerial scenes of the training. Several of the ACM sequences were done at very low altitude, almost inside rocky canyons and between peaks. Ludwig scoffed at this. "Most of our flying was done off the coast of Mexico, or over China Lake," he said. "We did some over ranges in Arizona. The 'soft deck' was at 10,000 feet so you'd never even notice the terrain." Scott wanted the aircraft flying low to get the effects of speed.

One of *Top Gun's* locations for aerial footage was at NAS Fallon in Nevada, using ground cameras. "It's not that exciting, really," said Ludwig. "The 'hard deck' is at 5,000 and you never got below that. Any ACM below that is a violation of our training rules."

The author did find differing opinions regarding the ACM and training. For this book he chose to outline certain informed comments that in some cases contradicted one another. Heatley said, "We often flew low and hid behind the mountains and went down on the deck during maneuvers. We often kicked up dust on the desert. But we didn't get below the hard deck during ACM." As for the training, Ludwig went on to say, "They took away from the true mission of Top Gun. We didn't pick the 'top one percent.' We looked for pilots who were not only good but also showed exceptional leadership and teaching ability. The idea was to train them to take the necessary skills back to their squadrons and teach their fellow pilots what they learned. We train the trainers." Ludwig explained that there was no use of call signs during debriefing. "We took the 'who' out of it and only referred to the aircraft and maneuvers. Also there is no Top Gun Trophy. We wanted to get the egos out of it."

Tom Cruise in a publicity shot as naval aviator Lt. Pete 'Maverick' Mitchell in *Top Gun.*

The success of *Top Gun* led to a huge increase in Naval Aviation cadet applications.

Maverick's actions and attitude were far off the board, according to Ludwig. "We would never have accepted anyone like that." The rebellious Maverick's ego was what made the movie so popular, whether or not he would have been accepted at Top Gun.

Ludwig was in a good position to see firsthand what Top Gun's skyrocketing popularity did for the image of the Navy fighter jock and, by extension, the Navy in general. "The Officer's Club on base was usually busy on Wednesdays or Friday nights, but after the movie came out it was full of what I called 'lots of Kellys looking for Toms.' The magnitude of the people at the club increased dramatically. One time I was coming out of a room in the O-Club in my flight gear with my name on it: *Top Gun C.O. Rick 'Wigs' Ludwig*. There was this woman standing there with this huge sourpuss look on her face. I stopped and said, 'Hey smile, will ya?' She saw my wings and with a starry-eyed look on her face asked, 'Will you dance with me?'"

Director Tony Scott managed to do what no other film in history had done since *Sergeant York* in 1942: Scott was responsible for a stunning increase in applications for military service. "Navy recruiting offices were inundated with applications for Naval aviation. So was the Air Force," said Ludwig.

What *Top Gun* did for the military might have been both a blessing and a curse, depending on the point of view. While every Type-A male wanted to be a fighter pilot, most were more interested in the dress white uniforms and being "chick magnets" than putting their lives on the line for their country. The Navy and Air Force must have spent a lot of time and manpower separating the "serious" grain from the "cool fad" chaff.

The immense popularity of *Top Gun* was proof that Americans were very susceptible to patriotic and action-themed movies. The film enjoyed a near-record run in the theaters and hit the top of the home video market. The soundtrack, with such hits as "Danger Zone" and "Unchained Melody," hit the top of the music charts.

Another aspect of the film's incredible success was what it did to Hollywood. Even before the box office receipts were fully tallied, the studios were suddenly looking seriously at screenplays that a year before wouldn't have made it past the agents. Scripts about jet planes and hot pilots were pulled from dusty bottom file cabinet drawers to be re-examined with a great deal more enthusiasm. While hoping to cash in on the *Top Gun* craze, few studios succeeded, and concentrated on the action popularity of Schwarzenegger, Willis, Stallone and Gibson.

Iron Eagle II arrived in theaters in 1988. Again Louis Gossett, Jr., is cast as the serious but still-daring pilot Chappy Sinclair, who managed to keep from being court-martialed for his little stunt in the previous film. With a reputation for unconventional missions, Chappy is called upon to form and lead a joint U.S./Soviet attack force of pilots to destroy a secret and heavily-defended nuclear weapons site in—where else? —the Middle East.

Chappy's job is made far harder than it should be. Babysitting the eclectic band of pilots causes him no end of grief, but it pales in comparison to what he learns: In the event their mission fails, a nuclear strike has been ordered on the site, even if his team is still there. All Chappy can do is race the clock and succeed in the mission, while blowing up as much enemy hardware as possible. With a beautiful Soviet woman as one of his team, Chappy also has to contend with overly macho Americans egos and one-upmanship. In an ever-building suspenseful climax the team manages to do its job and save the day, all to the accompaniment of rock music and bad jokes.

In a way the film, which didn't do nearly as well as its predecessor, did break the mold of the old "Evil Communist" image. The Soviets are suspicious of their American partners but slowly come to respect them as pilots. The Americans have a similar epiphany.

Again the Air Force, probably still smarting from director Sidney J. Furie's treatment of them in *Iron Eagle*, declined to cooperate with the production. And again it was filmed at Ramat David Air Base in Israel, using the same F-16s and Kfir fighters. Apparently the Soviet Union (now The Commonwealth of Independent States) also declined to be involved. The "Soviet" MiG fighter-bombers used are in fact McDonnell-Douglas F-4 Phantoms of Vietnam War vintage. The Soviet airliner bringing the Russians to the base is a Boeing 707 with a Soviet flag on the fuselage. The 'Libyan' weapons and vehicles are a mixed bag of modified American and Israeli equipment.

Once again the military personnel and leaders are laughingly overdramatized, harking back to the era of comic-opera villains. Of course this is a false impression but 1980s American audiences cared little about reality and only wanted to see the bad guys blown to bits while trying in vain to destroy the infidels.

Sidney Furie wasn't done hatching increasingly bizarre plots for Gossett and in 1992 released the third film of the series, *Aces: Iron Eagle III*. This time the "stars" are vintage World War II piston-engine fighters.

The film opens with Chappy as a member of a club which flies restored warbirds for air shows and public events. At the controls of a P-51 Mustang Chappy hasn't lost his zest for witty banter in the cockpit. Chappy learns of a large drug-smuggling ring at his air base and is determined to crush it. Along the way he discovers that a small Peruvian village is being held in virtual slavery by an ex-Nazi drug lord. A sexy woman named Anna, played by Rachel McLish, whose sculptured form is enough to make any male viewer forget about airplanes, escapes to tell what she knows. Several Americans are being held hostage, so Chappy collects a ragtag bunch of warbird pilots to join in a raid and save the villages. Amazingly, the FAA is never consulted, nor is the Peruvian government. Apparently the drug kingpin hadn't heard of what the Air Force colonel was capable of or he'd close down his operation and join a monastery. Chappy seems to have lots of free time to pursue his "off-duty" jaunts.

While the two previous films were wildly improbable, *Aces* does have some obvious elements of *The Magnificent Seven* in it. In the end, after a difficult period of coordinating the eclectic band of pilots and personalities, Chappy leads them down to South America and attacks the drug lord's headquarters. Even Doug Masters would have scoffed at this. Not much more than a chance to see a lot of World War II air hardware in every situation from fly-bys to strafing and bombing, *Aces* is a forgettable film. Even Gossett, who enjoyed working on it, felt it was stretching things too far.

The fighters run the gamut of American, British, German and Japanese planes. But all aren't what they appear to be. The Me-109 is a P-51A owned by Planes of Fame. The Me-262 jet is an American Scaled Composites Rutan ARES stunt jet. The Zero is again the usual North American T-6 Texan. Only the Mustang, the Spitfire and P-38 Lightning are real.

To break the *Iron Eagle* mold, director John Glen, who had larger budgets when doing several of the later James Bond 007 films, decided the Libyans were no longer suitable villains and went with the increasing threat of international drug smuggling. It's a fair bet the Libyan government might have protested the treatment of their nation in Furie's earlier *Iron Eagle* films. Be that as it may, *Aces* uses strong Republican and pro-American ideals to entice audiences to sit still for two hours and cheer on the vintage warbirds.

Louis Gossett's acting is far and away the best in the film, although a fair performance is put in by Horst Buchholz as the drug lord. The former Nazi's name is Leichmann, only a letter away from "Eichmann," just to make the point. Paul Freeman, best known for his role as the crafty Belloq in *Raiders of the Lost Ark* (1981), is another member of Chappy's team.

Chappy's Lockheed P-38 Lighting banks into a tight turn in *ACES: Iron Eagle III*. The P-38 is owned by Planes of Fame in Chino, California, and flown by the late Charlie Hillard.

The Supermarine Spitfire flown in *ACES: Iron Eagle III.*

Steve Hinton of Chino's Planes of Fame Air Museum did some of the stunt flying for *Aces*. "We flew the Spitfire, P-38, P-51A, which doubled as the Me-109, the T6 Zero and the B-25 camera ship," recalled Hinton. "The late Charlie Hillard was aerial coordinator. He'd worked with the production crew doing the Pancho Barnes TV movie. We painted the P-51A, added dummy rockets and the turbo booster device for the P-38." Hinton went on to describe some of the filming: "Charlie had never flown a P-38 so we trained him in our B-25 as part of the checkout in the P-38. Charlie had no problems at all. Kevin Eldridge and Walt Pine flew camera. I flew the Lightning and Spitfire while John Maloney flew the P-51A. Mike Melville flew the Rutan Jet. We were based out of Pinell Air Park [in Arizona] and flew 50 hours or so over four weeks around Tucson, Lake Havasu and down to Nogales, New Mexico."

According to Hinton the warbirds were fitted with smoke generators and propane machine guns. But he had one interesting experience. "I flew the Spitfire with a pair of fake steel legs," said Hinton. "The scene called for the pilot of the Spitfire to almost fall out. I ducked down after takeoff with this upside down torso sticking up in the air. I thought it was a stretch for sure, but whatever they wanted," he said with a grin. "We had a few sick camera operators in the B-25 a few times."

Furie made *Iron Eagle IV: On the Attack* in 1995. Chappy is now running a flight school, which only seems to accept misfits and rowdies. Doug Masters, the hero of the first film is back to help Chappy, but is now played by Jason Cadieux. Somehow Doug has been resurrected from the crash which killed him in *Iron Eagle II.*

This time the villains are rogue Air Force officers who are selling toxic waste, and Chappy has to mold his young pilots into a force capable of destroying the smuggling operation.

The filming took place in Ontario, Canada.

There is little point in detailing this movie as it is little more than a rehash of the first three.

The 'Me-109' in *ACES: Iron Eagle III* was Planes of Fame's repainted P-51A Mustang.

Air Force One (1997) starring Harrison Ford and Gary Oldman is one of the best action films of the last twenty years. President James Marshall (Ford) is on board the 747 Air Force One returning from Moscow after delivering a strong anti-terrorism speech. The aircraft is full of press, presidential staff and his family. Terrorists, under the leadership of Korshunov (Oldman), take control of the 747, vowing to kill hostages one by one until President Marshall agrees to their demands. The Secret Service tries to force Marshall into the escape pod. The pilots head to Ramstein Air Base, Germany, where F-15s take off to escort Air Force One. The base goes on full alert for the 747's arrival.

The terrorists kill the pilots. Then, with barely room to spare, they lift off again, missing the tower and parked aircraft. En route to Kazakhstan, Korshunov herds the passengers into the conference room. He contacts Vice President Kathryn Bennett (Glenn Close) in Washington. Until their demands to release their leader held in a Kazakhstan prison are met, the terrorists will kill hostages every half hour. Marshall's wife and daughter are first on the list.

Marshall was not ejected on the escape pod, but remains on board to fight back. What the terrorists fail to consider is Marshall as a Medal of Honor recipient and combat pilot. He kills one of the terrorists. Korshunov is enraged and demands Marshall's surrender.

The President slowly takes control away from the terrorists, dumping the fuel and forcing a mid-air refueling. He sneaks into the conference room where the hostages are held. His plan is to get the 747 down to 15,000 feet, where the hostages can escape by parachute. He and his remaining staff escort the hostages to the cargo hold. Only a few people are able to escape before their attempt is discovered by Korshunov's men. In the ensuing chaos some people fall out of the 747 while the refueling plane is damaged, causing the latter to explode.

Korshunov takes Marshall and others of his staff hostage. Korshunov threatens to kill the President's daughter unless Marshall makes the President of Russia meet his demands. A final fight takes place in the cargo hold when Marshall's daughter distracts Korshunov, allowing Marshall to throw him out while yelling, "Get off my plane!" Marshall turns the 747 to leave Kazakhstan but six MiG-29 Fulcrums piloted by men loyal to the terrorist leader launch in pursuit.

The Eagles arrive and fight the MiGs, losing one F-15 and its pilot, who sacrificed himself to protect the damaged Air Force One. Marshall knows he can't reach an airbase. An MC-130 Hercules is brought in to zip-line Marshall and the remaining passengers from the doomed 747 before it hits the water of the Caspian Sea. The Hercules crew manages to rescue Marshall's family and his wounded Chief of Staff. The President is winched to safety just as the 747 crashes into the water. The Hercules then assumes the call sign "Air Force One."

German-born Wolfgang Petersen, who brought the excellent *Das Boot* (1981) to the screen, directed the production. Jerry Goldsmith's powerful score has some elements of Arthur Rubinstein's *Blue Thunder* score from fourteen years earlier. An all-star cast and well-written dialogue serve the film well, bringing the audience to a fever pitch of excitement several times until the final confrontation. Without a doubt the plot is as convoluted as it can possibly get with many twists of fate and surprises.

This is every bit as much an aviation film as an action flick. It has everything: a 747, an MC-130, F-15 Eagles, MiG-29 Fulcrums, a KC-135 tanker and others. Whole planes explode and crash, break up in flight and dogfight.

Literally no expense was spared to make the aerial sequences as realistic as possible. The Air Force provided several F-15s and their crews, while only requesting that the studio pay for their hotel bills during the filming. Cinesite, a digital graphics company, animated the afterburner effects for the F-15 and MiG-29 miniatures. The final crash into the sea, even though it is a miniature, is very convincing, as are the shots when Marshall is spinning and twisting at the end of the tether in a 200-knot wind. The final crash took six months and $800,000 to film.

American International Airways rented the Boeing 747-146 to Columbia for the filming. It was repainted at a cost of over $300,000 to represent the president's 747-200 aircraft.

Despite the use of advanced aircraft and ultra-sophisticated technology seen in the film, the primary camera ship was once again the old tried and true B-25. With a top speed of 220 knots the converted Mitchell was capable of keeping up with the Boeing and the Lockheed MC-130 Hercules. Steve Hinton piloted the B-25 during the aerial shooting.

Paul Bishop, an experienced AIA pilot, flew the big 747 very close to the MC-130 during the mid-air transfer sequences, which were filmed over the Channel Island off the coast of California.

Air Force One was filmed in over a dozen locations, including Russia and California. The Ramstein AB sequences were shot at Rickenbacker International Airport in Columbus, Ohio.

For better or worse, the action films did serve their purpose: to make money and entertain the public. While many of these movies were unbelievable, they did advance the art of filmmaking to a level unknown or even dreamed in Wellman's time. Only history will tell whether that was a good thing or not.

CHAPTER ELEVEN

Gasbags and Whirlybirds

The public has grown so used to the sight of wings thrust forward by propellers and jets that it's often easy to forget there are other denizens of the blue with different modes of flight. For decades prior to World War II strange and beautiful machines as large as ocean liners soared over European and American cities. The airships were once the queens of the sky. They were massive silver behemoths carrying passengers on luxury flights across the oceans or crews on military missions.

They are all gone now, leaving behind an almost mystic legend. All that is left of their legacy are the diminutive present-day advertising blimps that tout tires, film or life insurance. Today the Goodyear blimp may seem huge, but it should be remembered that the zeppelins were as big to the blimp as the *Queen Mary* was to a tugboat. When the *Graf Zeppelin* or *USS Macon* flew overhead, they eclipsed the sun.

Only a few films showcased the era of giant airships. Howard Hughes' *Hell's Angels* (see Chapter Two) did a credible job of bringing a German Zeppelin to the screen. After a bombing raid the huge hydrogen-filled vessel fell to Earth in a pillar of flame.

Continuing the historical chronology of films is Warner's *Zeppelin* (1971), a mediocre romance drama set against the Zeppelin war of 1915. Michael York, five years before his performance as the "Sandman" of *Logan's Run*, was a British agent named Geoffrey Richter-Douglas. Of both Scottish and German descent, Geoffrey falls in love with a pretty German agent. Geoffrey has been given the assignment of entering Germany and stealing the plans for the new *LZ-36* Zeppelin. After he arrives in Germany—posing as a deserter—he meets up with German officers who bring him on board the new airship for its maiden flight. Richter-Douglas then learns of a plot to steal the priceless Magna Carta. The LZ-36 is the means for entering and escaping England. Geoffrey's loyalty to England is sorely tested, but in the end he foils the plot.

Simple plot notwithstanding, the special effects are above par. Several reproduction aircraft belonging to Lynn Garrison and previously used in *The Blue Max* were provided for the production, which was largely filmed in Ireland. Although the film takes place in 1915, the Fokker D.VII and S.E.5a did not enter service until early 1917. During the Ireland filming a disastrous collision between one of the S.E.5a fighters and an Allouette helicopter killed five people.

Michael York and Peter Carsten in the control gondola of the LZ-36 in *Zeppelin.*

The *LZ-36* was a detailed 40-foot long miniature with radio-controlled engines, rudder and elevators. Principal photography of the model was done in Malta. The real *LZ-36* was flown by the German Navy. In the film it is the Army that operates the ship. However, German Army zeppelins bore a different numbering system and deleted the "Z." *LZ-36* flew more than seventy reconnaissance and bombing missions over England and the North Sea before being destroyed in its shed in September 1916. The airship sheds seen in the film are at Cardington, Bedfordshire—once the airfield for the ill-fated *R-101* and her slightly more successful sister *R-100* in 1930.

Dirigible, produced by Harry Cohn's Columbia in 1931, was directed by Frank Capra. An explorer named Rondelle (Hobard Bosworth) asks the Navy to allow him to use the *USS Pensacola*, a giant rigid airship, to fly to the South Pole. A Navy officer, Jack Bradon (Jack Holt), and a pilot, "Frisky" Pierce (Ralph Graves, will fly the *Pensacola's* biplane. Disaster strikes when the ship crashes at sea, so Rondelle, Bradon and Pierce try again with a Ford Trimotor. This attempt too ends in near disaster when Frisky convinces Rondelle the landing site is safe, yet the Ford flips over and becomes a mass of flames. Rondelle and another crewman are seriously injured. To make matters worse, nearly all their supplies have been lost and they are 900 miles from help. After a long and desperate struggle in which Rondelle dies, Jack brings the new *USS Los Angeles* (ZR-3) into the area and saves the survivors.

The Luftschiff (airship) Zeppelin LZ-36 in 1916. The 40-foot miniature for the movie recreated the real ship in every detail but size.

Navy officer and screenwriter Frank Wead wrote the story and acted as technical advisor on a film that, while being largely forgotten, contains a wealth of rare 1930s aviation footage. *USS Los Angeles*, the Navy's most successful rigid airship, portrayed both herself and the fictional *Pensacola*. As the *LZ-126* she was a German-built Zeppelin and delivered to the United States Navy as part of war reparation payments. As the first airship to test the Navy's concept of a trapeze to launch and recover biplane fighters, the *Los Angeles* deserves a place in aviation history.

Most of the airship sequences were shot at NAS Lakehurst, New Jersey, the airship's base. The cavernous Hangar One at Lakehurst was also the American port for the *Graf Zeppelin* (LZ-127) and *Hindenburg* (LZ-129). The aircraft carrier *USS Lexington* (CV-2) appears in the background of one shot, and it is possible to see her short-lived 8-inch gun mounts.

Fay Wray, after working with Gary Cooper in *Legion of the Condemned*, was again cast in an aviation film, this time as Pierce's wife and Bradon's lover. Again the old "two men, one woman" love triangle appears, but it is hardly noticeable in this film. The aircraft fare better. Among the crew who contributed to *Dirigible*'s technical achievements was Aerial Cinematographer Elmer Dyer, the genius of *Wings*.

Rondelle's expedition was inspired by Commander Richard E. Byrd's flight over the South Pole in November 1929 aboard a Ford Trimotor. No dirigible was used in the actual attempt.

In 1934 Warner produced *Here Comes the Navy*, a flag-waving recruiting film with the team of a pugnacious Chesty O'Connor (James Cagney) facing off against a straight-laced Chief Biff Martin (Pat O'Brien).

Here Comes the Navy has two major elements of interest to military historians. Several scenes were shot aboard the battleship *USS Arizona* (BB-39), the favorite of the U.S. Pacific Fleet. Location shooting was done in Bremerton, San Pedro and San Diego, where the fleet was based prior to its 1940 deployment to Pearl Harbor. The footage shows the ship's decks and interiors, including men working inside the gun turrets.

(A poignant note here: *Arizona* was a prize posting for sailors. Many of her crew re-enlisted and remained on board the battleship long after 1935. When the Japanese 800-kg armor-piercing bomb exploded in her forward magazines at 0805 on December 7 many of the men seen in the film were killed.)

After the *Arizona* sequences, where O'Connor is awarded the Navy Cross for saving the lives of many of his crewmates, the movie shifts to the *USS Macon* (ZRS-5). The *Macon*, sister to the *USS Akron* (ZRS-4), was built as a long-range scout for the fleet in the Pacific. *Akron* crashed in a storm off New Jersey in 1933 and *Macon* met a similar fate near Monterey, California, two years later, ending the Navy's interest in rigid airships. But for a short time they were the darlings of aviation buffs as they flew over American coastal cities. *Macon*'s role in *Here Comes the Navy* is limited to stock footage and aerial shots over San Diego and Hangar No. 1 in Sunnyvale, but it is exciting to watch. Martin is caught up in a mooring line and yanked into the sky under the huge vessel. O'Connor, a member of her crew, slides down the line against orders and brings a parachute to his nemesis. Together they jump and survive. Martin no longer has any reservations about his savior marrying his sister (Gloria Stuart).

The U.S. Navy's dirigible *USS Macon* in the cavernous Hangar One at NAS Moffett Field in Sunnyvale, California. The *Macon* appeared in the finale of *Here Comes the Navy*. Hangar One is still there, but the airships are long gone.

The most ambitious film showcasing the bygone and romantic airships was Universal's 1975 thriller *The Hindenburg*, starring George C. Scott as a German Luftwaffe officer charged with ferreting out potential saboteurs. Based on the controversial book of the same name by Michael M. Mooney, *Hindenburg* tells a semi-historical account of the huge vessel's last voyage in May 1937.

The Luftschiff (airship) Zeppelin LZ-129 *Hindenburg* was the largest rigid airship ever built, utilizing the most advanced materials and over three decades of experience by German engineers. The airship was designed to carry as many as fifty passengers in unparalleled luxury between Friedrichshafen, Rio de Janeiro and Lakehurst, New Jersey, on regular service. For millions of Americans the silver titan was an object of wonder and beauty. But since the airship was funded, built and operated by organs of the Third Reich, it was also a propaganda tool and generated hatred among Jews, Europeans, and even many Germans.

After s successful season of flights in 1936, the LZ-129 waited out the winter in her hangar at Friedrischafen until May of the following year. Amid threats of sabotage, the Zeppelin Company made every effort to protect the huge airship's passengers and crew. But on the evening of May 6, as the *Hindenburg* approached the mooring mast at NAS Lakehurst, she erupted in a fireball which killed 13 passengers and 22 crew out of 97 aboard. It also ended the airship dream, leaving only the remains of a smoking skeleton to mark its passing.

What brought the mighty airship down is still debated to this day, but the most likely explanation is a series of small but related events. The ship had passed through a rain squall, adding a charge of static electricity to the aluminum-painted skin. A sharp turn into the final approach snapped wires holding the aft gas cell, allowing some volatile hydrogen to escape. When the crew dropped mooring lines to the wet soil it triggered a surge of electricity along the hull to the venting gas and ignited it. The rest is history.

But no reasonable explanation of a major event with such public exposure has ever been accepted without challenge. Therein lies the sabotage-and-bomb theory. Mooney's book notes that a German rigger named Erich Spehl planted a small bomb near an aft gas cell to bring down the symbol of Nazi superiority. His girlfriend had been killed by the Gestapo for her outspoken protests during the Spanish Civil War. This was perfect for the conspiracy-hungry moviegoers of the cynical 1970s.

Robert Wise's success with *The Sound of Music* (1965) and *West Side Story* (1961) allowed him to take on the big-budget project of bringing the *Hindenburg* back to life. With large-scale models and the best that Hollywood was capable of in the mid-1970s, the film follows some real and some fictional characters on the ill-fated voyage. Scott is Colonel Franz Ritter, a Luftwaffe pilot ordered to take the journey and spy on any Nazi-perceived threats to the ship. Along the way he interacts with vaudeville acrobat Joseph Spah, played by *Hogan's Heroes*' LeBeau (Robert Clary). Ritter has a personal acquaintance with a countess (Anne Bancroft) whose estate is on Peenemunde, where the Germans are secretly building the V-1 and V-2 rockets. Then a pair of card sharks (Rene Auberjonois and Burgess Meredith), preying on unwitting passengers are caught in the act and detained. An American businessman named Douglas (Gig Young) sends messages by code, and a Jewish family may harbor anti-Nazi feelings.

Ritter has his hands full trying to determine if any of the passengers or crew are a threat to the *Hindenburg*. Of those mentioned, only Spah is a real person.

On the voyage *Hindenburg* experiences a bout with an old sailing ship phenomenon (St. Elmo's Fire) and storm damage to her port stabilizer. Under great danger several of the ship's riggers go out in the swift slipstream to repair the damage. The moment is suspenseful and dramatic. Among the heroic riggers is Boath, a disgruntled German with ties to anti-Nazi factions. The character is based on Spehl and played by William Atherton.

Some of *Hindenburg's* more famous personages interact with Ritter, such as Ernst Lehmann, a longtime leader of the company, as well as the pro-Nazi Captain Max Pruss, played by Charles Durning. Ritter becomes aware of Boeth's plan to destroy the ship after it lands in Lakehurst, but is forced to assist or risk the bomb being detonated early. Ritter is beset by his own frustrations with the new power in Germany, especially how the Gestapo is destroying the lives of innocent people. A series of delays causes a late landing and even as Ritter finds and attempts to disarm the bomb, he accepts the inevitable and sets it off. The final cataclysm is shown in a series of vignettes as the ship's slow demise is halted periodically. Passengers fall to their deaths, crewmen die in the fire, heroes save and cowards run. In the end the ship is a roaring inferno.

A voice-over narrative cites the bomb as one of the causes of the blast, while pointing to static electricity as a possible cause. The final explosion and crash used actual newsreel footage of the May 6, 1937, event, colorized, cropped and enlarged.

The Hindenburg is an excellent technical achievement, and a very strong movie to boot. Scott is a bit old to be a Luftwaffe colonel, and it is ironic he took the role as a German five years after playing the vitriolic Nazi-hating General George Patton.

Some license was taken with history. The St. Elmo's Fire sequence and damage to the port stabilizer didn't happen to the *Hindenburg* but to her predecessor, the LZ-127 *Graf Zeppelin*, in 1928. A few characters are added for plot twists and suspense, but the film's portrayal of the long-vanished dirigible is virtually perfect.

A 25-foot long, detailed model was built for studio shots against a sky backdrop. It was fully operable with motors and control surfaces. Several full-scale mockups were constructed for interior and exterior scenes. They were based on archival photos of the Hindenburg, including the dining saloon, promenade and smoking room. The smoking room was a true innovation on a vessel filled with 7 million cubic feet of explosive hydrogen. The interior of the airship was crisscrossed by a complex web of duralumin girders, cables and struts. This too was carefully recreated for the production. During the crash scenes, the full-scale nose section was set afire. The sequence nearly got out of control, damaging cameras and threatening to engulf the sound stage.

Director Robert Wise and George C. Scott with the 25-foot detailed model of the *Hindenburg. SDASM Collection*

Other aspects of recreating the lost ship were given special attention. For instance, a giant airship makes a sound like no other aircraft in the world. Four powerful Daimler-Benz 16-cylinder engines with 20-foot propellers drove the huge ship through the sky at 80 knots. Inside, that sound is an all-pervasive presence. The author interviewed Sound Effects Editor Peter Berkos about his team's work on *The Hindenburg*. Berkos' resume included *The Great Waldo Pepper* and television's *Battlestar Galactica*. "I started at Universal in 1952," said Berkos. "I'd worked with Bob Wise before and he asked for me to work on *Hindenburg*."

"Bob Wise was a stickler for authenticity," Berkos said. "He wanted the sound to be perfect. I spent months researching all I could find out about what a large airship sounded like. I mean, every night for months I worked on it. I talked to George E. Lewis, who had worked with Goodyear-Zeppelin in the 1930s."

Lewis told Berkos about "structural stress" and the sound it makes when a huge complex structure bends under aerodynamic loads. Berkos' talents were put to the test. "We used the framework of the model and recorded the sounds of the twisting and bending metal," said Berkos. "When we played it to Bob, he said, 'That's just the sound of squeaking metal. I want to hear it flying.'" Berkos went back to his office, frustrated and determined to find the sound Wise wanted. "I sat down in my office chair and leaned back. I heard the groan and creak of metal, and did it again." The impromptu idea bore fruit, as after several attempts the sound effects team managed to expand the simple creaking of an office chair to be the noise of an 800-foot long duralumin structure twisting as it drove its way through the sky.

"I was nervous when we played it for Bob," Berkos said candidly. "But then he smiled and said, 'It's flying!'"

The engine noise was another challenge, since no existing aircraft engines sounded just right. "I recorded the noise of a PBY Catalina's engines," Berkos said. "We expanded and altered it, changed it in a lot of different ways to get the character of those big Daimlers in every evolution. Startup, idle, full power, all of it." The final result vindicated Berkos' long trial. What the audiences heard from the theater speakers was as close to the actual sound of the *Hindenburg*, inside and out, as could be recreated almost forty years after the last Zeppelin flew. "Bob Wise was a wonderful man," Berkos said. "I really liked working with him."

Berkos won the 1976 Academy Award for Best Sound Editing for *The Hindenburg*.

Only a few errors, primarily in the script, mar the smooth finish of the movie. But one is technical. When the riggers are outside repairing the damaged fin, wisps of simulated cloud slip past, but it is much too overdone, weakening the overall effect.

William Wellman again took to the skies by directing Wallace Beery and the ever-acerbic James Gleason in MGM's *This Man's Navy* in 1945. The plot tells of a Navy airship pilot named Ned "Old Gas Bags" Trumpet, who has been bragging about a nonexistent son in the service. He finds a young m man named Weaver (Tom Drake), who is eager to prove himself and get his pilot's license. Weaver joins forces with his "father" to fly patrols over Atlantic convoys to hunt U-boats. During one mission the younger man prematurely drops a bomb on a submarine, missing it but drawing fire on the blimp. Trumpet takes over and sinks the U-boat. Weaver is about to be court-martialed for disobeying orders, but Trumpet takes the fall.

Later Weaver goes to the China-Burma-India Theater as a ferry pilot and is shot down. Trumpet, feeling responsible, goes there with a search team to bring him out. They return to the Atlantic to fly blimps and hunt subs.

This Man's Navy is one of the only films to tell—albeit in an offhanded manner—the unsung but critical work of the U.S. Navy's blimps during the war. This was largely due to Commander Wallace Beery's goal of paying tribute to the service. The Navy provided the use of several Type K blimps, as well as full access to combat footage. Most of the ground scenes were shot at NAS Lakehurst and in California. Wellman's style is evident in some of the dialogue, and he manages to make the often slow airships into flying heroes.

Veteran actor Wallace Beery with Tom Drake in *This Man's Navy.*

Hangar 1 at the former NAS Santa Ana in Tustin, California. The hangar was used for location and effects filming for *This Man's Navy* and *The Hindenburg.* It also served as Starfleet Headquarters for *Star Trek* (2009).

From 1942 to 1945 scores of non-rigid blimps, in fifteen Airship Wings, flew patrols over the Atlantic. Prior to their emergence, over 520 Allied ships were sunk by U-boats. But after the blimps started staying with the convoys and providing round-the-clock coverage, only one ship was sunk by an enemy submarine.

The blimp had many advantages over fixed-wing aircraft: longer range, slow and stationary flight, and the ability to carry bombs, depth charges and torpedoes.

While the huge airships were soaring through the skies another, far smaller and almost unnoticed air machine was testing its wings, so to speak. The helicopter was born of a series of failed and strange craft. The first reasonably successful one was the Autogyro, or Gyrocopter, which didn't use powered rotors for lift. The blades spun from the forward motion imparted by a nose-mounted propeller as in an airplane.

By the end of World War II the first primitive but—if you'll forgive the pun—revolutionary Army helicopters were entering service,. However, it wasn't until the Korean War that they entered the public imagination. The cinema helped to make them more visible.

The most memorable film featuring helicopters was *M*A*S*H,* directed by Robert Altman in 1970. The bestselling book by Joseph Hooker inspired the film, which was a huge success. It told a blackly humorous account of the Mobile Army Surgical Hospitals' work in the back areas of Korea. The wounded were brought from the fighting by the Army's helicopters, most often Bell Model 47s. The image of the bubble-nosed choppers laden with stretchers has been ingrained into American popular culture by the film and the later TV series, which lasted eleven years.

For the film Fox acquired five civilian Bell 47s, most of which had been used by oil companies and forest fire battalions. Modified to the appearance of Army Medevac choppers, they were filmed for several weeks in every aspect of landing, takeoff, flyover and other needed footage. After that, and for most of the television series, at least two helicopters were available for specific shots on location.

The unpopularity of the Vietnam War drastically affected any film that showed even moderate support of the military until the late 1970s. Some of the most successful Vietnam War films showed the ordeal of the Marines and Army troops on the ground. In a way the films were meant to be nostalgic, but for the most part they lambasted the futility of an unpopular war. Taken as a film genre they had several things in common: young men in horrifying jungle and rice paddy combat; incompetent, martinet or bloodthirsty officers; and an implacable hidden enemy.

Led by the blockbuster *Apocalypse Now!,* the films included, among others, *Platoon, The Boys in Company C, BAT 21, Full Metal Jacket* and, some years later, *We Were Soldiers.*

One other common element in these films was the wealth of Army helicopter scenes, nearly always accompanied by rock 'n' roll music. This was pioneered by Francis Ford Coppola in *Apocalypse Now!* and was almost *de rigueur* for years afterward. It was so prevalent it would be easy for a viewer to assume that all Bell UH-1 Hueys were equipped with loudspeakers to blast rock music over Vietnam.

As we saw in Chapter Ten, a new genre of film took root in the early 1980s. This was the techno-thriller or action drama. The hallmark was usually high-tech military hardware, lots of guns and missiles, huge pyrotechnic explosions and—if the studio had the budget for it—a plot.

In 1983 Columbia's *Blue Thunder* screamed into the theaters with a bang and the helicopter hasn't been the same since. The "Metropolitan Police Department's Astro Division" keeps round-the-clock patrol over Los Angeles by providing support to the street cops with highly trained helicopter pilots and observers. One of those pilots is a Vietnam War veteran named Frank Murphy, who—unlike *Firefox's* Mitchell Gant—is personable and witty. His Vietnam flashbacks are an annoyance, not debilitating. Murphy is played by the unlikely sex symbol Roy Scheider, the hero of *Jaws*. With a Waldo Pepper-type disregard for rules, Murphy often pushes the limit in his work and earns the wrath of his superior, Captain Jack Braddock, played by the sour-faced Warren Oates.

Roy Scheider as Frank Murphy in the cockpit of Blue Thunder.

Murphy is teamed with a green street cop named Richard Lymangood, who is given the nickname of "JAFO"—"Just Another Fucking Observer." Daniel Stern, known as the adult voice of Kevin Arnold in *The Wonder Years*, plays Lymangood, who idolizes the older man.

Murphy is ordered to meet with a team of shadowy characters at a military test range where he witnesses a demonstration of a new helicopter for police use. Blue Thunder is a heavily armed stealthy attack chopper with sophisticated high-technology surveillance and eavesdropping systems. It is to be used in case of terrorist attack or hostage situations during the upcoming 1984 Olympics.

The chopper's pilot is a former Army colonel and bitter rival of Murphy's named Cochrane, cunningly portrayed by the aging Droog of Kubrick's *A Clockwork Orange*, Malcolm McDowell. Cochrane and Murphy square off against one another, an antipathy that stems from an incident during the war.

Despite its advanced technology, Blue Thunder is much too destructive for police use. Murphy and Lymangood are assigned to fly the helicopter during normal night patrols. By using the chopper's "Whisper Mode" as they trail Cochrane they begin to realize there is more to the military attack chopper than has been revealed. They discover its true purpose is for armed aerial suppression of civil unrest, particularly in the barrio and other ghetto areas with a project called THOR, for "Tactical Helicopter Armed Response."

The two cops find themselves marked men and are hunted by thugs of a quasi-government conspiracy. Lymangood is murdered, and Murphy steals Blue Thunder to hold his bargaining position until his girlfriend can deliver an incriminating videotape to the news station. During the standoff the Air Force launches two F-16 fighters to bring the rogue cop down, but the planes are cut to pieces and destroyed by Murphy's canny use of the cannon and other tactics.

Finally Cochrane goes up in another chopper with 20mm cannon and engages his rival in a never-before-seen helicopter dogfight over downtown Los Angeles. Murphy is seriously hurt but puts Blue Thunder into a loop and ends up behind the astonished Cochrane and shoots him down. Then Murphy lands the chopper in front of a moving freight train, which destroys the helicopter. As Murphy walks away a news anchor voiceover proclaims an investigation will begin on the intended use of the helicopter.

The film was dedicated to Warren Oates, who died shortly after filming concluded.

As mentioned, Blue Thunder was the most important "character" in the film. All of the actors were mere supporting characters to the helicopter in this, the first true techno-thriller. Murphy's candor in his skepticism about Blue Thunder's role—and his increasingly dangerous attempts to thwart the conspiracy and Cochrane—earn the audiences' respect. If *Firefox's* Mitchell Gant had been more likable to the audience, the film might have done better at the box office.

The helicopters used for Blue Thunder were two Aerospatiale SA-34 Gazelles, one of which had been owned by a coal mining company in the 1970s until it was bought by Columbia. Profoundly modified with "bolt-on" hardware, the chopper was painted a deep, metallic blue. With an operational 20mm six-barreled rotary cannon under the nose the helicopter was so nose-heavy it had to have a weight attached to the tail boom to compensate. Ross Davis, a former Navy helicopter pilot, told the author, "Blue Thunder, as a real military aircraft, would have been too dangerous to fly with all that extra stuff on it."

The Aerospatiale SA-34 Gazelle helicopter after being fitted with the 'bolt-on' hardware. Experienced helicopter pilots stated that a real Blue Thunder would have been very nose-heavy.

Yet record audiences cared little about reality. The film was a huge success, grossing more than $40 million in theater and video sales.

Cochrane's chopper was a Hughes 500, the same as was used in *Capricorn One*.

According to one source, a defense contractor offered to donate several million rounds of 20mm cannon ammunition to the production in return for screen credit. Director John Badham, despite being known for action-laced techno-thrillers, declined to accept the offer.

The LAPD decided not to cooperate with the studio, so the LAPD's Air Support Division was changed to "Astro Division" for the film. "LAPD" is not mentioned in the production.

When Murphy enters a duel with a pair of F-16s it seems he is doomed, but by using the hot reflection of the sun on the broad face of a high-rise building he misdirects a heat-seeking Sidewinder missile. The Air Force pilots are seen as comic buffoons. Murphy shoots one down by chopping off a wing with his rotary cannon. Though the aerial battle is happening over the center of one of the busiest cities in the world, no one seems to be hurt, even when the missile slams into the building and explodes. Another Sidewinder is led off to blow up a hot smokestack above a rotisserie chicken factory. The sky rains immolated poultry while the audience roars with delight.

The F-16s were miniatures made by famed model maker Gregory Jein, who worked on *Star Wars* and the *Star Trek* films. Coincidentally he also made the Firefox miniatures. Radio-controlled miniatures were used for several sequences, along with full-scale cockpit mockups. Blue Thunder was very tricky to fly, so many of the action sequences were done with the miniatures.

Malcolm McDowell was deathly afraid of flying and had to be ordered into the helicopter for the aerial shots. During the final battle, he displays several facial expressions which appear as if he was angry at Murphy's tactics. He is really showing his hatred of flying.

Blue Thunder's popularity spawned a short-lived television series of the same name and a more successful copycat series, *Airwolf*, starring Jan-Michael Vincent and Ernest Borgnine.

A full-color promotional brochure touted Blue Thunder's features and amazing abilities—all fictional of course—with detailed drawings and photographs. Again the actors were less important than the "star."

"I was amazed at the sophistication of the electronics and gear," said Colonel John Telles, USMC. The former Vietnam AH-60 Cobra pilot said the movie's concept was far ahead of reality. "I don't think even the military was able to put all that on a chopper back then," he said. As for looping a helicopter, Telles said, "I know of a pilot who even put a big Sikorsky H-53 into a loop years ago. The way rotors have been designed, it's no big deal."

Some of Blue Thunder's features were pure testosterone injections for the predominantly male audience, the sudden gut-twisting "turbo boost" and the macho rotary cannon being the most contrived.

The idea of a helicopter being capable of all the things Blue Thunder could do took hold in the public imagination. During a community debate in the Midwest to control helicopter noise, a man asked the police representative, "Why don't you use that 'whisper mode?'" The police officer, trying to keep a straight face, answered, "That is only available in Hollywood."

"I don't care where you have to go to get it, just get it."

In 1984's *Red Dawn*, a thriller about a Soviet invasion of the United States, a group of teenaged partisans fight a guerilla war in the mountains. Directed by John Milius (*Flight of the Intruder*), *Red Dawn* features a pair of Mil-24 Hind gunships that find and kill several of the resistance fighters, led by teen hunks Patrick Swayze and Charlie Sheen. The Hinds are modified Aerospatiale 330 Puma helicopters with gun turrets, rocket launchers and other external features.

Red Dawn's Soviet Mi-24 Hind attack helicopters were modified Aerospatiale 330 Pumas with added gun sponsons and simulated armor.

They also appear in two of the *Rambo* movies. While not real Soviet helicopters they are very menacing and believable.

CHAPTER TWELVE

Just for Fun: The Adventure Films

Over the last fifty years, a series of films not specifically about war, airlines, comedy or action have reached the screen. To be honest it wasn't easy to categorize the films into a particular genre. But they do have some commonalities. They're exciting and fun to watch.

The adventure films run the gamut of topics and plots. Some are suspenseful or dramatic, while others are whimsical and romantic. But a great number of them strive to show in detail a time only our grandparents knew: of flappers and flivvers, of Big Band music and pulp fiction heroes.

This chapter details several of these films, if for no other reason than to have a place to put them. Quite a few are not even aviation films. They merely have flying and airplanes in critical or important sequences.

In *The Flight of the Phoenix* (1965) James Stewart is Frank Towns, a grizzled, testy transport pilot flying oil company personnel in North Africa. An eclectic bunch of engineers, workers and assorted characters are aboard his weather-beaten old Fairchild C-82 twin-boom cargo plane. It is forced off course during a storm and crashes in the Libyan Desert. The survivors, with an ever growing sense of urgency and clashing personalities, struggle to live in the harsh conditions as they use the wreckage to build a working plane they can fly to safety.

James Stewart and Richard Attenborough struggling to survive the sand storm in Robert Aldrich's *Flight of the Phoenix.*

Towns, with his crushed peaked cap and week-old beard, appears much older than Stewart's 57 years. Unlike most of Stewart's screen roles, Towns is downright disagreeable, determined to always be right and in control. The men stuck in the desert with him are a motley mix of British Army officers, German engineers and American workers. Ernest Borgnine, already known for *McHale's Navy*, is Trucker Cobb, a burly worker whose immaturity causes no end of difficulty. George Kennedy, later the staple of the *Airport* films, is the competitive Bellamy; and Hardy Kruger is studious engineer Heinrich Dorfman, who designs the makeshift plane they stake their lives on.

Several days pass with members of the party dying of exposure or being killed by nomads. The slow work to cut apart the plane and move huge sections at night relentlessly saps their strength and spirit. The plane they cobble together uses one boom with its engine, the outer wing panels, and horizontal stabilizer. They attach the far side outer wing to the inside of the port boom and fit the stabilizer to it, building a plane with a single fuselage. Skids are welded on as landing gear. The elevator is cut from the one that formerly ran between the twin rudders. A pair of welded skids completes the ungainly design. Towns will sit on a makeshift cockpit behind the engine while the others lie flat on the wings holding welded fairings.

A Fairchild C-82 Packet, known as the "Flying Boxcar."
The Packet was also seen in *Always*.

When Towns learns that Dorfman's sole experience with aeronautical engineering is in designing model planes, Towns loses all faith in the idea. But having no choice, he trudges on with the dwindling pack of misfits to build the plane.

The suspenseful build-up to the flight was extremely well done. Towns gives every indication he doesn't believe the slapdash plane they've constructed will fly as he fires cartridge after cartridge to start the balky engine. After the first of the seven cartridges fails he says with a noticeable I-told-you-so tone, "That's number one."

The second and third fail to do more than make the propeller whirl a few times, then stop, despite the anxious pleading of the assembled men. Again and again Towns determinedly fires the cartridges in the starter until Dorfman, protesting to his nemesis, screams, "You're wasting the cartridges! You have only three left!"

Towns refuses to give in. "I know that," he says Then, taking command, he snarls, "I'm gong to use one cartridge, ignition off, clean out the cylinders."

Dorfman shouts "No! I forbid you!"

The audience knows no one will stop James Stewart as he defiantly sticks in the second-to-last cartridge and fires it against Dorfman's frenzied shouts to stop.

A cloud of black smoke erupts from the engine, bringing doom ever closer. Then Towns puts in the final cartridge and fires it to the accompaniment of a deep strident musical tone. The audience can read the fierce triumph in his eyes as the engine slowly turns over, going faster and faster until, in front of the jumping and cheering men, it roars to full and powerful life. Frank DeVol's evocative score seems to make the engine into a thrumming instrument.

Towns is once again in total control as he revs the engine until it drowns out all other sound. But the ordeal isn't over: the weary survivors have to pull the heavy plane to a flat space for take-off.

Phoenix was the last aviation film Stewart made. James Stewart was a Brigadier General in the U.S. Air Force with several decorations and citations for bravery in the skies over Germany. He had flown everything from biplanes to trainers to bombers and jets to B-52s. He seems at home in the makeshift cockpit of the *Phoenix*, perhaps remembering his early days of flying, when "by the seat of your pants" really meant something to a pilot.

The movie was largely filmed in California's Buttercup Valley near the Arizona border. The valley was the location for several desert movies, including 1926's *Son of the Sheik* with Rudolph Valentino and 1939's *Beau Geste*. In fact the location is called "*Beau Geste* Valley" on some maps. The place bears a great resemblance to the searing sands of Libya, including the daily high of 140 degrees.

Phoenix has a bloody history in that it cost the lives of three men during filming. Director Robert Aldrich's son William and his son-in-law Peter Bravos were killed in a crash scene.

The 'Phoenix' preparing to take off from Buttercup Valley, California.
Famed stunt pilot Paul Mantz was killed while flying the plane for *Flight of the Phoenix*.

Death finally took Paul Mantz on July 8, 1965. Mantz was apprehensive about the unproven *Phoenix*, yet against his better judgment he flew it anyway. The 62-year old aviation legend did it just one more time for a quick paycheck and as a favor to the production company. Mantz was killed while flying the plane in a series of touch-and-go passes to gather footage of take-offs and landings.

The author interviewed Zona Appleby, widow of famed stunt pilot Jim Appleby, who died in September 2010. Zona said the *Phoenix* had been damaged during flight. "At one point the fuselage was cracked behind the cockpit, but it was unnoticed by Mantz," Appleby said. "He was a short man and had to sit on several thick cushions to see over the cowling."

On the last take at 7 a.m., Mantz flew low into the narrow valley to get close to the No. 1 camera for a take off shot. When he applied full power to rise, the skids caught a hummock of soft sand. The plane nosed over and tore itself to pieces. Mantz was killed almost instantly. Bobby Rose, another veteran stunt pilot whose career went back to doubling for Mabel Normand, was injured as he was thrown from the disintegrating wreck. "Bobby was lying on the wing as one of the survivors," Appleby said.

Over 400 people attended Mantz' funeral at Hollywood's Church of the Recessional. Beirne Lay, Jr., read the eulogy.

Paul Mantz death was a powerful blow to Hollywood. Although he never called himself a "stunt pilot," preferring the term "precision flyer," the motion picture and aviation community knew an era had finally ended.

Phoenix did not do well at the box office but it does stand as an excellent film depicting a truly herculean struggle against nature, conflict and impossible odds.

One of the most memorable and downright fun films about the days of early flight was done by director George Roy Hill, known for highly spirited and successful films like *Butch Cassidy and the Sundance Kid* (1969) and *The Sting* (1973). *The Great Waldo Pepper* (1975) is a fictional bio-drama about a barnstormer named Waldo Pepper. Robert Redford was riding the crest of his popularity at the time.

A true aviation film, *Waldo Pepper* takes place in the early 1920s when barnstormers were plying their meager trade among the towns and farms of the nation. Waldo had been in the Air Service but was never in combat. This doesn't match the daring war hero image he has cultivated. He is struggling to eke out a living flying a nearly worn-out Jenny around Nebraska to finance a new aerobatic monoplane being constructed by his brother-in-law Ezra Stiles, played by Edward Hermann.

Waldo encounters another barnstormer who becomes instant competition. Tall, blond Swedish-born actor Bo Svenson portrays the confident Axel Olsson. Waldo works a bit of minor sabotage on Olsson's Jenny, causing the wheels to fall off on takeoff. Waldo then asks the assembled crowd of onlookers to contribute money to "see the famous Axel Olsson crash. Olsson survives a landing in a pond but his Jenny requires serious repair.

Waldo then woos Marybeth, a gullible but adventurous woman, in a movie house and tells her the story of his fateful meeting with the great German ace Ernst Kessler. Waldo

Robert Redford as the ambitious barnstormer Waldo Pepper in George Roy Hill's *The Great Waldo Pepper. SDASM Collection*

tells her his guns jammed during the dogfight. Waldo was about to be shot down by the German; but Kessler, in a gesture more suited to the Age of Chivalry, salutes Waldo and peels away. Marybeth believes Waldo's story, but then it turns out she is Olsson's girlfriend. She tells her beau that Waldo had been in combat and met up with Kessler.

This is an uncomfortable moment for Waldo, as Olsson had been in the very aero squadron in which the fateful meeting Waldo described had taken place. "I don't remember seeing any Waldo Pepper taking off with them," Olsson tells a bewildered Marybeth.

Eventually Waldo and Olsson not only begin working together but also become friends. They join up with Dillhoefer's Flying Circus but have to prove themselves with a new stunt. The wily Dillhoefer tells Waldo, "You dream up a stunt where people think you're gonna die."

The brief era of lone barnstormers is coming to an end: government safety regulations are limiting what pilots and performers can do in the air. When Marybeth dies in a failed wing-walking stunt, Waldo and Olsson are grounded. Waldo doesn't take it well and tries to make money to finance Ezra's plane, a sleek white monoplane designed to achieve the "last great stunt,"—the Outside Loop. Ezra does the stunt himself and crashes before a huge audience. While people look on in morbid fascination as Ezra burns to death Waldo takes a Jenny aloft to frighten them away with low swoops. He is banned from flying by federal order.

Meanwhile Olsson has become a Hollywood stunt man. Waldo meets him and begs for some work. They have heard a movie is being made about the famed Kessler dogfight. Olsson isn't sure about doing stunt flying. He is hoping to get a job with an airline. Waldo snorts, "You really want to get thrown to the lions, huh?"

"It's a lot better than being creamed by a Fokker," Olsson admits. But he gets a job as a stunt pilot and so does Waldo, going under the name of George Brown. Waldo meets Kessler, aptly portrayed by Bo Brundin, another Swede. The former scourge of the skies is in deep financial debt and is working as the technical advisor for the film. He knew about Stiles' death and Waldo being banned from flying. They find a mutual bond in being outcasts.

During the flying sequences, Waldo flies a Sopwith while Kessler is in a Fokker DR.1 Triplane. But very soon they are not acting for the camera planes. They begin dogfighting, pitting their skills against one another. Their guns only carry blanks but the pilots ram and tear at one another. The film ends with Waldo knowing his flying career is over, and with it all of the meaning in his life.

The Great Waldo Pepper is one of the best aviation films ever made. George Roy Hill did a superb job bringing to the screen an era long gone from the skies. The allure of barnstorming wing-walkers and early aviation movies are accurately depicted. It's very easy to believe Waldo Pepper was a real person and the film is in fact a whimsical biography. The opening credits are a series of old photos pasted in an album, accompanied by Henry Mancini's piano score.

One of the Curtiss JN-4Ds painted for Dillhoefer's Flying Circus in *The Great Waldo Pepper. SDASM Collection*

All the flying scenes in the film were done for real, with Frank Tallman, Jim Appleby, Art Scholl, Frank Pine and others doing the stunts. Hill had to recreate the daring exploits of the barnstormers in old biplanes while ensuring the safety of the pilots. Wing-walking and mid-air transfers, parachute jumps and crashes were among the stunts performed.

Assuredly the attention to safety was a great deal stricter than it had been in 1927. Frank Tomick, Frank Clarke, Dick Grace and their long-dead brethren would have been proud of their progeny.

Hill was a former Marine aviator and often flew one of the planes while directing. William A. Wellman, Jr., said, "Hill talked to my father about *Waldo Pepper*, and I'm sure he got a lot of ideas and inspiration from him."

Filming for the aerial sequences was done in Elgin and other locations in Texas. Several original JN-4s were used for the film, being repainted as needed. Redford, Svenson, Brundin and Hermann were filmed in real aircraft for close-up takes. There is no doubt of the realism as Waldo takes a boy up in the Jenny. The kid isn't acting; he's glowing with joy.

The camera mounts were the grandsons of those pioneered by Harry Perry in 1925.

Zona Appleby was present during her husband's work on *Waldo Pepper*. She provided several fascinating anecdotes about the filming. "George (Hill) had some planes with the front half painted one way and the back half painted another. If the actor was in the front cockpit, they used the plane with the front half painted. If the camera was to be on the pilot, they used another plane."

"The Jenny that lost its wheels had small caster wheels on it," she continued. "That permitted Tallman to land the plane. Then they did the crash with a Gypsy Moth."

Axel Olsson's plane loses its wheels in *The Great Waldo Pepper.* Note the tiny caster wheels on the landing gear spreader bar that permitted Frank Tallman to land safely.
SDASM Collection

One of the most gripping sequences occurs when Marybeth (Susan Sarandon) attempts to wing-walk while the Jenny is flying down the center of a street at nearly eye-level. The finished shot is so convincing audiences wondered how it was done. But there was no visual effects wizardry. "Frank Tallman was at the Jenny's controls," Zona said. Several cameras followed the Jenny as it flew down the street at less than ten feet altitude. The Jenny's 43-foot wingspan cleared the buildings on either side with a bare twenty feet to spare. "Jim was in the camera helicopter for that shot," she said.

Marybeth is too frozen with terror to climb back to the cockpit. Olsson begs her to come back as he can't land with her out on the wing. Jim Appleby appears as a pilot named Ace. When the stunt goes bad, Ace flies the plane carrying Waldo to assist. "I knew she wasn't worth top billing," Ace grumbles as he and Waldo climb into the plane.

Frank Tallman flies down the street in one of the most dangerous aerial stunts in *The Great Waldo Pepper*. Note how close the wingtips are to the buildings on either side of the street. *SDASM Collection*

The rescue was done with long-focus cameras on the camera plane. Redford climbed from the wing of his plane and onto Olsson's Jenny. After telling his friend to put the plane into a shallow glide in order to maintain stable flight with two people on one wing, he goes out to rescue Marybeth. But she makes a leap at Waldo and loses her grip. The next shot only shows Waldo, head down as the audience realizes the girl has fallen to her death.

Veteran wing-walker John Kazian worked on *Waldo Pepper*. "The Jenny with Redford on the wing was on a flatbed truck," he explained in a phone interview. "They filmed it moving along a cliff road so the view showed the distance to make it appear as if the plane was high in the air. Redford was in the close shots. I wore a half-mask of Redford's face below my goggles for the actual aerial shots." The former stunt man chuckled. "The makeup people took my black hair and made it blonde. I looked like a freak. But my wife married me because she thought I looked like Robert Redford!"

The author asked Kazian about working on the Jenny. He replied with a laugh. "With airspeed of about 40 miles per hour it's easy to hang on even without safety lines. I never had any trouble walking on a Jenny."

Ezra Stiles' "Skystreak" was a de Havilland DHC-1 Chipmunk shipped from Australia in 1972. Since it had to look like a homemade plane from the 1920s a few changes were made. Wire-spoke wheels and kingposts with bracing wire were fitted. The result is very convincing. "Jim test-flew that plane before Arc Scholl arrived to fly the plane in the movie," Zona commented.

Jim Appleby with his reproduction Fokker Dr.I Triplane. Appleby flew this aircraft in several films and Red Baron Pizza commercials. *Courtesy Zona Appleby*

George Roy Hill built the suspense to a fever pitch as Ezra Stiles attempted the Outside Loop. The stunt involves starting at high altitude, diving into a loop that is inverted at low altitude, and applying full power while climbing to complete the loop. The camera mounted behind Scholl's head gave the audience a good feel for the stomach-twisting sensation of pitching down at the ground while inverted. Hill cleverly goads the audience into willing the plane into the final climb. But each attempt ends in failure and Stiles falls from the sky in a fatal crash. The crash is not seen but only heard as a terrifying crunch.

Jimmy Doolittle was the first to successfully complete an Outside Loop in 1927 in a Curtiss P-1 Hawk.

Tallman flew the de Havilland DH-60 Gypsy Moth into the midway tents for Waldo's crash at the air show. He actually hit the trash barrels before nosing over into the tents.

In the shot where Waldo, hanging under Axel's plane, is flown into a barn roof, the filmmakers used a dummy. Zona said, "Johnny Kazian wanted to do that stunt but Jim said, 'No you're not.' Jim didn't have much confidence in Tallman's ability to be on target for something like that."

Kazian added his thoughts. "When Frank lost his leg he had a stirrup on the rudder pedal to keep his leg from slipping off because he had no feeling in the leg. The stirrup would hold the prosthetic foot in the proper place. I trusted Frank's flying but Applejack, which is what I called Jim Appleby, didn't think Frank could get me into the 'sweet spot.' I was the guy who grabbed the ladder and hung on but that was all."

According to Zona, there was supposed to be a scene in which a plane crashes into a house. But budget and time constraints prevented it. When Hill was approached to direct *The World According to Garp* (1982) he accepted on the condition that he'd be able to do such a stunt in the film.

Ernst Kessler is based on Ernst Udet, whose 62 victories made him the second-ranking German ace after Manfred von Richthofen. There is some truth in Waldo's story about the ace allowing the green pilot with jammed guns to escape. But it was France's second-ranking ace Georges Guynemer allowing none other than the young Ernst Udet with jammed guns to live.

Hill also manages a convincing job of showing the dangerous world of motion picture stunt flying in the 1920s. When the director of the movie talks to Olsson about bailing out of a burning plane, he says, "Make sure the plane is fully on fire before you get out. But don't open your chute too soon or otherwise you'll spoil the whole effect." Waldo smiles grimly as he says to Olsson, "Of course you could not pull your chute at all and that way you'll be sure to get the right effect."

In the manner of the old stunt pilots Olsson even has to devise and wire his own pyrotechnics on the plane. While showing some of the rushes, the director describes a crash, saying, "Actually Dick was lucky to get out of it alive. As it is he'll be in the hospital for at least a couple of months." This is almost certainly a salute to the greatest crash expert of the 1920s, Dick Grace.

Waldo goes outside and looks at the black- and-yellow Fokker Triplane. Mancini's music builds on the emotion Waldo must be feeling as he touches the legendary fighter.

In the final "battle" sequences, Kessler and Waldo duel in the skies to find out who is the better pilot. The camera operator uses hand gestures to indicate what he wants from the pilots in exactly the way it was done in the silent era before radios were available for communication. The pilots used exaggerated hand and head movements to convey intentions and understanding. There is no verbal dialogue, since that would have been impossible to hear above the engine noise in the 100 knot-plus slipstream. The duel was filmed at Lake Piru near Santa Paula. The pilots, according to Zona, were Jim in the Fokker DR-1 and Art Scholl in the Sopwith Camel. "Frank Pine had broken a Garland Lincoln 'flip plane,'" she said, referring to the notorious ground-looping Nieuport 28s rebuilt by Lincoln. The replicas are very nearly perfect and it's easy to accept them as the real thing. But one thing does stand out: the Sopwith's roundels are British rather than American, as the story would suggest.

The action is fast and furious with both unarmed planes trying to gain an advantage. Kessler uses his Fokker's propeller to shred the Camel's rudder. Some of the shots were done in flight; while others, particularly the close-up of the rudder being turned into confetti, were done with full-scale mockups. "That was done by studio effects," Zona said.

She related what Jim had said about flying a Fokker Triplane: "Jim said it wasn't an easy plane to fly. It was really hard to taxi because it was so hard to see forward. But it could turn on a dime and give you five cents change," she laughed.

The Fokker used in *Waldo Pepper* is now in the collection of Fantasy of Flight in Polk City, Florida.

In keeping with the public interest in conspiracy theories 1978 saw the Warner release of *Capricorn One*, starring James Brolin, Hal Holbrook and Elliott Gould. The plot was born from an old rumor that the Apollo Moon landings were all a hoax by NASA and the government. The theorists claimed that no man ever set foot on the Moon and it was all done with Hollywood special effects. Of course that's all pure rot. There are any number of verifiable indicators that twelve men walked the surface of the Moon between July 1969 and December 1972. In any case *Capricorn One* deals with the next "giant leap for mankind": the first landing on Mars.

In this particular case it was Hollywood wizardry. A crew of astronauts led by Charles Brubaker (Brolin), with Sam Waterston and O.J. Simpson, are about to lift off from Cape Canaveral to fly to the Red Planet. But just as the countdown approaches T-minus zero the astronauts are interrupted by a mysterious man who opens the hatch and tells them to follow him. After a hurried departure from the Cape and flight in an executive jet the men arrive at a remote base in the desert. Upon meeting NASA Director Kelloway (Holbrook) one of them quips, "Hiya Doctor Kelloway, nice to see you. A funny thing happened on the way to Mars."

Kelloway tells them the life-support system in the spacecraft would not have worked and all of them would have died in space. The astronauts learn that the whole mission is to be staged. In a hidden desert facility the crew reluctantly participates in a conspiracy to convince the world they are flying to and landing on Mars.

But upon their "return" something goes disastrously wrong just as the crew is being flown to the spot where they will emerge from the recently re-entered spacecraft. They are brought back to the facility. The spacecraft supposedly carrying them has burned up in re-entry—and now no one knows what to do. But Brubaker does. Realizing he and his men are now a liability and will probably be killed, they escape and attempt to make it back to civilization and expose the conspiracy. A hunt ensues in the desert. Meanwhile an intrepid reporter named Caulfield, played by Elliott Gould, has been suspecting something is not right. He continues to dig into the mystery, and eventually finds the hidden facility and the staged Mars landing site, complete with the Landing Module.

Convinced he has discovered the truth, Caulfield hires the services of a disreputable pilot to fly him in an N2S Stearman crop duster to find the missing crew. But Caulfield is not the only one searching. The bad guys, who are in actual "black helicopters," are determined to find and eliminate the escapees.

By the time Caulfield finds Brubaker in the desert the other two are already dead. Caulfield pulls Brubaker onto the wing of the biplane and tries to escape as the two government helicopters chasing them. The choppers attack with machine guns and try to drive the plane into cliffs, but they end up destroyed in crashes.

At the memorial services for the fallen crew, Brubaker, followed by a victorious Caulfield, runs to his shocked and bewildered wife while Kelloway suddenly realizes his troubles have just begun.

NASA cooperated fully with the production, despite being portrayed as the villain. In 1978 NASA needed all the publicity they could generate. The Apollo Program and its extension Skylab was over. Congress had cut NASA funding to the bone, which contributed greatly to the flawed Space Shuttle concept.

The early segments were done in a remarkable re-creation of Mission Control in Building 30 at the Johnson Manned Spaceflight Center in Houston. The voice-over of "Capricorn Control" is well done, with a great deal of technical jargon added to heighten the suspense. Several authentic terms and phrases common to all launch vehicle operations are heard. Actual footage of a Saturn V rocket in preparation for launch is used in the film. All of the footage was from the last of the Apollo flights in 1971 and 1972.

The aerial sequences in *Capricorn One* take place in the last suspenseful half-hour of the film. Director Peter Hyams—who would later direct the successful *2010: The Year We Make Contact* (1984)—brings the chase to a fever pitch. The runaway crew steals a Lear executive jet, but there is little fuel on board so they are forced to belly land in the desert. The studio didn't crash a real Lear nor did they use a miniature. A very low camera angle and carefully selected location allowed the plane to land on its gear while appearing to slide in on the belly. The dust from the landing shows three distinct rooster tails from the wheels, although they are hidden below the camera's close horizon.

The helicopters, twin Hughes MD 500s, are actually painted dark green, not black. But this may be the film that sparked the term "black helicopter." The chase and battle between a 1940s-era N2S Stearman and a pair of heavily armed choppers is not easily forgotten. Hyams makes the helicopters seem as malevolent living creatures. The 500 has a particularly insect-like appearance, and the use of tinted Perspex keeps the pilots invisible. Even the drone of the rotors is decidedly reminiscent of a locust swarm. In one shot the choppers "huddle" in the air as if talking to one another face-to-face.

Telly Savalas, who played the part of the grizzled and disagreeable Stearman pilot Albain, was actually afraid of flying. All the shots in which he is shown in the plane were done in a single day. Frank Tallman flew the Stearman for the film and later commented that it was the most dangerous stunt flying he'd ever done for a film. The scenes of the helicopter's skids thumping against the wing fabric of the Stearman were done in flight with cameras mounted on the choppers. Tallman had to do some very difficult piloting while flying through canyons and near cliff walls. The shadows of the plane on the crags give an indication of the nearness of the rocks during the 90-knot aerial sequences. John Kazian was the stuntman in the shots where a real person was needed on the wing. He recalls, "When you see the legs kicking, that's me. Peter Hyams never permitted telephoto lenses. He wanted the camera to see just what a person would see. When Tallman is zooming down Red Rock Canyon, it's just as close as it appears."

"I worked with Frank on a lot of films," continued Kazian. "I often had to be out on a Stearman or Jenny wing. We had to work as a team using hand or eye signals to communicate. If I had to go way out on the wing, I kept my eyes on Frank in the cockpit. He had to keep the plane balanced with my weight out there." Kazian explained there was often a counterweight on the opposite wing to help offset his own weight. "When Frank's eyes were the same size as his goggles I didn't go any farther," he laughed.

Kazian mentioned the helicopter chase scenes: "A helicopter doesn't respond like an airplane. It's scary as hell having one that close. Hyams wanted the chopper's skids to hit the wing hard enough to leave a dent. It took about half an hour of doing it before we had it." Kazian said at one point the skids actually caught under the wing, which could have led to a crash. "Frank saw that and kissed the throttle to pull the wing away."

A process shot of the Stearman with the acrophobic Telly Savalas at the controls, while Elliot Gould attempts to hang on to astronaut James Brolin in the climactic aerial chase in *Capricorn One*. For the distant shots, Frank Tallman flew the plane while stuntman John Kazian was on the wing. *Author's Collection*

The only weak point is the rear-screen projection of the wing as Brolin hangs on. It lacks the realism of the actual flying footage.

Capricorn One was Tallman's next-to-last film. He was killed in the crash of a Piper Aztec on Santiago Peak in the Santa Ana Mountains on April 15, 1978.

There are a few shots of an aircraft carrier that was to be used for the recovery of the spacecraft. The footage was of *USS Oriskany* (CV-34) from *The Bridges at Toko-Ri* (1954). Coincidentally Brolin's character name and that of William Holden in *Toko-Ri* is the same: Brubaker.

In 1981 Steven Spielberg, the talented and eclectic director of *Close Encounters of the Third Kind* began the first of a series of adventure films which came closer than most to capturing the 1930s serial movie and dime novel heroes. The main character for the film was Indiana Jones, an archaeologist and adventurer who found himself pitted against Nazis, hostile indigenous tribes, satanic cults and the Wrath of God while seeking rare artifacts. *Raiders of the Lost Ark* (1983) was the first of the "Indiana Jones" films. Harrison Ford, long over his less-than-sterling role in *Hanover Street*, portrayed the bullwhip-wielding swashbuckler who wore a battered felt fedora.

A wildly popular film, *Raiders* had Jones running from Nazi henchmen and an evil French archaeologist to find the long-lost Ark of the Covenant. During the quest Indy, as he is known, finds himself in more than a few aerial situations, not all successful. The first is just as Indy is running from maddened Amazonian tribesmen who, for some strange reason, feel Indy is desecrating their sacred temple. Indy runs pell-mell through the jungle until he reaches a river where his friend Jock is fishing from the float of a Waco seaplane. Indy screams "Get it up, Jock!" and dives into the river as poisonous darts and spears spray into the water around him. Then Indy scrambles into the front cockpit—still wearing his hat—and the plane lifts off.

The plane is a Waco UBF-2 fitted with pontoons. Sci-fi film buffs who pay attention will note the plane's "registration number" OB-CPO, a tongue-in-cheek nod to Spielberg's fellow USC alumni George Lucas and *Star Wars* (1977). The plane is now privately owned in Junction City, Oregon.

Indiana Jones' friend Jock fishing off the float of the Waco UBF-2 floatplane in an early sequence in *Raiders of the Lost Ark*.

Shortly afterward Indy travels from the United States to Asia via a Pan American Clipper flying boat. Since none of the original Martin M-130 or Boeing 314 Clippers still existed, Spielberg located a reasonable facsimile at the Oakland Aviation Museum. The aircraft is in fact a British-built Short Solent, closely related to the Sunderland flying boats used for long-range reconnaissance and U-boat hunting in World War II. The Solent does not fly anymore and remains on display outside the museum. For the short sequence in which Indy boards the plane unknowingly followed by a Nazi spy, the Solent was prepared by having one of its engines fixed enough to permit starting it to show the propeller turning. The foreground of water and dock are added by matte painting. The shot cuts to Indy sitting down in the plush passenger cabin and taking a nap. A moment later a model is shown winging its way over the Pacific into the sunset.

The Short S.45A Solent seen briefly in *Raiders of the Lost Ark* on public display at the Oakland Aviation Museum in Alameda, California. *Courtesy Oakland Aviation Museum*

The last time Indy deals with an airplane it is neither real nor a model. When the Nazis have taken the Ark from Indy it is to be loaded onto a Luftwaffe aircraft to be flown to Germany. Spielberg had his production artist Ron Cobb create a fictional German transport plane for the film. In keeping with the Nazi penchant for designing sinister-looking aircraft, Cobb drew up plans for the Flying Wing. Originally it was to be a four-engine design, but budget and time constraints reduced it to two. The Flying Wing may have been based on the Horten "Amerika Bomber" which was envisioned by the Nazis as a way of delivering heavy payloads across the Atlantic to the United States. The Wing was built in England by Vickers Aircraft—which must have raised a few staid British eyebrows—then painted at EMI Elstree Studios and shipped to Tunisia. The Wing never leaves the ground, instead being used as a huge prop in a fight scene. Indy is slugging it out with an ape-like German mechanic while Marion, the love interest, mans the machine gun to fight off German attackers. The whirling propellers pose a real threat to the actors as they duke it out while the plane pivots on one wheel.

Vickers Aircraft in England built the full-scale Flying Wing for one of the most dramatic scenes in *Raiders of the Lost Ark*.

Indiana Jones' next adventure, *Indiana Jones and the Temple of Doom* (1984) has only one aerial sequence, which involves a ford Tri-motor. A real Ford 5-AT was used for the exterior shots as a transport of Lao Che, the evil Mandarin gangster whom Indy foils. The aircraft is part of the collection of Fantasy of Flight.

At least three models were built by Industrial Light & Magic (ILM) for the film. One model with a three-foot wingspan was filmed over a snowy mountain set on ILM's main stage roof. A smaller one was used for the crash and explosion. A third six-foot wingspan model was used in detailed shots. A mockup of the flight deck and passenger cabin was built for interiors.

In *Temple of Doom* Indy admits he can't fly a plane but by the next film he seems to have picked up the knack.

Indiana Jones and the Last Crusade (1989) ranks with *Raiders* in thrills. The most interesting aviation sequence happens while Indy and his father Henry Jones, played with great spirit by Sean Connery, escape from the Nazis in a zeppelin. Father and son manage to get tickets for an unnamed dirigible, but it is apparently the *Hindenburg* (LZ-129) prior to its date with destiny over Lakehurst New Jersey in May 1937 (see Chapter Eleven).

Indy and his father are pursued by a villainous Gestapo officer whom Indy throws out of the window. After the ship has been airborne for some time Indy realizes they are turning around and returning to Berlin. He leads his father into the ship's interior, past crisscrossed aluminum girders and catwalks, to a ladder leading down and outside. Hanging from a trapeze is a small Luftwaffe biplane with an aft cockpit ring-mounted machine gun. Indy climbs into the pilot's seat while Henry sits at the gun, looking entirely out of place in his tweed suit. Indy starts the engine and the plane disengages from the airship. The men are immediately set upon by two fighters. An exciting but short air chase and dogfight ensues with Henry shredding the rudder in his inexperienced handling of the gun.

An SV4 Sampe biplane mockup was fitted with a ring gun mount for the German 'parasite' fighter in *Indiana Jones and the Last Crusade.*

They crash-land but are unhurt. Indy then steals a car from a local. Indy and his father hit the road, still pursued by the fighter. The car enters a tunnel, closely chased by the German plane, which flies into the tunnel and loses its wings. It is a typical Spielberg moment as the bewildered Luftwaffe pilot peers at his quarry while his burning wreck slides past.

Given his usual zeal for "getting on with the action," Spielberg was not concerned with historical accuracy. For one thing the *Hindenburg*, as a commercial airship, did not carry a "parasite" fighter, although there is evidence that there may have been a trapeze installed early in 1937. Only the United States Navy's *USS Macon* and *USS Akron* carried Curtiss F-9C Sparrowhawk fighters for air defense (see Chapter Eleven). In any case the plane is an SV4 Stampe biplane, used by the Belgian and French Air Forces as a primary trainer in the 1930s.

The entire chase was done with visual effects, but it is surprising Spielberg took it so lightly. The process shots are almost clumsy. When Indy and Henry are in the Stampe, even though they are in a slipstream of at least 100 knots, the two men show absolutely no sign of wind on their clothing or hats. Spielberg was clearly capable of great attention to detail. The Waco scene in *Raiders* was very well done. The Luftwaffe fighters are Pilatus P-2 training planes used by the Swiss. They don't even superficially resemble Messerschmitt fighters. The Indiana Jones films were meant to be fast and fun, not historical drama. It helps to suspend disbelief and just enjoy it.

The German fighter pursuing Indy and Henry Jones is a Swiss Pilatus P-2 trainer.

The Consolidated PBY Catalina flying boat is a big aircraft. But only the experience of nearly being run over by one while sitting calmly in a tiny rowboat can convey how huge it is. In the very first minute of Spielberg's *Always* (1989) that's exactly what happens. Spielberg has never been subtle in seizing the audience's attention. And he does just that with the sight and sound of a massive PBY growing closer and filling the screen until it rises just in the nick of time.

The main character in *Always* is *Jaws* and *Close Encounters of the Third Kind* alumnus Richard Dreyfuss as Pete Sandich—a slightly different name of the one familiar to fans of Spencer Tracy in *A Guy Named Joe* (1943). In fact, *Always* is a modern remake of the wartime classic, with more romantic involvement and contemporary action. The war being fought is against forest fires rather than Germans. The screenplay was adapted by Jerry Belson from Dalton Trumbo's original, and follows much the same storyline. Vivacious Holly Hunter's Dorinda is much the same as Irene Dunne's character in the original film but with more emotional vulnerability. Sandich is the hotshot fire tanker pilot with a zest for taking risks and flouting rules. Dorinda is a determined and lovestruck woman whom Pete cares for but is frequently angered by his daredevil tactics and flippant attitude about her feelings.

Ebullient John Goodman plays pilot Al Yackey, who compares their airbase to those in England during World War II. "Think about it," says Al. "The beer is warm, the dance hall is a Quonset, there are B-26s outside and hotshot pilots inside. It's England, man! Except that we go to burning places and bomb them until they stop burning."

Al tries to convince Pete to consider going to a new fire bomber training base in Flat Rock, Colorado, but Pete determinedly refuses. Pete does not have the same dreamy wonder about flying as Spencer Tracy, but at times his hidden side emerges to soften his acerbic demeanor. Dorinda is under constant fear that Pete might not survive his next flight. He agrees to go to Colorado. But then fate strikes and he is killed when an engine catches fire and his plane explodes.

Bob Schlaefli's huge PBY-5A Super Catalina N9505C looms over the hapless fisherman in the opening sequence of *Always*.

In a strange and ethereal place Pete meets Hap, a charming woman who takes him under her wing and explains he is dead. Hap is played by Hollywood legend Audrey Hepburn in her last role—Lionel Barrymore in drag, so to speak. Pete sees a Piper J-3 Cub flying past and nostalgically recalls his first solo. Hap explains he was not alone in the cockpit and he will soon be the "guardian angel" for new pilots. Thus Pete finds himself in Colorado at the tanker training school and meets Ted Baker (Brad Johnson), a new and nervous pilot. In time Pete provides Ted with the skills and intuition he needs to be a good tanker pilot. But Pete realizes he is also there to help Dorinda heal when she falls for Ted.

With Spielberg's very powerful point-of-view cinematography and rapid editing, *Always* is a compelling film for aviation buffs. Another World War II era plane is prominent in the film: a Douglas A-26 Invader twin-engine medium attack bomber. The second unit aerial filming was under the leadership of veteran aerial coordinator Jim Gavin. Steve Hinton of Planes of Fame was a valuable source of information about this and other films. Hinton is an experienced movie stunt pilot and has won several air races. Planes of Fame's B-25 *Betty Grable*—since renamed *Photo Fanny*—was on hand for the flying sequences. Some of the firefighting footage was actually from a 1988 fire in Redding, California. Both Gavin and Steve Hinton flew the camera plane for footage of the A-26s, PBYs and other aerial shots. "We did a lot of flying in clouds, over fires and of the A-26s," Hinton said.

A Douglas A-26C Invader dropping its load on a fire in *Always*.

In the shot where Pete runs out of fuel, the left propeller slows to a halt, and he radios, "I have a small inconvenience here. I may have overestimated my fuel just a tad, but I can see the base from here and my right engine is fine so I don't think there's going to be any..."—the right engine slows and stops— "...problem."

The tower calls back. "Pete, what do you need?"

Pete, with just a twinge of nervousness, responds, "Glider practice."

This is vintage Spielberg. The audience is immediately in Pete's corner. While trying to make the field Pete whistles "Garryowen," the marching tune of Custer's fabled Seventh Cavalry.

Author and aircraft restoration specialist Bruce Orriss fitted out two detailed fuselage sections of an A-26 and a PBY for use in the studio. The PBY had been used in *Midway* (1976). Every gauge and switch was perfect but it required a lot of scrounging to make it happen. The result of Orriss' work is the excellent cockpit footage in *Always*. The camera follows the A-26 as it banks in for a dead-stick landing. To add to the credibility of the scene, the A-26's propellers are feathered as it comes to a stop. Feathering propellers means to swivel the blades so their leading edges face directly into the airstream, thus preventing dangerous "windmilling" which can rip an engine off the wing. Denny Lynch and Hinton were at the controls.

"We never actually landed without engines," Hinton said. "The camera was on the fuselage and we got footage of the left engine feathered, then the right. We came in to the landing and feathered the props and came to a stop. With all the footage the editors were able to make it look as if we had landed with no power. I guess they liked it," Hinton chuckled.

The A-26s do some hairy low-level flying in the film, especially when Dorinda buzzes Pete and Al with wheels down. "That landing was my stunt," Hinton said. "It's nearly impossible to 'bounce' an A-26 because the center of gravity is far forward when the plane is light. I had some difficulty doing what they wanted. I did bring it down on the nose wheel pretty hard and broke the trunnion link." (The trunnion connects the landing gear to the underside of the aircraft.)

The base where Pete, Al, Dorinda and the others fly out of was located near Libby, Montana. The field was remote and perfect for the firefighting base. Amblin's set and production designers made it look so convincing that Jim McCown, a 20-year veteran of fighting fires from aircraft, remarked upon arrival, "I didn't know they had a retardant base here!"

The lake where the PBY loads up on water is Bull Lake; this is also where Dorinda puts her plane in the water. The Ephrata, Washington, Municipal Airport used for the Colorado sequences was a B-24 training base during World War II. Most of the hangars are original.

John Goodman said that the location only needed the music of Benny Goodman to make it perfect.

The A-26s are referred to as the "B-26," which was another designation for the aircraft—not to be confused with the Martin B-26 Marauder medium bomber of World War II. The PBY Super Catalina was one of six owned by Bob Schlaefli of Moses Lake, Washington. The Catalinas were fitted with Pratt & Whitney R-2800 radials. It was Schlaefli who was at the controls of the PBY as it scooped water before nearly running down the hapless fishermen.

The author interviewed Ray Chaney, battalion chief at CAL FIRE in San Diego County. With over eighteen years' experience in aerial firefighting, Chaney was able to provide some insight into the lives of the air tankers. "They are the last real 'stick and rudder' pilots in the world," said Chaney. "The way the movie shows them is more Hollywood than reality. They don't fly that close to tree lines or take risks like that. And they definitely don't drop retardant on a burning plane," Chaney concluded with a chuckle.

The final firefighting sequences were done with studio-staged fires. Since forest fires rarely go where they are supposed to a 5,000 gallon propane tank and piping were set up in woods with previously burned trees and brush. When it was filmed it looked very real and provided a dramatic setting for the finale. But nature in its capricious way also provided a fire at Yellowstone, which gave the film unit more footage of actual fire fighting efforts.

Bob Schlaefli credited the late Jim Gavin with the excellence of the flying sequences. Hinton said, "It was one of the best movie jobs I ever worked on."

Denny Lynch's A-26 is now owned by a collector in Palm Springs, California.

The author with Planes of Fame chief pilot Steve Hinton. Hinton flew the A-26s in *Always* and the B-25 in *Forever Young. Courtesy Linda Stull*

Another movie that captured the comic-book style of the 1930s was *The Rocketeer* (1991). The creation of director Joe Johnston, who had reached great success with *Honey, I Shrunk the Kids* (1989), *The Rocketeer* was based on a graphic novel of the same name by Dave Stevens.

The story takes place in the Los Angeles area. The main character is Cliff Secord, a young and ambitious pilot whose best friend and mentor Peevy has designed a sleek racing plane. Peevy, played by the veteran actor Alan Arkin, has his hands full keeping the impulsive Cliff from taking too many chances in his quest for fame and fortune. Bill Campbell plays Cliff with a boyish charm and not a little recklessness.

While testing their racing plane Cliff finds himself in the middle of a car chase between the FBI and German spies, firing submachine guns at one another. The plane catches several bullets and Cliff brings it down in a messy but non-fatal crash. It appears that his and Peavy's dream of making the National Air Races is at an end unless they can raise more money fast.

The Granville Brothers R-2 Super Sportster racer was both one of the fastest and most dangerous planes of the 1930s.

A stolen rocket pack built by Howard Hughes was hidden from the Feds in Cliff and Peevy's hangar. Cliff and his friend are of two minds as to what to do. Peevy thinks they should call the Feds, while Cliff wants to test it. The rocket pack is strapped to the back of a bronze statue of Charles Lindbergh. But things quickly go awry, resulting in total mayhem and a headless statue. Cliff says ruefully, "I'm gonna need a helmet." Undeterred, he buckles on the rocket pack himself, wearing a Buck Rogers-style helmet fitted with a rudder to provide control in flight. With a few mishaps, Cliff becomes adept at flying the rocket pack."

Finally Peevy gives in to Cliff's entreaty to use the rocket pack to join a flying show and make some real money. The show's owner dubs Cliff the "Rocketeer." A series of accidental adventures makes the Rocketeer famous.

Cliff's girlfriend Jenny, an aspiring actress, isn't impressed with her boyfriend's career, feeling he should find more stable work. The head of the spy ring is a famous actor named Neville Sinclair, not-too-subtly based on Errol Flynn. Flynn was wrongly suspected of pro-Nazi activity in the 1930s and 1940s. Former James Bond 007 actor Timothy Dalton is Sinclair, who learns that Jenny's beau is in possession of the rocket pack that Sinclair had intended to deliver to the Nazis.

Cliff is finally cornered by the Feds and learns the whole story. The Nazis have been testing—none too successfully—their own rocket packs to create a flying army of conquest. At a meeting inside an airplane hangar, Hughes asks Cliff to return the jetpack. But Cliff refuses, saying his girlfriend has been taken by Sinclair as bait for him to turn over the pack to the Nazis. Cliff escapes by throwing himself onto a large glider model of the Hughes HK-1 "Spruce Goose" and riding it out the window. Hughes smiles, "It *will* fly."

A furious fight aboard a zeppelin and at Griffith Observatory ensues with Sinclair's henchmen trading shots with gangsters and FBI agents on the same side. Sinclair leaps from the zeppelin's control gondola wearing the rocket pack but he is unaware of a fuel leak. The resulting blast turns him into a human torch that slams into the old "HOLLYWOODLAND" sign and removes the letters "LAND." The zeppelin also falls to the ground in a huge pyre. Hughes rewards Cliff and Peevy with a brand-new Gee Bee Model Z Racer just in time for the Nationals.

Much of *Rocketeer's* allure is in how beautifully Production Designer Jim Biesell and Art Director Christopher Burian-Mohr recreated the look and style of the Art Deco era. The rocket pack and Cliff's helmet—based on artist Dave Stevens' original designs—look like something right out of the Flash Gordon serials.

Several unique aircraft appear in the film. The Ford 5-AT Trimotor was a prop as Cliff's rocket pack literally puts him right next to the flying airliner. A comic moment ensues when he salutes the passengers and accidentally cuts off his rocket power. The film takes place around 1936, and by then the venerable "Tin Goose" was long gone from the mainstream airliner inventory. But audiences would more easily recognize it than a Boeing 247 or Douglas DC-1.

The airport sequences for the film were done at Santa Maria Airport, which still looks a great deal like an airfield of the 1930s. The film boasts a replica Granville Brothers (GB) Model Z Racer. It was the smaller forerunner of the R1 Super Sportster used to win the 1932 Thompson Trophy Race. Jimmy Doolittle set a world speed record of 296 knots in Gee Bee "Number 11." A replica of this plane is on display at the San Diego Air & Space Museum.

"*Rocketeer* was a wonderful movie. I really had a lot of fun on that," said Steve Hinton, one of the film's pilots. "The Gee Bee shots were real. We rigged smoke on the Gee Bee and flew between rows of trees. A Bell Jet Ranger helicopter did the air-to-air shots. Bill Campbell was in a Waco with the rear cockpit made to replicate the windscreen of the Gee Bee. The scene where he punched out the windscreen was done in flight."

The author asked Hinton about the experience of flying the racer, which had a reputation as a dangerous plane. Hinton said, "Craig Hosking was the aerial coordinator on the film. He was an experienced pilot who flew tricky planes for a living. He damn near ground-looped the thing. He and I were the only ones who flew it. It was just not a good flying airplane. The only way we learned how to land it was by mistake," Hinton laughed. "The plane was built as a replica just for looks and it might not have handled like a real Gee Bee. When it was time to fly the Gee Bee back to Chino, we both looked at each other and said, 'You gonna fly it home?' 'Nope.' 'You gonna fly it?' 'Nope.' So we just trucked it back," Hinton said, still chuckling.

The Gee Bee used in the film is now part of the collection of the Museum of Flight in Seattle, Washington.

Seattle's Museum of Flight has *The Rocketeer* Gee Bee Z-1 Racer on display. Craig Hosking and Steve Hinton both felt the Gee Bee was very tricky to fly. *Courtesy Museum of Flight*

Cliff's crash after being hit by bullets was done using a full-scale mockup. The mockup was pulled by a cable. Close examination of the shot reveals the cable under the plane.

The zeppelin was the *Luxembourg*, (LZ132), a totally fictional airship. George Lucas' ILM built the sections of the airship for the film. The control gondola and sections of the upper hull and elevators appear in the movie's climactic finale. It's never easy to simulate something as immense as the *Titanic* flying overhead, but the shot of the zeppelin coming into view over Griffith Observatory does a good job of it. No zeppelin ever exploded over Los Angeles, but Johnston, following Stevens' comic book stories, made it happen. When Tiny Ron Taylor, playing the hulking German spy Lothar, is caught on the upper hull he witnesses a hydrogen-filled airship explosion at close range, much to his chagrin.

The aircraft used to rescue Jenny and Cliff is an autogyro, a short-lived transportation fad in the 1930s, seen by many as the new "family vehicle" or way to get to work after traffic made the roads unusable. An autogyro is a rotary-winged aircraft like a helicopter. However, its rotor is not powered by the engine but spins by aerodynamic forces called autorotation. Since the rotor is not powered, an autogyro needs a separate source such as a propeller for propulsion to provide forward motion. The basic autogyro had a fuselage and engine with propeller and the same rudder and elevators as a fixed-wing aircraft.

In the movie Howard Hughes and Peavy fly close to the burning zeppelin, lower a rope ladder to Cliff and Jenny, and carry the couple away. An autogyro would never be able to handle the weight, since its lift wasn't a factor of engine power. But it looks good on screen.

The original "HOLLYWOODLAND" sign was an advertisement for a housing development. The letters "LAND" were removed in 1949, but not by Neville Sinclair.

A lot of work went into making *The Rocketeer* a fun film for audiences, but it also has appeal for pilots yearning for the romance of the old days. Even Beeman's Pectin Gum makes an appearance in the film. Beenman's was a traditional favorite of pilots.

Writer J.J. Abrams, later known for poignant films like *Regarding Henry* (1991) and television's *Lost* (2004) wrote the whimsical and moving *Forever Young* (1992). Again the film is less an aviation movie than a love story. But there are enough silver wings and whirling propellers to entice the aviation movie buff.

Forever Young is about a test pilot named Daniel McCormick, played by Mel Gibson at the peak of his popularity. Daniel is in love with Helen and intends to marry her. When she is injured in a car crash and ends up in a coma, he is devastated, unable to live without her constant presence in his life. He begs his scientist friend Harry to use him as a guinea pig in a cryogenic hibernation experiment so he won't have to endure his solitude.

But when Daniel is awakened, a bit more than the intended year has passed. It is now 1992 and the world has changed a great deal since 1939. Daniel befriends Nat Cooper, a young boy fascinated by flying, and teaches Nat the basics of piloting using a homemade rig of old junk and a computer flight simulator. Daniel and Nat go to an airshow. Daniel sees a vintage B-25 on display, which elicits a sense of what he had lost 53 years before. When he sits in the pilot's seat he smiles to himself, at last in a place he understands.

Daniel tries to cope, believing his girl is long gone. But the new, fast, loud and bewildering world of jets and computers, television and sex are too much for him. Daniel is aging rapidly.

Eventually he learns Helen is alive, and steals a B-25 bomber to find her. Now a widow, Helen is stunned but happy to see her old beau. They are able to live out their golden years together.

Planes of Fame's B-25 Mitchell, which appeared in *Forever Young.*
Courtesy Planes of Fame Air Museum

The opening sequence is of Daniel testing a North American B-25 Mitchell bomber in an incredibly steep dive. Just in time he pulls out of the dive but only manages a belly landing. Even though it is 1939, Mel Gibson displays his "wild man" persona that won him such acclaim in the *Mad Max* and *Lethal Weapon* films. The plane is B-25J *Photo Fanny*, owned by Planes of Fame in Chino, California. The aircraft has appeared in scores of films both in front of and behind the camera as a camera ship.

The pilot in *Forever Young* was Steve Hinton. Hinton said, "We took our B-25 and polished it to make it look like an early test model. For that ridiculous dive and belly landing they bought a hulk of a B-25 from Carl Scholl of Aero Trader and brought it up to where they filmed the landing. They dragged it across the ground." At no time, Hinton said, did Mel Gibson ever fly in the bomber. All the shots of the actor in the pilot's seat are studio mockups.

The dramatic theft of the plane stretched credibility to the breaking point, especially when Nat, with only ten minutes of instruction, manages to land a B-25. It's obviously only a way to bring the saga of Daniel and Helen full circle and because it was fun. Regarding this Hinton said, "Our plane was also used in the scene where Daniel goes to find his girlfriend he hasn't seen in a hundred years. It's at Point Arena on the coast north of San Francisco. They asked me how much runway I needed to land safely. So I said, 'If you give me a thousand feet with a very good approach, it's not a problem.' So they showed me a place nearby where they would have the landing area near the lighthouse set. I said, 'If you grade it and you can drive you car on it at eighty miles an hour without knocking your dentures out that will be good.'"

Needless to say the studio didn't deliver exactly what Hinton specified. They might have benefited from reading *Runways for Dummies*. Hinton continued: "So what happened is they built the set first, then they tried to clear the space for the runway. The result was very sloppy and bumpy. I said, 'I can't land a B-25 here; it'll tear the landing gear off.' They weren't happy with me. But coincidentally, when we were doing the airshow sequences at Los Alamitos Reserve Center, the military said the special ops guys had the capability of providing some aluminum landing mat. So as an exercise they laid about 800 feet at the site. I set the plane down as low and slow as I could right at the edge. It was noisy but at least I got it down."

The landing is a very dramatic moment in the film, but it's also funny how Helen hardly notices a World War II bomber landing in her front yard. As Mel Gibson says to Nat, "If you can land a B-25 you can land anything."

The reviews were mixed; most of the critics focused on the contrived script. But the box office considered *Forever Young* and Mel Gibson in particular to be a great draw with over $55 million in domestic receipts and sales. It only goes to prove that not all critics are to be taken seriously.

Hollywood, in its never-ending quest for subjects for motion pictures, all too often returns to previous efforts for ripe ideas. Rarely, this leads to a better film than the original. Not in the case of *Flight of the Phoenix* (2004). No matter how good a remake is, it can't escape being compared to an original film. Just imagine the scrutiny a remake of *Casablanca* or *Citizen Kane* would endure.

This time Dennis Quaid plays the role of Towns. The screenplay bears little resemblance to the original, with new characters more acceptable to the 21st century audience. In the cockpit at least, Quaid seems to have remembered some of his "Astronaut Gordo Cooper" cockiness from *The Right Stuff*. Tyrese Gibson, later known for the *Transformers* films, plays A.J, the co-pilot who adds a bit of welcome relief with witty repartee and banter.

Pretty red-haired Australian Miranda Otto changes the original cast in a way never conceived in Lukas Heller's screenplay. She is Kelly Johnson, a feisty wildcat oil prospector in Outer Mongolia who has just been pulled off her project by the powers-that-be back in the States. She is angry with the decision and matters don't improve as Towns arrives to take Johnson and her crew to Beijing. The first half hour of the film develops the characters and situation, instead of having the plane caught in a storm in the opening credits as in the original.

CGI was used for the storm and crash scenes, and is a little too obviously an attempt to overdramatize the violence of the event to appeal to the modern video game-era audience.

However, when the plane is in the storm and takes damage, the visual and sound effects are very convincing. Also instead of Towns and A.J. talking in "open air" they are only heard on one another's headsets. This adds more realism to the situation.

A large model of the *Phoenix* was built by Mike and Steve George at the cost of $250,000. Mike was also the radio control pilot for the miniature. As seen in *The Aviator*, radio control miniatures are perfectly capable of reproducing nearly every flight characteristic of a full-sized aircraft. In fact the *Phoenix* model was so well built it actually flew farther than expected. During one shot the model overflew the frame and hit a cameraman. The *Phoenix* was built from parts of three Fairchild C-119s in full-scale for the ground footage, but it was never flown—not surprising since it was an untested and dangerous design. Paul Mantz had met his end flying the original, and Moore had no intention of risking a life on the remake.

The construction of the plane was little different from the original, but Moore added a few lighthearted jokes expected by modern audiences. The engine start-up sequence is less dramatic than the original but the dialogue is nearly identical, right down to Towns' announcement that he is using one of the precious cartridges to clean out the dirty cylinders. The takeoff is given more drama when the group is attacked by bow-wielding Mongolian horsemen, adding a "stagecoach escaping from the Indians" touch to the film. There is no triumphant landing, just a flight into the skies with the jubilant survivors cheering.

If *Flight of the Phoenix* had not been a remake, it would stand on its own as a suspenseful drama about fighting and beating the odds against survival. But the film can't help being unfavorably compared to the 1965 version. In this case, more action doesn't translate to more drama and a better film.

Unfortunately, in the quest for more excitement and impact, Hollywood has either forgotten or ignored this fact.

The days of William Wellman, Howard Hawks, John Ford, Frank Capra, Raoul Walsh, Lloyd Bacon and Billy Wilder are long gone. The silver screen is a bit grayer as a result.

CHAPTER THIRTEEN

A Funny Thing Happened in the Air

The very first aircraft in films appeared in suspenseful dramas and comedy. Even in the days of Mack Sennett writers found it difficult to find a way to dispense laughs from a moving airplane. But in a very short time the third dimension of height added a lot of depth to potential guffaws and sidesplitting zany adventures. Only a few of the films reviewed in this chapter can be called "aviation" films. Most have some aerial sequences that stand out and add to the film's plot.

The earliest film the author decided to showcase is among Hollywood's lost films. Entitled *Now We're in the Air* (1927), the film features the sometime comedy team of Wallace Beery, Louise Brooks and Ray Hatton. Wally and Ray are inept fortune hunters who end up in the Army Air Service during World War I. A runaway observation balloon puts them over enemy lines, but for some reason the Germans see them as heroes and send them back to Allied lines as spies. They trio thinks they are safe—only to be caught and arrested as spies.

Paramount had some leftover *Wings* footage that was augmented by Frank Clarke and Harry Perry.

In 1931 *Air Tight* starred the Boy Friends, a long-forgotten comedy team of the Jazz Age. The plot is intended only to put the stars in an airplane and repeatedly bring them to the brink of death with madcap stunts. The biplane used is a 1929 Waco, one of the staples of civil aviation in the early 1930s. Using simple process and miniatures, the film isn't much to remember, but still deserves some recognition.

Bert Lahr, still eight years from his most memorable role as the Cowardly Lion in *The Wizard of Oz*, starred as an inventor in MGM's 1931 comedy *Flying High.* Rusty Krouse is an inventor with a new type of aircraft he calls an "Aero Copter." The machine is a variant on the Pitcairn Autogryo, one of the short-lived fads of the early 1930s. Rusty deals with trial after trial to get his machine into the air and prove its worth. But he can't do it as he's afraid of heights.

One of the most successful comedy duos of the 1930s was that of Stan Laurel and Oliver Hardy. With dozens of books relating their career and films in great detail, this book will only cover their sole "aviation" film, *The Flying Deuces* (1939). Even so, the flying scenes are nearly at the end of the film, when the boys are trying to escape execution by the French Foreign Legion. Once again, all the aerial sequences are done in the studio, and virtually no real aircraft other than what is shown on the ground appears on film. Stan's babyish squeals of fear and Ollie's howls of panic keep the audience in stitches while the uncontrolled biplane wheels around the sky.

The Pitcairn Autogyro enjoyed a brief popularity in the 1930s. Bert Lahr 'invented' one he called the'Auto Copter' in the 1931 comedy *Flying High.*

Two years later the equally successful team of Bud Abbott and Lou Costello also found their way into the sky in Universal's *Keep 'Em Flying.* Arthur Lubin directed Bud and Lou as he had learned to do from *Buck Privates* and *In the Navy*. That is giving them plenty of room to improvise. The success of their military-theme comedies was proof that it worked. Lubin later went on to be known for directing nearly all of the *Mister Ed* television series. In *Keep*

'Em Flying Bud and Lou are assistants to a handsome barnstorming pilot who decides to join the Air Corps. Of course the two comics join as well, but not by choice. The Air Corps is in for a hectic time with Lou Costello at the controls of a primary trainer.

The War Department supported Universal in the production, and upon the release set up a "*Keep 'Em Flying* Week" recruiting campaign. The original trailer was an Air Corps recruiting film that featured clips from the movie. Like their other 1941 military hits *Buck Privates* and *In the Navy, Keep 'Em Flying* shows a great deal of Air Corps training in progress. Most of the ground sequences were filmed at the Cal-Aero Air Flight Academy at Riverside Airport in Ontario (now Chino), California. More than 200 Boeing-Stearman PT-13 Kaydets and Vultee BT-13 Valiants were available at Cal-Aero during the filming. The base commander was Colonel Robert L. Scott, who very soon would go to China to fight with the Flying Tigers (see Chapter Seven).

Scott, who wrote the bestselling *God is My Co-Pilot*, also wrote *When I Owned the Sky*, and in it he relates working on this film. One sequence of *Keep 'Em Flying* has Lou at the controls of a primary trainer on the ground. He causes total havoc on the field while he careens around and through hangars. The shot in which he drives the plane through a hanger at high speed was filmed with Scott at the controls.

An ironic twist: The Japanese Navy's First Air Fleet of six aircraft carriers left Hitokkapu Bay Japan just two days before the film premiered. The Japanese were headed for Pearl Harbor.

Gasbags was a little-known but largely appreciated British comedy of 1941 in which a comedy team called the "Crazy Gang" have their mobile fish-and-chips shop carried away by a runaway barrage balloon. After landing in Nazi Germany and arrested as spies by the SS, the gang manage to escape by impersonating Hitler and return to England with a stolen secret weapon. The only "aircraft" of note is the barrage balloon, but the long-vanished team of Bud Flanagan, Chesney Allen, Jimmy Nervo, Teddy Knox and Charlie Naughton are worth looking for.

On the other hand, the Bowery Boys, with their popularity waning in the postwar years, made it into the Air Force in 1953's *Clipped Wings*. Once again the doofus, in the form of lanky Huntz Hall, is thrust into a plane with the inevitable consequences, but the film has little to offer any but the most ardent Bowery Boys fans.

Famed producer Stanley Kramer broke away from his traditional "message" films such as *On the Beach* (1959) and *Judgment at Nuremburg* (1961) with his epic comedy *It's a Mad, Mad, Mad, Mad World* in 1963. The plot follows the wild and greedy antics of one of the most colorful cast of comedy geniuses ever assembled in film history as they race the police and each other to recover a lost cache of money in a park along the California coast.

During the fast-paced melee a few airplanes manage to fill the screen. Frank Tallman did the flying sequences in two airplanes: a twin Beechcraft D-18 and a JN-4D Jenny. It is the Beech's appearance in the film that really stands out.

Buddy Hackett and the ever-busy Mickey Rooney are a pair of vaudeville comedians who are present during the film's opening to witness Jimmy Durante's last words to get the "three hundred and fifty G's" he has stashed under the "Big W." Rooney and Hackett—who had never worked together in a major film before—are a perfect team. Rooney's Ding Bell is the smart, levelheaded straight man to Hackett's mush-mouth babyish Benjy. They drive their red VW Beetle to an airport, intending to charter a plane to take them to Santa Rosita and recover the money. The only plane available at the exclusive flying club is the twin Beech 18 owned by Mr. Tyler Fitzgerald, played with great effectiveness by the future Thurston Howell III, Jim Backus. In fact it may be this role that made Sherwood Schwartz consider Backus for *Gilligan's Island* the following year.

Buddy Hackett and Mickey Rooney's hilarious piloting of the Beechcraft with an unconscious Jim Backus in the rear cabin is one of the highlights of *It's a Mad, Mad, Mad World.*

In any case the rich alcoholic Fitzgerald agrees to fly Benjy and Ding to their destination. But he insists on drinking several Old Fashioneds and ends up unconscious while Benjy attempts to control the plane. What results is some of the most impossibly wild flying in film history—and not a few very unusual stunts by Tallman. Benjy is trying to control the plane. In doing so, he pilots it through a billboard and a hangar. The billboard stunt is a classic and nearly everyone who has seen the film remembers it most.

In the foreword to Tallman's book *Flying the Old Planes*, Joe Brown said that Tallman had practiced with a simulated cloth-and-tape billboard frame for several weeks. Former wing walker John Kazian, who worked with Tallman on several movies, explained what was needed to do the stunt: "Frank told me the billboard was made of very light wood and paper. It was large enough to allow the Beech's wingspan, the propellers, vertical tail and the extended landing gear to pass through it. The trick was to hit the exact center, the 'sweet spot.' On the back side was a sort of bull's-eye for him to aim at. He intended to aim himself, not the plane, right at the center of it."

Famed stunt pilot Frank Tallman managed some of the most dangerous aerial stunts in motion pictures during his long career.

The billboard was constructed near the end of the former Orange County (now John Wayne) Airport runway, so Tallman could land as soon as he had passed through the board. "He went through it at about 160 knots with the propellers windmilling," Kazian said. "They stopped right when he hit the board and he was committed to landing." The Beech's windshield was shattered upon hitting the board.

Frank Tallman puts the Twin Beechcraft 18 through the billboard in *It's a Mad, Mad, Mad World.* Note the propellers which Tallman stopped just before he hit the sign.

As for the hangar fly-through, Tallman again had to thread the eye of the needle with a 47-foot wingspan at over a hundred miles an hour. The stunt was done at the Santa Rosa Airport in northern California. Kazian said, "Frank told me he felt pretty confident about it. It was going to be tricky, but Frank said if he had to, he'd just bring it in for a landing inside the hangar for one shot and then start and fly it out for the second shot. But he went right through."

Tallman did at least three practice approaches over the hangar before doing just one fly-through. He had to bank sharply to avoid some trees at the far end before flying away. The shot may not have been done at the same speed as is seen in the film but it appears to be at high speed.

Kazian added, "Frank did some 'falling leaf' stunts to appear as if Hackett was totally unable to control the plane." The interior shots of the Beech—with Hackett and Rooney in the pilots' seats while the hapless Backus is tossed about and finally knocked out—are memorable. Hackett's inept piloting causes the Beech to roll over several times. The unconscious Backus is thrown around the rear cabin.

At nearly 100 knots Tallman put the Beechcraft through the hangar at Santa Rosa Airport.

The Beechcraft just before its propellers shatter the restaurant windows in *It's a Mad, Mad, Mad World*. The scene was shot at the long-gone Rancho Conejo Airport in Newbury Park, California.

The final landing with the Three Stooges waiting in firefighting garb to effect a rescue is the last hair-raising event for the Beech. The landing scenes were done at the long-gone Rancho Conejo Airport in Newbury Park near Thousand Oaks, California. That is where the Beech, propellers whirling madly, comes to a stop just as it crashes into a large restaurant window. The weather-beaten and truly rickety Jenny does no stunt work but the pilot, portrayed by the ever-bewildered Ben Blue, looks as if a mere takeoff was enough to defy death.

In 1964 one of the most unusual films ever to emerge from the wildly fertile mind of Stanley Kubrick hit the silver screen. The dark anti-war comedy *Dr. Strangelove, or How I Learned to Stop Worrying and Love the Bomb*, created a cult of fans. *Strangelove* was shot in the studio at Shepperton, England, and featured a cast of improbable and innuendo-laden characters such as Col. Bat Guano, General Jack Ripper, and Major King Kong. The last is memorably played by six-foot-two former rodeo rider and actor Slim Pickens, brought over from the U.S. to replace the acrophobic Peter Sellers. John Wayne was approached to do the role but he refused. Sellers plays three other roles in the film, including an American president, a RAF officer and the sinister former Nazi-turned-nuclear-theorist Strangelove.

The story was based on Peter George's novel *Two Hours to Doom* (known as *Red Alert* in the U.S.). Kubrick made it a comedy to avoid confusion with *Fail Safe*, a similar nuclear-themed film that was released the same year. *Strangelove*'s stark black and white cinematography lends a raw tone to the comedy and imminent nuclear Armageddon.

The only aircraft in the film is a B-52 Stratofortress, which in the opening credits is a real plane being refueled to the lilting tune of "Try a Little Tenderness." After that all views of the bomber are miniatures in the studio, mostly in concert with the martial beat of "When Johnny Comes Marching Home." The USAF refused to provide access to a B-52 or even photos of the flight deck. Production Designer Ken Adam found photos in issues of *Flight Magazine*. He managed to assemble a nearly complete flight deck interior from these photos and illustrations. Air Force personnel who visited the set for publicity junkets were astonished at how Adam had been able to discover so much. The only thing they weren't able to obtain photos of were air-dropped atomic bombs.

Pickens is laid-back cowboy pilot Major King Kong, who is suddenly faced with having to invade the Soviet Union and bomb a missile base. The bombardier is played by future award-winning actor James Earl Jones. While trying to cope with the sudden crisis that has been created by a cigar-chomping SAC general gone mad, Kong puts on his battered cowboy hat and does his duty. The climactic sequence in which Kong rides an atomic bomb "rodeo-style" down to oblivion was a clever bit of special effects. In Kubrick's biography Ken Adam stated, "The B-52 was a huge, huge set, without bomb doors. Or at least not

The iconic scene from *Dr. Strangelove*. Major King Kong, played by former rodeo rider Slim Pickens, prepares to ride a nuclear bomb into eternity. Note director Stanley Kubrick's dark humor in the stenciling on the bomb, "NUCLEAR WARHEAD – HANDLE WITH CARE."

practical bomb doors. We had an old effects man named Wally Veevers. He would always help me when I had a problem. Wally said, 'Give me overnight to think about it.' We took an 8"x10" still of the bomb bay and cut the bomb doors out of the still. We had Kong get into the bay and mount the bomb. Then we cut away to him on the bomb outside the plane with the back projection of the photo behind him. Stanley was fascinated by this little bit of trickery.'

Some of the model flying scenes used stock wartime footage shot from a Boeing B-17. The shadow can clearly be seen behind the B-52 miniature in the sequence where Kong is reviewing the crew's survival kit.

A little-known fact, revealed in Kubrick's biography, is that the plane is named *Leper Colony*—a name from *Twelve O'clock High* (1949).

The film was being shot at the time of John F. Kennedy's assassination in November 1963. Kong's line, "Shoot, a fella could have a pretty good time in Dallas with all this stuff," was later re-dubbed to insert "Vegas" instead of "Dallas."

Strangelove is one of Kubrick's best remembered films. It brashly flips the finger to the patriotic dream world of *Strategic Air Command,* particularly in the lilting beauty of the opening credits and the bold sign at the SAC base claiming "Peace is Our Profession." Once the film was finished, the Pentagon insisted Columbia state that such an incident depicted could never take place, due to stringent checks and balances.

The author interviewed former SAC generals Chris Adams and Stan Brown and Sgt. Al Buckles regarding various films in this book. When asked about *Strangelove*, the response was universally partisan. They either never saw or would not admit to having seen the film and had nothing but negative opinions of the film's plot.

By their very nature, comedy films don't need to be technically accurate. But this isn't the case with one of the most clever, funny comedy movies of the 1960s, Blake Edwards' *The Great Race* (1965) with the semi-team of Tony Curtis and Jack Lemmon. Playing rival daredevils in 1912, the two constantly attempt to outdo one another in ever-more harrowing and crowd-pleasing stunts, ultimately leading to an automobile race from New York to Paris (the long way). Curtis' tooth-flashing good guy Leslie Gallant III is the foil to Lemmon's classic evil scientist Professor Phineas Fate, who is attended by not-so-subservient lackey Max, played by Peter Falk. Even his last name is given as "Mean."

'The Leper Colony' as it flies low over the Soviet Union towards its target. Note the model's upswept wingtips as a real B-52 would have in flight.

What makes *The Great Race* great is the beautiful cinematography, imaginative props, Arthur Ross' screenplay and, most particularly, Professor Fate himself. The author, long a fan of Lemmon's work, has rarely found an interview with the talented actor in which his role as the conniving, totally unscrupulous Fate is mentioned.

Be that as it may, the film has only one short aviation sequence, when Fate attempts a stunt in which he is snatched off the ground via a harness from an airplane flown by Max. With Fate dressed in his signature top hat and black "bat" cloak, the audience is eager to see what will happen, knowing that Fate will suffer some ignominious "fate."

The airplane is a modified replica of a Curtiss Pusher, c. 1912, painted black and sporting Fate's skull-and-crossbones insignia. Even the wing trailing edges are scalloped to appear bat-like. The engine appears to be either a Lycoming Flat Four or even a VW four-cylinder, and a large prop radiator was fitted behind Max's seat. The plane is a wonderful prop, fitting the film's imaginative production design.

Fate is yanked off the grass but isn't lifted high enough for his liking. He yells in his characteristic snarl, "Up, you idiot, up!" Max tries to comply but the Curtiss is totally unsuitable for the added weight. Then Max loses control, causing Fate to be dragged along the grass with a hilarious "Aaaaaarrrrrrgh!" Then Fate sees a barn looming before him and in one last appeal to be lifted is thrown into the roof. The next shot shows Max in the crashed plane amid a pigpen, covered with foul mud. Fate staggers out of the barn, festooned with chicken feathers. He spits a few out, and mumbles, "Let's see the Great Leslie try *that* one!"

While largely forgotten by all but the most ardent Lemmon and Curtis fans, *The Great Race* is one of Edwards' best works.

If *The Great Waldo Pepper* holds a place as one of the best true aviation film dramas, then its comedy twin is 1965's *Those Magnificent Men in their Flying Machines or How I Flew From London to Paris in 25 hours 11 minutes.* Ken Annakin, who directed *The Longest* Day in 1962, departed from serious epic war films to take on an epic comedy. Filmed entirely on location in England and at Pinewood Studios, the movie utilized 70mm Todd-AO cameras for the best image quality.

A true madcap comedy with shades of Mack Sennett's Keystone Kops, the film relates a 1910 aerial race sponsored by Lord Rawnsley, played by the quintessential British blueblood Robert Morley. Rawnsley was loosely based on the real Lord Northcliffe of the *London Daily Mail* who sponsored several early aviation feats including the first attempt to cross the English Channel in 1909. The race was to pit the most advanced aircraft and daring pilots from around the world to fly from London to Paris—a then-grueling 213 mile as the crow flies. The planes of the day were incapable of flying the distance in one leap, so a stop in Dover was arranged for refueling and night rest.

The contenders were as racially nationalistic as possible, from a haughty British officer to a strutting German, from a French lothario to a wealthy Italian inventor, and of course a laid-back fair-play American cowboy.

But what really makes the film fun isn't the zany comedy chases on the field at Croydon, nor even the rapscallion Terry-Thomas' evil deeds to win the race, but the wide variety of twenty accurate vintage aircraft reproductions. This is one film not to be missed by early aviation buffs Among the examples of pre-1914 airplanes are a Santos-Dumont Demoiselle monoplane, a 1910 Bristol Boxkite, an A.V. Roe IV Triplane, an Eardley Billing Tractor Biplane, and the graceful Levasseur "Antoinette" IV monoplane. The Eardley Billing played the role of two aircraft—the German and Japanese entries—with a few modifications. For instance, the Japanese plane was disguised with fabric panels on the wing struts and other places. Annakin's team built three of each of the flying aircraft, and at least one was in the air every day.

The sturdy 1910 Bristol Boxkite was reproduced as Stuart Whitman's 'Newton Flyer' in *Those Magnificent Men in Their Flying Machines.*

Some planes built for the film were not intended to fly and were used for ground or model shots. These were the strange Walton Edwards Rhomboidal, a Lee Richards Annular Biplane with circular wings, a Passat Ornithoper, a Picaut Dubrieul, and the Little Tiddler canard. The distinctive Philips Multiplane often appeared in old films of early flight. This last one was flown by the British airplane inventor in a "backwards" flight to his goal. He—that is, the aerial stuntman—also flew the wildly unstable Lee Richards circular-winged biplane and the unworkable Passat Ornithoper. Both of those were towed, rather than flown.

An original 1910 Deperdussin monoplane and a 1910 Blackburn Type D monoplane were seen in some of the ground sequences but not flown. Orville Newton's "Phoenix Flyer" was originally intended by Annakin to be a Wright Flyer, but the Bristol Boxkite—based on the sturdy Farman biplane—was used instead. It bore a resemblance to the American Curtiss and Wright pushers of the day.

The small "Demoiselle" monoplane, which greatly resembles the modern ultralight, was developed by the innovative Brazilian Alberto Santos-Dumont, who designed and successfully flew dozens of balloons and fixed-wing aircraft in France after the turn of the century. The replica was built so close to the original design that when it came time to fly the "Demoiselle" it refused to lift off and only bounced along the grass runway. Annakin learned from an aviation historian that Santos-Dumont had weighed only about 120 pounds. The man who was to fly the plane was far too heavy. A diminutive stunt pilot named Joan Hughes was able to fly the plane. All the aerial scenes of the "Demoiselle" are of Hughes at the controls, wearing a costume to appear as the male actor.

Derek Piggott, who flew in *The Blue Max*, was Stuart Whitman's double and pilot for the Bristol Boxkite.

The "Antoinette" monoplane is a nearly exact copy of the only one ever built. The original was intended to be a competitor for Louis Bleriot's monoplane in his attempt to fly the English Channel in 1909. But it was Bleriot who won the *Daily Mail* Prize of £1,000 for the July 25 flight simply because Hubert Latham, the British contender, overslept.

The winner of the air race from London to Paris in *Those Magnificent Men in Their Flying Machines* was a reproduction of Alberto Santos-Dumont's nimble Demoiselle monoplane. The plane so accurately fit the original design that the pilot who first tested it was unable to get off the ground because he was heavier than the diminutive Santos-Dumont.

At a cost of roughly $5,000 each, the planes were constructed by various builders to appear as close to the real thing as possible, using wood and fabric materials. Only the engines were modern, as dictated by the film's aviation consultant, RAF Air Commodore Allen Wheeler. Wheeler, long considered an expert on pre-war aviation, was relentless in his pursuit of authenticity and safety, two requirements that don't always work together. For example, the "Antoinette" was slightly changed from the original design. The real plane had "wing-warping" for controlling rolls in the air, but this proved to be too unstable and large ailerons were installed instead. A modern de Havilland Gypsy I four-cylinder in-line engine was used. Yet the final result is fairly faithful to the lovely "Antoinette."

Since the aircraft, modern or not, were fragile, aerial filming was done primarily in the morning and evening hours when the air was calm. When poor weather intervened, the production concentrated on ground and other sequences.

In the DVD commentary, Annakin describes some of the innovative means the production used to simulate flying. Two wheeled towers were set a few hundred yards apart. On wires between them were wheeled trolleys, from which was suspended a framework holding the aircraft to be filmed. An operator controlled the speed and orientation of the aircraft. This allowed the camera to film moving ground underneath. The apparatus, named "Dick Parker's Flying Rig" in honor of the American special effects coordinator, was only used on clear, blue-sky days, as the framework and wires were painted blue to blend in with the sky. The rig was used in the ground chase sequence where the tailless German plane "leaps" over other planes. "I defy anyone to see the wires," Annakin said with pride.

The graceful Levasseur IV 'Antoinette' monoplane landing with a clogged fuel line, which the pilot, using a pheasant's feather was able to clean out.

Other flying effects were achieved by using an Aerospatiale SA 313 Alouette II helicopter. In some cases, a mockup of a plane's forward section was built and mounted on the skids of the Alouette. This allowed the camera to shoot down on the pilot while in flight.

An airfield resembling what was seen in England in 1910 was found at the Booker Airfield in High Wycombe, Buckinghamshire. Several hangars emblazoned with the names "Sopwith," "A.V. Roe," "Humber" and "Vickers," among others, were built. A few historical notes here: Sopwith, the builders of the legendary Camel during the war, was not founded until 1912, two years after the film's era. Alliott Verdon Roe, whose company later became Avro, was the builder of the famous Avro Lancaster bomber of World War II.

The French government refused permission to film in the skies over Paris, so Annakin's model makers built a miniature Paris set complete with the Eiffel Tower for the model planes to fly over. A fake Calais was also constructed for the arrival over France.

Several downright funny if overly unrealistic scenes made it into the film. The German entry is flown by *Goldfinger* title lead Gert Frobe. As Colonel Manfred von Holstein, he toots German "oom-pah" music through his teeth as he attempts to fly the plane with the help of an instruction manual. During a test flight, the tail is torn off the German plane, prompting the Keystone Kops routine with Benny Hill as the fire brigade marshal leading his troops to the rescue. Careful examination of the footage reveals a small tail wheel under the broken end of the fuselage to keep it from dragging. When von Holstein loses the vital manual during the Channel crossing he climbs back along the open frame fuselage to retrieve it. Finally the pilotless plane turns over, and Holstein finds himself hanging over the water and tries to "run" before the crash.

Terry Thomas' character, the dastardly Sir Percy Ware-Armitage, is foiled in his sneaky attempts to win the race by cheating when he accidentally lands the A.V. Roe IV triplane on the back of a moving train. While trying to run forward to tell the engineer to stop he realizes the train is approaching a tunnel. Knowing he has no chance, Sir Percy throws himself to the deck and listens as his plane is shredded in the tunnel. When he opens his eyes he sees the torn remnants of the Roe with its wings ripped off. With the face only Terry Thomas can display, he yells "Blast!" through clenched teeth.

Sir Percy Ware-Armitage's distinctive Avro IV Triplane. Despite the dastardly Sir Percy's efforts, the plane ended up destroyed on the back of a train.

The UK-produced Twentieth Century Fox *Those Magnificent Men in their Flying Machines* was in every way a true and successful aviation film. In fact it would take more than a mere few pages in one chapter to do it justice. The opening sequence uses the highly visual comedy of Red Skelton, who plays various unsuccessful early aviation pioneers. Silent movie footage of some of the most ridiculous contraptions are shown, with cleverly inserted and carefully matched close-up shots of Skelton. The sequence sets the tone for the film very well. According to the DVD commentary by director Ken Annakin, the film's original title was *Flying Crazy*.

Sam Wanamaker, who plays Orville Newton's friend George, is less than enthusiastic about Orville's flying. Orville says, "You don't know what it's like up there, cause you ain't never been there."

Wilbur, deadpan, replies, "It ain't the goin' up that worries me; it's the different ways you find of comin' down."

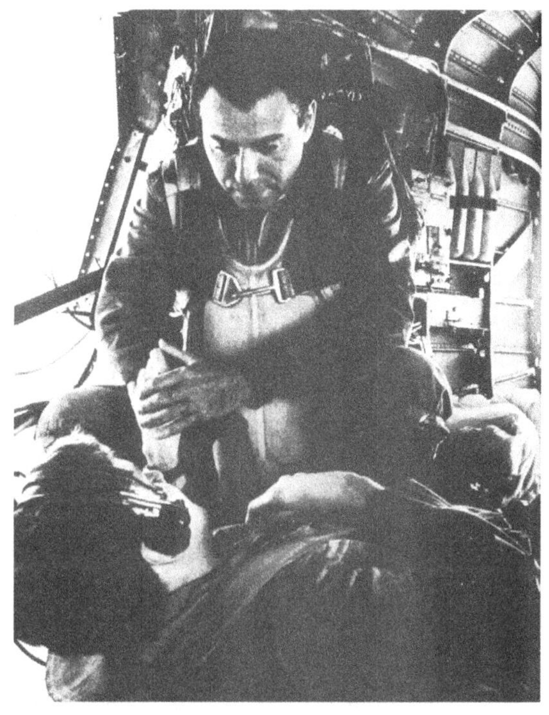

Alan Arkin as the frustrated Captain John Yossarian in *Catch-22*.

Paramount's 1970 production of Joseph Heller's bestseller, *Catch-22*, was—like *Dr. Strangelove*—another black comedy with a wartime theme. Released while the United States was deeply embroiled in the Vietnam War, the movie tells a very bleak view of the air war in the Mediterranean during World War II.

Captain John Yossarian (Alan Arkin) is a B-25 bombardier flying out of a small Italian island. Yossarian is desperate to get out of flying and the war. The only way to do it is to convince his commander he is insane. But insanity is the key to survival in an insane war.

Director Mike Nichols, who worked with Dustin Hoffman in *The Graduate* in 1967, gathered 18 flyable B-25 Mitchell bombers from Tallmantz Aviation for the production. This made it the largest formation of bombers ever assembled for a film, and the largest group of B-25s to be flown since the war. Nearly all the B-25s still fly today with various air museums around the country.

The movie was shot on locations in Sonora Mexico and Italy. *Catch-22* has some of the most spectacular flying sequences in any film, comedy or not.

The author interviewed Lt. Truman "Bud" Coble, a B-25 pilot who served with the 310th Bomb Group out of Corsica during the period covered by the film. "*Catch-22* was not a funny film, but I have to say the flying and combat are pretty well done," said Coble. "It was really like that. The plane shook like hell and you couldn't hear anything but the engines and flak."

Frank Pine and Tallmantz Chief Pilot Jim Appleby coordinated all the aerial footage with the Mitchells. Appleby gathered pilots and co-pilots with experience in military flying and particularly with tight formations. But that wasn't enough for Pine and Appleby, who put the aviators through a refresher B-25 training course and also taught the finer points of flying in front of a camera.

Process shots of the B-25 interiors are well done and convey the violent shaking of the cramped planes in combat. The actors have to shout to be heard, a novelty in air war movies. The author has flown in a B-25 and will attest to this.

For Coble, who flew over fifty missions against Italian and German targets, the film has some good points. "They did a good job of showing how miserable and hot it was there," he said. "I got nostalgic seeing those Mitchells flying."

Zona Appleby, the widow of stunt pilot Jim Appleby, recounted some of her husband's experiences on *Catch-22*. "In that scene where Lt. Milo Minderbinder (Jon Voight) was talking to the base commander about eggs, that's Jim coming in for a crash landing off camera."

The longest single sequence in the film has the entire force of bombers taking off. "That was kind of dangerous," Zona said. "They just took off one after another and had to get into the air. Jim was somewhere in the middle of the pack." Nichols wanted a single take for the sequence. Each plane had to get off the ground or crash in the bay lest the following B-25 crash into it from behind. "It was that close," Zona said.

Despite 1,150 hours of flight time accrued by the Mitchells, they appear on film for little more than ten minutes.

Yossarian's B-25 on yet another mission. Even though filming of the B-25s in Mexico took more than six months, less than fifteen minutes of aerial footage is seen in the final print.

Joseph Heller served in the 488th Bomb Squadron in the Mediterranean during 1943. In fact the squadron's patch of a nude woman riding a bomb is that of Heller's unit.

One of the seventeen B-25s used *in Catch-22* is on display at EAA AirVenture Museum in Oshkosh, Wisconsin. *Courtesy AirVenture*

Steven Spielberg stepped outside his usual comfort zone with his wild war comedy *1941* in 1979. The plot follows semi-historical events in Los Angeles during the weekend after the attack on Pearl Harbor. With an all-star cast, *1941* relates the story of several people as they cope with invasion hysteria, riots, air raids and a Japanese submarine off the Santa Monica Pier.

John Belushi's role as the slovenly wild man Bluto Blutarsky in *National Lampoon's Animal House* the previous year made him perfect for the role of Captain Wild Bill Kelso, U.S. Army Air Corps. Kelso is a P-40 pilot who has been chasing two Japanese squadrons all over the southwest, only to lose them over Fresno. The fact that the Japanese exist only in his imagination does not deter him from wreaking total havoc with the local populace.

Fellow Faber College alumnus Tim Matheson plays Captain Loomis Birkhead, a lecherous Army officer determined to seduce sexy Donna Stratton (Nancy Allen), a plane-crazy reporter. Donna is willing to submit to Birkhead's advances—but only if she is inside a plane. The fact that Birkhead washed out of flight school doesn't deter him from trying, even in a parked B-17.

Later Birkhead and Donna are in Barstow, California, where they secure the use of an unarmed Beechcraft twin-engine trainer. Birkhead, nervous but still horny, takes Donna up and flies towards Los Angeles. What they don't know is they are being tracked by skittish

Civilian Defense spotters and the trigger-happy Kelso, who only see Japanese. The aerial chase and battle result in the Beech being shot down in the La Brea Tar Pits. Kelso is shot down by a pistol bullet fired by a geeky air spotter on the Santa Monica Ferris Wheel.

Hang in there.

Kelso bellies in along Hollywood Boulevard, breaking up a riot between Zoot Suiters and military personnel. Kelso finally escapes to find his way back to Santa Monica, where he rides a motorcycle off the pier and climbs aboard the Japanese submarine to take its crew prisoner—or so he hopes.

All in all, a typical day's work for Spielberg.

The B-17 bomber was the CAF Arizona Wing's *Sentimental Journey*, a restored B-17G before the chin turret had been fitted. Left in its natural metal color, with early-war Air Corps markings, the Fortress merely had to stay on the ground. In the background sharp-eyed viewers can see the tall rudder of a B-52 Stratofortress. The sequence may have been filmed at the March Field Museum in Riverside.

The Boeing B-17G Flying Fortress in the airport sequence of *1941* is operated by the Arizona Wing of the CAF. This photo was taken prior to the installation of the chin turret. The plane, called 'Sentimental Journey,' currently appears at air shows around the country. *Courtesy Arizona Wing*

The twin Beechcraft was owned by Planes of Fame in Chino, California. Pilot Steve Hinton, who provided the author with some excellent information on many films in this book, said, "We filmed most of the ground sequences at Indian Dunes. I taxied the P-40 and the Beech. Tom Camp coordinated the sequences, including the shots where Kelso lands to get gas at the old station." The P-40 is painted with the ubiquitous "shark mouth" motif that audiences expected on the Warhawk. "During the flight over the Grand Canyon," said Hinton, "Tom Camp flew the Warhawk while Jim Gavin handled the aerial coordination. It was tight in there."

The FAA would not permit the studio to film any aerial sequences over the city at night. A huge miniature of Los Angeles circa 1941 was built with thousands of lights along detailed streets and intersections. Spielberg used nearly 75,000 flashbulbs to create the effect of bursting anti-aircraft fire over the city when the miniature Beechcraft and P-40 fly overhead. The searchlights were remotely controlled, with a thin hazy atmosphere to make them visible.

Hinton related that the shot in which Kelso, groggy and ill-tempered, falls of the wing of his plane, was actually not scripted. "[Belushi] caught his pants leg on something and fell off the wing. He was out for like two days," Hinton said with a chuckle. Considering the reputation Belushi gained for his antics both on and off screen the fall was hardly worth mentioning.

Even with Spielberg's magic touch, *1941* wasn't a major success. Stanley Kubrick had told him to consider making *1941* as a drama, as it would have great impact and appeal. But Spielberg did it his own way.

Jim Abrahams and David and Jerry Zucker, whose madcap *Police Squad* television series later spawned some successful movies, took on disaster films with Paramount's 1980 spoof, *Airplane!* Loosely based on Arthur Hailey's serious *Zero Hour!* (see Chapter Eight) the script takes great pleasure in shooting down all the cherished traditions of airline disaster movies. Nothing is sacred. Even the 707 jet is accompanied by propeller sound effects, and the FAA's air traffic controllers have to roll with the punches while their profession is reduced to the comedy equivalent of a kindergarten playground.

What makes *Airplane!* fun to watch over and over is the plethora of subtle and not-so-subtle sight gags, puns, witty dialogue and jabs at all the *Airport* films. *Airplane!* used the formulaic collection of misfits and Hollywood castoffs to fill an airliner and cast. Not surprisingly, the characters so prevalent in the "serious" airline disaster films fit right into the madcap *Airplane!* If a viewer were to step back and view the characters objectively, they might realize it took very little effort for the writers to take most of the passengers and crew from *Airport 1975*'s Columbia Flight 409 and—after a five-year layover—have them board *Airplane!*'s Trans America Airlines Flight 209. The cast of characters—from the sick child to singing nuns, from stable doctors to hysterical passengers, from serious pilots to zany air traffic controllers—add to the movie's appeal.

From the opening sequences, the film goes full tilt. Dramatic music reminiscent of the *Airport 1975* score shows cars unloading outside the terminal. It all seems perfectly serious, but then the airport announcers start arguing about whether the red or white zones are for loading and unloading only. From then on it's total mayhem.

In a pre-9/11 world, the filmmakers are able to poke fun at airport security, allowing obvious Middle East terrorists to board with weapons while innocent passengers are roughly searched.

The relation to *Zero Hour!* is seen when the passengers and flight crew are incapacitated by bad fish. According to patrician doctor Rumack (Leslie Nielsen), "We have to find someone who can not only fly this plane, but who didn't have fish for dinner." The stewardess Elaine, played by Julie Haggerty in her first role, flies the plane with almost as much success as Karen Black.

Otto Pilot, Leslie Nielsen and Robert Hays in *Airplane!*

Enter Ted Stryker, a former military pilot with emotional problems. A disastrous bombing raid during some unnamed war has left him with a drinking problem. But he is put in the driver's seat and flies the plane.

At the control tower, Chief Pilot Rex Kramer assists addled airport manager Steve McCroskey. Robert Stack, whose aviation film career goes back to *Fighter Squadron* in 1948, is hilarious as the overly serious Kramer. He is actually spoofing himself in *The High and the Mighty*. Lloyd Bridges, as McCroskey, displays an unbelievable skill at comedy.

Peter Graves of *Mission: Impossible* fame is the pilot, Captain Oveur. He also takes shots at his own role in the television disaster film *SST: Death Flight*. Stephen Stucker plays Johnny, a controller who does his level best to make the impending disaster into a cinematic pillow fight.

In the end Stryker lands the plane and wins the girl.

A favorite character is Otto Pilot, a grinning blow-up doll whose deflation requires Elaine, played by Julie Haggerty to "blow him" via a tube at his beltline.

Airplane! deflated Universal's long series of airline films with one prick—no pun intended.

An imaginative and fun re-hash of the old *Magnificent Seven* plot emerged in the *Three Amigos!* (1986). Lacking four of the seven gunfighters from the former film, the main characters in *Three Amigos!* are woefully ill-prepared for their task of saving a small Mexican village from the raids of the Infamous "El Guapo." Lucky, Dusty and Ned, played by Chevy Chase, Steve Martin and Martin Short, are three silent film heroes who find themselves pitted against a very dangerous Mexican bandito leader. The Three Amigos find the village to be trusting of their skills and finally end up using their unique Hollywood talents to foil the evil El Guapo and his German pilot crony.

While nowhere near what one would call an aviation film, the *Three Amigos* does hold a few aerial scenes of note. And it was also the last film of Jim Appleby. Director John Landis, with his usual skill at fast-paced action and madcap comedy, used the talents of Appleby for the aerial sequences. The first one occurs when a plane flies over the village.

Lucky: "What's that?"

Dusty: "It's a plane."

Ned, grinning: "Not just any plane, it's a Tubman 601. I flew one in *Little Neddy Goes to War*."

Lucky: "What's it doing here?"

Ned: "I think it's a mail plane."

Lucky (looking puzzled): "How can you tell?"

Ned: "Didn't you notice its little balls?"

Actually the plane is a Bücker Bu-131 Jungmann, and there is no such thing as a "Tubman 601." The Bu-131 was a two-seat biplane designed in 1935 and used by the Luftwaffe as an advanced trainer.

Zona Appleby related some of the behind-the-scenes trivia. "Ever since the *Twilight Zone* movie," she said, "John Landis was very intimidated by aircraft." Zona was referring to the 1982 accident in which actor Vic Morrow and two children were killed when a helicopter struck them during the filming of *Twilight Zone: The Movie*. Landis spent several months in court and had to contend with various legal battles.

Another pilot was to fly the Jungman, continued Zona, but he got into a dispute with Landis and was fired. "Then Jim and Jimmy Franklin were brought in to fly," said Zona. "Between the two of them they were flying the actual planes with the dummies on the wing and the studio plane on gimbals."

"Landis wouldn't even watch the filming if a plane was in a scene," Zona said. "In the scene where the Three Amigos land the plane and everybody was running around and kids were running up to the plane, he just wouldn't be there."

German-born actor Kai Wulff plays the unnamed German. Ironically he looks and acts more like Baron Manfred von Richthofen than any actor who played that role. To spotlight the German's evil role, the plane has German Air Service Iron Crosses painted on it.

Jim Appleby (1924 – 2010) in his 'work clothes' with the P-40 he flew in several movies. A veteran of the U.S. Army Air Force, USAF and countless stunt pilot roles, his last film was *The Three Amigos*. *Courtesy Zona Appleby*

CHAPTER FOURTEEN

The Edge of Flight: Non-Aviation Films

One of the most famous films in history ended with a huge ape clinging to the top of the tallest building in the world. The climactic ending of *King Kong* (1933)—with the terrified Fay Wray desperately trying to escape while Kong struggles to comprehend the strange new world around him—is burned into the collective memory of our culture. To the viewing audiences, Kong's last minutes were a curious mixture of pity and excitement. Seeing the huge ape holding onto the spire of the Empire State Building while Navy planes approach sent shivers of anticipation up the spines of viewers in front of the silver screen.

The planes were Curtiss OSC-2 biplanes with rear-cockpit gun mounts, filmed on takeoff and during attack sequences. In the DVD commentary, director Merian C. Cooper explained that he went out to Lockheed Air Terminal near Los Angeles to have the flying footage done. This is not consistent with other evidence that the planes were in New York. Most likely they were filmed in both locations. RKO paid the pilots $10.00 each under the table and $100.00 to the Navy Fund. It's amazing what could be bought during the Depression.

The miniatures were extremely detailed, and according to various sources had wingspans from 14" to 36" in length. Every strut and wire was meticulously duplicated. Stop-motion legend Ray Harryhausen stated that the Empire State Building in long shots was real and Kong was double-exposed onto the building. The process shots show a pilot and his gunner flying towards Manhattan. The gunner points, as if to say, "No, no it's the ape on *that* building over there!" An interesting bit of trivia is that the pilot and gunner are not actors; Cooper and producer Ernest B. Shroedsack sat in the plane. Cooper had said, "We should kill the sonofabitch ourselves."

Several aerial live shots and stop-motion shots were generated for Kong's final battle while the planes cut into the scene, firing their guns. The sequences manage a fair bit of visual trickery, forcing depth with the planes flying into a shot and away from the camera towards Kong. He catches a plane and pulls it down to crash and burn against the building's impervious façade.

In what is probably the most famous movie climax in Hollywood history, King Kong manages to snatch an attacking airplane while clinging to the top of the Empire State Building. The models used in the final sequences were built in three sizes to provide the illusion of distance.

Originally Kong's fall from the skyscraper was to use actual shots of the building but the effect was not satisfactory. RKO built a miniature of the Empire State Building.

Carl Denham, played by Robert Armstrong, is told by a policeman, "Well, Denham, the airplanes got him."

"Oh, no, it wasn't the planes," Denham says sadly. "'Twas beauty killed the beast."

That poignant line said it all in a way even the most pragmatic viewer couldn't ignore: it was sad to see Kong die.

There are literally hundreds of films about World War II with some aviation sequences in them. This book won't attempt to detail them all, but a few deserve mention, if for no other reason than they are favorites of the author.

The U.S. Navy provided several Curtiss O2C-2 Helldivers for the takeoff scene in *King Kong. Courtesy* The Hook *Magazine*

Humphrey Bogart starred in the excellent *Action in the North Atlantic* (1943), directed by Lloyd Bacon. Canadian Raymond Massey and Bogart are officers of a lone Liberty Ship pitted against a relentless U-Boat.

S.S. Seawitch was cut off from a convoy to Murmansk. The crew, which features such colorful character actors as Alan Hale and Dane Clark, fight to draw the sub away from the convoy. The Germans send a pair of seaplanes from Norway to find the rogue ship. The planes are Henkel He-59 biplanes each carrying a pilot and observer/gunner. Actual aircraft—possibly pre-war footage from the Luftwaffe or Finnish Navy—were used for the takeoff scenes. The miniatures had a wingspan of nearly six feet, and the attack was done with back projection on Stage 5 at Warner Bros. studios.

While *Action* is one of the best war movies ever made, the attack footage doesn't quite work. The models are shown doing formation maneuvers very slowly in order to keep them in the frame. But the final crash on the deck of *Seawitch* is spectacular. At the very close of the film, while the battered ship approaches the friendly port of Murmansk, a Soviet Hawker

Hurricane flies over. The pilot radios he has found an "Amerikantski freighter!" Then he guns his engine in a repeating pattern of three shorts and a long. This is Morse Code for "V for Victory." While long forgotten, it would have been very familiar to movie audiences of the war years.

Two He-50 Heinkel floatplane miniatures were built for the attack on the *SS Seawitch* in *Action in the North Atlantic.*

Sink the Bismarck! (1960) was based on the 1958 C.S. Forester bestseller *The Last Nine Days of the Bismarck.* With the help of veteran CBS radio reporter Edward R. Murrow in a series of explanatory links, the film follows the Royal Navy's desperate hunt for Germany's largest and most dangerous battleship in May 1941. *Bismarck* was directed by Lewis Gilbert, who also directed *Reach for the Sky* with Kenneth More. *Bismarck* was filmed both in the studio (using carefully detailed miniatures of ships and planes) and on location. The models were made by the masters of motion picture miniatures the Lydecker Brothers and filmed using spherical lenses to provide a "perspective and depth" effect. Location filming was done aboard some of the Royal Navy's last World War II warships. In fact, prewar training footage came from the 15" gun turrets on the battleships *HMS King George V* and the ill-fated *HMS Hood*. The latter was sunk in the Denmark Strait by the *Bismarck*.

The aircraft carrier *HMS Victorious* appeared in the film as herself and *HMS Ark Royal*. In 1960 *Victorious* had already been refitted with an angled flight deck but some of the interior shots were done on board as well as on *HMS Centaur*, another carrier. Three restored Fairey Swordfish torpedo biplanes were used in the film. The Swordfish, while appearing far less formidable than the Kates and Avengers of the Pacific war, were superb planes that destroyed and heavily damaged three Italian capital ships at Taranto in November 1940. They carried three men, a 1,600 lb. torpedo, and saw service until the end of the war.

The studio footage using full-scale mockups and actors with back projection are very realistic. Combined with footage of miniatures of aircraft and ships the cinematography was excellent for 1960. No Swordfish were lost in the attacks on the *Bismarck*, despite the film's assertion of three being shot down.

Unlike *Midway*, *Sink the Bismarck!* is an excellent example of how a semi-documentary film about a huge naval engagement can be done well, telling the story objectively, and still maintain a fictional subplot. And nowhere in the film, as in *Midway* (1976), is there a subtitle with the name of a ship, informing the audience what a good script would have told them.

Darryl F. Zanuck committed Fox to producing the biggest and most extravagant war movie ever made in 1962 with *The Longest Day*, based on Cornelius Ryan's bestseller. The big-budget epic of the Normandy Invasion has been the subject of many books, articles and documentaries, but here it will be just about the aviation sequences.

While most viewers recall the token appearance of two Luftwaffe fighters strafing Sword Beach during the landings, there were some stunning nighttime scenes of British gliders approaching the Orne River. The glider landing near Oistreham depicted the British 6th Airborne Division's Oxfordshire & Buckinghamshire Light Infantry's assault on Pegasus Bridge.

Richard Todd, who had played Wing Commander Guy Gibson in *The Dam Busters* in 1955, played the role of Major John Howard. Todd himself had been in the 6th Airborne and fought at Normandy. The British Horsa gliders are shown at night and first seen as silent black shapes towed by Avro Lancaster bombers. Then the shot cuts to the flight deck of a Horsa. The towing plane veers off. The camera frame is fixed with the glider, so every movement of the control column by the pilots result in the glider banking against the back projection. The audience, seeing the pilots turning the wheel almost reflexively, leans into the turn. It's very easy to believe the footage is real, right up to the almost-silent approach and violent, noisy landing.

Avro Lancasters tow the Airspeed Horsa gliders carrying the British 6th Airborne in *The Longest Day.*

Battle of Britain veteran Colonel Josef "Pips" Priller, played by the ebullient Heinz Reinke, leads his wingman in a strafing run along Sword Beach to attack the British 3rd Division. The planes are Messerschmitt Bf-108 Taifun monoplanes owned by the Spanish Air Force. Priller and his wingman, Heinz Wozardczyk, actually flew Focke-Wulf Fw-190s but in 1962they were even rarer than 109s. The strafing footage was done from a camera ship while long rows of squibs buried in the sand were detonated in sequence. The mass of troops running from the approaching fighters stretches for nearly half a mile and is extremely effective. Exploding trucks and gas fires erupt as the plane flies over. Priller then laughs that the "Luftwaffe has had its day."

1977's *A Bridge Too Far*, also based on a Cornelius Ryan book, makes extensive use of Douglas C-47 and C-53 aircraft in the early scenes. The movie tells a somewhat slanted view of Operation Market Garden, the Allied attempt to capture key bridges over the Rhine River and enter Germany in September 1944. Directed by Richard Attenborough, the star-studded cast included seven Oscar winners.

The aircraft used in the parachute scenes were a mix of DC-3s, C-47s and C-53s from French Somaliland, the Finnish Air Force and Portuguese Air Force. During September 1976, the planes dropped a total of 1,000 men—the largest airborne operation since the war. Ten Horsa gliders were built but a storm wrecked most of them. Eight were repaired. Careful camera placement kept the non-authentic tail supports out of view. While they were towed by a C-47 at high speed none were allowed to actually take off. The Royal Netherlands Air Force provided four AT-6 Texan/Harvards to be used as German fighters. Two Piper Aztecs mounted with several cameras captured the aerial footage.

Ed Pepping, a member of the famed Easy Company of the 506th Parachute Infantry Regiment of the 101st Airborne, had some praise for *A Bridge Too Far's* technical accuracy. "When you see the planes lining up for takeoff in the movie, that's what it looked like," he said. Pepping, a medic who jumped into Normandy on D-Day and later into Holland for Operation Market Garden, added, "That's how huge an operation it was. They got it just right." Pepping went on to say he was impressed by the appearance of the movie's airborne footage if not the acting and plot.

HBO's Emmy Award-winning miniseries *Band of Brothers* (2001) was based on Stephen Ambrose's best-selling book. While only short sequences in the first two episodes depict aerial operations, the cinematography and flying are unforgettable. Several C-47s and C-53s were obtained from various European and American sources. The aircraft were painted with the bold black and white Invasion stripes on wings and fuselage. The stripes on the planes appear sloppy and crude, which is exactly how it was done in 1944. Since thousands of fighters, bombers, transports and gliders had to be painted, only cursory care was taken to make the stripes neat and clear.

A Douglas C-53 Skytrooper carries the men of Easy Company, 503rd Parachute Infantry Regiment into history on the evening of June 5, 1944. Several vintage C-47s and C-53s were obtained from around Europe to participate in the filming of HBO's *Band of Brothers*.

With Michael Kamen's evocative score accompanying the loading scenes on the evening of June 5, it is easy for the viewer to become mesmerized by the scope of the event. The takeoff and assembly footage was given greater impact by the use of CGI and miniatures but it's hard to tell where.

HBO took great pains to assure technical accuracy, but a few minor concessions were made for the production. Instead of the normal 24 to 28 paratroopers normally carried in the C-53 Skytroopers, only twelve are seen in each aircraft. This may have been to keep from "crowding" the shot. The interior of a C-53 permitted little elbow room when fully loaded. Having flown in the last surviving Normandy C-53D, Inland Empire CAF's *D-Day Doll*, the author can say the sound effects of the shaking planes on takeoff and in flight fully convey what it was like on the way to Normandy. Ed Pepping agrees. "*Band of Brothers* was incredible."

Regarding the shots where the troopers climb into the planes, Pepping had this to say: "In my case I weighed 178 pounds, but that night my total was 305. It took four guys to get me into that plane. At the other end all I had to do was fall out," he laughed. "I remembered all my own experiences as I watched them climb into the planes and settle in. And the noise! It just hammered on your ears for hours. You could hardly hear anything and had to watch for hand signals."

All of the nighttime scenes over Carentan were done with miniatures and CGI to great effect. Pepping said the feeling of the plane shaking while flak burst outside was scary. "It was in every color," he recalled. "But you never heard anything of the bursts. The engine noise was too loud."

Steven Spielberg—in his quest for stories with powerful and poignant subjects—directed *Empire of the Sun* in 1987. Based on the autobiographical novel by J. G. Ballard, the film follows the life of young Jamie "Jim" Graham, a British diplomat's son left behind as the Japanese capture Shanghai in 1937. Jim is an impulsive and spoiled boy who is fascinated by the people who have imprisoned him and torn apart his family. He is also crazy about airplanes.

Early in the film Jim discovers the wreck of a Zero that was shot down during the fighting. He climbs in and, in the manner of all boys, pretends to be the pilot. The Zero is an AT-6 Texan conversion.

Near the end of the war, while in a prison camp near a Japanese airbase, Jim watches as a group of Kamikaze pilots drink their sake before flying off on their last mission. Jim is no longer enamored of the once-mythical Japanese and sees their weaknesses. One of the Zeros takes off into the sunset while Jim watches, wide-eyed. Suddenly the plane explodes into a ball of fire and falls to the ground. Jim is stunned, and a second later a sleek P-51 Mustang streaks past. Jim cheers, runs up to the roof of an abandoned hotel and sees the Mustang soaring by. The pilot salutes Jim, who has heard of the fighter from an American captive. He yells, "Whoa! P-51! Cadillac of the skies!"

Jim is released from the camp when the Japanese leave the area. While on the Chinese coast he stares out to sea one morning and witnesses the distant August 9, 1945, atomic blast at Nagasaki.

While the film is hardly an aviation movie, Jim's fascination for airplanes appeals to the audience. The B-29 that flies over Jim is a radio-controlled model with an 18-foot wingspan, fully operational landing gear, flaps and bomb bay doors. Six of the Mustangs and six Zeros in the final aerial battle are also radio-controlled models with 12-foot wingspans. They were built by Model Effects.

A rare Junkers Ju-52 twin-engine transport owned by the Swiss Air Force appeared in the opening sequence of *Where Eagles Dare* (1968) with Clint Eastwood, as Hitler's transport in the television production *Inside the Third Reich* (1982) with Rutger Hauer, and possibly at the end of Mel Brooks' 1983 remake of *To Be or Not To Be*.

In 1964, during the peak of the Cold War and the early years of the anti-war movement, Sidney Lumet directed *Fail Safe*. The film was the next in a series to showcase the horror of nuclear war after Nevil Shute's *On the Beach* (1959). Lumet, a master of monochrome filmmaking with 1957's *Twelve Angry Men*, made *Fail Safe* into a starkly raw drama. A technical glitch causes a bomb group to mistakenly attack targets in the Soviet Union. While very different from Kubrick's *Dr. Strangelove* the film was released at a time when Americans were just coming to grips with what nuclear war could mean.

Only a few minor aviation sequences are seen in *Fail Safe*: stock shots of a night takeoff and several curiously grainy images of Convair B-58 Hustler supersonic bombers in flight. In the short aerial sequences, the Hustlers—called "Vindicators" in the film—are seen in negative, appearing as white shapes on a dark sky. For a film that shines in nearly every technical field the images of the B-58 are almost clumsy. Other planes appear, such as the Lockheed F-104 Starfigther, Convair F-102 Delta Dagger and a Korean War-era Grumman F9F Cougar.

The 'Vindicator' bombers in *Fail Safe* were Convair B-58 Hustlers prior to their entering service with the United States Air Force.

Retired Chief Master Sgt. Al Buckles was a USAF nuclear technician in SAC's command center during the 1960s. In an interview for this book he said, "Lumet had to get file film from Convair. The Air Force wouldn't provide any. We didn't go operational with the B-58 until 1963. The cockpit shots are not B-58 interiors." Convair provided footage of flight tests of the new plane for the film with the proviso that the shots would be altered for the film. This is most obvious when the fighters are sent to shoot down the bombers. The USAF insignia is seen as a black star on a white circle. The jets appear as white shapes on a dark background.

Fail Safe isn't remembered for its aviation footage but for its reputation as a highly controversial film about accidental nuclear war.

George Clooney produced and starred in a 2000 television remake. The live broadcast was hosted by Walter Cronkite. It retained some of Eugene Burdick's original novel and utilized 1960s-era technology.

Al Buckles was a military advisor on the television version. "George Clooney got me to be the advisor," Buckles said. "Steven Frears, the director, took me aside and said, 'Now you own the red flag. You see anything you don't like or doesn't look right you throw the flag and we'll stop. You gotta make sure we know how it was done.' They lived up to that." Buckles said he was fanatical about uniforms and insignia. "I had to go to a base exchange and buy all the right ribbons so the actors had them on right," he laughed.

The Lockheed SR-71 Blackbird, once a top-secret Cold War reconnaissance plane, played a small role in 1985's *D.A.R.Y.L.*, a whimsical family action film about a technical Pinocchio, a robot who escapes his makers to be come a real boy. Daryl, played by future *Cocoon* star Barrett Oliver, steals the SR-71 and flies it to freedom, along the way duping the dimwitted USAF generals and government thugs.

The Blackbird's appearance in the film uses only full-scale mockups and miniatures, plus some short takeoff and flyby footage. The plane breaks Mach 2 during its flight—but at low altitude, which would have been devastating to communities below. There are a number of technical errors involving fuel and instrumentation but they can be forgiven. It's not intended to be accurate, just fun.

Real Genius, released by Columbia TriStar in the same year, has a gang of superminds plotting to stop the Air Force from using an airborne laser for long-distance assassinations. In the 1980s government and military entities were fair game and often the target of action and comedy films. Val Kilmer, two years after his co-starring role as Iceman in *Top Gun*, leads a fellow genius onto an airbase to sabotage a Rockwell B-1B Lancer bomber. The laser is used to ignite a huge "Jiffy Pop" mass of popcorn inside the home of an arrogant posturing scientist who masterminds the government project. The B-1B Lancer footage is all in miniature with predictable weaknesses. But again it's fun to watch.

Close Encounters of the Third Kind (1977) has a memorable opening sequence when the scientific team, led by French director François Truffaut, finds five World War II-era Grumman TBM Avenger torpedo bombers in the Sonoran Desert. Without going into the details of the plot, the planes have been "returned" by aliens as a goodwill gesture to Earth.

The Avengers of Flight 19 disappeared in December 1945 during a training flight out of NAS Fort Lauderdale, Florida. The vanishing of five planes and fourteen Navy crewmen was one of the most notorious events involving the Bermuda Triangle. For decades the mystery remained unsolved—that is, until Steven Spielberg "solved" it in his film. For the scene Spielberg was able to assemble four Avengers from various collections and private owners. A Grumman F6F Hellcat fighter was also used, which from a distance in a dust storm superficially resembles an Avenger.

One of the Martin-built Grumman Avenger torpedo planes seen in *Close Encounters of the Third Kind* is part of the collection of the Rocky Mountain Wing of the CAF. *Courtesy Rocky Mountain Wing*

Steve Hinton worked on *Close Encounters* as a pilot, although he did little flying in the film. "Ed Moloney, who was president of Planes of Fame at the time, helped to find the planes," recalled Hinton. "One came from Texas, one was from Chino, one was owned by Connie Edwards." Another TBM was operated by the CAF's Rocky Mountain Wing in Grand Junction, Colorado. Hinton appears, after a fashion, in the film: "My job was to start the engine and help coordinate the people who were running around trying to identify the planes. That's my hand you see tapping the instruments and flipping switches," Hinton said with a chuckle.

That sequence was filmed at El Mirage Dry Lake in California. "We had no idea what the movie was all about," Hinton explained. "We knew it had something to do with UFOs, but that was it. Spielberg was already famous for *Jaws*, and we thought it was really cool to be working with him."

When a team member says they want "the numbers off the engine blocks," it sounds good but a military aircraft often went through several engines while in service. It would not have been logical to determine the planes' authenticity in this manner. There would have been permanent numbers on a plate in the cockpit. The Avengers only appear for a few minutes but the audience is already hooked into the tantalizing mystery, which is only resolved at the end of the movie when the crews are released from the alien mother ship near Devil's Tower, Wyoming.

In 1980 Fox released the action comedy *The Stunt Man*, starring the multi-talented Peter O'Toole. The legendary Irish-born O'Toole plays Eli Cross, a temperamental film director working on a film when he suddenly finds himself in need of a stunt man. Steve Railsback, who recently completed the role of Charles Manson in the TV version of *Helter Skelter* in 1976, was cast as Cameron, a fugitive looking for a place to hide out. He stumbles on Cross' movie and joins the crew as a stunt man. The film they are making is called *The Devil's Squadron* (not to be confused with the 1936 movie of the same name).

The production was partially filmed on location at the historic Hotel del Coronado in San Diego, California, the site of many other classics such as *Some Like it Hot* (1959). The hotel's distinctive conical ballroom roof and other structures provide the setting for the aerial stunt work. The film is interesting with its view of a motion picture production. The first unit films the second unit filming the action.

Zona Appleby commented about her husband's work on the film: "Jim flew a replica Nieuport 28 and a Tiger Moth. There was one shot where they wanted Jim to fly close to the roof of the hotel and Jim refused to do it. He told them, 'You're not paying me enough to risk my livelihood to do that shot.' Chuck Bail did the stunt. That was a very scary thing that close to the hotel."

In that scene, one of Hollywood's leading stunt men, A.J. Bakunas, jumps from the cupola railing of the hotel ballroom roof and flip over to slide down the long 100-foot slope. He actually broke his leg, according to Chuck Bail on the DVD commentary.

When the Tiger Moth at and over the camera the fake cupola explodes. It's no wonder Appleby wasn't keen on the idea.

Zona related that one shot was to be done at Black's Beach, a secluded nude beach near La Jolla. "It took quite a while to get approval from the FAA to fly the Nieuport 28 at Black's Beach because it was a nudist beach," she said. "Jim said, 'I gotta go and check out the beach.' I asked him, 'Why? You're not gonna land there.' He said to me, 'But I might have to!'"

Waldo Pepper veteran John Kazian worked on *The Stunt Man*. When the author talked to Kazian, he had a great deal to say about the film and working with Appleby. "One day Jim was flying the Tiger Moth and there was a guy on the ground with a radio who was calling Jim in," said Kazian. "Every pass Jim made was closer and closer to the camera, but the guy wanted him in closer. He didn't know his butt from Beijing about airplanes. He kept telling Jim to move lower."

Appleby was unable to see where his wheels were and was getting nervous about how close he was getting to the cameraman. "Jim hit the camera and the guy landed on his butt and dislocated his shoulder," Kazian said. "Anyhow, Jim is circling. I took the radio from this guy and he says, 'Hey, I'm talking to him.' I said, 'No you're not, I am.'

Then I said into the radio, 'Jim, this is Johnny. Nobody is hurt badly, don't worry about it.' He was really worried but I said, 'Do me a favor. Give me a very slow fly-by so I can look you over.'" Appleby brought the plane down low and let Kazian examine his undercarriage. "Sure enough," Kazian recalled, "his right wheel was tweaked way out; it was pointing enough so he ain't gonna land on it. I told Jim that when he comes in to favor that left side, keep the right wheel off the ground as long as he can. I told him not to drop that wheel until he absolutely had to, even if he had to drag the wingtip. And you know, he did great. He came in on that left wheel and when he finally touched the right wheel the plane just twisted about three-quarters of the way around."

Appleby wanted to know about the cameraman. "He told Jim, 'Hell, when I could read the writing on your tires I got the hell away from the camera!'"

Kazian said he'd been insistent about having someone on the ground who knew how to direct a plane. "In the scene where we're up in the air and a guy is doing a jig on the wing, that's supposed to be Steve Railsback," Kazian said. "At 4,000 feet up it's me dancing on the plane."

The aerial footage for that sequence was done in the rain, according to the DVD commentary.

"For Steve they actually put a tail on a big 55-gallon drum painted to look like the plane," said Kazian. "And they had a wind fan blowing on him, a grip is rocking it back and forth, the pilot is singing 'How Ya Gonna Keep 'Em Down on the Farm When They've Seen Paree.' He's on that drum."

George Roy Hill finally got his chance to film a plane crashing into a house in 1982 during the making of *The World According to Garp*. There are only a few brief flying shots in the film, but the stunt crash bears mention. The plane flown by Jim Appleby is an Aeronca Model 7 Champ.

Zona Appleby commented on the stunt crash: "The house was built on a grassy area near the runway at Lincoln Park in New Jersey. The square blue vent on the side of the roof was his aiming point." Appleby practiced for weeks to perfect the stunt. "The whole inside of the fake house was a huge cargo net," said Zona. "Jim was adamant that it had to be made of a certain material so he wouldn't split the nut, or it wouldn't spring back and throw him right back outside the hole in the house. On the morning of the stunt visibility was too low to permit flying. But Jim convinced the local FAA officials that he would only be up about thirty feet."

Robin Williams was on location and in awe of what Appleby was about to do. "Jim had a full helmet on," said Zona, "and the air was so cold he had to use a small hair dryer to blow warm air under the faceplate to keep the condensation down."

The film grips asked Appleby, "How are you going to soften your landing?" Appleby, with his usual humor said, "Well, I'm going to hire Dolly Parton to sit on the net so I'll have a soft landing."

"Dolly was his girl," Zona said with a laugh.

The film crew gave Appleby the next best thing: "They took a *Playboy* centerfold and pinned it to the center of the net," Zona said. "And you know, when Jim hit that thing, the propeller hub went right through the middle." Zona admitted she still has that centerfold. "The wings were supposed to break off," she said, "but all they did was fold back. Jim had no egress when he tried to get out the door of the plane." George Roy Hill is the pilot who emerges from the wreck and asks to use the phone. He finally got the crash he'd wanted.

Jim Appleby flying the Aeronca Champ into the house *in The World According to Garp*, directed by George Roy Hill. Appleby was aiming at a Playboy centerfold in the center of a cargo net. He hit the playmate's belly with his propeller hub.

One of the most successful action films of 1996 was *Independence Day*, a thinly disguised remake of 1953s *War of the Worlds. ID4*, as it was known in the pre-release publicity, had a remorseless and totally unstoppable alien fleet systematically destroying human civilization. Only a determined effort by a Marine Corps aviator and a computer whiz are able to defeat the invading alien armada.

Several aerial sequences using F/A-18 Hornet fighters from El Toro and other bases were used in the film, which required a then unheard-of 3,000 visual effects. The Hornets were the "Black Knights" of VMFA-314, and they appear in both ground and flying shots. But the bulk of the battle scenes are done with miniatures in the studio.

A later battle—which presumably includes the last remnants of every squadron in the country—takes on the giant flying saucer about to destroy the Area 51 command base in the desert. Apparently only Hornets are left. A ragtag band of pilots and veterans brave the green alien death as they attack and destroy the huge invader.

The miniature and CGI effects are startling and incredibly dynamic. Over 3,900 Hornets were seen in the film, along with a like number of alien craft.

Incidentally, the resemblance to War of the Worlds is very clear. Both films used a Flying Wing bomber to hit the aliens with a nuclear weapon to no avail, and in both cases the aliens were finally defeated by a virus—in *ID4's* case, a computer virus.

With this big-budget retelling of *War of the Worlds*, this chapter concludes. And with the 2012 release of George Lucas' *Red Tails*, so does the century of aviation films covered in this book.

It has been a wild, fun and sometimes incredible 100 years. From those first shaky, grainy images of Mabel Normand in *A Dash Through the Clouds* in 1912, film and flying have reached heights no one in the age of *Wings* or *Those Magnificent Men in their Flying Machines*, *Strategic Air Command* or *The Dam Busters* could ever have dreamed.

While quality has certainly been sacrificed on the altar of box-office draw, this has been the trend ever since the first films appeared. Moviemaking is a business, and so is flying. No one can blame the studios for giving the audiences what they want. And if the audience wants more explosions and thrills, and less depth or substance, then Hollywood will deliver.

However, there will always be those—the author among them—who yearn for the days when real pilots flew real planes in front of real cameras to get the shots the directors wanted.

At least we have the films they created.

§

BIBLIOGRAPHY

BOOKS

Ault, P. (1978) *By the Seat of Their Paits – The Story of Early Aviation*
New York, Mead

Bartlett, D. (1979) *Empire: the Life, Legend, and Madness of Howard Hughes*
New York, W. W. Norton

Baxter, J. (1997). *Steven Spielberg; The Unauthorized Biogrphy*
London, Harper Collins

Baxter, J.(1997). *Stanley Kubrick: a Biography*
Emeryville, Carroll & Graf ed.

Berg, A.(1989). *Goldwyn: A Biography*
New York, Random House

Berg, A. (1998). *Lindberth*
New York, G.P. Putnam's Sons

Borgnine, E.(2008). *Ernie: An Autobiography*
New York, Citadel Press

Brickhill, P (1951) *The Dam Busters*
New York, W.W. Norton

Past Imperfect: History According to the Movies (1995)
Carnes, M. Ed.
New York, Henry Holt & co.

Chiles, J. (2007) *The God Machine – From Boomerangs to Black hawks: the Story of the Helicopter*
New York, Bantam Book

Davidson, B. (1988) *Spencer Tracy: Tragic Idol*
New York, Dutton

Davis, R.(1998). *Duke: The life and Image of John Wayne*
Norman, University of Oklahoma Press

Davis, R. (2001) *Van Johnson, MGM's Golden Boy*
University Press of Mississippi

Dwiggins, D. (1967) *Hollywood Stunt Pilot The Biography of Paul Mantz*
Camden, Doubleday

Dwiggins, D. (1968) *The Barnsormers – Flying Daredevils of the Roaring Twenties*
New York, Grosset & Dunlap

Eyman, S.(2005). *Lion of Hollywood: The Life and Legend of Louis B. Mayer*
New York, Simon & Schuster

Eyman, S. (1999) *Print the Legend – the Life and Times of John Ford*
New York, Simon & Schuster

Farmer, J.(1984). *Celluloid Wings: the Impact of Movies on Aviation*
Blue Ridge Summit, Tab Books

Fishcall, G.(2003). *Gregory Peck: A Biography*
New York, Scribner

Freedland, M.(2008). *Gregory Peck A Biography*
New York, W. Morrow

Greenwood, J. (1982) *Stunt Flying in the Movies*
Blue Ridge Summit, Tab Books

Harris, W. (2002). *Clark Gable: a Bigraphy*
New York, Harmony Books

Higham, C. (1980) *Errol Flynn: the Untold Story*
Garden City, Doubleday

Jourdan, D. (2010) *The Deep Sea Search for Amelia Earhart*
Cape Porpoise, ME, Ocellus Productions

Kramer, S.(1997). A Mad, *Mad, Mad, Mad World: a Life in Hollywood*
New York, Harcourt Brace

Linet, B. (1979) *Lad, the Life, the Legend, the Legacy of Alan Ladd*
New York, Arbor House

Louvish, S. (2004) *Keystone - The Life and Clowns of Mack Sennett*
New York, Faber and Fabeer, Inc.

Louvish, S. (2002) *Stan and Ollle: the Roots of Comedy - the Double Life of Laurel and Hardy*
New York, St. Martin's Press

Massey, R. (1979) *A Hundred Different Lives - an autobiography*
Boston, Little, Brown

McCabe, J. (1997) *Cagney*
New York, Random House

Meyers, J.(2008). *Gary Cooper: An American Hero*
New York, Morrow

Nelson, C. (2002) *The First Heroes: the extraordinary story of the Doolittle Raid-- America's first World War II victory*
New York, Viking

O'Brien, P. (1964) *The Wind at My Back – the Life and Times of Pat O'Brien*
Garden City N.Y, Doubleday

Orriss, B.W.(1984). *When Hollywood Ruled the Skies: The Aviation Classics of World War II*
Hawthorne, Aero Assoc.

Perret, G. (1993) Winged Victory – The Army Air Forces in World War II
New York, N.Y. Random House

Pettigrew, T. (1981) *Bogart – A Definitive Study of his Film Career*
New York, Proteus

Pickard, R.(1992). *Jimmy Stewart: A Life in Film*
New York, St. Martin's Press

Pisanos, S. (2008) *The Flying Greek*
Dulles. Virginia, Potomac Books

Roberton, J. (1993) *The Casablanca Man: The cinema of Michaal Curtiz*
New York, Routledge

Rooney, M. (1991) *Life is Too Short*
New York, Villard

Sikov, E. (2002) *Mr. Strangelove, A Biography of Peter Sellers*
New York, Hyperion

Schickel, R. (2006) *Bogie: A Celebration of the Life and Films of Humphrey Bogart*
New York. St. Martin's Press

Skogsberg, B. (1981) *Wings on the Screen: A Pictorial History*
La Jolla, A.S. Barnes & Company, Inc.

Smith, S.(2005). *Jimmy Stewart, Bomber Pilot*
Osceola, Zenith Press

Steen, M. (1974) Holllywood Speaks! An Oral History
New York, G.P. Putnam's Sons

Stout, J. (2010) *The Men Who Killed the Luftwaffe*
Menchanicsburg, Stackpole Books

Swintell, L.(1980). *The Last Hero: a Biography of Gary Cooper*
New York, 1st Edition, Garden City

Thomas, B. (1983) *Golden Boy" the Untold Story of William Holden*
New York, St. Martin's Press

Thompson, F. (1986). *Lost Films*
Secaucus, N.J. Carol Publishing Group

Thompson, F. (1983). *William A. Wellman*
Metuchen, N.J. Scarecrow Press

Warren, D.(1983) *James Cagney: The Authorized Biography*
New York, St. Martin's Press

Wellman, W. Jr. (2006*) The Man and His Wings*
Westport, CT, Praeger

Wood, D. (1975) *The Narrow Margin:* The *Battle fo Britain and the Rise of air Power*
Westport, CT Greenwood Peess

Wynne, H.(1987.) *The Motion Picture Stunt Pilots - And Hollywood's Classic Aviation Movies*
Missoula, Pictorial Histories Publishing

Yeager, C. & Janos, L.(1986). *Yeager: An Autobiography*
New York, Bantam First

PERIODICALS

Bowman, M. (1994) Dam Busters
Air Classics Vol. 30 No. 2 1994 54-75

Dwiggins, D. (1975) Paul Mantz: Kingpin of the Hollywood Air Force.
Air Classics Vol. 11. No. 12 1975 72-74

Farmer, J. (1998) The Aircraft of 'War and Rememberance.'
Air Classics Vol. 26, No. 11 1998 24-32

Farmer, J. (1994) Aviation Films we Love to Hate
Air Classics Vol. 30 No. 8 1994 14-32

Farmer, J. (1991) B-17: The Hollywood Legend.
Ari Classics Vol. 27, No.12 26-65

Farmer, J. (1988) Bomb 'em – A History of Hollywood's Bomber Moives.
Air Classics Vol. 24, No. 2 1988 60-71

Farmer, J. (1998) Empire of the Sun.
Air Classics Vol. 26, No. 1 1988 46-52

Farmer, J. (1983) Filming *The Right Stuff* (Part One).
Air Classics Vol. 19, No. 12 1983 46-81

Farmer, J. (1984) Filming *The Right Stuff* (part Two.
Air Classics Vol. 20, No. 1 1984 34-72

Farmer, J. (1989) Hollywood Goes to Edwards.
Air Classics Vol. 25, No. 8 1990 14-75

Farmer, J. (1998) Hollywood's World War One Films
Air Classics 2234Vol. 24, No. 12 1998 22-34

Farmer, J. (1989). Hollywood Goes to North Island, .
The Making of Great Aviation Movies Vol. 2, 1989 18-27

Farmer, J. (1989). Hollywood's World War One Aviation Films.
The Making of Great Aviation Movies Vol. 2, 1989 79-84

Farmer, J. (1990) The Making of *Air America.*
Air Classics Vol. 26, No. 10 1990 14-28

Farmer, J. (1990). The Making of *Always.*
Air Classics Vol. 26, No. 2 1990 24-67

Farmer, J. (1990) The Making of *Fighter Squadron.*
Air Classics Vol. 26, No. 5 1990 34-67

Farmer, J. (1990) Making of *Flight of the Intruder.*
Air Classics Vol. 26. No. 8 1990 30-75

Farmer, J. (1986) The Making of *The Iron Eagle.*
Air Classics Vol. 22, No. 2 1986 20-75

Farmer, J. (1990) The Making of *Memphis Belle.*
Air Classics Vol. 26, No. 11 1990 28-78

Farmer, J. (1990) The Making of *Thirty Seconds over Tokyo.*
Air Classics Vol. 26, No. 4 1990 14-26

Farmer, J. (1991) On Locaiotn: Santa Maria Airport
Air Classics Vol. 27, No. 10 1991 34-72

Farmer, J. (1989) *Test Pilot.*
Air Classics Vol. 25, No. 11 1989 20-28

Farmer, J. (1989) *Top Gun.*
The Making of Great Aviation Movies Vol. 2, 1989 36-39

Farmer, J. (1990) *Wings of the Navy.*
Air Classics Vol. 26, No. 9 1990 14-19

Farmer, J. (1991) You can't send a kid up in a crate like that!
Air Classics Vol. 27 No. 9 1991 1275

Kolchek, C. (1989). *The Hundenburg.*
The Making of Great Aviation Movies Vol. 2, 1989 28-35

O'Hara (1989). 633 Squadron.
The Making of Great Aviation Movies Vol. 2, 1989 85-88

O'Leary, M. (1986) Movie Birds.
Air Classics Vol. 26, No. 1 1986 24-29

O'Leary, M. (2001) *Pearl Harbor.*
Air Classics Vol. 37 No. 7 2001 48-71

Pockett, R. (1971) Cruse you, Red Baron!
Air Classics Vol. 8, No. 1 1971 16-21

Staff Writer, (1980) *Last Flight of Noah's Ark.*
Air Classics Vol. 16, No. 4 1980 56-59

Thompson, J. (2002) *Dark Blue World.*
Air Classics Vol. 38, No. 1 2002 12-31

Thompson, J. (1980) Hollywood Mitchells.
Air Classics Vol. 16, No. 9 1980 40-80

INDEX
of Films, Aircraft and Warships by Chapter

Chapter 1 The Silent Sky

A Dash Through the Clouds (1912)
    Wright Model B
Sky Pirate (1914)
    Wright Model B
Dizzy Heights and Daring Hearts (1915)
    Wright Model B
We Can't Have Everything (1918)
    Bleriot XI
The Great Air Robbery (1919)
    Curtiss JN-4D Jenny
Stranger Than Fiction (1921)
    JN-4C
The Grim Game (1919)
    JN-4D
The Eleventh Hour (1923)
    Standard J-1

The Woman with Four Faces (1923)
JN-4
The Sky Hawk (1924)
The Cloud Rider (1925)
JN-4, Standard J-1

Chapter 2 The Great War on the Screen

The Sky Raider (1925)
Harriot HD-1, Nieuport 12, Thomas-Morse Scout
Wings (1927)
Martin MB-2/3, Curtiss P-1 Hawk, Fokker D.VII, Thomas-Morse 2000, Boeing PW-3, SPAD VII
Legion of the Condemned (1928)
Airco DH-9A
Lilac Time (1928)
Waco 10
The Young Eagles (1930)
SPAD VII, Fokker D.VII, Waco 10, Travel Air 2000
The Sky Hawk (1929)
Travel Air 2000
Dawn Patrol/The Flight Commander (1930)
Pfalz D.VII, Thomas-Morse Scout, Travel Air Speedwing, Orenco D, Lincoln Nieuport 28
Hell's Angels (1930)
Sikorsky S-29, Fokker D.VII, Travel Air 2000/Fokker D.VII, reproduction
S.E.5a, Thomas-Morse S5C/Sopwith Camel, JN-4/Avro 504
The Last Flight (1931)
The Lost Squadron (1932)
The Eagle and the Hawk (1933)
Thomas-Morse S4C, Sopwith Camel, DH-4, DH-9, Waco ATO, Travel Air 2000
Ace of Aces (1933)
Fleet Model 2, Lincoln Nieuport 28, Travel Air 2000, Waco RNF
Dawn Patrol (1938)
Thomas-Morse Scout, Travel Air 2000/Wichita Fokker, reproduction S.E.5, Waco Model F

Lafayette Escadrille (1958)

Bleriot XI, Lincoln Nieuport 28, Reproduction SPAD VII

The Blue Max (1966)

Reproduction Pfalz D.III, Fokker D.VII, Fokker Dr.I, 3/4 scale S.E.5a, 1930 Morane-Saulnier 230/'Adler,' Cauldron Luciole

von Richthofen and Brown (1971)

Reproduction Fokker D.VII, Dr.I, S.E.5a,

Aces High (1976)

Stampe SV4/SE.5a and Fokker D.VII

Flyboys (2006)

CGI and reproduction Nieuport 17, Fokker Dr.I

Chapter 3 The Golden Age 1927 - 1939

The Air Mail (1925)

Catron & Fisk C-10 Triplane

Air Mail (1932)

Boeing M-3, Fairchild KR-21, Ford 4-AT Trimotor, Travel Air 16K

Central Airport (1933)

4-AT Trimotor, Pitcairn PA-5 (with floats), Stearman

Ceiling Zero (1936)

Northrop Gamma

Test Pilot (1938)

Seversky P-35/SEV-S2, Fairchild 24, Ryan STA, DC-3, PBY Catalina, Marcoux-Bromberg Special, Grumman F2F, A-17 Nomad, YB-17, Boeing 247, Harlow PJC, B-18 Bolo

Men With Wings (1938)

SPAD VII, Lincoln-Flagg LF-1 Nieuport 28, JN-4, Travel Air/Fokker D.VII, Lockheed Vega, Boeing 247, P-12

Only Angels Have Wings (1939)

Fokker F-10 (Ford Trimotor)

The Wings of Eagles (1957)

Curtiss Falcon/Helldiver, Douglas World Cruiser, F4U Corsair, *USS Bennington* (CVA-20)

Chapter 4 This is Your Life, Hollywood Style: Biographies

The Wright Brothers (1997)

Reproduction Wright Glider, 1903 Flyer, Model B

Gallant Journey (1946)

Reproduction Montgomery gliders

Court-Martial of Billy Mitchell (1955)

DH-4, JN-4D

The Spirit of St. Louis (1957)

JN-4D, Ryan NYP, Standard J-1

Flight for Freedom (1943)

Beechcraft 18

Amelia Earhart: The Final Flight (1994)

Beechcraft 18

Amelia (2009)

Reproduction Fokker F.VIIb, Vega, Lockheed Electra 12, 4-AT Trimotor

The Flying Irishman (1939)

JN-4, Ryan M2, Curtiss C-3 Robin

The Aviator (2004)

Reproduction/Radio control XF-11, H-1 Hercules

Reach for the Sky (1956)

Spitfire, Hurricane, Me-109 (model)

Chapter 5 The Approaching Storm

The Flying Fleet (1929)

Boeing F2B-1, Douglas T2B-1, Consolidated NY-2, *USS Langley* (CV-1)

Flight (1930)

Curtiss OSC-2

Hell Divers (1931)

F8C-4 Falcon, *USS Saratoga* (CV-3) *USS Los Angeles* (LZ-126/ZR-3)

Devil Dogs of the Air (1935)

Vought OCU Corsair, Loening OL-8, Boeing F-4B/P-12, Travel Air D-4000, Ford 4-AT Trimotor, Douglas Dolphin, RC-1 Kingbird

West Point of the Air (1935)

Reproduction Curtiss A-1 Triad, Fokker D.VII, JN-4, Curtiss P-3, Consolidated PT-4 Trusty

Wings of the Navy (1939)

Grumman F3F, N2N, PBY-2 Catalina, SNJ, NS-1 Stearman

Flight Command (1940)

F3F-2, F4F-2, *USS Enterprise* (CV-6)

I Wanted Wings (1941)

AT-6, A-17 Nomad, YB-17, B-17B, BT-9, BT-II Yale

Dive Bomber (1941)

Miles Mohawk, SB2C Vindicator, Beechcraft 18, *USS Enterprise* (CV-6)

Captains of the Clouds (1942)

Lockheed Hudson, AT-6, Fairchild 71, Waco EGC-7 and AGC-8, Noorduyn Norseman, Avro Anson, Northrop Nomad

Thunder Birds/Soldiers of the Air (1941)

AT-6, AT-9, AT-11, BT-9, BT-13

Ladies Courageous (1944)

AT-6, P-51, C-47

Chapter 6 The War in the Air: Europe

Spitfire / The First of the Few (1942)

Spitfire MkV, Supermarine S5, S6 Racers

The Battle of Britain (1969)

CASA 2.111/He-111, HA 1112 Bouchon/Me-109, CASA 352/Ju-52, Percival Proctor/Stuka, Spitfire MkI, MkIIa, MkIX, Hurricane

A Yank in the RAF (1941)

Lockheed Hudson, Spitfire MkV, Me-109 (mockup)

International Squadron (1941)

Boeing 100, Brown B3. Hudson, Travel Air Mystery Ship, Ryan ST

Eagle Squadron (1942)

Spitfire (various Mk)

Twelve O'clock High (1949)

B-17F, P-47

Memphis Belle (1990)

B-17F/G, P-51D, HA 2111/Me-109

The War Lover (1962)

B-17F/G

Command Decision (1948)

B-17E/F

A Guy Named Joe (1943)

B-25D, P-38

Hannover Street (1979)

B-25H

The Dam Busters (1955)

Avro Lancaster, B-17F

633 Squadron (1964)

DH98 Mosquito

Mosquito Squadron (1969)

DH98 Mosquito

Fighter Squadron (1948)

P-47D, P-51B/Me-109, B-17G

The Tuskegee Airmen (1995)

AT-6/SNJ, P-51D, B-17G

Red Tails (2012)

P-40E, P-51B, P-51D,

Chapter 7 The War in the Air: The Pacific

Flying Tigers (1942)

Reproduction P-40C, Capelis XC-12

God is my Co-Pilot (1945)

Republic P-43 Lancer, P-40E/f, B-25C/D, AT-6/Zero

Air Force (1943)

B-17C/D, P-39D, P-40C, AT-6, P-43, B-26C

Tora! Tora! Tora! (1970)

AT-6/A6M Zero, AT-6/B5N Kate, BT-13/D3A Val, B-17G, PBY-5 Catalina, N2S Stearman, P-40E, *USS Yorktown* (CV-10)

Pearl Harbor (2001)

Spitfire, Hurricane, HA 2111 Bouchon/Me-109, P-40E, P-40N, AT-6/Zero, B-25

Thirty Seconds Over Tokyo (1944)

B-25D

Midway (1976)

B-25D, SBD, AT-6/Zero, SB2U Vindicator, PBY Catalina, F4F Wildcat, *USS Lexington* (CV-16)

Wing and a Prayer (1944)

TBM Avenger, SB2C Helldiver, F6F Hellcat, *USS Yorktown* (CV-10)

Task Force (1949)
Boeing 100, Curtiss F8C-2, F4F, TBD, SBD, *USS Bairoko/Langley*, *USS Antietam* (CV-35)
Aerial Gunner (1943)
AT-6, AT-11, B-34, BT-9
Bombardier (1943)
B-17E/F, B-18 Bolo, AT-16
Winged Victory (1944)
BT-13, B-24
Flat Top (1952)
F4U Corsair, *USS Princeton* (CVL-23)
Flying Leathernecks (1951)
F6F Hellcat, AT-6 Texan/Zero, F4U Corsair
High Barbareee (1947)
PBY Catalina, Ryan ST
The Beginning or the End (1947)
B-29
Above and Beyond (1952)
B-29
Enola Gay (1980)
B-29

Chapter 8 Drama and Disaster: The Airliner Films

China Clipper (1936)
Douglas Dolphin, M-130, Ford 4-AT Trimotor,
Five Came Back (1939)
Capelis XC-12
Daredevils in the Clouds (1948)
No Highway in the Sky (1951)
Handley-Page Hallon (Rutland Reindeer)
Island in the Sky (1953)
C-47 Skytrain
High and the Mighty (1954)
C-54, PB-IG/B-17
Fate is the Hunter (1964)
Boeing 707 (modified)

Zero Hour (1957)

The Crowded Sky (1960)

T-33 Shooting Star, DC-6

Airport 1975 (1974)

Boeing 747-123, CH-53 Super Stallion, Beechcraft

Airport '77 (1977)

Boeing 747, S-3 Viking

The Concorde: Airport 1979 (1979)

Aerospatiale /BAC Concorde SST

Starflight: the Plane that Couldn't Land(1983)

Chapter 9 Blowtorches on Film: The Jets Take Over

Chain Lightning (1950)

Bell P-39N/JA-3

Breaking the Sound Barrier (1952)

de Havilland Comet, Vampire, Supermarine Spitfire and Swift

Towards the Unknown (1956)

Bell X-2, B-36/C-131, XF-92, B-66, F-94A,F-100, X-3 Stiletto, Martin XB-51, McDonnell F-101 Voodoo, Douglas D-558-2 Skyrocket

Jet Pilot (1957)

F-80/T-33 Shooting Star/Yak-12, F-86 Sabre, Bell X-1, B-36C, F-89, Peacemaker

Bridges at Toko-Ri (1954),

F9F Panther, AD-4 Skyraider, Sikorsky H-5, *USS Oriskany* (CV-34)

Men of the Fighting Lady (1954)

F9F Panther, AD-4, *USS Oriskany* (CV-34)

Strategic Air Command (1955)

B-36 Peacemaker, B-47 Stratojet. C-97

Bombers B-52 (1957)

B-47, B-52

The McConnell Story (1955)

T-33/F-80, Republic F-84F, F-86

The Hunters (1958)

F-86, F-84/MiG-15

X-15 (1961)

North American X-15, F-104 Starfighter, F-100 Super Sabre

The Right Stuff (1983)

Mockup Bell X-1, A4 Skyhawk, T-33, F-104G

Flight of the Intruder (1991)

A6E Intruder, A7 Corsair, AD-4 Skyraider, AD-6, F4 Phantom, Cessna 337, *USS Independence* (CVN-62)

Chapter 10 Faster, Louder, More Money: The Action Films

The Final Countdown (1980)

F-14 Tomcat, CH-46 Sea King, AT-6 Texan/Zero, A6 Intruder, *USS Nimitz* (CVN-68)

Firefox (1982)

MiG-31 (model/mockup)

Iron Eagle (1986)

Cessna 150, F-16C Falcon, IAI Kfir

Top Gun (1986)

F-14 Tomcat, A4 Skyhawk, F-5 Tiger, CH-46 Sea King, *USS Enterprise* (CVN-65)

Iron Eagle II (1988)

McDonnell-Douglas F4 Phantom II/MiG

Aces: Iron Eagle III (1992)

P-51B/Me-109, P-38, P-51D, Rutan ARES, Spitfire Mk.XIV, AT-6/Zero

Iron Eagle IV: On the Attack (1995)

Air Force One (1997)

747-300, MC-130 Hercules, CGI F-15 Eagles and MiG-29 Fulcrum, KC-135

Chapter 11 Gasbags and Whirlybirds

Zeppelin (1971)

Dirigible (1931)

USS Los Angeles (LZ-126)

Here Comes the Navy (1934)

USS Macon (ZRS-5), *USS Arizona* (BB-35)

The Hindenburg (1971)

HA 2111/Me-109

This Man's Navy (1945)

1938 ZPK K-Class Blimp

*M*A*S*H* (1970)

Bell 47

Blue Thunder (1983)

Aerospatiale SA-34 Gazelle, Bell JetRanger, Hughes 500, F-16 (models)

Red Dawn (1984)

Aerospatiale 500 Puma

Chapter 12 Just for Fun: The Adventure Films

The Flight of The Phoenix (1965)

C-82 Packet

The Great Waldo Pepper (1975)

JN-4D, Gypsy Moth, Reproduction Fokker Triplane and Standard J-1
Reproduction Sopwith Camel

Capricorn One (1978)

Lear Jet, N2S Stearman, Hughes 500

Raiders of the Lost Ark (1981)

Waco UBF-2, Short Solent, Ford 5-AT

Indiana Jones and the Temple of Doom (1984)

Ford 4-AT Trimotor (mockup and models)

Indiana Jones and the Last Crusade (1999)

Stampe SV4, Pilatus P-3

Always (1989)

PBY-5 Super Catalina, A-26, Beechcraft 18, Fairchild C-119, Csesna 337, Citabria Decathlon

Forever Young (1992)

B-25H

The Rocketeer (1991)

Ryan ST, Monocoupe 90A, Curtiss Robin, Travel Air Mystery Ship, Standard J-1, Reproduction Gee Bee ZI, de Havilland Tiger Moth, Pitcairn Autogyro

The Flight of the Phoenix (2004)

Fairchild C-119

Chapter 13 A Funny Thing Happened tin the Air: Comedies

Now We're in the Air (1927)

Leftover *Wings* footage

Air Tight (1931)

Flying High (1931)

Pitcairn Autogyro

Flying Deuces (1939)

Keep 'em Flying (1941)

PT-13, AT-6, A-17

Gasbags (1941)

Clipped Wings (1953)

It's a Mad, Mad, Mad, Mad World (1963)

Beechcraft 18, Standard J-1

Dr. Strangelove, Or, How I Learned to Stop Worrying and Love the Bomb (1964)

B-52H (model)

The Great Race (1965)

Replica Curtiss Pusher

Those Magnificent Men in Their Flying Machines (1965)

1910 Bristol Boxkite, Levasseur 'Antoinette, IV' A.V. Roe IV Triplane, Santos-Dumont 'Demoselle,' Eardley Billing Tractor Biplane, Walton Edwards Rhomboidal, Lee Richards Annular Biplane, Passat Ornithoper, Picaut Dubrieul, 'Little Tiddler Canard,' Philips Multiplane'

Catch-22 (1970)

B-25

1941 (1979)

P-40E, Beechcraft 18, B-17G

Airplane! (1980)

The Three Amigos (1986)

Bücker Bu-131 Jungman

Chapter 14 On the Edge of Flight: Non-Aviation Films

King Kong (1933)

Curtiss OSC-2

Action in the North Atlantic (1943)

He-50 Seaplane

Sink the Bismarck (1960)

Fairey Swordfish

The Longest Day (1962)

A Bridge Too Far (1977)

C-47, Avro Lancaster, Horsa, Me-108 Taifun

Band of Brothers (2001)

Douglas C-47, C-53, B-26, P-51D

Empire of the Sun (1987)

AT-6/Zero, P-51D, B-29 (model)

Where Eagles Dare (1968)

CASA 352/Ju-52

Fail Safe (1964)

McDonnell F-101 Voodoo, Convair B-58 Hustler/'Vindicator,'
F-102 Delta Dagger, F-104 Starfighter

D.A.R.Y.L. (1985)

Lockheed SR-71 Blackbird

Real Genius (1985)

B-1B Lancer

Close Encounters of the Third Kind (1977)

Grumman TBF/M Avenger

The Stunt Man (1980)

The World According to Garp (1982)

Aeronca Model 7 Champ

Independence Day (1996)

INDEX
of Film Titles
Page numbers in italics denote images

12 Angry Men 345
1941 331-333, *332*
633 Squadron 130-131, *131*

Above and Beyond 185-188, *186, 187*
Ace of Aces 37
Aces High 49-50
Aces: Iron Eagle III 261-263, *262, 263, 264*
Action in the North Atlantic 339-340, *340*
Adventures of Robin Hood, The 134
Aerial Gunner 178-179
Air Force 151-154, *152*
Air Force One 264-266
Air Mail 54-55
Air Tight 315-316
Airplane! 200, 333-325, *324*
Airport '77 206
Airport 1975 57, 203-205, *205,* 333
Always 302-306, *302, 303, 304*
Amelia 74-77, *75, 7+6, 77*
Amelia Earhart: The Final Flight 73-74

Apocalypse Now! 276
Apollo 13 208
Aviator, The 80-83, *80, 81*
Band of Brothers 343-344
BAT 21 276
Battle of Britain, The 107-111, *107, 108, 109, 110, 111*
Beau Geste 10, 286
Beggars of Life 25
Beginning or the End, The 185, 187
Big Sleep, The 216
Blue Max, The 43-46, *44, 45, 47,* 49
Blue Thunder 250, 277-280, *277, 279*
Bombardier 179-180
Bombers B-52 229-230, *229, 230*
Boys in Company C, The 276
Breaking the Sound Barrier or The Sound Barrier 210-212, *211, 212*
Bride Came C.O.D, The 101
Bridge Too Far, A 342-343
Bridges at Toko-Ri 219-222, *219, 220, 221, 225*
Buck Privates 317

Call Northside 777 169
Capricorn One 294-297, *297*
Captains of the Clouds 99-102, *100, 101, 102*
Catch-22 329-331, *329, 330, 331*
Ceiling Zero 33, 56-57
Central Airport 55-56
Chain Lightning 209-210, 219
Charly 200
China Clipper 189-191, *190, 191*
Clipped Wings 317
Close Encounters of the Third Kind 346-348, *347*
Cloud Rider, The 11
Command Decision 123, *123,* 143
Concorde: Airport 1979, The 206-207
Court-Martial of Billy Mitchell, The 66-69, *67, 68, 69*
Crowded Sky, The 201-203, *202, 203*

D.A.R.Y.L. 346
Dam Busters, The 125-130, *126, 127, 128, 129,* 341

Daredevils in the Clouds 193
Dash Through the Clouds, A 1, *2*
Dawn Patrol (1938) 38-39, *38*, *39*, *43*, 55, 134, 182, 232
Dawn Patrol/The Flight Commander (1930) 33-35, *35*, 37, 182, 232
Devil Dogs of the Air 57, 91-93, *92*, *93*
Dirigible 268-269
Dive Bomber 96-99, *97*, *98*, *99*, 101
Dizzy Heights and Daring Hearts 2
Doctor Zhivago 212
Dr. Strangelove, Or, How I Learned to Stop Worrying and Love the Bomb 321-322, *322*, *323*

Eagle and the Hawk, The 36-37
Eagle Squadron 113-114
Eleventh Hour, The 10
Empire of the Sun 344-345
Enemy Below, The 230
Enola Gay 188
Exorcist, The 205

Fail Safe 345-346, *345*
Fate is the Hunter 199-200, 204
Father Goose 200
Fighter Squadron 134-139, *135*, *136*, *138*, 151, 181, 334
Final Countdown, The 162, 246-249, *247*, *248*, 253
Firefox 249-250, *249*, 257
Five Came Back 191-193, *193*
Flat Top 182
Flight 90
Flight Command 94-95
Flight for Freedom *72*, 73
Flight of the Intruder 239-243, *240*, *242*, *243* 281
Flight of The Phoenix (1965) 180, 283-287, *284*, *285*, *286*
Flight of the Phoenix, The (2004) 312-313
Flyboys 50-52, 83
Flying Deuces 8, 316
Flying Fleet, The 90
Flying High 316, *316* *Flying Irishman, The* 77-79, *79*
Flying Irishman, The 77-79, *79*

Flying Leathernecks 182-184, *183*
Flying Tigers 146-148, *146, 148,* 182, 193
Forced Landing 9
Forever Young 310-312, *306, 311*
Friendly Persuasion 66
From the Earth to the Moon 208
Full Metal Jacket 276

Gallant Journey 65-66, *66*
Gasbags 317
God is my Co-Pilot 148-151, *149, 150*
Goldfinger 328
Gone With the Wind 180
Great Air Robbery, The 6
Great Race, The 323-324 *Great Waldo Pepper, The* 287-294, *288, 289, 290, 291, 292,* 348
Grim Game, The 3, 9-10
Guy Named Joe, A 123-125, *124*

Hannover Street 125, 232
Have and Have Not, To 216
Hell Divers 90-91
Hell's Angels 27-33, *28, 29, 30, 32,* 35-36, 216, 219, 267
Helter Skelter 348
Here Comes the Navy 93, 269-270, *270*
High and the Mighty 197-199, *198,* 334
High Barbareee 184-185 *High Noon* 66
High Sierra 134
Hindenburg, The 180, 271-274, *273*
How the West Was Won 169
Hunters, The 232-233

In the Navy 317
I Wanted Wings 95-96, *96*
Independence Day 349-350
Indiana Jones and the Last Crusade 300-302, *301, 302*
Indiana Jones and the Temple of Doom 300
Inside the Third Reich 345
International Squadron 112-113
Iron Eagle 250-253, *251, 252*
Iron Eagle II 261
Iron Eagle IV: On the Attack
Island in the Sky 196-197, *196*

It's a Mad, Mad, Mad, Mad World 317-321, *318, 319, 320*

Jazz Singer, The 27
Jet Pilot 62, 216-219, *216, 217, 218*
Judgment at Nuremburg 317

Keep 'em Flying 316-317
King Kong 37, 113, 337-339, *338, 339*
Ladies Courageous 103-104
Lafayette Escadrille 40-42, *40, 41, 42,* 200
Last Flight, The 36
Lawrence of Arabia 212
Legion of the Condemned 22-25, *25*
Lifeboat 192
Lilac Time 25-26
Lilies of the Field 200
Longest Day, The 341-342, *342*
Lost Squadron, The 36

*M*A*S*H* 276
McConnell Story, The 230-231, *231, 232*
Memphis Belle 117-122, *118, 119, 121*
Men With Wings 8, 41, 59-62, *60, 61*
Midway 170-175, *171, 172, 173,* 224, 341
Mission: Impossible 335
Mosquito Squadron 131-134, *133*
Mutiny on the Bounty 62, 184

New York, I LoveYou 74
No Highway in the Sky 194-196, *194, 195*
Now We're in the Air 315

On the Beach 317, 345
Only Angels Have Wings 33, 62-63, *63*

Passage to India, A 212
Pearl Harbor 162-164
Petrified Forest, The 176, 191
Platoon 276
Poseidon Adventure, The 192
Pride of the Yankees, 178

Raiders of the Lost Ark 262, 297-299, *298, 299, 300*
Rambo 281

Reach for the Sky 83-86, *84, 85, 86, 87,* 110
Real Genius 346
Red Dawn 281, *281*
Red Tails 142-143
Right Stuff, The 234-239, *235, 236, 237, 238,* 257
Roaring Twenties, The 134
Rocketeer, The 306-310, 307, 309

Sergeant York 33
Sink the Bismarck 174, 340-341
Sky Devils 33
Sky Hawk, The 11, 33
Skywqyman, The 6
Sky Pirate 2
Sky Raider, The 17
Spirit of St. Louis, The 69-71, *70, 71*
Spitfire/The First of the Few 105-107, *106*
Starflight: the Plane that Couldn't Land 206-208
Star Trek 193, 198
Star Wars 125, 129, 143, 208, 280
Stranger Than Fiction 7
Strategic Air Command 224-229, *226, 227, 228*
Streets of San Francisco, The 229
Stunt Man, The 348-349

Task Force 175-178, *176, 177*
Test Pilot 8, 57-59, *58*
Ten Commandments, The 174
Thirty Seconds Over Tokyo 58, 164-167, *165, 168, 169*
This Man's Navy 274-276, *275*
Those Magnificent Men in Their Flying Machines 41, 47, 324-328, *325, 326, 327, 328*
Three Amigos, The 335-336, *336*
Thunder Birds/Soldiers of the Air 103, *103*
Titanic 120
To Be or Not To Be (1983) 345
Top Gun 253-260, *254, 256, 257, 258*
Tora! Tora! Tora! 154-162, *155, 157, 158, 159, 160, 161,* 249
Towards the Unknown 212-216 , *213, 214, 215*
True Grit 169
Tuskegee Airmen, The 139-142, *140*

Twelve O'clock High 114-117, *115, 116*, 120, 322
Twilight Zone: The Movie 132, 335

von Richthofen and Brown 47-49, *48*

War Lover, The 122-123
We Can't Have Everything 4
We Were Soldiers 276
West Point of the Air 93
When Worlds Collide 188
Where Eagles Dare 345
White Squaw, The 12
Wing and a Prayer 168-170, *170,* 192
Winged Victory 180-182, *182*
Wings 8, 17-24, *18, 19, 20, 22, 23,* 27, 33, 37, 178, 315
Wings of Eagles, The 63-64
Wings of the Navy 93-94
Woman With Four Faces, The 10
World According to Garp, The 349-350, *350*
World War III, 132
Wright Brothers, The 65

X-15 233-234, *234*

Yank in the RAF, A, 111-112, 113
Young Eagles, The 26-27, 37

Zeppelin 267-268, *268, 269*
Zero Hour 200-201

INDEX
of Interviews
Page numbers in italics denote images

Adams, Chris 230, 322
Appleby, Zona 287, 290-294, 330, 335-336, 348-349
Armanini, Joe 180
Astin, Sean 121-122
Bader, Virginia 86
Beauchesne, Charles 241-243, *242*
Berkos, Peter 273-274
Boyne, Walter 210, *210*, 214, 218, 219, 233
Brown, Roscoe 141-142, *142*
Brown, Stan 322
Buckles, Al 322, 346
Caswell, Dean 184
Cardenas, Robert 235-236, *237*
Chaney, Ray, 305-306
Coble, Truman 329-330
Corrigan, Douglas Jr. 79
Davidson, Edwin 116-117, *117*
Davis, Ross 279
Douglas, Walter 227
Evert, Dick 247-248
Finn, John W. 161, *161*, 164

Frewin, Leon 213
Gossett, Louis 253
Griffin, W.S. 98-99, *99*, 182
Heatley, C.J. 257
Hempel, Bill 80-82
Herrick, Greg 75-76, *75*
Hinton, Steve, 73-74, 162-163, 263, 305, *306*, 311-312, 332-333, 347-348
Kazian, John 291-293, 296-297, 319-320, 348-349
Laird, Dean 155-161
Larson, Jack 137-139, *135, 138*
Ludwig, Rick 247-248, 255, 258-260
Lyles, A.C. 17-18
McCallum, David, 133-134
McGuire, Grace 76-77
Martin, Dewey 223
Orriss, Bruce 166
Parr, Ralph 217, *232*
Pepping, Ed 343-344
Pisanos, Steve 112, *112*, 113, 135, 137
Ramage, James 220-221, *222*
Robertson, Cliff 131, *131*, *171*, 174
Sexton, Frank 122
Shepherd, Joe 74-75
Silverstone, Ed 120, 123
Simon, Bob 204
Simpson, Geoff 108-110, 128-129
Stubbs, John 241-243
Telles, John 64, 280
Thatcher, David 164, 167-168, *168*
Tipton, Lynn 180
Warden, Rex 221-222
Wellman, William Jr. 24-25, 26, 41-42, *41*, *42*, 55-56, 199, 290,
Zimbalist, Efrem, Jr. 202-203, *202, 203*, 204, 230

ABOUT THE AUTHOR

Mark Carlson is an aviation historian, writer, classic film buff and student of filmmaking. He has written articles for several national aviation magazines and organizations. As a docent and researcher at the San Diego Air & Space Museum and member of many aviation-related organizations, Carlson has gained an insight into the people who lived the world of airplanes and the movies.

He and his wife live in San Diego